GREEN PLANET BLUES

A project of the Harrison Program on the Future Global Agenda

SECOND EDITION

GREEN
PLANET
BLUES

Environmental Politics from Stockholm to Kyoto

KEN CONCA
University of Maryland, College Park

GEOFFREY D. DABELKO
Woodrow Wilson International Center for Scholars

Westview Press
A Member of the Perseus Books Group

Copyright © 1998 by Westview Press, A Member of the Perseus Books Group

Published in 1998 in the United States of America by Westview Press, 5500 Central Avenue, Boulder,
Colorado 80301-2877, and in the United Kingdom by Westview Press, 12 Hid's Copse Road, Cumnor
Hill, Oxford OX2 9JJ

Library of Congress Cataloging-in-Publication Data
Green planet blues : environmental politics from Stockholm to Kyoto /
edited by Ken Conca and Geoffrey D. Dabelko. — 2nd ed.
    p.   cm.
  A project of the Harrison Program on the Future Global Agenda.
  Includes bibliographical references.
  ISBN 0-8133-6882-0 (pbk.)
    1. Environmental policy—Political aspects.   2. Sustainable
development.   3. Green movement.   I. Conca, Ken.   II. Dabelko,
Geoffrey D.   III. Harrison Program on the Future Global Agenda.
HC79.E5G6916   1998
363.7—dc21   98-19814
                                                                           CIP

The paper used in this publication meets the requirements of the American National Standard for Per-
manence of Paper for Printed Library Materials Z39.48-1984.

10   9   8   7   6   5   4   3   2   1

Contents

Part Three: The Prospects for International Environmental Cooperation

Part Four: Institutions as Though the Earth Mattered

Part Five: The Sustainable Development Debate

Part Six: From Ecological Conflict to Environmental Security?

Part Seven: Ecological Justice

Preface

This book is a project of the University of Maryland's Harrison Program on the Future Global Agenda. We are grateful to Horace Harrison for making the program a possibility and to its current director, Dennis Pirages, for logistical, financial, and moral support. We appreciate the support of the Woodrow Wilson International Center for Scholars, its Environmental Change and Security Project, and the Project's primary funder, the U.S. Agency for International Development Office of Population. We thank Melissa Brown, Madhavi Chavali, Beth DeSombre, Daniel Deudney, Aaron Frank, Joanne Grossi, Peter Haas, Margaret Keck, Deepa Khosla, Jennifer Knerr, Karen Litfin, Michael Maniates, Christa Matthew, Richard Matthew, Kristin Milavec, Ron Mitchell, Laura Munley, Kate O'Neill, Tim O'Riordan, Dennis Pirages, Jessica Powers, Rebecca Ritke, Natasha Shur, Marvin Soroos, Peter Stoett, Peter Taylor, Michael Vaden, Stacy VanDeveer, Paul Wapner, and Leo Wiegman for their help, advice, and support. Finally, our heartfelt thanks to our coeditor on the first edition, Michael Alberty.

For the second edition we have updated the text to cover developments since the 1992 Earth Summit, while preserving our original goals to discuss cross-cutting issues of power and authority, juxtapose different environmental paradigms, and present a diversity of voices. In making revisions we benefited greatly from the advice of several colleagues who responded to a survey on their teaching experiences with the first edition. At the end of the introduction to each part, we have included a list of questions that we have found useful in stimulating critical thought, discussion, and learning. We also have appended to each part a number of suggestions for further reading and addresses of useful internet sites related to the themes developed in that part of the book. These are by no means comprehensive lists, but they will provide readers with entry points for the abundance of printed and electronic resources available on environmental matters.

Because many of the selections presented in this volume are excerpts, a brief explanation of our editing philosophy is in order. In those cases where space limitations precluded reprinting an entire essay, our goal has been to edit in such a way as to emphasize the underlying ideas and concepts. In many cases, this has meant leaving out complex elaborations, trenchant asides, or supporting examples. We have preserved the original notes corresponding to the material reproduced here but have left out notes corresponding to passages of text not included.

For two essays with a large number of in-line citations in the original (those by Feeny et al. and Lélé), we have preserved all of the factual citations but removed several of the more general references in order to save space and enhance readability. Readers seeking further background, greater detail, or additional references should consult the original material.

Ken Conca
Geoffrey D. Dabelko

GREEN PLANET BLUES

Twenty–five Years of Global Environmental Politics

Chris J. Calwell, Ecos Consulting

$\mathbb{T}$*hink globally, act locally. Spaceship Earth. The common heritage of human-*
ity. Pollution does not respect national borders. The Earth is one, but the
World is not. We have not inherited the Earth from our parents; we have bor-
rowed it from our children. The global commons. Each of these well-known
phrases invokes similar themes: the interconnectedness of the global environment; the close ties between environmental quality and human well-being;
and the common fate that these realities impose upon all of the planet's occupants, present and future. We live, as we have for some time, in an era of
global environmental politics.

Pollution, ecosystem destruction, and natural resource depletion are not
new problems. Many regions and localities were grappling with these issues
long before the industrial revolution or even the emergence of the modern
system of nation-states. And just as environmental problems have a long-
standing history, so do the political struggles that inevitably accompany those
problems. Thus, severe wood shortages led to conservation efforts in Babylo-
nia during the time of Hammurabi.[1] Measures to protect wetlands in recognition of their importance as sources of fish, game, and fuel have been traced
to the sixth century A.D. in the Huang-Huai-Hai plain of northeastern China.[2]
Air-quality crises in London during the early stages of the industrial revolution led to the formation of smoke-abatement societies advocating legisla-
tive action.[3] One can easily imagine the political controversies that must have
engulfed each such case, given that these measures protecting environmental
quality or altering access to natural resources would have offended powerful
economic interests.

Today, the dramas of environmental politics are increasingly played out on
a global stage. It is generally agreed that human transformation of the environment is a global problem. In some cases this is because the system under
stress is globally interconnected in a physical sense, as in the case of the
Earth's climate, the oceans, or the atmosphere's protective ozone layer. In
other cases, accumulated local events produce consequences of global significance, as in the depletion of the world's fisheries or the reduction of the
planet's biological diversity.

The Earth as Transformed by Human Action, a book published in 1990, provides the most comprehensive description to date of the cumulative and expanding effects of human activities on the environment.[4] For the purposes of
assessment and comparison, the authors divide the world into seven ecologi-

cal regions; they then describe the historical "trajectory" by which population growth, technological development, changes in consumption patterns, and different forms of social organization in each region have generated profound environmental changes. Although the specific pattern that emerges differs significantly from region to region, the common theme is the expanding scale of human impact, from local to regional to global.

People increasingly speak of global environmental problems. But what do we mean when we speak of *global environmental politics*? To answer this question, consider what people see when they look at a forest. Some see a stock of timber to be exploited for economic gain. Others see a complex ecological system that holds the soil in place, stabilizes the local water cycle, moderates the local climate, and fosters biological diversity. Still others see the forest as a home for people and other living things, or perhaps as an ancestral burial ground. Finally, some see the forest as a powerful cultural symbol: The forest as a living system reflects the potential harmony between humanity and nature, and provides a link between the past and the future.

We live in a world that is at once fragmented by the political division into sovereign states and reassembled by pervasive flows of people, goods, money, ideas, images, and technology across borders.[5] In such a world, conflicting visions of the forest take on international significance. Some see in the forest an important source of international economic power, giving those who control it influence in international markets and a reliable source of foreign exchange. Others see it as a powerful symbol of global interdependence: The forest reflects the global consequences of local acts in that its destruction may alter the global climate or deplete the global stock of biological diversity. Still others see a very different sort of international symbol: The forest represents national sovereignty in that it confirms the right of a nation to do as it sees fit within its territory. Such rights may seem luxuries that a crowded planet cannot afford. But this is not often the view of people who feel their sovereign rights immediately threatened—particularly if those rights were won in a struggle for independence that forged their very nation.

Often these competing visions reflect different interests held by individuals, groups, and perhaps even entire nations. They are also a product, however, of the structures that govern world politics. The institution of national sovereignty, the division of labor in the capitalist world economy, the rise of transnational networks of environmentalists, the predominance of powerful beliefs about the links between consumption and "progress"—all of these underlying features of contemporary world politics shape what people see when they look at the forest.

Competing visions, values, and interests often lead to conflict. Actors disagree about the nature of the problem, the effectiveness or fairness of proposed solutions, and the appropriate location of responsibility. Thus, studying global environmental politics means understanding the conflicts of interest that surround environmental issues as well as asking how interests, values, and visions related to the environment are shaped.

The study of global environmental politics also involves the search for cooperative solutions to ecological dilemmas. The idea that global environmental problems require "international cooperation" is widely accepted; but the appropriate scope and content of such cooperation are hotly contested. Does international cooperation mean formal, treaty-based agreements among governments? Does it mean a broader "global bargain" between North and South, linking a number of issues in a single package? Or does it refer to a still broader process of global dialogue not limited to governments, in which different societies move toward a global convergence of values? Does an increasingly global network of environmental organizations represent an effective new form of international cooperation, or is it simply one more way in which the strong impose their will upon the weak? Is the goal to create an increasingly dense web of transnational linkages, one that binds nations to a common future and a common commitment to environmental protection? Or would it be wiser to work toward delinking an already tightly coupled world system, so that various localities and regions have more flexibility to pursue responses appropriate to their unique circumstances?

Finally, an important dimension of the study of global environmental politics is connecting the patterns of international conflict and cooperation we see over the environment to some of the larger changes under way in world politics. If studying the structure of world politics gives us insight into the character of global environmental problems, the reverse is also true. It is no surprise that as the world stands on the edge of the twenty-first century, environmental problems have emerged as a critical theme in the study of international relations and world politics. At a time when much conventional wisdom in international relations is under challenge, studying the politics of the global environment may also give us greater insight into the emerging patterns of world politics as a whole.

From Stockholm to Rio—and Beyond

For twelve days in June 1992, representatives of 178 nations gathered in the city of Rio de Janeiro, Brazil. Diplomats debated the causes of environmental problems, the nature of the linkages between the environment and economic development, and the appropriateness of various policy responses. By the end of the conference, they had produced international agreements on climate change and biological diversity, a statement of general principles on environment and development, and "Agenda 21," an ambitious, eight-hundred-page document on a broad array of environmental problems, setting guidelines for action into the twenty-first century.

The political elites gathering in Rio, including more than a hundred heads of state, were joined by more than eight thousand journalists from all over the world, as well as more than 1,400 nongovernmental organizations (NGOs).[6] Some of the NGOs, including business groups and mainstream environmental organizations, enjoyed substantial access to the official and unofficial discussions among governments; others, including many grassroots environmental organizations, indigenous peoples' groups, human rights advocates, and women's groups, found themselves relegated to outsider status. Many participated in a parallel "Global Forum" of NGOs, held on the other side of the city. Many activists left frustrated at the relative lack of action on pressing problems, but many also left convinced that the Global Forum was a major step toward the creation of a global social movement of environmentalism.[7]

The Rio Conference—formally known as the United Nations Conference on Environment and Development (UNCED) and popularly dubbed the Earth Summit—was not the first United Nations conference focused on the planet's environmental predicaments. Two decades earlier, representatives of many nations' governments had gathered in Stockholm, Sweden to discuss many of the same issues. The 1972 Stockholm Conference—formally known as the U.N. Conference on the Human Environment—did not attract nearly the level of broad participation, public interest, or media attention seen in Rio de Janeiro two decades later. But the fundamental question was the same: how to respond to urgent environmental problems in a politically, economically, and culturally divided world.[8]

The contrasts between Stockholm and Rio reflect many underlying changes that took place in the world during the intervening two decades. Stockholm occurred in the shadow of the Cold War; the governments of Eastern Europe and the Soviet Union boycotted the conference after a dispute over the representation of divided Germany. Rio, in contrast, took place in the relatively optimistic afterglow of the end of the Cold War, amid a general sense of new opportunities for global cooperation.

The 1992 Earth Summit also reflected the tremendous growth in scientific understanding of environmental problems during the previous two decades. Whereas Stockholm had focused attention principally on relatively narrowly defined problems of air and water pollution, Rio embraced a far broader and more complex agenda. This shift reflected in part a changing scientific paradigm—one that views the Earth as a single integrated system with complex linkages among the large-scale ecological systems of land, oceans, atmosphere, and biosphere.[9] The discussion at Rio, especially the ambitious goals embodied in "Agenda 21," also reflected the greater capacity of scientists to measure, monitor, and model complex processes of environmental change.[10]

Another clear change from Stockholm to Rio was the emergence of global public awareness and concern. Many of the participants at Stockholm—particularly those from the North—framed environmental problems as the by-products of an affluent, industrialized lifestyle. The implication was that the poorer regions of the world do not suffer as much from environmental problems as do the wealthy, nor exhibit the same level of concern about such problems. In the ensuing two decades, however, the notion that there is both a "pollution of affluence" *and* a "pollution of poverty" has gained much broader acceptance. As the environmental causes of poverty have become clearer, what many of those suffering from poverty have presumably known all along has become more generally understood: Environmental concerns are not the exclusive property of affluent people or industrialized countries.

Public opinion data support this claim of broad public concern. In a fascinating comparison of polling data from several nations, Riley Dunlap, George Gallup Jr., and Alec Gallup found a remarkably uniform pattern: Large majorities in each country revealed deep concern about environmental problems, attached significant value to a healthy environment, and expressed fear about the future.[11] The findings (summarized in Table I.1) suggest that even if different peoples, classes, regions, and cultures define the problem somewhat differently, concerns about the environment cut across simplistic distinctions between rich and poor, North and South, overdeveloped and underdeveloped.[12]

Rio also differed from Stockholm in that the governments and other actors gathering to discuss global environmental problems themselves had undergone notable changes in the intervening decades. Virtually all of the governments converging on Rio de Janeiro had some form of national environmental bureaucracy; almost none had at the time of the Stockholm conference. In many cases, these agencies enabled governments to take advantage of the growth of environmental knowledge so as to analyze more effectively the causes and consequences of environmental problems. And in some cases these agencies had evolved into advocates for various environmental protection programs, producing more complex internal debates within national delegations.

Table I.1 Selected Results of the 1993 "Health of the Planet Survey"

Percentage of respondents who say that environmental problems are a "very serious" issue in their nation

Industrialized Nations		Developing Nations	
Germany	67	South Korea	67
Switzerland	63	Poland	66
Canada	53	Mexico	66
United States	51	Russia	62
Portugal	51	Turkey	61
Japan	42	Chile	56
Norway	40	Hungary	52
Great Britain	36	India	51
Ireland	32	Brazil	50
Netherlands	27	Nigeria	45
Denmark	26	Uruguay	44
Finland	21	Philippines	37

Percentage of respondents who rate the quality of the world environment as "very" or "fairly" bad

Industrialized Nations		Developing Nations	
Denmark	92	Chile	88
Norway	88	Uruguay	74
Germany	86	Poland	73
Switzerland	86	Hungary	71
Netherlands	84	Mexico	70
Canada	79	Russia	66
Great Britain	76	South Korea	65
Portugal	75	Brazil	64
Finland	73	Philippines	58
Ireland	73	Turkey	45
Japan	73	India	42
United States	66	Nigeria	24

SOURCE: Figures 2 and 4 of Riley E. Dunlap, George H. Gallup, Jr. , and Alec M. Gallup, "Of Global Concern: Results of the Health of the Planet Survey," *Environment* 35, 9 (November 1993): 6–15, 33–39.

Nongovernmental environmental organizations also underwent substantial changes from Stockholm to Rio. These changes included growth in numbers (more than 1,400 NGOs were officially accredited participants at Rio, as opposed to 134 at Stockholm) and a shift toward greater global representation (one-third of the groups at Rio were from the South, as opposed to only about one-tenth at Stockholm).[13] During the 1970s and 1980s many of these groups turned their attention to the international arena, forming coalitions among local- or national-level environmental organizations.[14] Although environmentalists face many of the same obstacles to North-South cooperation that confront governments, the emergence of this global network fundamentally altered the terms of the debate at Rio.

A final measure of the changes from Stockholm to Rio is the growth in the number of international environmental treaties, agreements, and cooperative accords. By one estimate there are now more than nine hundred such international agreements in operation.[15] Many of these are relatively narrow in scope, including bilateral accords on specific environmental problems or regional agreements involving small numbers of countries and narrow agendas. But the list also includes several major international accords adopted since the Stockholm Conference, including agreements on ocean pollution, acid rain, preservation of the ozone layer, the international trade in endangered species, and environmental protection in Antarctica.[16] The designers of international accords at Rio had a much broader set of examples upon which to draw than did their predecessors at Stockholm; as a result, they also had at least a crude understanding of what makes various approaches to international environmental cooperation effective.[17]

It is equally important to stress what did *not* change in the twenty years between the conferences. Many of the stumbling blocks to effective global response seen at Stockholm were also in full evidence at Rio. These include the tremendous mistrust and suspicion governing relations between North and South in world politics; the tenacious embrace of traditional conceptions of national sovereignty by governments, even as they acknowledge the need for coordinated global response to problems that do not respect borders; and the tensions between the long-term vision necessary for ecologically sane planning and the short-term concern for economic growth and political stability that preoccupies most governments.

These obstacles were equally evident when the world's governments met in Kyoto, Japan five years after the Earth Summit, in December 1997, to discuss the problem of global climate change. As a follow-up conference of the parties to Rio's framework convention on climate, Kyoto had been envisioned as a chance to strengthen and clarify the original agreement by adding specific, binding targets and timetables for reducing "greenhouse" gases implicated in global warming. Kyoto did produce an agreement—the industrialized countries committed to reducing their annual emissions by varying amounts below 1990 levels by 2008 or 2012. But behind the technical discussion of differentiated responsibilities, joint implementation, tradable permits, caps, bubbles, and other seemingly arcane themes lay many of the same fundamental questions—of North and South, sovereignty and globalism, state and society, growth and limits—confronted at Stockholm.

Perhaps the most important continuity in the more than twenty-five years since Stockholm is that global environmental change has continued at an alarming rate. Between 1970 and 1990, global commercial energy consumption, a major source of environmental impacts, increased by roughly 62 percent; other global indicators of human impact on the environment, including food production, overall economic activity, and population, increased in roughly similar proportions.[18] To be sure, these very crude indicators of human stress on environmental systems can mask as much as they reveal. They say nothing about how underlying activities actually affect the environment, about who or what may be responsible, or who suffers the consequences most directly and immediately. But they do indicate the scale of the problem and the enormity of the challenge of reorienting fundamental practices that drive growth, production, consumption, and environmental transformation in the current world system.

This mixed picture of continuity and change raises an obvious question: Compared to where things stood at Stockholm, does the glass appear half empty or half full as we enter the twenty-first century? Does the period since Stockholm tell an optimistic story of global society moving to meet the challenges of ecological interdependence, or does it chronicle a continued unwillingness or inability to grapple with the root causes of the problem? There are more than enough ways to measure change, and more than enough definitions of progress, to support either interpretation. Perhaps both are true: Just as some of the differences between Stockholm and Rio may reveal important possibilities for change, learning, and effective global cooperation, so the enduring patterns and divisions highlight the depth of the political challenge posed by global environmental problems.

Conflicting Views of the Environmental Problematique

Growing scientific understanding and shared levels of public concern do not automatically translate into a shared understanding of the social causes of environmental problems. One of the first challenges facing students of global environmental politics is to sort out a potentially bewildering debate on the causes of pollution and environmental degradation. Some of this uncertainty lies in the realm of science. The physical, chemical, and biological mechanisms involved in processes such as climate change, desertification, and deforestation are sometimes quite poorly understood by leading experts, to say nothing of the general public, policymakers, or interest groups. The global inter-action of oceans, atmosphere, land, and biosphere has only recently become a central concern of disciplines like oceanography, atmospheric science, and terrestrial ecology. Although knowledge is expanding rapidly on many fronts, scientific uncertainty remains substantial in the face of the complexity of processes of environmental change.

These aspects of technical complexity are matched by similar controversies, debates, and uncertainties surrounding the social dimensions of environmen-tal change. In explaining why human populations have had such a substantial impact on planetary ecosystems, different analysts invoke factors as diverse as values, technology, culture, ideology, public policies, demographic change, and social structures of class, race, or gender. Some observers elevate one or a few of these factors to the role of central cause, treating the others as mere symptoms. Others have sought to develop more complex models that stress the interaction of these various forces and processes.

Some see the problem as essentially one of values—in particular, the value that modern societies attach to consumption. Alan Durning of the World-watch Institute, a Washington-based environmental policy institute, writes that

> The soaring consumption lines that track the rise of the consumer society are, from another perspective, surging indicators of environmental harm. The consumer soci-ety's exploitation of resources threatens to exhaust, poison, or unalterably disfigure forests, soils, water, and air. We, its members, are responsible for a disproportionate share of all the global environmental challenges facing humanity.[19]

Our consumer culture translates wants into needs, stresses material-intensive forms of social gratification, and overwhelms older, more ecologically sustain-able traditions that stand in its way. As consumerism spreads through increas-ingly sophisticated advertising, pop culture, and the global media, more and more regions of the planet adopt the aspirations of the consumer society.

Technology is another commonly cited culprit. Barry Commoner, a key fig-ure in raising public awareness about environmental problems in the United States through books such as *The Closing Circle*, uses the simple example of the production of beer bottles in the United States to illustrate the techno-logical dimension.[20] In the mid-1970s, Commoner investigated the impact of three factors commonly cited as causes of environmental problems—popula-tion growth, rising levels of consumption per capita, and technological change. He found that the number of beer bottles produced in America in-creased by a dramatic 593 percent from 1950 to 1967, even though the popu-lation grew by only 30 percent and beer consumption by only 5 percent per capita. Clearly, a technological change—the replacement of kegs and returnable bottles with single-use, throwaway ones—led to the bulk of the increase, and hence, to the bulk of the environmental impact in terms of energy use, trash, and so on. Commoner argues that similar technological changes that have occurred across most of the key sectors of modern society are at the heart of the environmental crisis.

Some observers argue that prevailing technologies and values are expressions of underlying power dynamics in society. For example, Murray Bookchin—though not necessarily disagreeing with Durning's assessment of the consumer society or Commoner's cautions about technology—stresses the importance of social inequality. He warns against attributing environmental problems to such vague and impersonal formulations as "values," "technology," and "humanity." Such reasoning "serves to deflect our attention from the role society plays in producing ecological breakdown."[21] According to Bookchin,

A mythic "Humanity" is created—irrespective of whether we are talking about oppressed ethnic minorities, women, Third World people, or people in the First World—in which everyone is brought into complicity with powerful corporate elites in producing environmental dislocations. In this way, the social roots of ecological problems are shrewdly obscured. A new kind of biological "original sin" is created in which a vague group of animals called "Humanity" is turned into a destructive force that threatens the survival of the living world.[22]

According to Bookchin, the key to understanding lies instead in seeing how social inequality feeds environmental degradation and resource overexploitation. Societies constructed upon hierarchies of race, class, and gender are, in this view, fundamentally based on exploitation, and thus have an inherent tendency to seek domination over nature rather than a means of living in harmony with it, just as they favor the domination of some people by others.[23]

Vandana Shiva, who has written extensively about forestry issues in postcolonial India, provides a model aimed at linking such diverse causal forces as technology, values, and social structure.[24] For Shiva, history is key: Technological and demographic change, hierarchical patterns of social structure, and consumption-oriented values are coevolutionary products of Indian society's dominant historical experience—the political, economic, and social transformations brought about by more than a century of British colonial rule. Thus, in her view, "causes" of environmental degradation in India as diverse as the industrial revolution, the capitalist world economy, and the destructive power of modern science and technology are "the philosophical, technological and economic components of the same process."[25]

Sorting out this diverse array of claims requires carefully detailed, historical study of the ways in which economic, social, and political institutions in society coevolve over time.[26] Many of the selections in this volume present models of the causes of environmental problems, at varying levels of detail and complexity. It will become apparent to the reader that these various causal claims are based on very different understandings of the sources of power, interest, authority, and legitimacy in society. Sorting out such diverse claims does not guarantee that effective policies and institutions will be designed. Actors may agree on the causes of a problem but still disagree on the appropriate responses; they may see their interests affected differently, or hold different views about the fairness or effectiveness of a particular response. But grappling with the complex array of causes does seem to be a necessary preliminary step if appropriate responses are to be crafted. Perhaps just as importantly, examining the diversity of claims also helps us to understand the equally diverse beliefs about history, justice, and responsibility that various actors bring to the debate.

Global Environmental Politics: Power, Ideas, and Voices

The material in this book has been selected with three goals in mind. One goal has been to pay particular attention to underlying questions of power, interest, authority, and legitimacy that shape global environmental debates. The challenge of the global environment is often framed as a narrowly technical task of promoting policy coordination among governments. Clearly, rational policies and effective intergovernmental cooperation will be a crucial part of any meaningful response to the challenge. But a narrow focus on governments, treaties, and public policies can blur our understanding of some of the deeper components of the problematique. The environmental problems facing the global community also raise deeper questions of governmental authority and legitimacy; of the relationship between the state and society; and of processes of economic and cultural globalization that challenge state sovereignty.

Second, we have tried to emphasize the *ideas* that have most powerfully shaped the evolving debate over the global environment. By assembling under one cover some of the most influential voices in the debate, we hope to provide a firsthand sense of how ideas have shaped action, while at the same time stressing the obstacles to changing the world through new ideas. Thus we examine some of the most powerful paradigms that prevailed at the time of the Stockholm Conference, and the controversies engendered by those views. We also explore the powerful and controversial new paradigms that have emerged, in the two decades since Stockholm, around themes of sustainability, environmental security, and ecological justice. Comparing these sets of ideas over time reveals how many people's thinking has changed at the same time as it highlights enduring themes: for example, the obstacles to cooperation in a politically fragmented international system, or the tremendously destructive potential of modern technology and current economic practices.

Our third goal has been to present a broad range of voices in what is and must be a *global* debate. This goal might appear to conflict with our previously stated intention of presenting the most powerful and influential ideas: One might be tempted by a sense of urgency to favor a narrowing of the debate to what the most powerful voices consider feasible or desirable. However, in our view any such narrowing of the debate would be deeply troubling on moral grounds, as well as potentially disastrous given the current lack of global consensus on so many fundamental issues. The poor and powerless might lack the ability to shape the ecological future they desire, but they might well have the power to veto proposed "solutions" that ignore their needs and interests. Although universal agreement is a utopia difficult to imagine, durable responses to global environmental problems can be achieved only through a broader social consensus. Thus we have chosen essays for this book with the intent of broadening the debate to include perspectives from South as well as North; voices that are rural as well as urban, female as well as male, and critical of existing institutions as well as broadly sympathetic toward them.

The book's organization is meant to serve these goals. We begin in Part One with a discussion of dominant paradigms and controversies that shaped debate at the time of the Stockholm Conference, and during the conference itself. The views and debates that prevailed in that era provide a useful reference point for measuring what has changed since Stockholm. Part One focuses in particular on three provocative and influential ideas of the Stockholm era: first, the notion that there are inherent "limits to growth" on a planet of finite natural resources and limited ecological resilience; second, the claim that self-interested individual behavior often adds up to a global "tragedy of the commons"; and third, the idea that environmental threats increasingly demand controlling, authoritarian responses.

In Part Two we examine how the structure of the international system shapes the types of problems we face and the types of solutions we can imagine. The discussion focuses on the role of national sovereignty, transnational capitalism, and prevailing beliefs about "modernization" and "progress" that shape political and economic institutions. Part Two also examines environmentalism as a global social movement, asking whether we might be seeing the emergence of new and different forms of political authority that challenge these dominant aspects of system structure.

Parts Three and Four examine challenges of international cooperation and institutional reform. Part Three focuses on international cooperation, presenting a range of views on the prospects for cooperation and the appropriate form and substance of such cooperation. Part Four examines the possibilities for reforming existing international institutions so as to foster environmental protection. The section focuses in particular on international trade and international development assistance, two institutionalized practices that have been at the center of the ongoing debate about the relationship between the world economy and the global environment.

The volume concludes with three powerful and controversial new paradigms that crystallized in the two decades between Stockholm and Rio: sustainable development (Part Five), environmental security (Part Six), and ecological justice (Part Seven). For some observers, these three paradigms are complementary and potentially harmonious facets of a single vision. Others see only the tensions and trade-offs inherent in the simultaneous pursuit of development, security, and justice, and fear that each particular paradigm favors certain values at the expense of others. However, these paradigms might be sufficiently broad that they can either complement or contradict one another, depending on the specific choices made in implementing them. In any case, they are likely to be the conceptual building blocks for the environmental initiatives of the future.

In compiling this material, we have deliberately avoided organizing the book around a conventional list of environmental "issue areas" (climate change, deforestation, toxic substances, acid rain, and so on) or generic "classes" of environmental problems (as in the common distinction between local, cumulative processes, transboundary issues, and the global commons). To be sure, these are important and insightful ways to organize one's thinking about complex, multidimensional problems. However, by focusing on crosscutting issues of power, authority, and responsibility, we hope this book will provide a useful complement to these other approaches, which are already well represented in the literature.

PART ONE

The Debate at Stockholm

As discussed in the introductory chapter, the 1972 U.N. Conference on the Human Environment, held in Stockholm, was a seminal event in the history of global environmental politics. Many important international agreements had already been concluded by the time of the Stockholm Conference, including a treaty governing Antarctica (1959), a partial nuclear test-ban treaty (1963), a treaty governing the exploration and use of outer space (1967), and several international agreements on ocean-related matters, such as whaling, the use of marine resources, and ocean pollution.[1] But the Stockholm Conference was the first broadly international effort to evaluate and discuss the environment in systematic, comprehensive terms, and it helped establish the trajectory of future efforts—the complex array of diplomatic initiatives and debates, attempts at transnational institution building, and global movements for social change that unfolded during the two decades that followed.

Although the Stockholm Conference took place more than twenty-five years ago, many of its central debates are still current. These include several key questions revisited later in this book: Is global pollution mainly a problem of poverty or a problem of affluence? What is the balance of responsibility between North and South in global environmental degradation? Does the institution of national sovereignty help or hinder the effort to construct international responses to environmental problems? An understanding of the dominant ideas and controversies at Stockholm provides an important historical perspective on the debates and disputes that dominate contemporary global environmental politics.[2]

In this section we introduce some of the ideas that shaped debate during the Stockholm era. We pay particular attention to three powerful and controversial claims from that era: the idea that there are inherent "limits to growth" facing the international economy, the world's population, and global consumption; the idea that self-interested individual behavior toward the environment adds up to a collective "tragedy of the commons"; and the claim that the environmental crisis demands a firm, authoritarian state to deal with the problems facing a "scarcity society."

Although thinking about the environment has evolved considerably in the years since Stockholm, these themes are not just of historical interest. They have strongly influenced the nature of scientific and social-scientific inquiry since Stockholm, with many analysts and activists working to either prove or disprove the existence of limits to growth, a tragedy of the commons, or a political basis for ecological authoritarianism. These ideas also have shaped the political strategies pursued by governments, corporations, environmentalists, and other actors seeking to promote or hinder various forms of international environmental cooperation.

For the industrialized countries of the North, the Stockholm Conference was a response to mounting public anxiety over the environmental consequences of industrial society. By the early 1970s, concerns over problems as diverse as air and water pollution, wilderness preservation, toxic chemicals, urban congestion, nuclear radiation, and rising prices for natural-resource commodities began to fuse into the notion that the world was rapidly approaching natural limits to growth. The best-selling book *The Limits to Growth* did much to galvanize public fears. Using a technique known as systems modeling, the authors tried to predict the consequences of unlimited growth in human numbers and consumption. As the passage presented here indicates, they concluded that the convergence of several trends—accelerating industrialization, rapid population growth, widespread malnutrition, depletion of nonrenewable resources, and a deteriorating environment—was moving the world rapidly toward overall limits on global growth. In order to avoid a potentially catastrophic collapse of the world's economic and social systems, it would be necessary to implement planned restraints on growth in population and in resource consumption.

Critics of *The Limits to Growth* argued that the book overstated the urgency of the problem, overlooked the possibility of substituting less-scarce inputs, and underestimated the possibility for technological solutions.[3] (These arguments foreshadowed the emergence in the 1980s of the concept of "sustainable development," which argues that some forms of economic growth can be compatible with natural limits; see Part Five.) The book's central claims were highly controversial, and most Northern governments were reluctant to fully endorse or embrace its findings. But the fears articulated in *The Limits to Growth* found widespread popular support in industrial societies, where they converged with the arguments of the growing coalition of environmental organizations.

Not surprisingly, the idea of limits to growth, and the controversy surrounding it, was received quite differently in the South. Among the less-industrialized countries, the idea of limits to growth evoked not only intellectual skepticism but also political suspicions. These suspicions were expressed eloquently in a 1972 essay by João Augusto de Araujo Castro, at that time Brazilian ambassador to the United States and an influential voice in North-South diplomacy. The South has never been monolithic in its views on problems of development and the environment. But as Castro made clear, many in the South linked the North's environmental concerns to the broader pattern of North-South relations. Thus, there was widespread agreement among Third World governments at the Stockholm Conference that the North was responsible for the global environmental crisis; that the North, having reaped the fruits of industrialization, now sought to close the door on the South; that the environmental problems of poverty differed fundamentally from those of affluence; and that solutions crafted with the North's problems in mind would be ineffective, or worse, if imposed on the South.

The South's unity at Stockholm made it clear that a *global* response to environmental problems would require linking the environmental debate to the development concerns of the South, and to a broader dialogue about the political and economic "rules of the game" in the international system. The message was clear: If such connections were not drawn, the South would not participate.

Just as the idea of limits to growth dominated the debate over the *consequences* of environmental problems, the debate over *causes* crystallized around the powerful and controversial idea of the "tragedy of the commons." This view was popularized by biologist Garrett Hardin in a now-famous essay that appeared in the influential scholarly journal *Science* in 1968. According to Hardin, the "tragedy" occurred when self-interested actors enjoyed open access to, or unlimited use of, natural resources or environmental systems. Because consumers could benefit fully from additional exploitation while bearing only a small part of the "costs" of that exploitation (for example, environmental degradation)—costs shared with all other users—the overwhelming tendency would be toward greater exploitation of the resource. Each actor would pursue this logical individual behavior until the result for the system as a whole was the destruction or degradation of the resource in question. Individual logic would produce collective disaster—hence the notion of tragedy. Using the example of overgrazing on the town commons of medieval England (hence the "tragedy of the commons"), Hardin suggested that the same combination of self-interest and open access that had caused this earlier catastrophe was at the root of current problems of pollution and overpopulation. The solutions offered by Hardin were either to replace open access with enforceable private property rights, so that individual users would reap the full costs as well as the full benefits of their actions, or to impose governmental restrictions on access.

Hardin's model has been enormously influential in shaping thinking about global environmental problems, particularly for the so-called "global commons" such as the oceans and atmosphere, which fall under the domain of no single government. One reason for its influence is the model's simple elegance: The tragedy of the commons combines a recognizable human motive (self-interest) with a recognizable set of social rules (those allowing open access to natural resources and the environment) to produce a result that most would recognize as undesirable (rapid depletion or destruction of the resource in question).

Yet Hardin's model is, at heart, just a metaphor: The English commons is invoked as a simplified representation of the complex social rules, customs, goals, and behavioral incentives that shape how people interact with the environment individually and collectively. Whether such a "tragedy" actually lies at the center of global environmental problems depends on whether this abstraction is in fact an accurate representation of human behavior and social institutions. Even if the tragedy seems plausible conceptually, how widely does it apply as a description of the real world?

Susan J. Buck argues that despite its widespread acceptance, Hardin's tragedy does not even describe accurately the situation of the commons in medieval England on which the metaphor is based. According to Buck, access to the town commons was never unrestrained but rather was governed by a complex set of community rules that ensured sustainable use. The commons system was not destroyed by population growth and self-interested individual behavior, as Hardin asserted, but by changing political and economic conditions in Britain, which gave powerful actors the incentive and ability to privatize the commons and to overwhelm community-based systems of property rights. Thus, rather than representing a tragedy, the endurance of the commons system, in some cases for several hundred years, shows that there may be possibilities other than the stark choice Hardin poses between purely private property and purely open access.

In an article published more than two decades after Hardin's classic essay, David Feeny and his colleagues reviewed a large body of empirical evidence addressing the question of whether Hardin's tragedy actually exists. The authors examined a wide range of studies of natural-resource and environmental systems potentially subject to the "tragedy," including fisheries, wildlife populations, surface water, groundwater, rangelands, and forests. The authors concluded that Hardin's formulation, though sometimes applicable, is by no means universal. Whether a "tragedy" of overconsumption ensues depends, in their view, on the type of social rules governing these natural resources or environmental systems. The enforceable private property rights advocated by Hardin are just one such set of rules, and not necessarily the most appropriate for all situations. The authors cited numerous examples of societies that had developed sets of rules to collectively manage local common-property resources. These ideas are developed in detail in Elinor

Ostrom's influential book *Governing the Commons*, which provides both theory and evidence that self-organizing, sustainable management of shared resources is possible under certain conditions.[4]

The work of Buck, Ostrom, Feeny, and others is of critical importance in the effort to craft international responses to environmental problems. If Hardin's tragedy does apply to the global commons, it will be exceedingly difficult to craft effective international responses to global environmental problems. This is so because Hardin's preferred solutions, privatizing the commons or subjecting it to the control of a powerful central authority, are infeasible in the current international system. If these are the only choices, the tragedy seems likely to proceed apace. However, if systems of collective management can be shown to have been effective on the local or regional level, it may also be possible to design such systems to operate on the international level.[5] Under these circumstances there could still be a tragedy of the commons, but it would result from our lack of skill and effectiveness in designing fair and efficient international responses, rather than from some ironclad logic of nature.

What would be the political consequences of the limits to growth and the tragedy of the commons? A provocative answer to this question was provided by William Ophuls in his 1977 book *Ecology and the Politics of Scarcity*, on which the later essay excerpted in our book was based. According to Ophuls, a new era of scarcity would be marked by an authoritarian political response, just as scarcity in the past had been the trigger for various forms of violence, oppression, and war. The "scarcity society" that Ophuls described would perceive "the necessity for political control" in order to avoid "ecological self-destruction." The result Ophuls foresaw was a political future "much less libertarian and much more authoritarian, much less individualistic and much more communalistic than our present." Ophuls did see an alternative to this grim scenario, which he labeled a "democracy of restraint." In this scenario, it would be possible to forge an ecologically rational future without coercive authority, provided that human gratification could be decoupled from material consumption. But a democracy of restraint would demand a prompt response to environmental problems and a broad social consensus on the importance of taking action—circumstances that Ophuls deemed unlikely.

Ophuls's notions about the likelihood of authoritarian responses to environmental problems remain controversial. Nor is it clear that authoritarian responses would be effective. In Part Seven, on the question of ecological justice, we present a very different interpretation of the links between freedom, democracy, justice, and the environment. But the questions Ophuls raised about the ability of today's governments to respond effectively and in a timely fashion, and the attention he drew to the close link between control of nature and control of people, remain critical themes in environmental politics.

Despite their critics, and despite changes in our understanding in the decades since Stockholm, the concepts of "limits to growth," "the tragedy of the commons," and "the scarcity society" remain powerfully influential in global environmental politics. Not only did they help shape the pathway from Stockholm to Rio; they are also readily seen in contemporary controversies. The dispute about growth limits has reemerged in current debates over the environmental consequences of international trade (see Part Four) and the prospects for sustainable development (see Part Five). Similarly, skeptics about the prospects for effective international cooperation invoke both the logic of self-interested behavior and the commons-like features of global environmental systems (see Part Three)—just as Hardin did thirty years ago. And the increasingly widespread fear that environmental degradation threatens national and international security raises for some the specter of authoritarian solutions, as posited by Ophuls (see Part Six). The evolution of global environmental politics cannot be understood without examining the history of these ideas; weighing their claims carefully and critically is as important today as it was in the Stockholm era.

Thinking Critically

1. How well have the essays by Meadows, Castro, Hardin, and Ophuls withstood the test of time? Do they still provide an adequate framework for understanding and addressing global environmental problems? What aspects of their essays seem anachronistic? What aspects ring true today? Imagine what a dialogue among these thinkers would be like if they were to meet today and discuss the durability of each other's claims.

2. Contrast Castro's claims about the environment and development with the essays on sustainability in Part Five. Do either the advocates or the critics of the sustainability paradigm frame the problem in the same way that Castro has?

3. Do the criticisms of Hardin presented in the essays by Buck and Feeny invalidate his central claim about the tragedy of the commons? In other words, can Hardin still be right about the larger problem even if he misread the history of the English commons, and even if exceptions to his pessimistic scenario can be found? What do you think Hardin would say to his critics?

4. If Buck and Feeny are correct to argue that sustainable governance of the commons is feasible on a local scale, can we imagine similar forms of governance on a larger scale? What are the limits of scale for these forms of governance, and at what scale are these limits likely to be encountered?

5. Contrast Ophuls's arguments about the need for strong command-and-control governance with the essays on environmental justice in Part Seven. Is

the concentration of power in the hands of the state part of the problem or part of the solution? In an era in which many governments face profound skepticism and frequent crises of authority, are people likely to look to the state for solutions to the problems of the "scarcity society"?

Additional Reading

Stockholm-Era Classics

Carson, Rachel, *Silent Spring* (Boston: Houghton Mifflin, 1962).

Ophuls, William, *Ecology and the Politics of Scarcity* (San Francisco: W. H. Freeman, 1976).

Sprout, Harold, and Margaret Sprout, *Toward a Politics of the Planet Earth* (New York: Van Nostrand Reinhold, 1971).

Ward, Barbara, and Rene Dubos, *Only One Earth* (New York: W. W. Norton, 1972).

The Limits to Growth

Buttel, Frederick H., Ann P. Hawkins, and Alison G. Power, "From limits to growth to global change," *Global Environmental Change* 1 (December 1990):57–66.

Daly, Herman E., *Steady-State Economics: The Economics of Biophysical Equilibrium and Moral Growth* (San Francisco: W. H. Freeman, 1977).

Nordhaus, W. D., "World Dynamics: Measurement without Data," *Economic Journal* 83, no. 332 (December 1973):1156–1183.

Simon, Julian, and Herman Kahn, *The Resourceful Earth* (Oxford: Basil Blackwell, 1984).

Governing the Commons

Hardin, Garrett, and John Baden, eds., *Managing the Commons* (San Francisco: W. H. Freeman, 1977).

Keohane, Robert O., and Elinor Ostrom, eds., *Local Commons and Global Interdependence: Heterogeneity and Cooperation in Two Domains* (London: Sage Publications, 1995).

Ostrom, Elinor, *Governing the Commons: The Evolution of Institutions for Collective Action* (Cambridge: Cambridge University Press, 1990).

Handy References

Bergesen, Helge Ole, and Georg Parmann, eds., *Green Globe Yearbook of International Co-operation on Environment and Development 1997* (New York: Oxford University Press, 1997).

Caldwell, Lynton, *International Environmental Policy,* 3d ed. (Durham, NC: Duke University Press, 1996).

Porter, Gareth, and Janet Welsh Brown, *Global Environmental Politics*, 2d ed. (Boulder, CO: Westview Press, 1995).

Tolba, Mostafa K., Osama A. El-Kholy, E. El-Hinnawi, M. W. Holdgate, D. F. McMichael, and R. E. Munn, eds., *The World Environment 1972–1992: Two Decades of Challenge* (London: Chapman & Hall, 1992).

Turner, B. L. II, et al., *The Earth as Transformed by Human Action* (New York: Cambridge University Press, 1990).

World Resources Institute, *World Resources* (New York: Oxford University Press, biannual).

Worldwatch Institute, *State of the World* (New York: W. W. Norton, annual).

Internet Resources

United Nations Environment Programme (UNEP), *http://www.unep.org/*. Created in the wake of the Stockholm Conference, the United Nations Environment Programme has the assignment of catalyzing and coordinating U.N. activities on the environment. This site provides information on the UNEP's organization, mandate, activities, and cooperative ventures.

United Nations Division for Sustainable Development, *http://www.un.org/dpcsd/dsd/*. This site contains the major documents from UNCED, as well as information on follow-up activities of the United Nations.

ECONet, *http://www.igc.org/igc/econet/index.html*. ECONet connects to a vast array of research resources, environmental listserves, organizations, and on-line resources related to the environment.

International Human Dimensions Program on Global Environmental Change, *http://ibm.rhrz.uni-bonn.de:80/IHDP/*. This program, established by the International Social Science Research Council, coordinates a wide range of social-science research on global change.

International Association for the Study of Common Property, *http://www.indiana.edu/~iascp/*. An academic association formed to study and promote the collective management of commons environmental resources. This site contains information on the group's publication *CPR Digest* as well as useful bibliographies and links.

Project on Teaching Global Environmental Politics, *http://merlin.alleg.edu/mmaniate/GepEd/geped.html*. This site features syllabi, reading lists, simulations, classroom exercises, information on video materials, and other resources for the study of global environmental politics.

Ronald Mitchell, University of Oregon. *http://darkwing.uoregon.edu/~rmitchell/*. A useful model for using the Internet as a teaching tool.

DONELLA H. MEADOWS,

DENNIS L. MEADOWS, JØRGEN RANDERS

& WILLIAM W. BEHRENS III

1

The Limits to Growth

Problems and Models

Every person approaches HIS problems . . . with the help of models. A model is simply an ordered set of assumptions about a complex system. It is an attempt to understand some aspect of the infinitely varied world by selecting from perceptions and past experience a set of general observations applicable to the problem at hand. . . .

Decision-makers at every level unconsciously use mental models to choose among policies that will shape our future world. These mental models are, of necessity, very simple when compared with the reality from which they are abstracted. The human brain, remarkable as it is, can only keep track of a limited number of the complicated, simultaneous interactions that determine the nature of the real world.

We, too, have used a model. Ours is a formal, written model of the world.* It constitutes a preliminary attempt to improve our mental models of long-term, global problems by combining the large amount of information that is already in human minds and in written records with the new information-processing tools

---

Excerpted from Donella H. Meadows, Dennis L. Meadows, Jørgen Randers, and William W. Behrens III, *The Limits to Growth* (Washington, DC: Potomac Associates, 1972). Reprinted with permission.

*The prototype model on which we have based our work was designed by Professor Jay W. Forrester of the Massachusetts Institute of Technology. A description of that model has been published in his book *World Dynamics* (Cambridge, Mass.: Wright-Allen Press, 1971).

that mankind's increasing knowledge has produced—the scientific method, systems analysis, and the modern computer.

Our world model was built specifically to investigate five major trends of global concern—accelerating industrialization, rapid population growth, widespread malnutrition, depletion of nonrenewable resources, and a deteriorating environment. These trends are all interconnected in many ways, and their development is measured in decades or centuries, rather than in months or years. With the model we are seeking to understand the causes of these trends, their interrelationships, and their implications as much as one hundred years in the future.

The model we have constructed is, like every other model, imperfect, oversimplified, and unfinished. We are well aware of its shortcomings, but we believe that it is the most useful model now available for dealing with problems far out on the space-time graph. To our knowledge it is the only formal model in existence that is truly global in scope, that has a time horizon longer than thirty years, and that includes important variables such as population, food production, and pollution, not as independent entities, but as dynamically interacting elements, as they are in the real world. . . .

In spite of the preliminary state of our work, we believe it is important to publish the model and our findings now. Decisions are being made every day, in every part of the world, that will affect the physical, economic, and social conditions of the world system for decades to come. These decisions cannot wait for perfect models and total understanding. They will be made on the basis of some model, mental or written, in any case. . . .

Our conclusions are:

1. If the present growth trends in world population, industrialization, pollution, food production, and resource depletion continue unchanged, the limits to growth on this planet will be reached sometime within the next one hundred years. The most probable result will be a rather sudden and uncontrollable decline in both population and industrial capacity.
2. It is possible to alter these growth trends and to establish a condition of ecological and economic stability that is sustainable far into the future. The state of global equilibrium could be designed so that the basic material needs of each person on earth are satisfied and each person has an equal opportunity to realize his individual human potential.
3. If the world's people decide to strive for this second outcome rather than the first, the sooner they begin working to attain it, the greater will be their chances of success.

These conclusions are so far-reaching and raise so many questions for further study that we are quite frankly overwhelmed by the enormity of the job that must be done. We hope that this book will serve to interest other people . . . to raise the space and time horizons of their concerns and to join us in understanding and preparing for a period of great transition—the transition from growth to global equilibrium.

. . .

A Finite World

We have mentioned many difficult trade-offs . . . in the production of food, in the consumption of resources, and in the generation and clean-up of pollution. By now it should be clear that all of these trade-offs arise from one simple fact—the earth is finite. The closer any human activity comes to the limit of the earth's ability to support that activity, the more apparent and unresolvable the trade-offs become. When there is plenty of unused arable land, there can be more people and also more food per person. When all the land is already used, the trade-off between more people or more food per person becomes a choice between absolutes.

In general, modern society has not learned to recognize and deal with these trade-offs. The apparent goal of the present world system is to produce more people with more (food, material goods, clean air, and water) for each person. . . . We have noted that if society continues to strive for that goal, it will eventually reach one of many earthly limitations. . . . It is not possible to foretell exactly which limitation will occur first or what the consequences will be, because there are many conceivable, unpredictable human responses to such a situation. It is possible, however, to investigate what conditions and what changes in the world system might lead society to collision with or accommodation to the limits to growth in a finite world.

. . .

Technology and the Limits to Growth

Although the history of human effort contains numerous incidents of mankind's failure to live within physical limits, it is success in overcoming limits that forms the cultural tradition of many dominant people in today's world. Over the past three hundred years, mankind has compiled an impressive record of pushing back the apparent limits to population and economic growth by a series of spectacular technological advances. Since the recent history of a large part of human society has been so continuously successful, it is quite natural that many people expect technological breakthroughs to go on raising physical ceilings indefinitely. These people speak about the future with resounding technological optimism.

. . .

The hopes of the technological optimists center on the ability of technology to remove or extend the limits to growth of population and capital. We have shown that in the world model the application of technology to apparent problems of resource depletion or pollution or food shortage has no impact on the essential problem, which is exponential growth in a finite and complex system. Our attempts to use even the most optimistic estimates of the benefits of technology in the model did not prevent the ultimate decline of population and industry, and in fact did not in any case postpone the collapse beyond the year 2100.

. . .

Applying technology to the natural pressures that the environment exerts against any growth process has been so successful in the past that a whole culture has evolved around the principle of fighting against limits rather than learning to live with them. . . . But the relationship between the earth's limits and man's activities is changing. The exponential growth curves are adding millions of people and billions of tons of pollutants to the ecosystem each year. Even the ocean, which once appeared virtually inexhaustible, is losing species after species of its commercially useful animals. . . .

There may be much disagreement with the statement that population and capital growth must stop soon. But virtually no one will argue that material growth on this planet can go on forever. . . . Man can still choose his limits and stop when he pleases by weakening some of the strong pressures that cause capital and population growth, or by instituting counterpressures, or both. Such counterpressures will probably not be entirely pleasant. They will certainly involve profound changes in the social and economic structures that have been deeply impressed into human culture by centuries of growth. The alternative is to wait until the price of technology becomes more than society can pay, or until the side-effects of technology suppress growth themselves, or until problems arise that have no technical solutions. At any of those points the choice of limits will be gone. Growth will be stopped by pressures that are not of human choosing, and that, as the world model suggests, may be very much worse than those which society might choose for itself.

. . . Technological optimism is the most common and the most dangerous reaction to our findings from the world model. Technology can relieve the symptoms of a problem without affecting the underlying causes. Faith in technology as the ultimate solution to all problems can thus divert our attention from the most fundamental problem—the problem of growth in a finite system—and prevent us from taking effective action to solve it.

. . .

The Transition from Growth to Global Equilibrium

We can say very little at this point about the practical, day-by-day steps that might be taken to reach a desirable, sustainable state of global equilibrium. Neither the world model nor our own thoughts have been developed in sufficient detail to understand all the implications of the transition from growth to equilibrium. Before any part of the world's society embarks deliberately on such a transition, there must be much more discussion, more extensive analysis, and many new ideas contributed by many different people. . . .

Although we underline the need for more study and discussion of these difficult questions, we end on a note of urgency. We hope that intensive study and debate will proceed simultaneously with an ongoing program of action. The details are not yet specified, but the general direction for action is obvious. Enough is known already to analyze many proposed policies in terms of their tendencies to promote or to regulate growth.[53] . . . Efforts are weak at the moment, but they could be strengthened very quickly if the goal of equilibrium were recognized as desirable and important by any sizable part of human society. . . .

Taking no action to solve these problems is equivalent to taking strong action. Every day of continued exponential growth brings the world system closer to the ultimate limits to that growth. A decision to do nothing is a decision to increase the risk of collapse. We cannot say with certainty how much longer mankind can postpone initiating deliberate control of his growth before he will have lost the chance for control. We suspect on the basis of present knowledge of the physical constraints of the planet that the growth phase cannot continue for another one hundred years. Again, because of the delays in the system, if the global society waits until those constraints are unmistakably apparent, it will have waited too long.

If there is cause for deep concern, there is also cause for hope. Deliberately limiting growth would be difficult, but not impossible. The way to proceed is clear, and the necessary steps, although they are new ones for human society, are well within human capabilities. Man possesses, for a small moment in his history, the most powerful combination of knowledge, tools, and resources the world has ever known. He has all that is physically necessary to create a totally new form of human society—one that would be built to last for generations. The two missing ingredients are a realistic, long-term goal that can guide mankind to the equilibrium society and the human will to achieve that goal. Without such a goal and a commitment to it, short-term concerns will generate the exponential growth that drives the world system toward the limits of the earth and ultimate collapse. With that goal and that commitment mankind would be ready now to begin a controlled, orderly transition from growth to global equilibrium.

JOÃO AUGUSTO DE ARAUJO CASTRO

2

Environment & Development: The Case of the Developing Countries

Introduction

Interest in the field of ecology, which is centered in the developed countries, has recently increased due to the sudden discovery of a possible imbalance between man and earth. Resulting from the population explosion and the misuse of existing and newly developed technologies, this potential imbalance could bring about an environmental crisis menacing the future of mankind. In several countries the emergence of an interest in ecological problems has not been confined to the realm of the scientific community. It has aroused public concern which has expressed itself, although sometimes vaguely, in such initiatives as Earth Week, celebrated in the United States in April 1970, and the mushrooming of a specialized literature.

As would be expected, the methods envisaged to resolve on a world basis the so-called environmental crisis were inspired by the realities of a fraction of that very same world: the family of the developed countries. Furthermore, the bulk of

Excerpted from "Environment and Development: The Case of the Developing Countries," in *World Eco-crisis: International Organizations in Response,* eds. David A. Kay and Eugene B. Skolnikoff. © 1972. Reprinted by permission of the University of Wisconsin Press, Madison, WI.

the solutions in hand, mainly of a technical nature, seek primarily to make healthier the consequences of the Industrial Revolution without necessarily providing a tool for a further distribution of its benefits among states.

This study seeks to introduce some neglected aspects of the interests of developing countries into discussions about a world ecological policy. The working hypothesis is that the implementation of any worldwide environmental policy based on the realities of the developed countries tends to perpetuate the existing gap in socioeconomic development between developed and developing countries and so promote the freezing of the present international order. . . .

Developed Countries

Although there does not yet exist a systematic body of doctrine, the new ecological policy of the developed countries contains several elements that have already stimulated important developments in academic thought, as indicated by the growing literature on the matter, and attitudes of governments and private sectors in these countries, mainly in their relations with the developing countries.

A short historical digression may help in analyzing the rationale of this ecological policy. As a localized phenomenon in the countries of the Northern Hemisphere, the Industrial Revolution of the eighteenth century was not brought about by one single factor. It was not, for instance, the result of inventions or the coming into operation of new machines. As in the case of other major movements in history, it was the result of the interplay of many factors, some obscure in themselves, whose combined effort laid down the foundations of a new industrial system. Growing organically, cell by cell, new patterns of industrial organization were soon translated into the establishment of a new international order. Around the group of countries enjoying the benefits of the Industrial Revolution there existed an increasing family of countries, trying, mostly unsuccessfully, to modernize their own means of production.

This new international order and the relatively uneven distribution of political power among states, based on the use and monopoly of advanced technologies, may be considered one of the most enduring effects of the Industrial Revolution. And since then, as a normal corollary of the new order, the technologically advanced countries have been endeavoring to maintain their political and economic position in the world while the technologically less endowed countries have been seeking to alter, through development, this global status quo.

This permanent struggle between the two groups of countries persists in the present days and it is unlikely that it will cease in the near future. For this to happen one would have to assume a perfectly homogeneous world community whose conflicts would have been eliminated through a perfect satisfaction, on a homogeneous basis, of all human needs. This condition is most likely to be found only in the realms of utopia. . . .

According to a helpful image taken from academic and governmental sources in the developed countries our planet could be visualized as a "spaceship earth," where life could only be sustained, nay simply possible, through maintenance of a delicate equilibrium between the needs of the passengers and the ability of the craft to respond to those needs. Undisturbed until recently, this equilibrium would now be menaced by an excess of population and the consequences of the use of both previously existing and newly developed technologies. Elaborating the same image, "spaceship earth" would be divided into two classes of passengers, the first coincident with the technologically advanced countries and the second representative of the technologically less endowed countries, which would necessarily have to trade off positions with a view to maintaining the equilibrium of the vessel. . . .

In order to maintain the equilibrium of the vessel the problems created by population explosion and the use of both previously existing and new technologies should, in the view of developed countries, now be dealt with globally, irrespective of the unequal distribution, on a world scale, of the benefits and related destructive effects on the environment engendered by the Industrial Revolution. Germane to such a global ecological policy is the need for world planning for development which, to be successful, might purposely aim at freezing the present relative positions of the two classes inside the vessel.

Provided that the first class already enjoys low average rates of population growth and is unlikely to opt for a slower rate of industrial growth for the sole purpose of guaranteeing a purer atmosphere or cleaner water, the new ecology-saving policy would be more successful if applied in the areas where the environmental crisis has not yet appeared, even in its least acute forms. Actually, these areas would mainly comprise the territory of the second class. Thus: the second class should be taught to employ the most effective and expeditious birth control methods and to follow an orderly pollution-reducing process of industrialization. In the case of industrialization, the mainstream of socioeconomic development, the lesson must be even harsher: The second class must organize production in accordance with environment-saving techniques already tested by the first class or be doomed to socioeconomic stagnation. . . .

Nowadays some ecologists do not hesitate to say that the developing countries can never hope to achieve the consumption patterns of the developed countries. Some seemingly appalling calculations are offered as proof of this. To raise the living standards of the world's existing population to American levels the annual production of iron would have to increase 75 times, that of copper 100 times, that of lead 200 times, and that of tin 250 times. Were a country such as India to make use of fertilizers at the per capita level of the Netherlands, it would consume one-half of the world's total output of fertilizers. Clearly, the parity of the developing countries with the developed ones is no longer compatible with the existing stocks of natural resources. Again, according to those wise men, the increasing expectations in developing countries, which are sometimes associated with something approaching a revolution, are nothing more than expectations of elites and therefore must be curbed. Most of the population of these countries, it is claimed, do not have an ambition to reach Western standards and do not even know that "such a thing as development is on the agenda."

Now, the alleged exhaustion of natural resources is accompanied, in general, by forecasts of the fateful coming of formidable ecological hecatombs. The continuing progress of developed countries would require an economic lebensraum in the Southern Hemisphere. In the name of the survival of mankind developing countries should continue in a state of underdevelopment because if the evils of industrialization were to reach them, life on the planet would be placed in jeopardy. . . .

Very few reasonable people underwrite these fanciful ideas. Yet, it cannot be denied that the environment in developed countries is threatened and that it should be preserved. The difficulty in dealing with environmental problems nowadays is that they have become a myth. . . . From an uttermost neglect of ecological problems public opinion in the United States has swung to an outright "geolatry." The environment has been rediscovered and Mother Earth now has a week dedicated to her in the calendar. School children crusade to clean up the streets; college students organize huge demonstrations; uncivilized industries that dump their wastes in the air, in the water, or on the ground are denounced as public enemies.

. . . The simplistic concepts that ecology is disturbed because there are "too many people" or because they "consume too much" must be discarded as nothing more than fallacies. There is abundant evidence that the earth is capable of supporting a considerably greater population at much higher levels of consumption. The simple fact that in half a century mankind found it possible to wage four major wars, with a terrible waste of wealth, is a clear indication that we are not after all so short of resources although we may be short of common sense. . . .

Environmental problems not only pose a new and compelling argument for disarmament and peace but also call attention to the question of efficiency in the organization of production. It is widely known, but seldom remembered when the availability of natural resources is discussed, that in developed countries billions of dollars are spent every year to purchase so-called farm surpluses. Millions of tons of agricultural products have been regularly stored or destroyed to keep prices up in the world markets. . . . These figures and these facts evidently do not agree with the superficial statements which have been made about the irreparable strain being put on natural resources.

Pollution of the air and water and related damages to the environment are loosely attributed, in general, to faulty technologies, but few have bothered to assess objectively the exact proportions of the problem. According to experts at the Organization for Economic Cooperation and Development (OECD) safeguarding the environment in the United States would require annual expenditures of . . . less than 2 percent of the American GNP [Editors' note: gross national product]. Clearly, there is no real cause for most of the fuzzy agitation about the environment. Put in their proper perspective, environmental problems are little more than a question of the reexamination of national priorities. . . .

When discussing the environment some ecologists and other wise men, as often happens in many other instances, try haphazardly to superimpose peculiar situations prevailing in developed countries onto the realities of the developing countries. . . . If the peculiarities of developing countries are taken into account, it will not be difficult to recognize that, in broad terms, they are still at a prepollution stage or, in other words, have not yet been given the chance to become polluted. . . . The 24 countries of Latin America, the least under-developed region in the developing world, have less than one-tenth of the total number of motor vehicles in the United States. Only a few ecologists and other wise men would say that Latin Americans should rather have fewer cars and cleaner air.

There is a pollution of affluence and a pollution of poverty. It is imperative to distinguish between the two lest some pollution be prevented at the cost of much economic development. Were it not for the dangers arising from the confusion between the two kinds of pollution, there would be no need for calling attention to the precarious housing conditions, poor health, and low sanitary standards not to mention starvation in developing countries. The linear transposition of ecological problems of the developed countries to the context of the developing ones disregards the existence of such distressing social conditions. Wherever these conditions prevail, the assertion that income means less pollution is nonsense. It is obvious, or should be, that the so-called pollution of poverty can only be corrected through higher incomes, or more precisely, through economic development.

The most sensible ecologists are of the opinion that the pollution levels can be attributed not so much to population or affluence as to modern technologies. In the United States the economy would have grown enough, in the absence of technological change, to give the increased population about the same per capita amounts of goods and services today as in 1946. The ecological crisis has resulted mainly from the sweeping progress in technologies. Modern technologies have multiplied the impact of growth on the environment and, consequently, generated most of the existing pollution. Those who haphazardly transpose developed countries' situations to the milieu of an underdeveloped country repeatedly warn the latter against the dangers of modern technologies and rapid industrialization. "Don't let happen to your cities what happened to New York; keep your beautiful landscapes." It is ironic that developed countries, which create and sell modern technologies, should caution developing countries against utilizing them. Is this done to justify the second-hand technologies that sometimes accompany foreign direct investments?

Developing Countries

A somewhat apathetic attitude on the part of the developing countries regarding the environmental issue does not imply negation of the relevance of the matter and the need for true international cooperation to solve the problem it poses for the survival of mankind. This apathetic attitude, however, clearly is derived from the developing countries' socioeconomic experience which differs, to a large extent, from that of the developed countries. Consequently, one has to bear in mind that, not having enjoyed the opportunity to experience their own Industrial Revolution, the developing countries have not been stimulated to think about the environmental crisis as posed in the present days. The phenomenon of urbanization in the Southern Hemisphere, even in the countries experiencing a considerable degree of progress, may raise questions about poor living standards in some areas but has not thus far led to industrial congestion.

As indicated in the elements of the ecological policy of the developed countries, the equilibrium of "spaceship earth" would depend on the enforcement of measures bearing on population and on the use of the previously existing and new technologies chiefly in the second class of the vessel or, in other words, in the territory of the developing countries. Even if applied to their full extent, those measures would not result at some foreseeable date in a single-class carrying vessel, preferably closer to the first steerage. This ecological policy, which aims primarily at the equilibrium of the vessel, could better succeed if the relative positions of the classes were maintained, for the emergence of one single class would presuppose a considerable change in the living standards of the first class, something that may not be attained in the light of present global socioeconomic realities. . . .

On the question of the preservation of the environment the passenger's survival would call for the enforcement of a drastic decision, globally applied, to maintain a "green area reserve" which would have to coincide mainly with the territories of the developing countries. This step would safeguard, against complete exhaustion, the natural elements (soil, atmosphere, and water) still available on the planet just to provide some sort of counteraction to the spoilage of the same natural elements used up in the countries where the benefits of the Industrial Revolution were massively concentrated.

Besides the ethical question raised by this policy, as expressed in the ostensive imbalance between responsibility for the damage and obligation for repair, the developing countries, in abiding by its prescriptions, would make a commitment to conservatism rather than to conservation. Furthermore, the possibility of a widespread application of developed countries' ecological policy, theoretically conceived to secure the equilibrium of "spaceship earth," may risk transforming the Southern Hemisphere countries into the last healthy weekend areas for the inhabitants of a planet already saturated with the environment created by the Industrial Revolution. As a token of compensation the Southern Hemisphere countries could claim to have resurrected, and adequately preserved, the environmental milieu for the living and the survival of Rousseau's "happy savage." In expressing their concern over the environmental crisis the developing countries cannot accept, without further refinement, the ecological policy devised by the developed countries whose socioeconomic structure was deeply influenced by the unique phenomenon of the Industrial Revolution.

The first step toward the refinement of that policy may be the rejection of the principle that the ecology issue, taken on a global basis, can be dealt with exclusively through a technical approach, as suggested by the developed countries. Given the implications for the international order, including the freezing of the status quo, any environment-saving policy must necessarily be imbued with a solid and well-informed political approach. This would provide an opportunity for the developing countries, by preserving their national identities, to join safely in the effort of the international community to preserve the equilibrium of "spaceship earth."

As a normal corollary of the political approach, ecological policy should not depart from the broader framework of socioeconomic development. In this regard a second step of refinement would require a corresponding universal commitment to development if the task of preserving the environment is to be shared by the world community. . . .

Evidently, no country wants any pollution at all. But each country must evolve its own development plans, exploit its own resources as it thinks suitable, and define its own environmental standards. The idea of having such priorities and standards imposed on individual countries or groups of countries, on either a multilateral or a bilateral basis, is very hard to accept.

That is why it is disturbing to see the International Bank for Reconstruction and Development (IBRD) set up its own ecological policy. Repercussions on the environment, defined according to IBRD ecologists, have become an important factor in determining whether financial assistance by that institution should be granted for an industrial project in developing countries. It seems reasonable that the preservation of the environment should not exclude the preservation of national sovereignty. Ecological policies should rather be inserted into the framework of national development.

It is perhaps time for the developing countries to present their own views on the framing of an environmental policy in spite of the fact that the developed countries have not yet ended their own controversial debate or furnished definite and convincing data on the issue. In adopting a position the developing countries recognize the existence of environmental problems in the world and the possibility of finding solutions through both national efforts and international cooperation.

The first point to be touched on concerns the question of national sovereignty. In this regard any ecological policy, globally applied, must not be an instrument to suppress wholly or in part the legitimate right of any country to decide about its own affairs. In reality this point would simply seek to guarantee on an operational level the full exercise of the principle of juridical equality of states as expressed, for instance, in the Charter of the United Nations. . . . Sovereignty, in this context, should not be taken as an excuse for isolationism and consequently for escapism in relation to international efforts geared to solving environmental problems. For the developing countries it is crucial to consider, in the light of their own interests, nationally defined, the whole range of alternative solutions devised or implemented in the developed countries. Naturally, it is assumed that all countries can act responsibly and that none is going to deliberately favor policies that may endanger the equilibrium of "spaceship earth."

Closely linked to the problem of sovereignty, the question of national priorities calls for an understanding of the distinction between the developmental characteristics of developed and developing countries. As has been previously pointed out in this article, while the ecological issue came to the forefront of public concern as a by-product of postindustrial stages of development, it is not yet strikingly apparent in the majority of the developing countries. And different realities, of course, should be differently treated or, at least, given the fittest solutions.

In the developing countries the major concern is an urgent need to accelerate socioeconomic development, and a meaningful ecological policy must not hamper the attainment of that goal in the most expeditious way. . . . In this context the developing countries, while rejecting the implementation of any ecological policy which bears in itself elements of socioeconomic stagnation, could only share a common responsibility for the preservation of the environment if it was accompanied and paralleled by a corresponding common responsibility for development.

. . .

Conclusion

This study has probed very briefly some aspects of an ecological policy in the light of the interests of the developing countries. . . . Emphasis has been laid on the undesirability of transposing, uncritically, into the realities of the developing countries the solutions already envisaged by the developed countries to eliminate or reduce the so-called environmental crisis to the extent that those solutions may embody elements of socioeconomic stagnation. . . . Finally, a preliminary and broad picture of a position of the developing countries has stressed the relation between preservation of environment and the urgent need to speed up socioeconomic development and the desirability of a common world effort to tackle both these aspects simultaneously. This common effort, however, should not preclude or trespass on national interest as a departing point for the setting up of concepts and operational guidelines of an ecological policy for the developing countries.

In conclusion, a discussion of any meaningful ecological policy for both developed and developing countries . . . would better reflect a broad socioeconomic concern, as tentatively suggested in this article, rather than confine itself to a strictly scientific approach. Man's conceptual environment, and nothing else, will certainly prevail in shaping the future of mankind, for the preservation of the environment presupposes a human being to live in it and a human mind to conceive a better life for man on this planet. From the point of view of man—and we have no other standpoint—Man, Pascal's "roseau pensant," is still more relevant than Nature.

GARRETT HARDIN

3

The Tragedy
of the Commons

Tragedy of Freedom in a Commons

... The tragedy of the commons develops in this way. Picture a pasture open
to all. It is to be expected that each herdsman will try to keep as many cattle as
possible on the commons. Such an arrangement may work reasonably satisfacto-
rily for centuries because tribal wars, poaching, and disease keep the numbers of
both man and beast well below the carrying capacity of the land. Finally, however,
comes the day of reckoning, that is, the day when the long-desired goal of social
stability becomes a reality. At this point, the inherent logic of the commons re-
morselessly generates tragedy.

As a rational being, each herdsman seeks to maximize his gain. Explicitly or implicitly, more or less consciously, he asks, "What is the utility to *me* of adding one
more animal to my herd?" This utility has one negative and one positive component.

1. The positive component is a function of the increment of one animal.
   Since the herdsman receives all the proceeds from the sale of the additional animal, the positive utility is nearly +1.
2. The negative component is a function of the additional overgrazing created by one more animal. Since, however, the effects of overgrazing are

Originally published in *Science* 162 (December 13, 1968):1243–1248. Copyright © 1968 by the
American Association for the Advancement of Science. Reprinted with permission.

shared by all the herdsmen, the negative utility for any particular decision-making herdsman is only a fraction of -1.

Adding together the component partial utilities, the rational herdsman concludes that the only sensible course for him to pursue is to add another animal to his herd. And another; and another. . . . But this is the conclusion reached by each and every rational herdsman sharing a commons. Therein is the tragedy. Each man is locked into a system that compels him to increase his herd without limit—in a world that is limited. Ruin is the destination toward which all men rush, each pursuing his own best interest in a society that believes in the freedom of the commons. Freedom in a commons brings ruin to all.

Some would say that this is a platitude. Would that it were! In a sense, it was learned thousands of years ago, but natural selection favors the forces of psychological denial.[8] The individual benefits as an individual from his ability to deny the truth even though society as a whole, of which he is a part, suffers. Education can counteract the natural tendency to do the wrong thing, but the inexorable succession of generations requires that the basis for this knowledge be constantly refreshed. . . .

In an approximate way, the logic of the commons has been understood for a long time, perhaps since the discovery of agriculture or the invention of private property in real estate. But it is understood mostly only in special cases which are not sufficiently generalized. Even at this late date, cattlemen leasing national land on the western ranges demonstrate no more than an ambivalent understanding, in constantly pressuring federal authorities to increase the head count to the point where overgrazing produces erosion and weed dominance. Likewise, the oceans of the world continue to suffer from the survival of the philosophy of the commons. Maritime nations still respond automatically to the shibboleth of the "freedom of the seas." Professing to believe in the "inexhaustible resources of the oceans," they bring species after species of fish and whales closer to extinction.[9]

The National Parks present another instance of the working out of the tragedy of the commons. At present, they are open to all, without limit. The parks themselves are limited in extent—there is only one Yosemite Valley—whereas the population seems to grow without limit. The values that visitors seek in the parks are steadily eroded. Plainly, we must soon cease to treat the parks as commons or they will be of no value to anyone.

What shall we do? We have several options. We might sell them off as private property. We might keep them as public property, but allocate the right to enter them. The allocation might be on the basis of wealth, by the use of an auction system. It might be on the basis of merit, as defined by some agreed-upon standards. It might be by lottery. Or it might be on a first-come, first-served basis, administered to long queues. These, I think, are all the reasonable possibilities. They are all objectionable. But we must choose—or acquiesce in the destruction of the commons that we call our National Parks.

Pollution

In a reverse way, the tragedy of the commons reappears in problems of pollution. Here it is not a question of taking something out of the commons, but of putting something in—sewage, or chemical, radioactive, and heat wastes into water; noxious and dangerous fumes into the air; and distracting and unpleasant advertising signs into the line of sight. The calculations of utility are much the same as before. The rational man finds that his share of the cost of the wastes he discharges into the commons is less than the cost of purifying his wastes before releasing them. Since this is true for everyone, we are locked into a system of "fouling our own nest," so long as we behave only as independent, rational, free-enterprisers.

The tragedy of the commons as a food basket is averted by private property, or something formally like it. But the air and waters surrounding us cannot readily be fenced, and so the tragedy of the commons as a cesspool must be prevented by different means, by coercive laws or taxing devices that make it cheaper for the polluter to treat his pollutants than to discharge them untreated. We have not progressed as far with the solution of this problem as we have with the first. Indeed, our particular concept of private property, which deters us from exhausting the positive resources of the earth, favors pollution. The owner of a factory on the bank of a stream—whose property extends to the middle of the stream—often has difficulty seeing why it is not his natural right to muddy the waters flowing past his door. The law, always behind the times, requires elaborate stitching and fitting to adapt it to this newly perceived aspect of the commons.

The pollution problem is a consequence of population. It did not much matter how a lonely American frontiersman disposed of his waste. "Flowing water purifies itself every 10 miles," my grandfather used to say, and the myth was near enough to the truth when he was a boy, for there were not too many people. But as population became denser, the natural chemical and biological recycling processes became overloaded, calling for a redefinition of property rights.

How to Legislate Temperance?

Analysis of the pollution problem as a function of population density uncovers a not generally recognized principle of morality, namely: *the morality of an act is a function of the state of the system at the time it is performed*.[10] Using the commons as a cesspool does not harm the general public under frontier conditions, because there is no public; the same behavior in a metropolis is unbearable. A hundred and fifty years ago a plainsman could kill an American bison, cut out only the tongue for his dinner, and discard the rest of the animal. He was not in any important sense being wasteful. Today, with only a few thousand bison left, we would be appalled at such behavior. . . .

That morality is system-sensitive escaped the attention of most codifiers of ethics in the past. "Thou shalt not . . ." is the form of traditional ethical directives which make no allowance for particular circumstances. The laws of our society follow the pattern of ancient ethics, and therefore are poorly suited to governing a complex, crowded, changeable world. Our epicyclic solution is to augment statutory law with administrative law. Since it is practically impossible to spell out all the conditions under which it is safe to burn trash in the back yard or to run an automobile without smog-control, by law we delegate the details to bureaus. The result is administrative law, which is rightly feared for an ancient reason—*Quis custodiet ipsos custodes?*—"Who shall watch the watchers themselves?" John Adams said that we must have "a government of laws and not men." Bureau administrators, trying to evaluate the morality of acts in the total system, are singularly liable to corruption, producing a government by men, not laws.

Prohibition is easy to legislate (though not necessarily to enforce); but how do we legislate temperance? Experience indicates that it can be accomplished best through the mediation of administrative law. We limit possibilities unnecessarily if we suppose that the sentiment of *Quis custodiet* denies us the use of administrative law. We should rather retain the phrase as a perpetual reminder of fearful dangers we cannot avoid. The great challenge facing us now is to invent the corrective feedbacks that are needed to keep custodians honest. We must find ways to legitimate the needed authority of both the custodians and the corrective feedbacks.

Freedom to Breed Is Intolerable

The tragedy of the commons is involved in population problems in another way. In a world governed solely by the principle of "dog eat dog"—if indeed there ever was such a world—how many children a family had would not be a matter of public concern. Parents who bred too exuberantly would leave fewer descendants, not more, because they would be unable to care adequately for their children. David Lack and others have found that such a negative feedback demonstrably controls the fecundity of birds.[11] But men are not birds, and have not acted like them for millenniums, at least.

If each human family were dependent only on its own resources; *if* the children of improvident parents starved to death; *if,* thus, overbreeding brought its own "punishment" to the germ line—*then* there would be no public interest in controlling the breeding of families. But our society is deeply committed to the welfare state,[12] and hence is confronted with another aspect of the tragedy of the commons.

In a welfare state, how shall we deal with the family, the religion, the race, or the class (or indeed any distinguishable and cohesive group) that adopts overbreeding as a policy to secure its own aggrandizement?[13] To couple the concept of freedom to breed with the belief that everyone born has an equal right to the commons is to lock the world into a tragic course of action. . . .

Conscience Is Self-Eliminating

It is a mistake to think that we can control the breeding of mankind in the long run by an appeal to conscience. . . .

People vary. Confronted with appeals to limit breeding, some people will undoubtedly respond to the plea more than others. Those who have more children will produce a larger fraction of the next generation than those with more susceptible consciences. The difference will be accentuated, generation by generation. . . . The argument has here been stated in the context of the population problem, but it applies equally well to any instance in which society appeals to an individual exploiting a commons to restrain himself for the general good—by means of his conscience. To make such an appeal is to set up a selective system that works toward the elimination of conscience from the race.

Pathogenic Effects of Conscience

. . . To conjure up a conscience in others is tempting to anyone who wishes to extend his control beyond the legal limits. Leaders at the highest level succumb to this temptation. Has any President during the past generation failed to call on labor unions to moderate voluntarily their demands for higher wages, or to steel companies to honor voluntary guidelines on prices? I can recall none. The rhetoric used on such occasions is designed to produce feelings of guilt in noncooperators.

For centuries it was assumed without proof that guilt was a valuable, perhaps even an indispensable, ingredient of the civilized life. Now, in this post-Freudian world, we doubt it.

Paul Goodman speaks from the modern point of view when he says: "No good has ever come from feeling guilty, neither intelligence, policy, nor compassion. The guilty do not pay attention to the object but only to themselves, and not even to their own interests, which might make sense, but to their anxieties."[18]

One does not have to be a professional psychiatrist to see the consequences of anxiety. We in the Western world are just emerging from a dreadful two-centuries-long Dark Ages of Eros that was sustained partly by prohibition laws, but perhaps more effectively by the anxiety-generating mechanisms of education. . . .

Since proof is difficult, we may even concede that the results of anxiety may sometimes, from certain points of view, be desirable. The larger question we should ask is whether, as a matter of policy, we should ever encourage the use of a technique the tendency (if not the intention) of which is psychologically pathogenic. We hear much talk these days of responsible parenthood; the coupled words are incorporated into the titles of some organizations devoted to birth control. Some people have proposed massive propaganda campaigns to instill responsibility into the nation's (or the world's) breeders. But what is the meaning of the word responsibility in this context? Is it not merely a synonym for the word conscience? When we use the word responsibility in the absence of substantial sanctions are we not trying to browbeat a free man in a commons into acting against his own interest? Responsibility is a verbal counterfeit for a substantial quid pro quo. It is an attempt to get something for nothing.

If the word responsibility is to be used at all, I suggest that it be in the sense Charles Frankel uses it.[20] "Responsibility," says this philosopher, "is the product of definite social arrangements." Notice that Frankel calls for social arrangements—not propaganda.

Mutual Coercion
Mutually Agreed Upon

The social arrangements that produce responsibility are arrangements that create coercion, of some sort. Consider bank-robbing. The man who takes money from a bank acts as if the bank were a commons. How do we prevent such action? Certainly not by trying to control his behavior solely by a verbal appeal to his sense of responsibility. Rather than rely on propaganda we follow Frankel's lead and insist that a bank is not a commons; we seek the definite social arrangements that will keep it from becoming a commons. That we thereby infringe on the freedom of would-be robbers we neither deny nor regret.

The morality of bank-robbing is particularly easy to understand because we accept complete prohibition of this activity. We are willing to say "Thou shalt not rob banks," without providing for exceptions. But temperance also can be created by coercion. Taxing is a good coercive device. To keep downtown shoppers temperate in their use of parking space we introduce parking meters for short periods, and traffic fines for longer ones. We need not actually forbid a citizen to park as long as he wants to; we need merely make it increasingly expensive for him to do so. Not prohibition, but carefully biased options are what we offer him. A Madison Avenue man might call this persuasion; I prefer the greater candor of the word coercion.

Coercion is a dirty word to most liberals now, but it need not forever be so. As with the four-letter words, its dirtiness can be cleansed away by exposure to the light, by saying it over and over without apology or embarrassment. To many, the word coercion implies arbitrary decisions of distant and irresponsible bureaucrats; but this is not a necessary part of its meaning. The only kind of coercion I recommend is mutual coercion, mutually agreed upon by the majority of the people affected.

To say that we mutually agree to coercion is not to say that we are required to enjoy it, or even to pretend we enjoy it. Who enjoys taxes? We all grumble about them. But we accept compulsory taxes because we recognize that voluntary taxes would favor the conscienceless. We institute and (grumblingly) support taxes and other coercive devices to escape the horror of the commons.

An alternative to the commons need not be perfectly just to be preferable. . . . The alternative of the commons is too horrifying to contemplate. Injustice is preferable to total ruin.

It is one of the peculiarities of the warfare between reform and the status quo that it is thoughtlessly governed by a double standard. Whenever a reform measure is proposed it is often defeated when its opponents triumphantly discover a flaw in it. As Kingsley Davis has pointed out,[21] worshippers of the status quo sometimes imply that no reform is possible without unanimous agreement, an implication contrary to historical fact. As nearly as I can make out, automatic rejection of proposed reforms is based on one of two unconscious assumptions: (i) that the status quo is perfect; or (ii) that the choice we face is between reform and no action; if the proposed reform is imperfect, we presumably should take no action at all, while we wait for a perfect proposal.

But we can never do nothing. That which we have done for thousands of years is also action. It also produces evils. Once we are aware that the status quo is action, we can then compare its discoverable advantages and disadvantages with the predicted advantages and disadvantages of the proposed reform, discounting as best we can for our lack of experience. On the basis of such a comparison, we can make a rational decision which will not involve the unworkable assumption that only perfect systems are tolerable.

Recognition of Necessity

Perhaps the simplest summary of this analysis of man's population problems is this: the commons, if justifiable at all, is justifiable only under conditions of low-population density. As the human population has increased, the commons has had to be abandoned in one aspect after another.

First we abandoned the commons in food gathering, enclosing farm land and restricting pastures and hunting and fishing areas. These restrictions are still not complete throughout the world.

Somewhat later we saw that the commons as a place for waste disposal would also have to be abandoned. Restrictions on the disposal of domestic sewage are widely accepted in the Western world; we are still struggling to close the commons to pollution by automobiles, factories, insecticide sprayers, fertilizing operations, and atomic energy installations.

In a still more embryonic state is our recognition of the evils of the commons in matters of pleasure. There is almost no restriction on the propagation of sound waves in the public medium. The shopping public is assaulted with mindless music, without its consent. Our government is paying out billions of dollars to create supersonic transport which will disturb 50,000 people for every one person who is whisked from coast to coast 3 hours faster. Advertisers muddy the airwaves of radio and television and pollute the view of travelers. We are a long way from outlawing the commons in matters of pleasure. Is this because our Puritan inheritance makes us view pleasure as something of a sin, and pain (that is, the pollution of advertising) as the sign of virtue?

Every new enclosure of the commons involves the infringement of somebody's personal liberty. Infringements made in the distant past are accepted because no contemporary complains of a loss. It is the newly proposed infringements that we vigorously oppose; cries of "rights" and "freedom" fill the air. But what does "freedom" mean? When men mutually agreed to pass laws against robbing, mankind became more free, not less so. Individuals locked into the logic of the commons are free only to bring on universal ruin; once they see the necessity of mutual coercion, they become free to pursue other goals. I believe it was Hegel who said, "Freedom is the recognition of necessity."

The most important aspect of necessity that we must now recognize is the necessity of abandoning the commons in breeding. No technical solution can rescue us from the misery of overpopulation. Freedom to breed will bring ruin to all. At the moment, to avoid hard decisions many of us are tempted to propagandize for conscience and responsible parenthood. The temptation must be resisted, because an appeal to independently acting consciences selects for life disappearance of all conscience in the long run, and an increase in anxiety in the short.

The only way we can preserve and nurture other and more precious freedoms is by relinquishing the freedom to breed, and that very soon. "Freedom is the recognition of necessity"—and it is the role of education to reveal to all the necessity of abandoning the freedom to breed. Only so, can we put an end to this aspect of the tragedy of the commons.

S U S A N   J .   B U C K

4

No Tragedy
on the Commons

Introduction

In 1951, Josephine Tey published her classic detective story *Daughter of Time.* In this defense of Richard III, she coined the term *Tonypandy,* which is the regrettable situation which occurs when a historical event is reported and memorialized inaccurately but consistently until the resulting fiction is believed to be the truth.[1] History is not the only field in which Tonypandy occurs. A prime example of Tonypandy in the field of economics is the "tragedy of the commons."

Academics are often too facile in labeling an article as "seminal," but Garrett Hardin's 1968 article, "The Tragedy of the Commons," deserves the accolade.[2] The article has been reprinted over fifty times,[3] and entire books have been devoted to exploring the meaning and implications of Hardin's memorable title.[4] The phrase "tragedy of the commons" has slipped into common parlance at colleges and universities and is rapidly becoming public property.[5] Discussion of the inevitability of such a tragedy is the lawful prey of economists, sociologists, philosophers, and theologians. Certainly we cannot deny that the phenomenon exists: the ruination of a limited resource when confronted with unlimited access by an expanding population. Where, then, lies Tonypandy in the tragedy of the commons?

Although the tragedy of the commons may occur, that it regularly occurred on the common lands of medieval and post-medieval England is not true; the histor-

Originally published as Susan Jane Buck Cox, "No Tragedy on the Commons," in *Environmental Ethics* 7 (Spring 1985):49–61. Reprinted with permission.

ical antecedents of the tragedy of the commons as developed by Hardin and others following the 1968 article, and as commonly understood by students and professors, are inaccurate.[6] . . . Decline was not the result of unlimited access, but rather was the result of the historical forces of the industrial revolution, agrarian reform, and improved agricultural practices.

"The Tragedy of the Commons" Defined

. . . [Hardin's original] language is relatively free of cultural phenomena. . . . Later references to Hardin's tragedy of the commons, however, reflect a more explicit historical perspective. In 1977 Hardin used allusions to the Enclosure Acts of the late eighteenth and early nineteenth centuries to explain how the tragedy might be cured.[10] In 1969, Beryl Crowe wrote:

> The commons is a fundamental social institution that has a history going back through our own colonial experience to a body of English common law which antedates the Roman conquest. That law recognized that in societies there are some environmental objects which have never been, and should never be, exclusively appropriated to any individual or group of individuals. In England the classic example of the commons is the pasturage set aside for public use, and the "tragedy of the commons" to which Hardin refers was a tragedy of overgrazing and lack of care and fertilization which resulted in erosion and underproduction so destructive that there developed in the late 19th century an enclosure movement.[11]

. . . Perhaps the most extensive anglicization of the commons is found in *This Endangered Planet* by Richard Falk. He writes that Hardin "has evolved an effective metaphor of [the paradox of aggregation] from a historical experience, the destruction of the common pastures of English country towns in the 1700s and 1800s through overgrazing herds."[13]

Further examples can be found, almost ad infinitum and certainly ad nauseam. Moreover, questioning of graduate students in economics or planning or public administration elicits the same historical background on the tragedy of the commons as described by Falk. Such evidence suggests that there is a general impression among most people today that the tragedy was a regular occurrence on the common lands of the villages in medieval and post-medieval England—a belief which, despite its wide acceptance as fact, is historically false.

The Commons Defined

In order to dispel the myth of the tragedy of the commons, we must first discover the definition of *commons* as it was understood in medieval England. The legal right of common is "a right which one or more persons have to take or use some portion of that which another's soil produces . . . and is a right to part of the profits of the soil, and to part only, the right of the soil lying with another and not with the person who claims common."[14] This right is an ancient one: "Recent archaeological and historical work indicates that in many places nucleated villages did not come into being until the ninth, tenth, or even the eleventh centuries. . . . But whatever their origins, the classic common field system probably developed with them. . . ."[15] These rights "were not something specifically granted by a generous landlord, but were the residue of rights that were much more extensive, rights that are in all probability older than the modern conception of private property. They probably antedate the idea of private property in land, and are therefore of vast antiquity."[16] The right of common was a right granted to specific persons because these persons had some prior claim to the land or because the actual owner of the land granted them that right in return for their services.

Our modern-day notions of *common* as a public right does not accurately describe the medieval commons. Gonner wrote in 1912:

> [Common] now is taken as denoting the claims, somewhat vague and precarious, of the public as against those holding the land and engaged in its cultivation. But this finds no sanction in a time when over very many, if not most, cultivated districts common was a result of claim to land, and formed a necessary condition of its proper management. . . . The early rights of common were anything but vague, and were invariably vested in those employed in cultivation of their representatives; they were anything rather than a general claim on the part of the public. . . . [Common rights] were a necessary element in the agricultural system, they were involved in the ownership and cultivation of the land, and they were largely the source of the profits obtained from the land and the means of rendering its cultivation effective.[17]

Clearly our use of common to describe public access to national parks or to deep-sea fishing is at variance with the original use of the term. . . .

We thus have a picture of the legal status of a common. Either by common-law right as freehold tenant or through usage and grants, a villager was entitled to pasture limited numbers of specific animals on the lord's waste. It is important to note that even from the beginning, the use of the common was not unrestricted: "Common pasture of stubble and fallow was a feature of open-field husbandry from the start . . . and with it went communal control."[24] The English common was not available to the general public but was only available to certain individuals who owned or were granted the right to use it. Use of the common even by these people was not unregulated. The types and in some cases the numbers of animals each tenant could pasture were limited, based at least partly on a recognition of the limited carrying capacity of the land.

The Management of the Commons

The earliest records for communal farming regulations are the manor court rolls of the mid-thirteenth century.[25] The earliest record for a village meeting is the fourteenth century. Joan Thirsk writes:

> From these dates the evidence points unequivocally to the autonomy of village communities in determining the form of, and the rules governing their field system. . . . In villages which possessed no more than one manor, matters were agreed in the manorial court, and the decisions sometimes, but not always, recorded on the court roll. Decisions affecting villages which shared the use of commons were taken at the court of the chief lord, at which all the villages were represented. In villages where more than one manor existed, agreement might be reached at a village meeting at which all tenants and lords were present or represented.[26]

. . . Such agreements among the neighbors are recorded in the village bylaws. These bylaws "emphasize the degree to which . . . agricultural practice was directed and controlled by an assembly of cultivators, the manorial court, who coordinated and regulated the season-by-season activities of the whole community. Arable and meadowland were normally thrown open for common pasturing by the stock of all the commoners after harvest and in fallow times, and this necessitated some rules about cropping, fencing, and grazing beasts. Similarly, all the cultivators of the intermixed strips enjoyed common pasturage in the waste, and in addition, the rights to gather timber, peat and other commodities were essential concomitants of the possession of arable and meadow shares."[28] There was, however, an extraordinary diversity of bylaws among the various regions of England. In one Lincolnshire fenland village, for example, "strangers coming into the town but having no land could enjoy free common for their cattle for one year. After that they had to abide by the rules governing all other inhabitants. These were generous provisions that reflected the abundance of grazing."[29] In contrast, in 1440, the village of Launton decreed that "any tenant who has a parcel of meadow in East Brokemede shall not mow there now or ever until his neighbors are agreed under pain of 3s.4d."[30], a clear reflection of the need to conserve and to regulate. What is important to note here is the detail with which the open fields were regulated. Ault notes that bylaws covered such points as where field workers were paid (at the granary rather than in the field, where payment in kind might lead to accusations of theft), and at what age boys could begin to pasture sheep on the common (sixteen). The commons were carefully and painstakingly regulated, and those instances in which the common deteriorated were most often due to lawbreaking and to oppression of the poorer tenant rather than to egoistic abuse of a common resource.

Abuses of the Commons

The commons were subject to several forms of abuse. Often the regulations governing the commons were broken, as when greedy farmers took in unauthorized animals, or when wealthy landowners or squatters took grazing to which they were not entitled because of lack of agreement among the tenants. The common thread in these abuses is their illegality.

One of the methods of controlling grazing was "stinting," allocating the number and type of beasts that could be grazed on the waste. Stinting developed more from lack of winter feed when stock was pastured on the arable land than from a desire to protect the summer grazing. This summer grazing "was as carefully controlled as the manorial courts could make it."[31] . . . In Westmorland in 1695, "Occasionally, these stinting rules were broken, resulting in the 'Townfield . . . being sore abused and misorderly eaten.' The remedy was to employ a pounder who had to make sure the stints were carefully maintained."[35] Hence, we have one abuse of the common: simple lawbreaking which was remedied by resort to the law.

A similar problem with a less happy solution occurred when the wealthier landholders took advantage of the poorer tenants. In the early sixteenth century, Fitzherbert noted that the rich man benefitted from overcharging the common.[36] According to Gonner, it was "pointed out alike in the sixteenth, seventeenth and eighteenth centuries that the poor owning rights may be largely kept out of their rights by the action of large farmers who exceed their rights and thus surcharge the common to the detriment of all, or by the lack of winter feed in the absence of which summer grazing could be of little worth. . . . The unfortunate poor tenant was denied his remedy at law for the illegal abuses of the more powerful landowners. The ultimate conclusion was the enclosure of the common land, most effective in the parliamentary enclosure acts from 1720 to 1880."[39] Such change was perhaps inevitable, but it is social change and the perennial exploitation of the poor by the less poor rather than Hardin's tragedy.[40]

A third problem arose on unstinted land. In the sixteenth century the "unstinted common was almost invariably overburdened. . . . This state of things was largely to the advantage of rich commoners or the lord of the manor, who got together large flocks and herds and pastured them in the common lands to the detriment of the poorer commoners, who, unlike them, could do little in the way of providing winter feed, and now found themselves ousted even from their slender privileges in the commons."[41] . . . By 1800 in the East Riding, "there was a good deal of overstocking. Some of the commons were stinted but others were not, and it was here that overstocking occurred. Many of the commons were frequently waterlogged when a small expenditure would have drained them, but what was everyone's business was nobody's business."[43] Of course, by 1800 parliamentary enclosure was well under way and this report from East Riding was made by an employee of the newly formed board of agriculture, established in response to a "widespread campaign for the more effective use of the land-resources of the country, with particular reference to the large areas of remaining open fields and to the vast areas of common lands and wastes."[44] Sponsored by wealthy landowners, the land reform was frequently no more than a sophisticated land-grab, justified in part by the admittedly striking increase in productivity of enclosed common land.

The Inevitable Decline of the Commons

The increased productivity was often touted by land reformers—wealthy or otherwise—as proof of the evils of the commons system. However, the change was the result of many factors, and not just of enclosure. Some of the increase would probably have occurred without enclosure, but enclosure hastened the process. The common land was not the best land. The lord's waste was often reclaimed land, cultivated from forest and marsh. . . . Enclosure took the better land and subjected it to the new and improved methods of agriculture which had been all but impossible under the common system, for the management of the common could not be changed unless all commoners agreed and, just as important, remained agreed.[46] Improved roads and transportation facilities made marketing easier, and of course, the land had fewer people to support. Economies of scale made it profitable to use improved stock. In 1760, Robert Bakewell, the founder of modern methods of livestock improvement, began selective breeding of farm animals.[47] Previously forbidden by ecclesiastical authorities as incest, inbreeding of animals with desirable qualities soon led to dramatic improvements in stock.[48] Planting the enclosure with nitrogen-fixing crops such as clover improved the soil; drainage improved livestock health. Animals were disturbed less by driving to and from land pasture. All of these factors combined to improve the productivity of the formerly common land.

That enclosure improved productivity is neither a surprise nor a shame to the commons. The commons system "was falling into disuse, a new system was taking its place, and with the change the actual use made of the common or common rights declined. It might indeed have been retorted [to advocates of inclosure] that what was wanted was a stricter enforcement of the whole common right system."[49] A related view was expressed in 1974 by Van Rensselaer Potter:

When I first read Hardin's article [on the tragedy of the commons], I wondered if the users of the early English commons weren't prevented from committing the fatal error of overgrazing by a kind of 'bioethics' enforced by the moral pressure of their neighbors. Indeed, the commons system operated successfully in England for several hundred years. Now we read that, before the colonial era in the Sahel, 'overpasturage was avoided' by rules worked out by tribal chiefs. When deep wells were drilled to obtain water 'the boreholes threw into chaos the traditional system of pasture use based on agreements among tribal chieftains.' Thus, we see the tragedy of the commons not as a defect in the concept of a 'commons' but as a result of the disastrous transition period between the loss of an effective bioethic and its replacement by a new bioethic that could once again bring biological realities and human values into a viable balance.[50]

Conclusion

Hardin writes that the "view that whatever is owned by many people should be free for the taking by anyone who feels a need for it . . . is precisely the idea of the commons."[51] Why should it matter if this "idea of the commons" is historically inaccurate?

Any academic should feel an aversion to Tonypandy, but the issue is more important than a possible pedantic dislike of inaccuracy. It is beyond dispute that issues such as depletion of limited resources, environmental quality, fisheries economics, and national land management are of great and increasing concern. How those issues are dealt with depends in large part on our perceptions of the disposition of similar issues in the past. If we misunderstand the true nature of the commons, we also misunderstand the implications of the demise of the traditional commons system. Perhaps what existed in fact was not a "tragedy of the commons" but rather a triumph: that for hundreds of years—and perhaps thousands, although written records do not exist to prove the longer era—land was managed successfully by communities. That the system failed to survive the industrial revolution, agrarian reform, and transfigured farming practices is hardly to be wondered at.

Our reexamination of the commons requires a dual focus. The first is to search for the ideas and practices which led to successful commoning for centuries and to try to find lessons and applications for our own times. The second focus is epistemological: are our perceptions of the nature of humankind awry? Since it seems quite likely if "economic man" had been managing the commons that tragedy really would have occurred, perhaps someone else was running the common.

In 1968, Hardin wrote that "'ruin' is the destruction toward which all men rush, each pursuing his own best interest in a society that believes in the freedom of the commons. Freedom in a common brings ruin to all."[52] But the common is not free and never was free. Perhaps in the changed perception of the common lies a remedy for ruin.

DAVID FEENY, FIKRET BERKES,

BONNIE J. MCCAY & JAMES M. ACHESON

5

The Tragedy
of the Commons:
Twenty–two Years Later

Introduction

Garrett Hardin's *The Tragedy of the Commons* was published 22 years ago (Hardin, 1968). Although it focused attention on overpopulation, the dominant legacy of the paper has been its metaphor of common-property resource management. In the intervening years, the ideas that Hardin popularized have become the most widely accepted explanation for overexploitation of resources that are commonly held. The essential idea was that resources held in common, such as oceans, rivers, air, and parklands, are subject to massive degradation. . . .

This conclusion has been accorded by some the status of scientific law. The tragedy of the commons has become part of the conventional wisdom in environ-

Originally published in *Human Ecology* 18, 1 (1990):1–19. Reprinted with permission from Plenum Publishing Company.

The authors acknowledge the helpful comments of Mina Kislalioglu, Donald McCloskey, Stuart Mestelman, Elinor Ostrom, Henry Reiger, and Darrell Tomkins. Interested readers are referred to *The Common Property Resource Digest,* available from the International Association for the Study of Common Property, School of Forestry and Environmental Studies, Yale University, 205 Prospect Street, New Haven, CT 06511

mental studies, resource science and policy, economics, ecology, and political science and is featured in textbooks. . . . It has also been used in formulating resource-management policy. . . .

To avoid the tragedy, Hardin concluded that the commons could be privatized or kept as public property to which rights to entry and use could be allocated. Hardin has been widely cited as having said that resource degradation was inevitable unless common property was converted to private property, or government regulation of uses and users was instituted. In a later paper, Hardin (1978) specifically recognized two general solutions, and presumably no others: private enterprise and socialism (control by government). Hardin argued that if we do not act in one of these two ways, we "acquiesce in the destruction of the commons" (Hardin, 1968, p. 1245). . . .

Definitions and Concepts

Common-property resources include fisheries, wildlife, surface and groundwater, range, and forests. It is important to delineate the characteristics shared by these resources, and to distinguish between the resource and the property-rights regime in which the resource is held.

Common-property resources share two important characteristics. The first is excludability (or control of access). That is, the physical nature of the resource is such that controlling access by potential users may be costly and, in the extreme, virtually impossible. Migratory resources such as fish, wildlife, and groundwater pose obvious problems for regulating access. Similarly, range and forest lands typically pose problems of exclusion. For large bodies of water, the global atmosphere, and radio frequency bands, exclusion is even more problematic.

The second basic characteristic of common-property resources is subtractability, that is, each user is capable of subtracting from the welfare of other users. Even if users cooperate to enhance the productivity of their resource, for instance by replanting trees, the nature of the resource is such that the level of exploitation by one user adversely affects the ability of another user to exploit the resource. Subtractability (or rivalry) is the source of the potential divergence between individual and collective rationality. If one user pumps more water from an aquifer, other users will experience an increase in pumping costs as aggregate use approaches or exceeds recharge capacity. If one user harvests fish, the catch per unit of fishing effort of other fishermen declines. Hence, we define common-property resources as *a class of resources for which exclusion is difficult and joint use involves subtractability*. . . . In order to facilitate analysis, we define four categories of property rights within which common-property resources are held: open access, private property, communal property, and state property. These are ideal, analytic types. In practice, many resources are held in overlapping, and sometimes conflicting combinations of these regimes, and there is variation within each. It is nevertheless important to distinguish these four basic property-rights regimes.

Open access is the absence of well-defined property rights. Access to the resource is unregulated and is free and open to everyone. Many offshore ocean fisheries before the twentieth century, or the global atmosphere provide examples.

Under *private property,* the rights to exclude others from using the resource and to regulate the use of the resource are vested in an individual (or group of individuals such as a corporation). Private-property rights are generally recognized and enforced by the state. Unlike rights under open access, private-property rights usually are exclusive and transferable. Examples include forests and rangelands that are held privately.

Under *communal property,* the resource is held by an identifiable community of interdependent users. These users exclude outsiders while regulating use by members of the local community. Within the community, rights to the resource are unlikely to be either exclusive or transferable; they are often rights of equal access and use. Some inshore fisheries, shellfish beds, range lands, and forests have been managed as communal property; similarly, water-users associations for many groundwater and irrigation systems can be included in this category. The rights of the group may be legally recognized. In other cases the rights are de facto, depending on the benign neglect of the state. . . .

Finally, under *state property,* or state governance, rights to the resource are vested exclusively in government which in turn makes decisions concerning access to the resource and the level and nature of exploitation. Examples include forests and rangelands held by the government or crown-owned, and resources such as fish and wildlife that may be held in public trust for the citizenry. . . . The nature of the state property regime also differs from the other regimes in that, in general, the state, unlike private parties, has coercive powers of enforcement.

. . . One theme of the paper is that one must understand a whole host of institutional arrangements governing access to and use of the resource. Knowledge of the property rights is necessary but not sufficient. Many of the misunderstandings found in the literature may be traced to the assumption that common property is the same as open access. Hardin's prediction of the inevitability of overexploitation follows from this assumption. Yet the assumption is inaccurate and it has led to a great deal of confusion. Based on our definition of common property, an approach to testing Hardin's hypothesis is to examine two broad challenges in the management of common-property resources: (1) the exclusion of other potential users, and (2) the regulation of use and users to ameliorate the problems associated with subtractability. . . .

Evidence on Exclusion

Open Access. The evidence supports Hardin's argument concerning degradation due to the inability to regulate access to resources held as open access. Examples are many, and include the classic case of the historical depletion of various whale stocks in the open ocean. Several examples, however, reveal a point not mentioned by Hardin. In many cases, the tragedy occurred only after open-access conditions were created, often as a consequence of the destruction of existing communal land-tenure and marine-tenure systems. A number of these cases involved the imposition of colonial rule, as in sub-Saharan Africa, the Pacific Islands, and northwest North American salmon rivers.

Private Property. The establishment and enforcement of private property rights have frequently provided the institutional arrangements for successful exclusion. Private-property rights may not, however, be sufficiently precise for solving the exclusion problem. A classic example is the exploitation of oil pools in much of the United States. In an 1889 Pennsylvania Supreme Court decision, the doctrine of law of capture was applied to oil. Private property rights in oil were assigned only upon extraction. In practice, this means that each owner of surface rights has the incentive to accelerate their pumping of oil to the surface. The result is a duplication of drilling and other capital costs, substantial reduction in the overall rate of recovery, and dissipation of economic rents. A remedy to the problem has long been recognized—to define property rights in the underground pool as a unit (unitization) before extraction rather than after. In jurisdictions (such as Wyoming) in which unitization is required before drilling on land leased for oil exploration, greater efficiency has been achieved. In spite of the potential gains for all users through unitization, this form of contract is uncommon in other jurisdictions (such as Texas and Oklahoma) because the high cost of private contracting inhibits its adoption. Private property rights and the incentives they afford are not always sufficient to achieve efficient exploitation.

There is an enforcement problem with all types of property rights, including private property. For common-property resources, which by definition pose exclusion problems, such enforcement can be costly. Well recognized de jure rights of the medieval lord, and even contemporary landlords, to fish and game have been routinely violated by poachers. The extent to which the community regards private-property rights as legitimate affects the cost of enforcement. The difficulty of enforcing private claims to common-property resources is exacerbated by competing claims to communal rights in those resources. This is evident in the United States oyster industry, where a private property regime, including leasehold, is not politically acceptable in many areas regardless of the fact that it is logical, feasible, and demonstrably more efficient.

Communal Property. Hardin did not consider the possibility of exclusion under communal-property regimes. By exclusion we mean the power to exclude people other than members of a defined community. Evidence suggests that successful exclusion under communal property is the rule rather than the exception. Well-documented contemporary cases include Amerindian community hunting and fishing lands in James Bay, eastern subarctic Canada. Here, the communal-property regime collapsed as a result of incursions by outsiders and recovered with the re-establishment of exclusion at least twice since the nineteenth century.

Other examples come from the Pacific islands where communal-property regimes have collapsed in some areas but continue to be viable in many others.

Communal property is not confined to remote and sparsely populated areas. Cooperative-based coastal fisheries in Japan provide many successful examples of communal-property systems. These fishing communities hold legally guaranteed exclusive fishing rights in coastal areas. One of the major conclusions of the National Research Council conference was that legal recognition of communal rights, as in Japanese coastal fisheries, was crucial for the success of communal-property regimes. . . . Even when there is no legal recognition of communal property, the exclusion of outsiders by local users through such means as threats and surreptitious violence is not uncommon. The persistence of community-based lobster fishing territories in Maine is merely one example, but an important one because it occurs in a country and culture in which the belief in right of free access is deeply held.

The examples given thus far are for fish and wildlife for which exclusion is particularly difficult because of the migratory nature of the resource. Successful exclusion can also be found for other resource types, including grazing lands, forests, and water resources.

Pressure on the resource because of human population growth, technological change, or economic change, including new market opportunities, may contribute to the breakdown of communal-property mechanisms for exclusion. The role of population growth is especially controversial. For example, some argue that in the case of East Africa, the carrying capacity of rangelands under any management regime has been exceeded. Other cases indicate that population is merely one of many interrelated social and economic problems.

Communal-property regimes fail to provide for exclusion for other reasons as well. Many of these failures are associated with the appropriation of the resource by politically or militarily powerful groups, or by other factors such as land reform that disrupt existing communal management systems. Others are associated with problems of scale and internal organization. The social and political characteristics of the users of the resource and how they relate to the larger political system affect the ability of local groups to organize and manage communal property.

State Property.   Exclusive state governance of the resource has in many cases been sufficient to provide for adequate exclusion. However, difficulties in exclusion are not necessarily overcome by declaring the resource to be state property. A vivid example comes from Nepal. Alarmed by deforestation, the government nationalized forests in 1957, converting what were often communal forests into de jure state property. But the result more closely approximated the creation of de facto open access. Villagers whose control of nearby forests had been removed often succumbed to the incentives of law of capture. Deforestation accelerated instead of decelerated. In the face of worsening conditions the government began to experiment in 1976 with the re-creation of communal-property rights. . . .

Another problem with state governance is that imperfections in the political process will often be mirrored in resource management. In some cultures, free access to certain resources for citizens at large is viewed as a right. In other cases, the state is especially responsive to the interests of the elite. Some instances of apparent tragedies of the commons are more accurately construed as examples of government failure.

The logic of the argument of *The Tragedy of the Commons* is that we should not observe sustainable management of common-property resources and the exclusion of some uses or users, under regimes other than private or state property. But as we have illustrated, exclusion is feasible, if not always successful, under private, state, *and* communal-property regimes. Furthermore, private or state ownership is not always sufficient to provide for exclusion.

Evidence on Regulations of Use and Users

Open Access. Hardin's predictions that incentives for successful resource management are absent from or weak in open access regimes are in general consistent with the evidence. In such regimes, under conditions in which demand exceeds the capacity of the resource to sustain itself, and where the technology is available to exploit the resource at a high level, many species, including the North American passenger pigeon and the bison, have become extinct, or virtually extinct. In the context of the day, free and unregulated use of resources such as the bison initially made sense. To illustrate the individual rationality that lay behind ecological tragedy, Hardin (1978) invokes the image of Kit Carson shooting bison on the plains, taking only the tongue and leaving the rest. This is not economically irrational if one considers that the game was then abundant but the hunter's time was scarce. Depletion occurred rapidly, before countervailing institutional arrangements or changing cultural values could prevent it.

Private Property. Privatization usually provides incentives for rational exploitation of the resource. If the owner has property rights in the resource and those rights are tradeable, both the costs and benefits will accrue to the same owner and will be reflected in the market price of the resource, giving the owner the pecuniary incentive to refrain from destructive use. These incentives, however, are not necessarily consistent with sustainable use. Suppose a redwood planted for $1 is worth $14,000 at maturity—which may take 2000 years. The implied rate of return would be less than 0.5%, well below the rates of return generally available to investors. Although planting a redwood may make ecological sense, it does not make economic sense under a private-property regime.

More realistically, Clark (1973) has shown that for relatively slow-growing and late-maturing species such as whales, it may be economically optimal to deplete the resource rather than to use it sustainably. . . . [Private property] rights permit the owner to maximize the present value of the resource, yet the resource is not protected from extinction.

Communal Property. There is abundant evidence, contrary to Hardin, on the ability of social groups to design, utilize, and adapt often ingenious mechanisms to allocate use rights among members. The medieval English commons featured in Hardin's paper, like many other historic and contemporary commons, were often subject to comprehensive systems of regulation. For example, stinting was often practiced, that is, limiting the number of head that each owner could graze. Not only was access exclusive to certain members of the village, but their rights were often closely regulated. A plethora of scholars have noted in passing that the commons operated successfully for several hundred years in medieval England, and have questioned if a tragedy of the sort described by Hardin (1968) ever occurred widely.

Forest and meadow commons in Japanese villages were also the subject of elaborate regulations. Village leaders set opening and closing dates for the harvest of certain products. In some villages, thatch was harvested collectively; bundles were then randomly assigned to each household. This device permitted the aggregate level of utilization to be controlled while giving each household an incentive to be reasonably conscientious in its harvesting effort. Guards patrolled the common lands to prevent poaching both by villagers and outsiders. Written rules provided a graduated schedule of fines for violators. Harvesting tools were also regulated. Regulations legislated by villagers ensured sustainable use of common lands for generations.

In the Japanese case, forest and meadow lands and irrigation works were held as communal property while crop lands were held privately. This is not an isolated example of the co-existence of two property-rights regimes. There are other cases indicating the ability of users to match appropriately the resource with the regime. In some societies, the same resource may alternate back and forth between communal and private control seasonally or over the long term.

Not all examples of successful regulation are historic or based on longstanding tradition. In a study of Turkish coastal fisheries, successful regulation was found to have evolved within 15 years in two cases (Alanya, Tasucu), and 9 years in one case. Alarmed by the increasing numbers of users and escalating conflicts, fishermen in Alanya developed a system to regulate use: fishing sites were spaced sufficiently apart to avoid interference, and fisherman agreed among themselves to fish in rotation to ensure equitable access to best sites, with their starting position determined by drawing lots. Although only half of the licensed fishermen belonged to the local marketing cooperative, the authority under which the system was operated, all participated in the process for creating and maintaining it.

Self-regulation of resource use to improve livelihood was also achieved by a local marketing cooperative of New Jersey fishermen. Because large catches depressed prices on the New York fresh fish market, a cooperative was formed to enhance producers' bargaining power. This cooperative decided on total catch levels for the fleet, and provided for the sharing of revenues regardless of the catch levels of individual boats. The pooling of revenues reduced the incentives to over-fish. Although the system was devised to raise prices, a spillover benefit may have been conservation. . . .

These case studies illustrate that people are not helpless but are able to organize, to monitor resource use by members, to allocate use rights among members, and to adjust aggregate utilization levels to maintain sustainable use of the resource. . . . Under the appropriate circumstances, voluntary collective action is feasible and effective.

State Property. Government ownership (state governance) permits the formulation of appropriate regulations for resource use. It also provides for the expression of public interest and for accountability. But state governance does not necessarily ensure sustainable use. Given that the officials who make decisions do not have the same time horizon or interests as private owners, the general public, or the government itself, this is not surprising.

One of the oft-mentioned problems of state ownership is the proliferation of such regulations. Smith points out, for example, that in a New England regional fishery, the combination of quotas, allocations, and trip limitations generated more than 100 different limits, with the result that there was widespread violation of the law. Noncompliance of users and de facto open access has led to an assertion by some that better protection can be achieved under private- rather than state-property regimes.

State ownership is seldom associated with successful management in less-developed countries. The professional resource-management infrastructure of the state is usually poorly developed and enforcement of regulations problematic. In India, for example, communally-held forests were nationalized before the state had developed the capacity for management. Local communities are, however, starting to re-assert their cultural traditions of conservation. . . . Repetto argues that "villagers who ruthlessly cut trees for firewood and fodder in government forests will zealously nurture and protect groves that belong to them or—if their community is sufficiently strong—to their village" (Repetto, 1986, pp. 30–31).

The logic of the argument of "The Tragedy of the Commons" is that private owners or state managers can and often do manage resources successfully. That is, these two property-rights regimes would provide the incentives to regulate use in a fashion consistent with sustainability. Implicitly Hardin argues that these incentives would be absent or weak for other regimes. However, the evidence indicates that complex interactions among the characteristics of the resource, the property-rights regime and other institutional arrangements, and the socio-economic environment contribute to the degree of management success. Success in the regulation of uses and users is not universally associated with any particular type of property-rights regime. Communal property, private property, and government property have all been associated both with success and failure.

Conclusions

Hardin's model is insightful but incomplete. His conclusion of unavoidable tragedy follows from his assumptions of open access, lack of constraints on individual behavior, conditions in which demand exceeds supply, and resource users who are incapable of altering the rules. Actual common-property situations often do not conform to all four of these assumptions. This leads us to amend Hardin's (1968) heuristic fable. The "tragedy" may start as in Hardin. But after several years of declining yields, the herdsmen are likely to get together to seek ways to (1) control access to the pasture, and (2) agree upon a set of rules of conduct, perhaps including stinting, that effectively limits exploitation. Whether or not the intended self-regulation works depends on a number of factors. Here the simple model breaks down—no single metaphor can tell the full story. The medieval English commons usually were regulated by the community, sometimes effectively, sometimes not. The outcome was never so clear and deterministically predictable as in Hardin's model. . . .

The original Hardin paper did, however, allude to the potential viability of communal property. Hardin's (1968, p. 1247) phrase, "mutual coercion, mutually agreed upon" is consistent with communal-property arrangements, although he appears to have meant state institutions under representative government. Societies have the capacity to construct and enforce rules and norms that constrain the behavior of individuals. In many societies and in many situations, the capacity for concerted social action overcomes the divergence between individual and collective rationality. The cases discussed in this paper provide ample evidence of the ability of groups of users and local communities to organize and to manage local resources effectively. Contrary to assumptions by many common-property analysts, these communal-property arrangements have persisted. A diversity of societies in the past and present have independently devised, maintained, or adapted communal arrangements to manage common-property resources. Their persistence is not an historical accident; these arrangements build on knowledge of the resource and cultural norms that have evolved and been tested over time. . . .

Further, the logic of communal property can also be applied to resources that are global (rather than local) in scope. Here, tragedies are more difficult to prevent. This is perhaps why the World Conservation Strategy (1980) and the World Commission on Environment and Development (1987) both emphasized the global commons. Problems such as ozone depletion and carbon dioxide accumulation in the atmosphere are clearly global tragedies of the commons in the making. The solution of such problems will necessarily involve co-management on a large scale. The 1987 Montreal Protocol to protect the ozone layer is an example of international co-management. The case of oil pollution on the high seas, with various international conventions going back to 1954, and leading to reductions in accidental oil spills in the 1980's, the Alaska spill notwithstanding, demonstrates that international cooperation can be effective.

The problem posed by Hardin over 20 years ago captured the attention of a multi-disciplinary collection of scholars and practitioners, including anthropologists, development planners, ecologists, economists, geographers, political scientists, resource scientists, and sociologists. . . . However, as with many seminal but simple models, Hardin's analysis has been shown by subsequent studies to be overly simplified and deterministic. . . . A new and more comprehensive theory for common-property resources must be able to account for sustainable resource management under communal-property regimes. The theory should be capable of accommodating user self-organization or the lack of it. Such a model can better explain whether and under what conditions sustainable resource management will occur, rather than simply predicting the demise of all resources held in common.

[Editors' note: See the original publication for full references list.]

References

Clark, C. W. (1973). The Economics of Overexploitation. *Science* 181:630–634.

Hardin, G. (1968). The tragedy of the commons. *Science* 162:1243–1248.

Hardin, G. (1978). Political requirements for preserving our common heritage. In Brokaw, H. P. (ed.), *Wildlife and America*. Council on Environmental Quality, Washington, D.C., pp. 310–317.

Repetto, R. (1986). *World Enough and Time*. Yale University Press, New Haven.

World Commission on Environment and Development (1987). *Our Common Future*. Oxford University Press, Oxford.

World Conservation Strategy (1980). *World Conservation Strategy: Living Resource Conservation for Sustainable Development*. IUCN/UNEP/WWF, International Union for the Conservation of Nature and Natural Resources, Gland.

WILLIAM OPHULS

6

The Scarcity Society

. . .

For the past three centuries, we have been living in an age of abnormal abundance. The bonanza of the New World and other founts of virgin resources, the dazzling achievements of science and technology, the availability of "free" ecological resources such as air and water to absorb the waste products of industrial activities and other lesser factors allowed our ancestors to dream of endless material growth. Infinite abundance, men reasoned, would result in the elevation of the common man to economic nobility. And with poverty abolished, inequality, injustice, and fear—all those flowers of evil alleged to have their roots in scarcity—would wither away. Apart from William Blake and a few other disgruntled romantics, or the occasional pessimist like Thomas Malthus, the Enlightenment ideology of progress was shared by all in the West.*The works of John Locke and Adam Smith, the two men who gave bourgeois political economy its fundamental direction, are shot through with the assumption that there is always going to be more—more land in the colonies, more wealth to be dug from the ground, and so on. Virtually all the philosophies, values, and institutions typical of modern capitalist society—the legitimacy of self-interest, the primacy of the individual and his inalienable rights, economic laissez-faire, and democracy as we know it—are

*Marxists tend to be more extreme optimists than non-Marxists, differing only on how the drive to Utopia was to be organized.

the luxuriant fruit of an era of apparently endless abundance. They cannot continue to exist in their current form once we return to the more normal condition of scarcity.

Worse, the historic responses to scarcity have been conflict—wars fought to control resources, and oppression—great inequality of wealth and the political measures needed to maintain it. The link between scarcity and oppression is well understood by spokesmen for underprivileged groups and nations, who react violently to any suggested restraint in growth of output.

Our awakening from the pleasant dream of infinite progress and the abolition of scarcity will be extremely painful. Institutionally, scarcity demands that we sooner or later achieve a full-fledged "steady-state" or "spaceman" economy. Thereafter, we shall have to live off the annual income the earth receives from the sun, and this means a forced end to our kind of abnormal affluence and an abrupt return to frugality. This will require the strictest sort of economic and technological husbandry, as well as the strictest sort of political control.

The necessity for political control should be obvious from the use of the spaceship metaphor: political ships embarked on dangerous voyages need philosopher-king captains. However, another metaphor—the tragedy of the commons—comes even closer to depicting the essence of the ecopolitical dilemma. The tragedy of the commons has to do with the uncontrolled self-seeking in a limited environment that eventually results in competitive overexploitation of a common resource, whether it is a commonly owned field on which any villager may graze his sheep, or the earth's atmosphere into which producers dump their effluents.

Francis Carney's powerful analysis of the Los Angeles smog problem indicates how deeply all our daily acts enmesh us in the tragic logic of the commons:

> Every person who lives in this basin knows that for twenty-five years he has been living through a disaster. We have all watched it happen, have participated in it with full knowledge.... The smog is the result of ten million individual pursuits of private gratification. But there is absolutely nothing that any individual can do to stop its spread.... An individual act of renunciation is now nearly impossible, and, in any case, would be meaningless unless everyone else did the same thing. But he has no way of getting everyone else to do it.

If this inexorable process is not controlled by prudent and, above all, timely political restraints on the behavior that causes it, then we must resign ourselves to ecological self-destruction. And the new political strictures that seem required to cope with the tragedy of the commons (as well as the imperatives of technology) are going to violate our most cherished ideals, for they will be neither democratic nor libertarian. At worst, the new era could be an anti-Utopia in which we are conditioned to behave according to the exigencies of ecological scarcity.

Ecological scarcity is a new concept, embracing more than the shortage of any particular resource. It has to do primarily with pollution limits, complex trade-offs between present and future needs, and a variety of other physical constraints, rather than with a simple Malthusian overpopulation. The case for the coming of ecological scarcity was most forcefully argued in the Club of Rome study *The Limits to Growth.* That study says, in essence, that man lives on a finite planet containing limited resources and that we appear to be approaching some of these major limits with great speed. To use ecological jargon, we are about to overtax the "carrying capacity" of the planet.

Critical reaction to this Jeremiad was predictably reassuring. Those wise in the ways of computers were largely content to assert that the Club of Rome people had fed the machines false or slanted information. "Garbage in, garbage out," they soothed. Other critics sought solace in less empirical directions, but everyone who recoiled from the book's apocalyptic vision took his stand on grounds of social or technological optimism. Justified or not, the optimism is worth examining to see where it leads us politically.

The social optimists, to put their case briefly, believe that various "negative feedback mechanisms" allegedly built into society will (if left alone) automatically check the trends toward ever more population, consumption, and pollution, and that this feedback will function smoothly and gradually so as to bring us up against the limits to growth, if any, with scarcely a bump. The market-price system is the feedback mechanism usually relied upon. Shortages of one resource—oil, for example—simply make it economical to substitute another in more abundant supply (coal or shale oil). A few of these critics of the limits-to-growth thesis believe that this process can go on indefinitely.

Technological optimism is founded on the belief that it makes little difference whether exponential growth is pushing us up against limits, for technology is simultaneously expanding the limits. To use the metaphor popularized during the debate, ecologists see us as fish in a pond where all life is rapidly being suffocated by a water lily that doubles in size every day (covering the whole pond in thirty days). The technological optimists do not deny that the lily grows very quickly, but they believe that the pond itself can be made to grow even faster. Technology made a liar out of Malthus, say the optimists, and the same fate awaits the neo-Malthusians. In sum, the optimists assert that we can never run out of resources, for economics and technology, like modern genii, will always keep finding new ones for us to exploit or will enable us to use the present supply with ever-greater efficiency.

The point most overlooked in this debate, however, is that politically it matters little who is right: the neo-Malthusians *or* either type of optimist. If the "doomsdayers" are right, then of course we crash into the ceiling of physical limits and relapse into a Hobbesian universe of the war of all against all, followed, as anarchy always has been, by dictatorship of one form or another. If, on the other hand, the optimists are right in supposing that we can adjust to ecological scarcity with economics and technology, this effort will have, as we say, "side effects." For the collision with physical limits can be forestalled only by moving toward some kind of steady-state economy—characterized by the most scrupulous husbanding of resources, by extreme vigilance against the ever-present possibility of disaster should breakdown occur, and, therefore, by tight controls on human behavior. However we get there, "Spaceship Earth" will be an all-powerful Leviathan—perhaps benign, perhaps not.

A Bird in the Bush

The scarcity problem thus poses a classic dilemma. It may be possible to avoid crashing into the physical limits, but only by adopting radical and unpalatable measures that, paradoxically, are little different in their ultimate political and social implications from the future predicted by the doomsdayers.

Why this is so becomes clear enough when one realizes that the optimistic critics of the doomsdayers, whom I have artificially grouped into "social" and "technological" tendencies, finally have to rest their different cases on a theory of politics, that is, on assumptions about the adaptability of leaders, their constituencies, and the institutions that hold them together. Looked at closely, these assumptions also appear unrealistic.

Even on a technical level, for example, the market-price mechanism does not coexist easily with environmental imperatives. In a market system a bird in the hand is always worth two in the bush.* This means that resources critically needed in the future will be discounted—that is, assessed at a fraction of their future value—by today's economic decision-makers. Thus decisions that are economically "rational," like mine-the-soil farming and forestry, may be ecologically catastrophic. Moreover, charging industries—and, therefore, consumers—for pollution and other environmental harms that are caused by mining and manufacturing (the technical solution favored by most economists to bring market prices into line with ecological realities) is not politically palatable. It clearly requires political decisions that do not accord with current values or the present distribution of political power; and the same goes for other obvious and necessary measures, like energy conservation. No consumer wants to pay more for the same product simply because it is produced in a cleaner way; no developer wants to be confronted with an environmental impact statement that lets the world know his gain is the community's loss; no trucker is likely to agree with any energy-conservation program that cuts his income.

We all have a vested interest in continuing to abuse the environment as we have in the past. And even if we should find the political will to take these kinds of steps before we collide with the physical limits, then we will have adopted the essential features of a spaceman economy on a piecemeal basis—and will have simply exchanged one horn of the dilemma for the other.

Technological solutions are more roundabout, but the outcome—greater social control in a planned society—is equally certain. Even assuming that necessity always proves to be the mother of invention, the management burden thrown on our leaders and institutions by continued technological expansion of that famous fishpond will be enormous. Prevailing rates of growth require us to double our capital stock, our capacity to control pollution, our agricultural productivity, and

---

*Of course, noneconomic factors may temporarily override market forces, as the [1973] Arab oil boycott illustrates.

so forth every fifteen to thirty years. Since we already start from a very high absolute level, the increment of required new construction and new invention will be staggering. For example, to accommodate world population growth, we must, in roughly the next thirty years, build houses, hospitals, ports, factories, bridges, and every other kind of facility in numbers that almost equal all the construction work done by the human race up to now.

The task in every area of our lives is essentially similar, so that the management problem extends across the board, item by item. Moreover, the complexity of the overall problem grows faster than any of the sectors that comprise it, requiring the work of innovation, construction, and environmental management to be orchestrated into a reasonably integrated, harmonious whole. Since delays, planning failures, and general incapacity to deal effectively with even our current level of problems are all too obvious today, the technological response further assumes that our ability to cope with large-scale complexity will improve substantially in the next few decades. Technology, in short, cannot be implemented in a political and social vacuum. The factor in least supply governs, and technological solutions cannot run ahead of our ability to plan, construct, fund, and man them.

Planning will be especially difficult. For one thing, time may be our scarcest resource. Problems now develop so rapidly that they must be foreseen well in advance. Otherwise, our "solutions" will be too little and too late. The automobile is a critical example. By the time we recognized the dangers, it was too late for anything but a mishmash of stopgap measures that may have provoked worse symptoms than they alleviated and that will not even enable us to meet health standards without painful additional measures like rationing. But at this point we are almost helpless to do better, for we have ignored the problem until it is too big to handle by any means that are politically, economically, and technically feasible. . . .

Another planning difficulty: the growing vulnerability of a highly technological society to accident and error. The main cause for concern is, of course, some of the especially dangerous technologies we have begun to employ. One accident involving a breeder reactor would be one too many: the most minuscule dose of plutonium is deadly, and any we release now will be around to poison us for a quarter of a million years. Thus, while we know that counting on perfection in any human enterprise is folly, we seem headed for a society in which nothing less than perfect planning and control will do.

At the very least, it should be clear that ecological scarcity makes "muddling through" in a basically laissez-faire socioeconomic system no longer tolerable or even possible. In a crowded world where only the most exquisite care will prevent the collapse of the technological society on which we all depend, the grip of planning and social control will of necessity become more and more complete. Accidents, much less the random behavior of individuals, cannot be permitted; the expert pilots will run the ship in accordance with technological imperatives. Industrial man's Faustian bargain with technology therefore appears to lead inexorably to total domination by technique in a setting of clockwork institutions. C.S. Lewis once said that "what we call Man's power over Nature turns out to be a power exercised by some men over other men with Nature as its instrument," and it appears that the greater our technological power over nature, the more absolute the political power that must be yielded up to some men by others.

These developments will be especially painful for Americans because, from the beginning, we adopted the doctrines of Locke and Smith in their most libertarian form. Given the cornucopia of the frontier, an unpolluted environment, and a rapidly developing technology, American politics could afford to be a more or less amicable squabble over the division of the spoils, with the government stepping in only when the free-for-all pursuit of wealth got out of hand. In the new era of scarcity, laissez-faire and the inalienable right of the individual to get as much as he can are prescriptions for disaster. It follows that the political system inherited from our forefathers is moribund. We have come to the final act of the tragedy of the commons.

The answer to the tragedy is political. Historically, the use of the commons was closely regulated to prevent overgrazing, and we need similar controls . . . to prevent the individual acts that are destroying the commons today. Ecological scarcity imposes certain political measures on us if we wish to survive. Whatever these measures may turn out to be—if we act soon, we may have a significant range of responses—it is evident that our political future will inevitably be much less libertarian and much more authoritarian, much less individualistic and much more communalistic than our present. The likely result of the reemergence of scarcity appears to be the resurrection in modern form of the preindustrial polity, in which the few govern the many and in which government is no longer of or by the people. Such forms of government may or may not be benevolent. At worst, they will be totalitarian, in every evil sense of that word we know now, and some ways undreamed of. At best, government seems likely to rest on engineered consent, as we are manipulated by Platonic guardians in one or another version of Brave New World. The alternative will be the destruction, perhaps consciously, of "Spaceship Earth."

A Democracy of Restraint

There is, however, a way out of this depressing scenario. To use the language of ancient philosophers, it is the restoration of the civic virtue of a corrupt people. By their standards, by the standards of many of the men who founded our nation (and whose moral capital we have just about squandered), we are indeed a corrupt people. We understand liberty as a license for self-indulgence, so that we exploit our rights to the full while scanting our duties. We understand democracy as a political means of gratifying our desires rather than as a system of government that gives us the precious freedom to impose laws on ourselves—instead of having some remote sovereign impose them on us without our participation or consent. Moreover, the desires we express through our political system are primarily for material gain; the pursuit of happiness has been degraded into a mass quest for what wise men have always said would injure our souls. We have yet to learn the truth of Burke's political syllogism, which expresses the essential wisdom of political philosophy: man is a passionate being, and there must therefore be checks on will and appetite; if these checks are not self-imposed, they must be applied externally as fetters by a sovereign power. The way out of our difficulties, then, is through the abandonment of our political corruption.

The crisis of ecological scarcity poses basic value questions about man's place in nature and the meaning of human life. It is possible that we may learn from this challenge what Lao-tzu taught two-and-a-half millennia ago:

> Nature sustains itself through three precious
> principles, which one does well to embrace and follow.
>
> These are gentleness, frugality, and humility.

A very good life—in fact, an affluent life by historic standards—can be lived without the profligate use of resources that characterizes our civilization. A sophisticated and ecologically sound technology, using solar power and other renewable resources, could bring us a life of simple sufficiency that would yet allow the full expression of the human potential. Having chosen such a life, rather than having had it forced on us, we might find it had its own richness.

Such a choice may be impossible, however. The root of our problem lies deep. The real shortage with which we are afflicted is that of moral resources. Assuming that we wish to survive in dignity and not as ciphers in some ant-heap society, we are obliged to reassume our full moral responsibility. The earth is not just a banquet at which we are free to gorge. The ideal in Buddhism of compassion for all sentient beings, the concern for the harmony of man and nature so evident among American Indians, and the almost forgotten ideal of stewardship in Christianity point us in the direction of a true ethics of human survival—and it is toward such an ideal that the best among the young are groping. We must realize that there is no real scarcity in nature. It is our numbers and, above all, our wants that have outrun nature's bounty. We become rich precisely in proportion to the degree in which we eliminate violence, greed, and pride from our lives. As several thousands of years of history show, this is not something easily learned by humanity, and we seem no readier to choose the simple, virtuous life now than we have been in the past. Nevertheless, if we wish to avoid either a crash into the ecological ceiling or a tyrannical Leviathan, we must choose it. There is no other way to defeat the gathering forces of scarcity.

PART TWO

Ecology and the Structure of the International System

As discussed in the introductory chapter to this volume, environmental problems are the result of a complex array of social forces, including technology, political and economic institutions, social structures, and human values. In this part we are particularly interested in the subset of causes that can be attributed to the structure of the international system. The term *structure* is sometimes used by scholars in international relations to refer to the international distribution of power among states. Thus, during the Cold War, the structure of the system was often said to be bipolar in that the two superpowers wielded by far the most power in international affairs. Here we use the term more generally to refer to the relatively stable, unchanging characteristics of world politics, such as the political division of the world into sovereign states, or the capitalist global economy, which shapes transactions among societies.[1] These relatively permanent features of the world system give shape and definition to the interactions among governments, international organizations, multinational corporations, nongovernmental organizations, and other agents of world politics.

Three aspects of system structure seem particularly important in shaping the array of global environmental problems we face and the possibilities for responding to those problems. The first is state sovereignty, which many scholars take to be the central feature of world politics. As the World Commission on Environment and Development put it, "The Earth is one, but the world is not."[2] One of the main reasons for this absence of unity is the sovereignty of individual states, which gives them, at least in principle, decision-making autonomy over matters falling within their territorial jurisdiction.

The tensions between ecology and sovereignty are largely due to the fact that the boundaries of states and the boundaries of ecosystems do not perfectly coincide, meaning that individual states cannot effectively manage many of their most serious environmental problems. Most large-scale environmental problems cross national borders; many are tied to global systems, such as the atmosphere and oceans, that are beyond the control of individual states. And yet governments have clung tenaciously to the notion that they retain exclusive authority over activities taking place within their territory that affect the global environment. The primacy of state sovereignty was one of the few points on which governments could agree during the contentious Stockholm Conference:

> States have . . . the sovereign right to exploit their own resources pursuant to their own environmental policies, and the responsibility to ensure that activities

within their jurisdiction or control do not cause damage to the environment of other states or of areas beyond the limits of their national jurisdiction.[3]

Although this principle refers not only to the sovereign *rights* of states but also to their *responsibilities,* it has generally been seen as a reinforcement of state sovereignty. In most instances, states have guarded this right emphatically when pressured by the global community—whether the state in question is a tropical rain-forest country, such as Brazil, or a leading emitter of greenhouse gases, such as the United States.

Some observers see global environmental challenges as eroding sovereignty, as states are forced to accept restrictions on domestic actions. Others argue that international environmental cooperation is boosting the problem-solving abilities of many states, thereby reaffirming their sovereign authority. But as Ken Conca points out, sovereignty is more complex than simply the right of nations to do as they please or the authority of governments to act. Conca argues that sovereignty is indeed being changed by global ecological interdependence, but in many ways at once. Using the example of the Brazilian Amazon, Conca sees Brazilian sovereignty as simultaneously being bounded by new international norms, broadened as the state is made the foundation for forest protection strategies, and rendered more brittle as the enormity of the task and likelihood of failure put state legitimacy at risk. Seen in this light sovereignty is not an unchanging structural feature of the world system but rather a historical social institution that may or may not successfully adapt to global ecological interdependence.

A second crucial feature of system structure is the existence of an increasingly interconnected capitalist world economy. Economic processes do not respect national borders any more than do ecological realities. This has long been the case for international trade, which predates the founding of the modern state system. Today the pattern of economic interconnectedness established by international trade is being deepened by the increasing mobility in the world economy not only of goods and services but also of money, people, technology, and ideas.

Jim MacNeill, Pieter Winsemius, and Taizo Yakushiji have developed the concept of "shadow ecologies" to capture the ecological consequences of this economic interconnectedness. The authors point out that the world's major centers of industrial production and consumption, including the United States, Europe, and Japan, are not "ecologically self-contained." These regions rely upon imports of a wide range of commodities, both as raw materials for production and as food for consumption. As a result, the core industrial regions of the world economy draw upon the "ecological capital" of the places that supply those inputs. The production that takes place in the industrialized world thus casts an ecological shadow far beyond the borders of individual industrialized countries.

The fact that national economies cast ecological shadows beyond their borders has important consequences. Individual states may exert only a limited degree of control over economic processes occurring within their territories and thus over the environmental consequences of the processes. The pollution and destruction of the ecosystem may be driven as much by the workings of these transnational economic processes as by the choices made by individual governments or local actors. Governments of the South, for example, have long argued that international debt is one of the principal driving forces behind the accelerating resource depletion and environmental degradation in the Third World. Similarly, economic globalization raises anew the question of whether governments have the capacity to hold multinational corporations accountable for the environmental impacts of their activities.[4]

The ecological shadows cast by individual states in an interdependent world economy make the enforcement of international environmental agreements much more difficult. Even when governments are willing to enforce domestically the rules to which they agree internationally, they might be unable to do so in the face of powerful transnational economic pressures.

The transnational character of modern capitalism also raises important questions of responsibility. Who is responsible for the destruction of tropical rain forests, when the "causes" of that destruction range from the chain saws in the hands of local timber cutters to the global economic system that creates a demand for tropical timber products? Do we blame local people, the transnational banks and corporations that carry economic practices across borders, third parties who may benefit from these activities, or the structure of the world capitalist economy as a whole?

State sovereignty and transnational capitalism have complex implications for the global environment. As discussed in subsequent parts of this book, some observers see great potential for these structures to become the foundation of solutions to environmental problems, while others see them as root causes. What is clear is that just as state sovereignty imposes a pattern of political authority that does not correspond exactly to the underlying ecological reality, so transnational capitalism imposes patterns of economic activity that do not wholly correspond to the prevailing pattern of political authority. Both features of system structure give environmental problems an inherently "international" dimension, and both greatly complicate the prospects for global cooperation.

While the limits imposed by these global structures must be addressed by any serious analysis of environmental problems and solutions, it is important also to remember that these "structural" properties of world politics are not natural or automatic properties of the international system—they are the results of human choice and behavior. This leads us to the question of how ideas, beliefs, and worldviews give structure to the behavior of the various actors in world politics. Obviously, sovereignty and capitalism are two ideas that have had a powerful structuring influence. Some observers have argued that these two ideas are embedded in the more fundamental ethos of "modernity"—a complex set of beliefs that came to dominate European culture in the modern era and subsequently spread to the Americas, Africa, and Asia via colonialism and other manifestations of European power.[5] Some of the principal ideas that make up the modern worldview involve beliefs about the autonomy of the individual, the power of science and technology, the desirability of increased consumption, and the inevitability of progress. Thus, the ideological bedrock of modernity gave rise to the political structure of state sovereignty, and to the economic structure of global capitalism.[6]

Dennis Pirages argues that the modern worldview lies at the core of contemporary world politics, with important environmental implications. Pirages describes a "dominant social paradigm"—a core set of ideas that shape our understanding in ways that most people never question. Pirages sees underlying technological and economic forces as creating the dominant social paradigm of any given era. The paradigm in turn legitimizes prevailing technological, economic, political, and social practices. The current paradigm is for Pirages a legacy of the industrial revolution and the era of relative resource abundance in which it occurred. Pirages argues that modern industrial society is currently trapped within this paradigm, even though the paradigm is increasingly unsuited to a world of resource scarcity and environmental vulnerability. Cracks have begun to appear in the paradigm but have not yet allowed a new paradigm to take its place.

Different observers differently weight the role of ideas in shaping world politics.[7] Pirages sees the dominant social paradigm as a product of underlying economic and technological processes. But he also argues that once in place, the paradigm exerts an independent influence that makes other possibilities harder to imagine.

Not all actors embrace the dominant social paradigm, of course. Indeed, many environmentalists argue that environmentalism is a social movement that rejects core features of the dominant paradigm. Is this the case? Does environmentalism transcend the limits of state sovereignty, oppose the unfettered operation of global capitalism, and reject many central tenets of the modern worldview? Is it possible that the idea of environmentalism is itself building a new global structure: a network of individuals and groups with an "antisystemic" orientation in the sense that they reject many values and preferences of the dominant social paradigm?[8] These questions are hotly debated by environmentalists and their critics. There may be no single answer to this question: The environmental movement consists of a patchwork of groups with widely differing goals and views, working at levels ranging from local to global. If environmentalism is to be effective as an "antisystemic force," it will be because of effective collaboration among these diverse groups, on a global scale. As Parts Five, Six, and Seven make clear, the diversity of ideas driving various groups and individuals can make such collaboration difficult.

Nevertheless, the environmental movement has emerged as a force to be reckoned with in international affairs. We conclude this part with three essays that present three important ways in which environmental NGOs and movement groups are changing world politics: through domestic political struggles, transnational networking, and the promotion of large-scale sociocultural change.

The autobiography of Brazilian activist Chico Mendes reminds us that environmentalism around the world has historically drawn most of its energy from the grass roots. Despite the growing internationalization of environmental politics, domestic political struggles remain the most important pathway to change. Mendes was a labor activist and environmentalist working in the western Amazon state of Acre. He led a movement for the preservation of the Amazon forest and the livelihood of its occupants. Mendes advocated a brand of environmentalism that struggled as much against the oppression of people as the destruction of nature. Mendes was killed in 1988, assassinated by powerful local landowning interests that were threatened by his efforts to organize rural workers in the region. The powerful vision he expressed, which made him an important political leader of the forest peoples' movement in Brazil, also made him in death a martyr and an international symbol. The global outcry following his murder greatly enhanced the pressures on the Brazilian government to reverse policies that promote deforestation in the Amazon region.[9]

Mary Barker and Dietrich Soyez illustrate the increasingly transnational character of such local struggles. Drawing their examples from recent environmental disputes in Canada, the authors point out that urban industrial societies cast an ecological shadow over their domestic "hinterlands" (analogous to the process described in global terms by MacNeill, Winsemius, and Yakushiji in Part Two). Canadians resisting the effects of this shadow have increasingly reached across borders to network with allies, to lobby governments and corporations that have dealings with Canada, and to bring external pressures to bear on the Canadian government. Their activities reverse one of the traditional axioms of environmentalism: As the authors point out, these communities are thinking locally but acting globally.

If a sustained global movement of environmentalism is to exert political power, it will be because movement groups as diverse as those seen in these Brazilian and Canadian examples can find a way to establish effective, durable international networks to coordinate efforts, exchange information, and pool resources. The barriers to such cooperation are formidable: a lack of resources compared to the activities they oppose; the frequent opposition of governments, corporations, and other powerful actors; conflicting viewpoints on goals and means; and unequal power between relatively well-heeled and influential groups from the North and some of the less institutionalized, grassroots groups of both North and South. Nor can we assume that international environmentalism automatically produces environmental or social benefits; Part Seven presents troubling cases in which transnational environmental groups have sought to preserve Latin American rain forests or African wildlife in ways that fail to involve local communities and perhaps even contribute to their continued oppression.

Despite these obstacles and potential pitfalls, there have been examples of effective international networking among environmentalists, as in the case of the internationally coordinated campaign to change the environmental practices of the World Bank during the late 1980s (see the selection by Bruce Rich in Part Four). Moreover, as Paul Wapner reminds us in the final essay of this part, the activities of transnational environmental networks need not be limited to lobbying efforts by well-heeled organizations with access to power. Wapner argues that too much attention has been paid to the lobbying activities of environmental NGOs and movement groups, and not enough to the ways in which they cross borders to alter directly the practices of large numbers of people. Groups such as Greenpeace, the World Wildlife Fund, and Friends of the Earth use available political resources—including symbolic gestures, boycotts, economic pressures, and local networking—to promote the environmental agenda in ways that often bypass governments entirely. Wapner sees this as a form of "world civic politics" rooted in a thin but expanding global civil society.

As Ronnie Lipschutz suggests,

The notion of 'civil society' is one with a long history, but it generally refers to those forms of association among individuals that are explicitly not part of the public, state apparatus, the private, household realm or the atomistic market. Civil society is important in global politics in that it is a sector of the state-society complex where social change often begins. This does not mean that global civil society is a unity; it is riven by many divisions, more than one finds in even the international state system. Nonetheless, there are segments of this global civil society that are oriented in ways that specifically promote social and political change.[10]

Whether it makes sense to extend to the global realm the idea of "civil society," which originated with the study of domestic politics in industrial democracies, remains the subject of much debate. But even for skeptics, the idea serves as an important reminder that the state is not the sole or even the primary source of political, social, and cultural change.

Thinking Critically

1. Are the problems confronting the Brazilian state in the Amazon generalizable? Is the pattern of transformation of Brazilian sovereignty hypothesized in Conca's essay likely to be found on a broader scale? What makes sovereignty endure in the face of such pressures?

2. Does the problem of "shadow ecologies" identified by MacNeill and colleagues promote or inhibit international environmental cooperation? Which seems to be growing more quickly—the pressures on countries to solve problems collectively or the loss of control in an increasingly transnationalized world economy?

3. What forces drive the sort of paradigm shift that Pirages describes? Are "failures and anomalies" the only pathway to change? Or are anticipatory, learning-based social transitions possible? If growth, control, distribution, and work roles are indeed the central dilemmas of the industrial paradigm, how might a postindustrial paradigm address these challenges?

4. Contrast the activities of the environmental organizations and movement groups discussed in the essays by Mendes, Wapner, and Barker and Soyez. Are the forces that push people to mobilize politically the same in each case? Are the political resources available to these groups the same in each case? What gives these groups power? What limits their power?

5. Do the cases from Canada and Brazil provide evidence for Wapner's claim that we are seeing the emergence of a global civil society? Or do they describe locally grounded political struggles that have little in common beyond occasional, expedient cooperation?

Additional Reading

The Structure of the International System

Choucri, Nazli, *Global Accord: Environmental Challenges and International Responses* (Cambridge, MA: MIT Press, 1995).

Korten, David C., *When Corporations Rule the World* (West Hartford, CT: Kumarian Press, 1995).

Kuehls, Thom, *Beyond Sovereign Territory* (Minneapolis: University of Minnesota Press, 1996).

Lipschutz, Ronnie D., and Ken Conca, eds., *The State and Social Power in Global Environmental Politics* (New York: Columbia University Press, 1993).

Schreurs, Miranda, and Elizabeth Economy, eds., *The Internationalization of Environmental Politics* (Cambridge: Cambridge University Press, 1997).

Environmentalism as Local Struggle and Global Movement

Dawson, Jane, *Econationalism: Anti-nuclear Activism and National Identity in Russia, Lithuania, and Ukraine* (Durham, NC: Duke University Press, 1996).

Keck, Margaret, and Katherine Sikkink, *Activists Beyond Borders: Advocacy Networks and International Politics* (Ithaca, NY: Cornell University Press, 1998).

Lipschutz, Ronnie D., with Judith Mayer, *Global Civil Society and Global Environmental Governance: The Politics of Nature from Place to Planet* (Albany, NY: SUNY Press, 1996).

Princen, Thomas, and Matthias Finger, eds., *Environmental NGOs in World Politics: Linking the Local and the Global* (London: Routledge, 1994).

Taylor, Bron, ed., *Ecological Resistance Movements: The Global Emergence of Radical and Popular Environmentalism* (Albany, NY: SUNY Press, 1995).

Wapner, Paul, *Environmental Activism and World Civic Politics* (Albany, NY: SUNY Press, 1996).

Internet Resources

Regional Environmental Centre for Eastern and Central Europe (REC), *http:// www.rec.org/Default.shtml*.

Bellona Foundation, *http://www.bellona.no/e/index.htm*

Green Korea, *http://soback.kornet.nm.kr/~baedal*

Brazilian Institute of Social and Economic Analyses (IBASE), *http://www. ibase.br/ibase/ibase.htm*

Pesticide Action Network (PAN), *http://www.igc.apc.org/panna/index.html*

These five sites illustrate the diversity of local environmental organizations and movement groups around the planet. REC, based in Budapest, Hungary, provides training and information for NGOs and links to other sites on Central and Eastern Europe. The Bellona Foundation is a Norwegian NGO that gathers information on radioactive contamination in the Russian Northwest. Green Korea "seeks to restore the traditional harmony between the Korean people and the Korean peninsula's ecosystems." IBASE is a Brazilian organization that promotes information campaigns and social activism on a wide range of issues. PAN is a network of local organizations in North America working on issues related to pesticide pollution, health and safety, and sustainable agriculture.

Greenpeace, *http://www.greenpeace.org/index.shtml*

World Wildlife Fund, *http://www.panda.org*

Friends of the Earth, *http://www.foe.org*

These three transnational environmental NGOs are featured in Wapner's essay.

International Rivers Network, *http://www.irn.org*

Rainforest Action Network, *http://www.ran.org*

These sites, which provide examples of two global networks linking local environmental groups, are focused on forestry and river issues, respectively.

Environment Liaison Centre, *www.unep.or.jp/cgi-bin/keyword_ietc.csh?/WWW/SERVERS/ietc/ESTdire /orga/arki0001.html+Kenya+arki0001.html.* This Nairobi-based organization works closely with the U.N. Environment Programme and serves as a clearinghouse for a variety of environmental organizations worldwide, with particular emphasis on the global South.

KEN CONCA

7

Rethinking the Ecology–Sovereignty Debate

How do mounting international pressures for environmental protection affect state sovereignty? Does it even make sense to speak of sovereignty in a world marked by tight ecological interdependence, massive transboundary pollutant flows and severe threats to key global environmental services? How will the evolving roles, rules and understandings that have institutionalised sovereignty adapt to these new ecological realities?

These questions are of particular concern in the South, where the full range of rights and opportunities promised by sovereignty have rarely been realised to the extent enjoyed in the industrialised world. When Third World governments have voiced resistance to the institutionalisation of new standards of environmental behaviour, they have often done so on the grounds that such rules violate their sovereignty.[1]

In this paper I present a critique of prevailing perspectives on the sovereignty-ecology link. Though the focus is not exclusively on the Third World, the critique illustrates the limited utility of prevailing formulations in a Third World context. I also point the way toward some elements of an alternative conceptualisation, and illustrate these propositions with a brief discussion of the case of the Brazilian Amazon.

© *Millennium: Journal of International Studies.* This article first appeared in *Millennium* 23, no. 3 (1994):701–711 and is reproduced with the permission of the publisher.

Two Perspectives on Ecology and Sovereignty

My reading of the ecology-sovereignty literature is that two perspectives dominate the debate. The first argues that we are in fact seeing an erosion or weakening of sovereignty. Environmental concerns are said to be erecting new and effectively global standards for state behaviour. These new global standards are said to manifest themselves in several ways: in formal dealings among states (such as the creation of international environmental regimes), in rules of environmental conditionality, attached to the actions of international organisations such as the World Bank;[2] in the evolving norms of a growing body of international environmental law;[3] and in the political pressures brought to bear on governments by increasingly transnational environmental movements, citizens' networks, and non-governmental organisations.[4] Such pressures and constraints are unevenly applied and imperfectly enforced, to be sure; but they are beginning, it is claimed, to constrain the autonomy of state action by imposing limits on the menu of policy choices available to states.

This perspective is sometimes, though not inevitably, tied to the view that sovereignty and ecology are inherently at odds. Because ecosystems and environmental processes do not respect state borders, sovereignty itself becomes a key institution of global-scale environmental destruction. It creates a scale for decision-making, adjudication, and authority that does not coincide with fundamental ecological realities, and thus frustrates ecologically responsible management.[5]

These claims about eroding sovereignty can be contrasted with a second identifiable point of view in the literature. Here the claim is that international processes and, in particular, the emergence of multilateral institutions for environmental protection, do not inevitably erode state sovereignty and may even strengthen it. By placing states at the centre of institutional responses and strengthening their capacity to act collectively, it is argued, the menu of choices available to states is being expanded, not restricted.

For example, Levy, Keohane and Haas have argued that, although environmental regimes may limit the scope of governments to act unilaterally, they also facilitate collective state-based problem solving.[6] The authors draw a distinction between 'operational' sovereignty, defined as the legal freedom of the state to act under international law, and 'formal' sovereignty, defined in terms of the state's legal supremacy and independence.[7] International environmental institutions constrain operational sovereignty, but formal sovereignty remains largely intact. Implicit in this reasoning is the argument that enhanced problem-solving capabilities more than offset the external limitations on the scope of state authority.

A Critique

These two perspectives inevitably embody normative stances toward the state. In one view, the state is a large part of the problem, whereas in the other it is the foundation for solutions—or, at the very least, a central feature of the terrain on which solutions will have to be built. We can also examine them, however, as claims of what is happening to sovereignty, for better or for worse. Here, although they do make different sets of claims, the two are not necessarily irreconcilable. It is perfectly plausible, for example, that the scope of state autonomy is being narrowed (as the first claim would suggest) at the same time that the problem-solving capacity of states is increasing (as the second claim would argue).

However, before concluding that this represents the full range of consequences for sovereignty in an ecologically interdependent world, several observations are in order. The picture sketched above is in fact seriously incomplete, particularly when applied to contemporary international politics in the Third World. I hypothesise that for many Third World states, sovereignty is in fact being transformed as a result of global ecological interdependence, but not in the manner sketched by either of the above claims, or even by the net effect of the two taken together.

I base this hypothesis on two sets of observations. First, both arguments fail to disaggregate what is in fact a complex and highly unevenly distributed set of international pressures on states to solve environmental problems. Second, both are based on an incomplete characterisation of sovereignty itself. They only partially capture what has made sovereignty endure over time, and therefore misrepresent what sovereignty has actually meant for most states.

Let me stress here that the point is not to set up two straw arguments for easy dismissal. There are important insights in both of these perspectives. But they also appear to miss some potentially important effects on sovereignty, in part because their conceptual approaches to sovereignty limit the range of hypotheses they entertain.

Characterisation of Environmental Pressures on the State

One problem is an overly general representation of the types of environmental pressure states feel. Clearly, governments do feel mounting pressure to respond to international environmental problems. Cross-national comparisons of public opinion data show consistently high levels of public awareness and concern.[8] While not all peoples, classes, regions and cultures define the problem in exactly the same terms, widespread concerns about environmental quality cut across simplistic distinctions between rich and poor, North and South, overdeveloped and underdeveloped.[9] The growth of pressures on states can also be seen in the contrast between the 1992 UNCED Conference in Rio de Janeiro and the UN Conference on the Human Environment, held two decades earlier in Stockholm. Stockholm was a gathering of 114 nations but was attended by only 2 heads of state; Rio represented an assemblage of more than 150 nations, including over 100 heads of state. The 134 non-governmental organisations at Stockholm were dwarfed by the 1400 non-governmental organisations and more than 8000 journalists from 111 countries who attended the Rio Conference.[10]

If it is clear that pressures are mounting, it is also clear that there have been consequences for the range of choices available to states. It has become much more difficult (though by no means impossible) to construct large dams, indiscriminately export toxic wastes, clear-cut forests, traffic in endangered species, or emit unlimited quantities of chemicals that destroy the ozone layer. That governments of both the North and the South so often see these limits (at least when applied to them) as interference in their sovereign right to use natural resources as they see fit, indicates a strong perception that the consequences are real.

However, while we may very well be seeing the birth of a generalisable, universal norm of environmental responsibility, the specific pressures on states have thus far followed a much more selective pattern. First, to the extent that a new norm is emerging, it is manifest in a highly segmented set of activities, including the lobbying of scientists, the pressure of public opinion, the calculations of governments, and the targeted political pressures of eco-activists. There is no reason to suppose that these all carry the same implications for sovereignty, or even push in the same general direction.

Second, regardless of their origin, the pressures states are feeling typically flow through multiple channels, including intergovernmental relations, dealings with international organisations, transnational linkages among environmental groups, and the workings of the media. Can pressures to join state-based international regimes be assumed to affect sovereignty in the same manner as pressures to accept the World Bank's environmental conditions on lending?

Third, current pressures clearly do not touch all states equally. Instead, what we have seen is something akin to assigning ecological pariah status to specific states on specific issues, whether it be Brazil and Indonesia in the case of tropical deforestation, China and India on dam construction, Japan on the trade in endangered species, or the former Soviet Union on reactor safety. Whatever the implications for sovereignty, they are unevenly distributed.

Fourth, and perhaps most important, responding to international environmental pressures can create resources and purchase legitimacy at the same time that it may constrain the menu of policy choices. This is in fact generally acknowledged when the gains for states are directly linked to efforts at environmental management. But these are not the only plausible effects; some of the resources gained or legitimacy purchased may speak to more general questions of the state's legitimacy and capacity to govern.[11]

Conceptions of Sovereignty

A second set of problems involves the specific conceptualisation of sovereignty itself that underlies these perspectives. One problem is that both sovereignty and the challenge to it are viewed in essentially functionalist terms. By this reasoning, states exist because they perform key functions better than alternative forms of social organisation, and pressures on the state exist because one increasingly important function—environmental protection—is being performed inadequately. The problems with functionalist arguments are well known, and stem from their *post hoc* character: causes are imputed from observed effects.[12] Problems emerge when the function is incorrectly specified—that is, when causal significance is given to an observed effect that is in reality an unintended consequence or less-than-central function. A straightforward example: the notion that international environmental regimes exist because states want to solve environmental problems may in fact be wrong. Regimes may be thrust on states by increasingly powerful non-state actors, or they may serve other fundamental purposes of state, e.g., those having to do with state legitimacy and perceptions of effectiveness. Functionalist interpretations based on each of these widely differing "functions" would lead us to dramatically different conclusions about the implications for sovereignty.

The conceptualisation of sovereignty is also excessively general. Sovereignty in historical practice has carried with it the presumption of a complex *bundle* of rights: equality among states, non-intervention, exclusive territorial jurisdiction, the presumption of state competence, restrictions on binding adjudication without consent, exclusive rights to wield violence, and the embeddedness of international law in the free will of states.[13]

There is no reason to expect that a particular set of international pressures affects these various component norms of sovereignty equally or in parallel fashion. Indeed, to the extent that ecological interdependence highlights *tensions* among such norms, one would expect just the opposite—that some normative pillars of sovereignty can be strengthened as others are undermined or eroded. Consider transboundary pollutant flows: institutional mechanisms to control them could erode the sovereign right to exclusive territorial jurisdiction, but at the same time *strengthen* aspects of the principle of non-intervention, if the flows themselves are viewed as unjustified interventions.

Third, the view of sovereignty is largely ahistorical. What rules, practices or beliefs reproduce sovereignty as an institution? Has this process of reproduction been broadly similar in all entities we regard as states, or is there more than one way to reproduce oneself as a sovereign entity? Are there differences in what sovereignty has meant for states whose organised existence is largely a product of colonialism? Does the territorial basis of the state differ fundamentally in frontier societies or in multi-ethnic ones? Clearly, the answers are unlikely to be uniform across time and for all states. This suggests that we cannot describe in universal terms either the processes rendering states sovereign or the way in which they may be changing as a result of ecological interdependence. Sovereignty as a global institution changes because of what happens to different states over time, at different rates and in different ways.

These weaknesses—functionalist logic, excessive generality, and ahistorical character—are symptoms of more fundamental conceptual problems. One of these is the unresolved tension over whether sovereignty represents, as Robert

Jackson has put it, "a norm or a fact". In other words, is sovereignty based on the "fact" of material capabilities that enable organised entities to claim standing as states? Or is it based on the selective extension of recognition as a legitimate state? As Jackson and others have argued, we need to understand sovereignty as at once *both* "fact" *and* "norm".[14]

The perspectives examined here tend instead to fall on one or the other side of this divide. The ecology-erodes-sovereignty view typically frames sovereignty as a formal legal right, de-emphasising the foundations of the state that make it able to claim domestic authority and international standing. Alternately, the claim of enduring sovereignty in the face of environmental pressures stresses states as problem-solvers (albeit with varying degrees of capability). It thus emphasises sovereignty as the maintenance of a certain set of capabilities with which to act.

Finally, and perhaps most importantly, sovereignty in both perspectives is essentially conceived as freedom from external constraints on state action and choice. This one-dimensional view overlooks the fact that sovereignty looks inward as well as outward. It finds its basis not only in autonomy relative to external actors, but also in the state's jurisdictional power over civil society. According to Ruth Lapidoth:

> Usually, a distinction is made between the internal and external aspect of sovereignty. The former [internal] means the highest, original—as opposed to derivative—power within a territorial jurisdiction; this power is not subject to the executive, legislative, or judicial jurisdiction of a foreign state or any foreign law other than public international law. The external aspect of sovereignty underlines the independence and equality of states and the fact that they are direct and immediate subjects of international law.[15]

John Ruggie's definition of sovereignty as "the institutionalisation of public authority within mutually exclusive jurisdictional domains" also captures this internal dimension.[16]

Historically, the ability to control rules of access to the environment and natural resources—to define who may alter, and to what extent, which specific natural materials, systems, and processes—has been a central component of state authority and legitimacy.[17] Thus the full effects of international environmental pressures on state sovereignty as a collective institution cannot be understood without examining this inward-looking dimension. This is particularly so for much of the South, given the legacy of colonialism and the orientation of so many Third World political economies toward commodity exports.

Like the outward-looking dimension, the state-society dimension of sovereignty represents both fact and norm. It demands not only some minimal level of social recognition of the state's legitimacy, but also a complex bundle of state capabilities. Joel Migdal, for example, disaggregates the notion of state capacity into such varied components as the penetration of civil society, the regulation of social relations, the extraction of resources from civil society, and the use of those resources for defined state purposes.[18] International pressures, whether manifest in state-state, state-IO, or state-NGO interactions, are unlikely to affect these varied capabilities equally. Moreover, state capacity and social legitimacy may be at odds, as appears to be the case when coercive means are used to "protect" ecosystems from local use and encroachment.[19]

Toward an Alternative View of the Sovereignty-Ecology Link

What would an alternative conceptualisation look like? Clearly, it will require a multi-dimensional, less readily operational definition of sovereignty. Sovereignty must be conceived as having both external and internal dimensions; it must be seen as having a basis in both norms of recognition and material capabilities; and both its normative and material bases must be seen as consisting of multi-faceted bundles of norms and capabilities, respectively. These complexities should make us humble about drawing general conclusions outside the context of specific cases. A corollary is that there is little to be gained in speaking in general unified terms about sovereignty being 'strengthened', 'eroded', or 'maintained', either with regard to specific states or the institution of state sovereignty as a whole.

The multiple dimensions of sovereignty should not, however, automatically lead us down the path of static 2x3 matrices and reductionist thinking. The focus should be on whether and how *specific* state actions and *specific* aspects of state-society relations create the conditions of authority, legitimacy, and capability necessary for states to make effectively sovereign claims. When the Brazilian government builds a road through the jungle, this must be seen as an act that speaks to *each* of the dimensions of sovereignty alluded to above: legitimacy as well as capability, international as well as domestic. If the idea of a two-level game is an apt metaphor (and it may not be, for this reason), it is a game in which most of the moves resonate on both boards at once.

An Example: The Brazilian Amazon

Consider the example of the Brazilian Amazon, perhaps the single most widely noted and contentious case to date in the ecology-sovereignty debate.[20] Before the ink had dried on the major agreements signed at the 1992 UNCED Conference in Rio de Janeiro, Brazilian diplomat Marcos Azambuja offered the following analysis:

> Brazilian interests are reinforced in the majority of the documents. At no time did we face opposition to our basic interests.... (W)e came out of the negotiations without the slightest scratch to our sovereignty.[21]

As evidence, the ambassador could have pointed to the conference declaration of principles on environment and development. Here the sovereign right of states to 'exploit their own resources' is reaffirmed using exactly the same language enshrined in the well-known Principle 21 of the Stockholm Conference 20 years earlier.[22] Or, the ambassador could turn to the specific agreements on climate and biodiversity, which did little to contradict this principle.

The absence of 'scratches' on the wall of Brazilian sovereignty was particularly noteworthy with respect to the issue of predominant concern to the Brazilians at the conference: the fate of tropical rainforests, and of the Amazon in particular. Efforts to scratch that wall, by constructing a regime for the preservation (or at least controlled depletion) of the world's remaining rainforests, were soundly defeated. Key points of disagreement included whether to link the regime specifically to an agreement on climate change and whether to cover temperate as well as tropical forests.

But walls have two surfaces, and in the Brazilian case the inside surface has suffered more than a slight scratch. Consider the following testimony of one veteran field researcher in the Amazon:

> Wherever one looks in the Amazonian economy, the state is in retreat: unable to finance tax breaks or build highways without the aid of multilateral banks, unable to include more than one per cent of the rural population in official colonisation schemes, unable to control land titling or land conflicts, unable to register or tax the greater part of the Amazonian economy, unable to enforce federal law on more than a sporadic basis.[23]

The irony is that this assessment of the limits of state capabilities comes at a time when the Brazilian state has been placed squarely at the centre of most schemes for sustainable development in the region. Clearly, some state actions have been proscribed by international pressures. But, far from prohibiting state action, the net effect of international pressures has been to stimulate a more active, interventionist state role in the region, under the rubric of supporting sustainable development. Far from simply "eroding" sovereignty, these pressures strengthen the presence of the state in the region and in Brazilian society as a whole. They also create opportunities for state actors to pursue longstanding goals having little to do with ecology. In the specifically Brazilian case such goals include the control of remote territories or indigenous peoples, the demarcation and fortification of Brazil's borders, and the reorganisation of existing patterns of land tenure.[24]

These extensions of the state are not without cost, however; they can only be realised at substantial risk to state legitimacy, given the enormous complexity of the task of sustainable development and the limited effectiveness of many state actions as sketched in the above quote. Moreover, the risk to state legitimacy may extend beyond the relatively narrow realm of environmental management. Consider the following commentary in the leading Brazilian newsweekly, *Veja*, discussing the highly publicised murder of a group of indigenous people at the Haximu settlement. "The Haximu massacre shows that, in reality, these minorities [indigenous peoples] are protected with the same courage and efficiency that guard the public hospital network and the pensions of the retired".[25] The state's inability to protect the lives and land of indigenous peoples is being linked directly to its other widely perceived inadequacies.

Under such circumstances, it means little to say that Brazilian sovereignty over the Amazon is eroding, strengthening, or maintaining the *status quo*. Rather, it seems that we are seeing a more complex, dynamic process in which sovereignty is simultaneously being narrowed in scope (by international prohibitions), deepened (by strengthening state capacities and state penetration of civil society), and rendered more brittle (by eroding state legitimacy).

Conclusion

. . .

A strong case can be made for both of the perspectives sketched at the outset of this paper. Clearly, the freedom of states to undertake, promote or tolerate processes of environmental degradation is being limited, and many of the limits emanate from sources external to the state itself. At the same time, there is little doubt that new international institutions have made some governments more effective problem solvers (although we should always be careful about assumptions that the problem to be solved is, from the point of view of state actors, environmental and not political). That both effects could be happening at once is testimony to the multi-faceted character of sovereignty.

Whether these represent the full set of effects is another matter. Consider an analogy to the origins of the modern welfare state. States were faced with a new set of challenges (macroeconomic stabilisation, creating a social safety net, and so on). In response, states evolved new institutions, some national and some international, and in the process thrust themselves into a whole new set of state-society relationships. The consequences were hardly a lessening of the state's penetration of civil society or a decline in the size and reach of state institutions. At the same time, however, by assuming these new tasks, state legitimacy (both domestic and international) was put substantially at risk. The entire process was of course intensely politicised and political, with both state and non-state actors seeking to turn the new agenda to maximum advantage.

Much the same process may be at work with the challenge of environmental protection. New tasks, for which states are poorly suited and to which they are often opposed, have been thrust upon them by rising social demands. This challenge renders some choices more remote, but it also creates new opportunities, in the form of international resources for state responses and new mandates for state management and regulation. However, because most of the solutions being promulgated have a strongly statist cast, state legitimacy is put at substantial risk. A growing body of evidence suggests that participation, democracy, and legitimate authority are the keys to solving environmental problems. If so, the implications for state legitimacy may ultimately be the greatest consequence, both for sovereignty and for ecology.

JIM MACNEILL, PIETER WINSEMIUS
& TAIZO YAKUSHIJI

8

The Shadow Ecologies of Western Economies

Many nations, both industrial and developing, impose large burdens on the earth's environmental systems. Some do so through wealth, some through poverty; some through large and rapidly growing populations, others through high and rapidly growing levels of consumption of environmental resources per capita. The aggregate impact of any community on the environment can usefully be thought of as the product of three factors: its population, its consumption or economic activity per capita, and its material or energy flow per unit of economic activity. . . . A nation can therefore impose a heavy burden on the environment through any combination of high population growth, high consumption, and the inefficient use of materials and energy.

This simple formulation is complicated by one major factor: the environment and resource content of trade between nations. Economic activity today is concentrated in the world's urban/industrial regions. Few, if any, of these regions are ecologically self-contained. They breathe, drink, feed, and work on the ecological capital of their "hinterland," which also receives their accumulated wastes. At one time, the ecological hinterland of a community was confined to the areas immediately surrounding it, and that may still be true of some rural communities in developing countries. Today, however, the major urban/industrial centers of the world are locked into complex international networks for trade in goods and services of all kinds, including primary and processed energy, food, materials, and other resources. The major cities of the economically powerful Western nations constitute the nodes of these networks, enabling these nations to draw upon the ecological capital of all other nations to provide food for their populations, energy and materials for their economies, and even land, air, and water to assimilate their waste by-products. This ecological capital, which may be found thousands of miles from the regions in which it is used, forms the "shadow ecology" of an economy. The oceans, the atmosphere (climate), and other "commons" also form part of this shadow ecology. In essence, the ecological shadow of a country is the environmental resources it draws from other countries and the global commons.[13] If a nation without much geographical resilience had to do without its shadow ecology, even for a short period, its people and economy would suffocate.

Third World economies seek to be drawn into these trading networks. It is the only way they can hope to attract the investment and technologies needed to develop and trade in world markets. But participation in such networks is a two-edged sword. The economies of most developing countries (and parts of many industrialized countries) are based on their natural resources. . . . Their soils, forests, fisheries, species, and waters make up their principal stocks of economic capital. The overexploitation and depletion of these stocks can provide developing countries with financial gains in the very short term, but can also result in a steady reduction of their economic potential over the medium and long term.[14]

Western nations heavily engaged in global sourcing should be aware of their shadow ecologies and the need to pursue policies that will sustain them. Some countries, of course, are more dependent on them than others. Japan is a case in point. Being a resource-poor country, the world's second largest economy has to import most of its energy and renewable resources as raw materials and export them as finished products. Japan's vast population also depends on access to its shadow ecology. Seventy percent of all cereal (corn, wheat, and barley) consumption and 95 percent of soybean consumption are supplied from abroad. Poor crop yields in exporting countries due to environmental degradation or bad weather could have a grave impact on Japan's food supplies. Japanese imports of round-woods account for one-third of the world total, and more than 50 percent of Japanese consumption is supplied from abroad. . . .

Japan's vulnerability to the effects of global environmental change is not limited to the outsourcing of basic materials; it is also found in the exports of finished products. Nearly 30 percent of Japan's export income is earned by the sale of automobiles, the use of which depends on the availability of sufficient ecological space to handle their waste emissions, especially air pollution, in the cities and towns that form their principal markets. The fact that Japan's automobiles have been more energy and environmentally efficient than those of its competitors has had much to do with their success in export markets. The margin, however, is growing smaller, partly because Japanese firms have begun to produce and export more large, high-consumption automobiles. This should concern the Japanese government. If environment can be used to justify controls on imports of food-stuffs, it can also be used to justify controls on imports of automobiles. Japan must remain sensitive to global environmental trends, lest its exports be limited by stringent measures to protect the "ecological space" available in foreign markets. The same is true of other countries.

... These dependencies are large and growing and they apply to North America and Europe as well as to Japan. The figures on exports and imports reveal that the dependencies are also reciprocal. The environment and resource content of trade flows, which is usually hidden in the trade figures, is increased by the global reach of domestic policies, especially policies to increase trade. The agencies that make decisions on trade policies, however, are usually unaware of, and unresponsive to, their environmental connections. Trade in agriculture, energy, forestry, and a range of industrial products suffers from government interventions that are designed to distort markets in ways that protect domestic producers and give exporters an unfair advantage. But, as noted earlier, they also destroy the ecological capital on which prospects for future trade and economic prosperity depend.

Trade in tropical timbers provides a good example. Some industrialized countries impose levies that favor the importation of raw logs rather than processed products from tropical countries. They thus gain the value-added in processing the logs. As a result, the countries exporting the logs, usually developing countries, have to cut far more forest than they otherwise would in order to earn the foreign exchange that they need for development. This overexploitation now threatens the trade itself. Export revenues from tropical timber have been falling for years and are now worth about $8 billion. They are expected to continue to fall to $2 billion by the turn of the century because the resource is simply disappearing.[15] Even the industry concerned now agrees that the trade policies and domestic incentive frameworks which govern the exploitation and trade in tropical forests must be changed. In 1986 a commodity agreement was ratified that incorporated a specific commitment by governments and industry to invest in measures to sustain the growth and production of the forests being traded. It was the first international agreement that attempted to employ novel funding arrangements to address a global issue by bridging the concerns of the importing nations, mainly in the North, and the exporting nations, mainly in the South. The International Tropical Timber Organization (ITTO), based in Yokahama, Japan, was established to implement the agreement, but it is much too early to say whether it will work.

DENNIS PIRAGES

9
Global Technopolitics

. . .

Technology, Revolutions, and Social Paradigms

Many scholars interpret the last decades of the twentieth century as a departure from established patterns of social evolution and the beginning of a period of revolutionary change in mature industrial societies.[27] The term *revolution* has a myriad of meanings and is often used loosely. Here it refers to large-scale discontinuities in the structural and value realms of societies. There have been only two such major revolutionary transformations in world history that have impacted the majority of the earth's population. The first large-scale revolutionary transformation of human culture was the agricultural revolution, which apparently began simultaneously in several different places in the Middle East around 8000 B.C. and then subsequently spread slowly outward to the rest of the world. The second was the industrial revolution, which began to gather momentum in the fifteenth and sixteenth centuries in Western Europe and is currently spreading spasmodically to the more remote areas of the world.

Both of these previous revolutions were driven by significant technological innovations and related ecological changes, which created social surplus, or capital over and above what was needed for subsistence.[28] The agricultural revolution

Excerpted from Dennis Pirages, *Global Technopolitics* (Pacific Grove, CA: Brooks/Cole, 1989). Reprinted with permission of the author.

was initially driven by innovations in farming that permitted humans to exploit nature more efficiently. These innovations included domestication of plants and animals, and they provided social surplus resulting in enhanced diets, more dependable food supplies, and more sedentary populations. . . . The agricultural revolution eventually produced enough surplus in some countries to support military castes and organized warfare and culminated in the development of several large empires.

The industrial revolution gained much of its impetus from technological innovations that utilized fossil fuels—coal, petroleum, and natural gas—to do the work previously done by human beings and draft animals. This second revolution, which now has moved into advanced stages in much of the world, originally produced social surplus of unprecedented magnitude by enhancing human productivity through a much more intricate division of labor feeding on a generous natural subsidy stored in coal, petroleum, and eventually natural gas.[29] New political, economic, and social institutions were shaped by these technological changes as significant social surplus permitted unprecedented social and political change. . . .

The tumultuous events of the last twenty years are evidence that resource dislocations are pushing and new technologies are pulling the world into a third revolutionary period. But unlike the previous two revolutions, which swept aside tradition on the strength of new technologies and related economic benefits, as yet no positive vision has been articulated by advocates of a new way of life. Thus, the industrial countries seem caught between two ages, experiencing the economic stagnation and political uncertainty brought on by the worldwide slowing of industrial growth while not having yet developed a positive vision and related values appropriate for a new age.

The mental product of these revolutions and related long periods of social evolution, generations of human learning experiences translated into social survival rules, can be called a dominant social paradigm (DSP).[30] These survival rules—individual beliefs, ideas, and values transferred from one generation to the next—are carried as part of the larger culture and transmitted through socialization processes. During normal times of slow change, only simple maintenance learning is required to sustain a dominant social paradigm. Indeed, in the absence of perceived threats to the established ways of doing things, it is very difficult to avoid problems of social stagnation. The industrial paradigm or world view has been shaped by generations of material-intensive economic growth and seemingly gives technological optimists a recipe for future success. But just as natural selection in the biological realm cannot anticipate future environments—witness the fate of the unfortunate dinosaur—the cumulative survival information contained in the present dominant industrial paradigm may not give relevant guidance for coping with the turmoil of a post-industrial transformation.

. . .

Cracks in the Industrial Paradigm

Change in dominant social paradigms can be slow or rapid, destructive or constructive, minor or major, depending on the rate at which failures and anomalies
mount up and the ability of leaders to respond with appropriate policies. Over the
course of the industrial period, constant small changes have taken place within
the overriding world view that now defines the industrial DSP. But in the last two
decades of the twentieth century, considerable evidence is mounting to indicate
that the paradigm currently prescribing and shaping behavior within and among
nations is not providing adequate guidance for coping with rapidly changing
technological and environmental realities.

The current cracks in the industrial paradigm are not easily noticed, because in
the early stages of a paradigm shift it is difficult for people caught up in it to realize that a transition is taking place. But such periods are detectable, because they
are times when old rules no longer seem to apply and conventional explanations
for mounting anomalies no longer make sense. Under such conditions of uncertainty, individuals may return to old ideologies, authority figures, and religious
practices in a desperate attempt to cope with an increasingly unexplainable and
threatening world. . . .

Harman has suggested four key dilemmas or anomalies within the industrial
paradigm that cannot be resolved without a major system transformation.[35] The
growth dilemma has developed because economic expectations associated with
the industrial paradigm require continued rapid growth in material consumption, while on a planetary scale it is impossible to live with the consequences. The
control dilemma results from a need for more government capacity to control
techno-ecological change at the same time that social values portray such control
as evil and a brake on progress. The *distribution dilemma* revolves around a growing need for wealthy individuals and nations to develop mechanisms to help those
less fortunate while in reality the rich attempt to insulate themselves from the rising expectations among the growing numbers of the world's poor by building
walls around their spheres of prosperity. Finally, a *work roles dilemma* results from
the fact that not enough industrial jobs can be created to keep unemployment low
and meet the expectations of future generations. Harman links these four dilemmas to the emergence of a new scarcity. Old scarcities involved shortages of things
needed to meet basic human needs and were overcome by developing new technologies and using more land and resources. The new shortages, however, result
from ecological scarcity, approaching technological and resource limits to growth
on a planetary scale.[36]

Manifestations of the politics of new scarcity and the approach of ecological
limits have been obvious in international relations over the last two decades. The
twin oil crises of 1973–74 and 1979–80 and subsequent events in the Persian Gulf
have called attention to the longer-term problem of petroleum and natural gas
depletion as well as the more immediate problem of reserve location. The food

and basic commodity crises of the mid-1970s indicated how rapidly an over-heated global economy can exhaust resource inventories and drive up prices. The food crises in Africa in the 1980s highlighted the anomaly of a world in which farmers in industrialized countries hold land out of production while millions starve for lack of food. The global recession, debt crisis, and stock market crash of the 1980s stressed the interdependence of capital markets and the need for careful management of surplus (capital) available for investment on a global scale. . . .

These and many related assessments of the acute problems of advanced indus-trial societies could well indicate that the industrial revolution has now peaked and that a "third wave," or high-tech revolution focusing on telecommunications, biotechnologies, and information processing, is now under way.[41]

. . .

Theoretical Paradigms in International Relations

Scholarly analysis of international relations has developed within and therefore is difficult to separate from the dominant social paradigm of industrial societies. In-ternational relations theory has been very much influenced by a Western indus-trial world view that is closely related to more general developments in the behav-ioral and social sciences. Theories, concepts and research are dominated by an exclusionist view of the world that may well lend itself to inappropriate interpre-tations of current trends and events.

The history of international relations as a discipline, or subdiscipline, has been characterized by a search for a unifying scholarly paradigm. The most commonly accepted explanatory framework within the field is an exclusionist, state-centered, power-politics view of reality. It is firmly anchored in explanations originating in the structural and value domains and depicts nations as frequently in conflict be-cause leaders cannot refrain from attempting to exercise their power within the international hierarchy. According to this view, these industrial-paradigm politi-cal "realists" aggressively pursue short-term national interests leading to in-evitable conflicts among the nations making up the international system.

Mansbach and Vasquez have characterized the essentials of this exclusionist, state-centered paradigm as follows.

1. Nation-states and/or key decision makers and their motives are the starting point in accounting for international political behavior.
2. Political life is bifurcated into domestic and international spheres, each subject to its own characteristic traits and laws.
3. International relations can be most usefully analyzed as a struggle for power. This struggle constitutes the major issue occurring in a single system and entails a cease-less and repetitive competition for the single stake of power. Understanding how

and why that struggle occurs and suggesting ways for regulating it is the purpose of the discipline.[51]

... These basic ideas have guided generations of international relations scholars and provided policy prescriptions or ideological justifications for political leaders as diverse as Joseph Stalin and Ronald Reagan. The inadequacies of this framework are found in its exclusionist nature, which stresses the autonomy of decision makers and limits causal explanations to leaders and their motives. It assumes that leaders operate in a vacuum rather than an environment of pressures and issues shaped by technological and ecological change. Its basic weaknesses have been illuminated, over time, by numerous scholars, who have contributed pieces of a possible new explanatory paradigm to replace the one now in a state of decay.[53]

The emphasis in this book is on building an inclusionist approach to the theory and practice of international relations that could provide the glue needed to hold many of these new ideas together. ... Nations are viewed as organized human populations coping with physical laws and resource requirements similar to those confronting other species. Nations compete and cooperate within a system composed of a physical ecosphere, a structured set of practices and rules referred to as the international political economy, and an ideological realm characterized by value conflicts among proponents of different organizational methods. How well nations perform is primarily a function of the ways that they organize internally and the domestic and international policies that they choose to deal with nature's challenges and the imperatives of technology.

Global technopolitics, then, refers to the dynamics of an emerging post-industrial international system increasingly driven by the imperatives of technology. It is different from the expansionist system of the industrial period in a number of ways. There is now no country clearly in charge of maintaining order and prescribing rules of conduct within the international system. The former hegemony of the United States has been repeatedly challenged in different ways by Western Europe, Japan, the Soviet Union, newly industrializing countries such as Korea and Taiwan, and more recently by coalitions of less developed countries. ...

This contemporary period of transition to a post-industrial international system is not unexpectedly beset with crises: a food and raw materials crisis, two energy crises, a protracted world debt crisis, and a collapse of world economic confidence. ... Thus, the nature and exercise of power are changing dramatically as "low politics" economic, ethical, and ecological concerns are replacing "high politics" issues involving potential use of military force. ...

10

Fight for the Forest

Building Bridges

We realised that in order to guarantee the future of the Amazon we had to find a way to preserve the forest while at the same time developing the region's economy.

So what were our thoughts originally? We accepted that the Amazon could not be turned into some kind of sanctuary that nobody could touch. On the other hand, we knew it was important to stop the deforestation that is threatening the Amazon and all human life on the planet. We felt our alternative should involve preserving the forest, but it should also include a plan to develop the economy. So we came up with the idea of extractive reserves.

What do we mean by an extractive reserve? We mean the land is under public ownership but the rubber tappers and other workers that live on that land should have the right to live and work there. I say "other workers" because there are not only rubber tappers in the forest. In our area, rubber tappers also harvest brazil nuts, but in other parts of the Amazon there are people who earn a living solely from harvesting nuts, while there are others who harvest babaçu and jute. . . .

Where did we get the idea of setting up the CNS [Editors' note: National Council of Rubber Tappers]? We discovered there is something called the National Rubber Council which represents the interests of landowners and businessmen but not the interests of the rubber tappers, so we thought, why not create an organisation as a counterweight to all that bureaucracy and try to stop the govern-

Originally published in Chico Mendes with Tony Gross, *Fight for the Forest: Chico Mendes in His Own Words* (London: Latin America Bureau, 1989). Reprinted with permission.

ment messing the rubber tappers about? The First National Congress set up the CNS and elected a provisional executive committee.

The CNS is not meant to be a kind of parallel trade union, replacing the Xapuri Rural Workers' Union, for example. [Editors' note: Xapuri is the town where Mendes lived and worked until his assassination in December of 1988. It is located in the western Amazonian state of Acre, near the Brazilian border with Bolivia.] It is just an organisation for rubber tappers. The growth of the trade unions was very important for us, but other agricultural workers including day labourers and so on are also members of the same union. Other kinds of agricultural workers have been seen as having particular needs and interests, but not rubber tappers; it's as though we were something that existed only in the past. So one of the reasons for creating the CNS was to recognise the rubber tappers as a particular group of workers fighting for a very important objective—the defence of the Amazon forest. The idea went down very well.

The Indians

We also wanted to seek out the leaders of the Indian peoples in Acre and discuss how to unite our resistance movements, especially since Indians and rubber tappers have been at odds with each other for centuries. In Acre the leaders of the rubber tappers and Indian peoples met and concluded that neither of us was to blame for this. The real culprits were the rubber estate owners, the bankers and all the other powerful interest groups that had exploited us both.

People understood this very quickly, and from the beginning of 1986 the alliance of the peoples of the forest got stronger and stronger. Our links with the Indians have grown even further this year. For example, a meeting of the Tarauacá rubber tappers was attended by 200 Indians and six of them were elected to the Tarauacá Rubber Tappers' Commission. Indians are now beginning to participate in the CNS organising commissions. In Cruzeiro do Sul about 200 Indians are active in the movement and this year they have even joined in our *empates* [Editors' note: The term *empate* means "tie" or "stand-off" in Portuguese. It refers here to a common tactic of the movement in which local people physically occupy the area threatened by deforesters. The goals are to create a standoff that inhibits the destruction of the forest and to convince the workers involved in deforestation that their interests lie in forest preservation].

Our proposals are now not just ours alone, they are put forward together by Indians and rubber tappers. Our fight is the fight of all the peoples of the forest.

When the Minister of Agriculture met a joint commission of Indians and rubber tappers in his office, he was really taken aback. "What's going on?", he said, "Indians and rubber tappers have been fighting each other since the last century! Why is it that today you come here together?"

We told him things had changed and this meant the fight to defend the Amazon was stronger. People really took notice of that.

. . .

The Landowners Strike Back

We know we face powerful opposition. As well as the landowners and business-men who dominate the Amazon region, we are up against the power of those who voted against land reform in the Constituent Assembly. The voting power of these people in Congress has been a problem for us and has encouraged the growth of the right-wing landowners' movement, the Rural Democratic Union (UDR). The defeat of the land reform proposal was a big victory for the landowners and land speculators. Now, since the establishment of the UDR in Acre, we've got a real fight on our hands. However, we also believe our movement has never been stronger.

You can already see how strong the UDR is in Acre—it's just organised its first cattle auction to raise funds. We know, through people who have been to UDR meetings here, that their aim is to destroy the Xapuri union by striking at the grassroots organisations of the Xapuri rubber tappers. They think if they can de-feat Xapuri they can impose their terms on the whole state and further afield in the Amazon region as well. The Governor of Acre himself told me this. Just to give you an idea, it was after the UDR's official launch here in Acre that the first drops of blood were spilt in Xapuri. . . .

The Government Takes Sides

There was a time when the state government seemed to be paying a lot of atten-tion to environmental problems and to the rubber tappers.[2] But we soon realised it was just putting on a show of defending the environment so the international banks and other international organisations would approve its development projects.

We can't see how the authorities can say they defend the ecological system while at the same time deploying police to protect those who are destroying the forest. That happened, for example, in the case of the Ecuador rubber estate where there were many nut and rubber trees. The Governor was warned several times about what was going on there. In fact, I personally warned him and sug-gested he go and look at what was happening for himself. I told him he was being very hasty in sending police there. Fifty acres of virgin forest were cut down, but thanks to the pressure, thanks to the hundreds of telegrams sent to the Governor by national and international organisations, we managed to get him to withdraw the police from the area and so saved about 300 hectares of forest.

In the area they destroyed there, the last harvest produced 1,400 cans of brazil nuts,[3] a good crop. We challenged the owner of the land and the Governor himself to work out the annual income per hectare produced by forest products such as brazil nuts and rubber and then compare it with that produced by grazing cattle there. They refused because they knew we could prove the income from one hectare of forest is 20 times greater than when the forest is cleared and given over to cattle.

We quoted decree law 7.511 of 30 July 1986 and regulation 486 of 28 October 1986 which prohibit the cutting down and sale of brazil nut and rubber trees and the deforestation of hillsides. There were two hillsides in the area being cut down on the Ecuador rubber estate and the law was completely flouted. After the second empate, when the rubber tappers managed to stop work going ahead, the local IBDF [Editors' note: Brazilian Forestry Development Institute] representative appeared and without even inspecting what was going on, told the landowner he could go ahead and clear the forest. He gave the landowner a licence even though the landowner did not present, as he should have done, a written plan for managing the area.

Another law—I can't remember its number—says you can only clear up to 50 hectares of forest without presenting a forestry management plan. Further on it adds that it's forbidden to cut down any area of forest on hillsides or where there is a concentration of brazil nut and rubber trees. None of these laws were respected. The Governor himself didn't even consider them and the IBDF certainly didn't.

We do have a good relationship with the Acre Technology Foundation (FUNTAC) which is a state government agency.[4] They really understand how difficult the lives of rubber tappers are and recognise that deforestation is a problem. But despite the good relationship we've got with FUNTAC, we have no confidence left in the state government. How can we believe a Governor who says he defends the forest, and visits Rio and Japan to talk about defending the forest, but who then orders the police to go and protect the people who are destroying it? He ought to be using the political power that his office gives him. If he used his power in favour of the workers he'd certainly get their support. . . .

The rubber tappers aren't saying that nobody should lay a finger on the Amazon. No. We've got our own proposals for organising production. The rubber tappers and the Indians have always grown their subsistence crops but they've never threatened the existence of the forest. It's the deforestation carried out by the big landowners to open up pasture for their cattle that is threatening the forest. Often, these people are just speculating with the land. What happens in Xapuri and other parts of the Amazon is that these people cut down 10,000 hectares, turn half of it into pasture for their cattle and let the other half grow wild. They are really just involved in land speculation.

The landowners use all the economic power at their disposal. They bribe the authorities; it's common knowledge that they've bought off the IBDF staff in the Amazon region. They also use the law. They request police protection for the workers hired to cut down the trees, saying it is their land so they can do whatever they like with it. They accuse the rubber tappers of trespassing when we try and stop the deforestation. They turn to the courts for support and protection, claiming the land is private property. But the rubber tappers have been here for centuries!

There has been less pressure from the police in the last two years because we are able to present reasoned arguments to them. When we organise an *empate,* the main argument we use is that the law is being flouted by the landowners and our *empate* is only trying to make sure the law is respected.

The other tactic the landowners use, and it's a very effective one, is to use hired guns to intimidate us. Our movement's leaders, not just myself but quite a few others as well, have been threatened a lot this year. We are all on the death list of the UDR's assassination squads. Here in Xapuri, these squads are led by Darlí and Alvarino Alves da Silva, owners of the Paraná and other ranches round here. They lead a gang of about 30 gunmen—I say 30 because we've counted them as they patrol the town. Things have changed recently because we managed to get an arrest warrant issued in Umuarama, in the state of Paraná, for the two of them. I don't know whether it was the federal police, but somebody tipped them off. Now they're both in hiding and have said they'll only give themselves up when I'm dead.

We are sure this will be the landowners' main tactic from now on. They are going to fight our movement with violence and intimidation. There's no doubt in our minds about that. The level of violence that has been common in the south of the state of Pará is already spreading to Xapuri, to Acre.

MARY L. BARKER AND DIETRICH SOYEZ

11

Think Locally, Act Globally? The Transnationalization of Canadian Resource-Use Conflicts

Conflicts over resource use and development projects in northern Canada are being played out increasingly in the international arena. When transboundary impacts or water diversion and export are at issue, the interactions are primarily among people, organizations, and processes in Canada and its neighbor, the United States.[1] Foreign investment in resource projects can trigger even wider-ranging interactions, as in the case of Japanese involvement in large-scale clearcut logging and pulp mill construction in northern Alberta. Canadian aboriginal peoples and environmental groups, concerned about the impacts of logging in the northern boreal forest, have attempted to gain support in the "end-user" country (where the wood or wood products are used) by forging links with Japanese environmentalists and by developing an information campaign aimed at Japanese tourists visiting Canada.[2]

Environment 36, no. 5 (June 1994):12–20 and 32–36. Reprinted with permission of the Helen Dwight Reid Educational Foundation. Published by Heldref Publications, 1319 Eighteenth St. N.W., Washington, D.C. 20036-1802. © 1994.

In the last three years, the German media have frequently covered clearcut logging in western Canada, and, in 1993, the German Greenpeace organization initiated a publicity campaign against logging the remaining oldgrowth temperate rain forest in coastal British Columbia. German activists participated in roadblock protests on the Canadian west coast and organized a domestic lobbying campaign against German publishing companies that use paper imported from Canada and Scandinavia.[3] Because of these activities, the Canadian forest industry and government attempted to counteract the spread of what they considered to be misinformation in the European end-user countries about temperate rain forests, logging methods, and forest products.

The strategies of internationally based interest groups have been an effective political catalyst in the past. In the early 1980s, for example, controversies surrounding the Newfoundland offshore seal hunt and the trapping of northern fur-bearing animals pitted the international animal rights movement and Greenpeace International against the Canadian government, the fur industry, and both aboriginal and nonaboriginal hunters. The European Common Market became the main arena for the dispute, which led to a consumer fur boycott, an import ban on seal products, and major repercussions for the subsistence economy of aboriginal peoples.[4] Increasingly, opponents as well as proponents of particular resource-use regimes or large development projects seek to influence the political outcome of the conflicts by forging and capitalizing on international linkages.

The common denominator and triggering mechanism behind many such conflicts are the "ecological shadows"[5] that urban-industrial societies cast over their hinterlands. These shadows include the negative impacts of resource extraction as well as pollution from distant sources.[6] They are caused by social and cultural conceptions and institutional failures that prevent an adequate assessment and fair distribution of the risks and benefits of economic growth and consumption patterns. The concept of the ecological shadow has been applied to the global debate between the "North" and "South" over the inequitable relations between developed and developing nations.[7] In Canada, this north-south dichotomy is reversed: The environmental and social costs often are borne by economically and socially marginalized groups in the sparsely populated north, whereas the large majority of Canadians, who live in the south, reap most of the benefits.[8] Comparable north-south patterns exist in Norway, Sweden, Japan, and Australia. The costs are engendered not only by resource projects but by water- and airborne pollutants from distant sources; the perceptions, values, and economic strategies of a distant but powerful urban society (such as the seal-hunt opponents in Europe) also may have major repercussions on northern environments, economies, and peoples.

Both the injection of large-scale technologies—with international financing and external end-users—and the imposition of outside ideologies meet with opposition from indigenous peoples in the affected regions. Many no longer expect their concerns to be addressed appropriately within their own nation-state, and so, increasingly during the last few years, they have appealed to the international public, the media, and international organizations. These appeals have built on expressions of solidarity, information strategies, and links established in the 1970s among indigenous peoples around the world.[9] Indigenous peoples have also tried to forge alliances in end-user regions at home and abroad. Thus, the catch phrase of sustainable development—"think globally, act locally"—has been reversed, as populations seek outside support for their causes to "think locally, act globally." These interactions are transnational in nature not only because more than one nation is involved but also because the players often include multinational corporations, international banks, and indigenous peoples active in international forums, such as United Nations organizations.[10]

A Question of Rights

International resource transfers and the reactions of northern aboriginal peoples who bear the environmental and cultural impacts exported by the end-user states are a special example of a much broader problem: the adverse distributional effects of facilities siting and environmental degradation borne by any marginal group whose property rights are not recognized or adequately protected by the state.[11] Northern aboriginal peoples occupy a geographically, economically, and socially marginal position in today's world. But urban ethnic minorities and the nonaboriginal rural and elderly poor also lack the political empowerment and resources to resist externally imposed impacts.

Northern Canadian development conflicts involve several interwoven themes, including sustainable resource use, center-periphery relations, transboundary impacts, and minority-majority relations. Sustainable resource use has become a key theme in public debates over megaproject proposals in the north, where the dominant development-oriented interests impinge on aboriginal communities, many of which are showing severe symptoms of cultural dislocation but are seeking to return to or at least maintain remnants of a world view that values long-term stability.[12]

Environmental damage and land (or water) losses from resource extraction and construction projects, along with resource competition (such as hunting pressures) from incoming workers, can undermine or block aboriginal subsistence activities. Thus, the concept of sustainable resource use relates not only to resources but also to the ecological and cultural rights that enable people to choose future paths in keeping with their cultural aspirations.[13] When such rights are not recognized or guaranteed, populations often seek public (and media) support and forge alliances with other groups to exert pressure on political decision-makers. If their efforts meet with little success in their own country, people begin to explore and develop transnational links.

In Canada, aboriginal aspirations and the complex issue of First Nation rights have gained increasing public attention over the last 20 years. Aboriginal leaders have long argued the need to redefine the relationship of the First Peoples with the Canadian state in order to fulfill their aspirations: self-government, settlement of outstanding land claims, and guaranteed rights that reflect their special histor-ical status.[14] Section 35 of the Constitution Act of 1982 "recognized and con-firmed" existing aboriginal and treaty rights, but there has been much disagree-ment and legal uncertainty about what this actually means. Decisions handed down by the Supreme Court of Canada in 1990 clarified some of the key issues, such as those concerning wildlife harvesting.

Aboriginal peoples assert a special relationship with the land—one that is inex-tricably linked with their cultural distinctiveness. The settlement of outstanding land claims is therefore crucial in areas where aboriginal title has never been ex-tinguished by treaty. In 1973, the federal government adopted a policy of accept-ing for negotiation land claims based on traditional land use and occupancy. The first two comprehensive claims of aboriginal groups to be settled dealt with the James Bay Territory. Other Indian and Inuit organizations are now negotiating land claims with the Canadian government and, where applicable, provincial gov-ernments. These negotiations cover a wide range of issues, including ownership of certain land areas, guaranteed wildlife-harvesting rights, participation in re-source-management decisions, resource revenue-sharing, and financial compen-sation. Although aboriginal leaders consider self-government to be an essential component, the federal government argues that this is a topic for later, separate negotiation.

The settlement of comprehensive land claims, even if successful, involves years of negotiation. The legal interpretation of broad, inherent aboriginal rights—for example, via Supreme Court decisions—is also a lengthy process. Until such rights are established and land claims settlements are negotiated to the satisfac-tion of the aboriginal peoples, some will seek to attain their goals by influencing political opinion within Canada and abroad.

Two Northern Conflicts

Two large projects in northern Canada, Phase 2 of the James Bay hydroelectric power scheme in Quebec and military low-altitude flight training over Labrador and eastern Quebec by member countries of the North Atlantic Treaty Organiza-tion (NATO), have generated conflicts featuring pervasive transnationalization. At first glance, the two cases have little in common: One concerns energy supply and demand, and the other, NATO defense policy. The James Bay project involves end-users in southern Quebec and the northeastern United States, but the aquatic environment, wetland habitats, wildlife, and aboriginal communities pursuing subsistence hunting and fishing are greatly affected. Although low-level flight training is not a permanent construction project like a storage reservoir or power station, its impacts are nonetheless serious. The key issues are rights over territory and airspace; noise impacts on people and wildlife; and the economic, social, and environmental effects of the project. The end-users are European NATO partners who export low-level flight training from their own densely populated countries because of increasing public opposition.

The James Bay Project

The government of Quebec and the provincial power utility, Hydro-Quebec, are committed to harnessing 28,000 megawatts of hydroelectric capacity from northern rivers whose total catchment area covers almost 400,000 square kilometers. Phase 1, which has harnessed La Grande River, is nearly completed, and Phase 2, which would place three dams on the Great Whale River is just now undergoing environment review.[15] A third phase of development is projected for the turn of the century. The end-users—consumers of electricity generated from the dams—live in southern Quebec, New York, and the New England states. Ultimately, Europeans and the Japanese may also be end-users if electricity-based hydrogen production and liquid hydrogen export (by tanker) prove to be feasible.

The project is greatly modifying the hydrological regime—including water volumes, discharge rates, temperature patterns, and ice formation—of the rivers flowing into James Bay and thus should result in substantial changes to the inland waters and coastal region. Although the scale of the project makes impact prediction and evaluation difficult, substantial habitat loss as well as changes in habitat and wildlife populations are already evident, especially in highly biologically productive wetland areas.[16] The accumulation of methyl mercury in the storage reservoirs and its concentration in food chains constitute a critical problem. Mercury contamination of fish has had a serious impact on the traditional subsistence economy of the aboriginal population in the region.[17]

Impacts seen by project proponents as controllable or capable of mitigation are viewed by opponents as irreversible and existence-threatening.[18] The affected peoples are mostly Cree Indians and Inuit living on the northern fringe of the project area and a small population (450) of Naskapi near Schefferville in northeastern Quebec. Some 4,700 aboriginal people live in two Cree and four Inuit communities located within the area of the Great Whale project alone. (More than 10,500 Cree and 8,500 Inuit live in Quebec.)[19]

In response to a Cree court challenge aimed at halting Phase 1, the Quebec government negotiated a treaty with the Cree and Inuit in 1975 that became known as the James Bay and Northern Quebec Agreement.[20] This agreement exchanged future provincial development rights for protection of aboriginal subsistence rights and monetary compensation. The Naskapi band, left out of this original treaty, signed a separate James Bay and Northeastern Quebec Agreement in 1978. Confronted with Phase 2 and possibly a third phase of development, the Cree are now challenging the provisions of the 1975 agreement. Key actors in the current dispute include the government of Quebec, local and international corporations, the Grand Council of the Cree, and environmental and human rights groups in Canada and the United States. The conflict has been played out before the courts, in state energy hearings in the northeastern United States, and in the heated constitutional dispute between French-speaking Québécois and the rest of Canada.

Military Flight Training

The Department of National Defence and Canada's NATO partners are engaging in low-level military flight training over a 100,000-square-kilometer area in Labrador and eastern Quebec. NATO training began in 1979, using the existing Canadian Forces Base at Goose Bay, Labrador, and expanded in 1986, when Canada signed 10-year agreements with its NATO partners Germany, Great Britain, and the Netherlands. These agreements allow up to 18,000 flights a year at elevations as low as 30 meters above ground level in two designated training areas connected by three flight corridors.[21] A proposal for a NATO tactical training center, which would have involved up to 40,000 flights a year, an offshore bombing range, and the use of live ammunition, was dropped in 1991 in response to profound shifts in the world strategic balance of power.

In 1992, approximately 7,400 low level flights were flown in the two designated areas during the April to October training season. The impact of noise (especially the "startle effect" of fast, low-flying jets) on human health and wildlife,[22] pollutant discharges on vegetation and water bodies, and the social impacts of the base on the local communities should be weighed against the benefits to the local economy, which is almost totally dependent on the military presence.

The aboriginal peoples affected by the overflights are mostly Montagnais and Innu Indians in Quebec and Labrador, respectively, as well as Inuit living on the Labrador coast and, more distantly, the small Naskapi band near Schefferville.[23] There are approximately 9,500 Montagnais living in Quebec and some 1,100 Innu and 4,500 Inuit and Settlers (people of mixed Inuit and European ancestry) living in Labrador. In the fall, about 1,200 Innu, Montagnais, and Naskapi engage in wildlife harvesting in the two flight training areas in Quebec and Labrador.[24] The Labrador Inuit are less immediately affected, but caribou hunters from the northernmost coastal community, Nain, have been overflown when they travel inland in April and May. Nonaboriginal hunters and commercial outfitters also use the two flight-training areas.

The flight-training proponents argue that there is no permanent population living within the two designated training areas and that potential effects—on the estimated 600,000 caribou of the George River herd and on local resource users, for example—can be mitigated by an impact-avoidance program, which was recently put in place. The aboriginal peoples who use the flight area for seasonal subsistence hunting express grave concerns about the environmental and health effects, question the justification for low-level flight training, and doubt the effectiveness of the avoidance program.[25] The Innu and Montagnais also object to the militarization of their homeland.

The Montagnais, Innu, and Labrador Inuit have never signed treaties with Canada or the former British colonial authorities. All three groups have engaged in lengthy land-claim negotiations with the federal and respective provincial governments to define their "homeland" rights.[26] Each group has taken a different position and adopted a particular political strategy with respect to the low-level flight training and land-claim negotiations. Since 1986, the ongoing military project has been the subject of a federal environmental assessment, which will not be concluded before mid-1994 at the earliest. Key actors in the conflict include the federal Department of National Defence and the three NATO partners, the provincial governments of Quebec and Newfoundland-Labrador, regional business interests, the Montagnais and Naskapi in Quebec, the Innu and Inuit in Labrador, and peace, church, and aboriginal support groups in Canada and Europe.

A Match of Scale

These two cases can be viewed at three different scales: global, supraregional, and regional/local. At the global level, the concepts of sustainable resource use and equitable development have been mentioned already. At the supraregional scale, where the two basic issues are energy and defense, the broad global concepts manifest themselves as specific elements, many of which are common to both conflicts even though they take place in different physical settings and political arenas with, to a large extent, different actors. The James Bay dispute must be seen in the context of Quebec's sovereignty aspirations as well as the energy debate in potential end-user states. Two themes are unique to the military flying dispute: the NATO defense debate in Europe (and the role it played in justifying low-level flight training in the past) and the regional development policy of Newfoundland-Labrador, which has encouraged any development that held the promise of income and employment in remote Labrador. All the other elements at this supraregional level are common to both conflicts. These include the question of First Nation rights, the environmental behavior of corporations (the public utility, Hydro-Quebec) and of state institutions (the Canadian Department of National Defence), and the intercultural communication barriers, which go well beyond language differences and involve contrasting perceptions, values, and knowledge systems.[27]

At the regional/local scale of analysis, other elements appear that are embedded in and interact with the larger themes already mentioned. At this microscale, it is important to recognize not only that there are differences between aboriginal and nonaboriginal peoples but also that subgroupings of both peoples vary in their perceptions, values, aspirations, degree of empowerment, and political strategies. For example, in both conflicts, the Inuit and Indian leaderships have pursued different strategies. The Inuit traditionally have sought negotiated solutions through existing institutional channels, such as the land-claim negotiations. In specific resource-use or management conflicts, their aim has been to convince people by presenting factual documentation. The Montagnais and Innu have sponsored research and published reports documenting their traditional land use, culture, and the perceived impacts of military flying.[28] But they have also followed a different course, which has included nonparticipation in formal proceedings in which they have little or no faith. The Labrador Innu have refused to recognize Canadian ju-

risdictional authority in some cases and have pursued strategies of civil disobedience, publicity-seeking, and alliances with other groups.[29]

Returning once more to the global and supraregional scales, both projects are located in peripheral, or "frontier," regions in the boreal and sub-Arctic north, which
is, to a high degree, economically, politically, and socially dependent on southern,
urban core regions. The indigenous peoples occupy a "Fourth World"[30] within an
urban-industrial state, and there is a collision of the constitutional rights and claims
of Canada, the provinces of Quebec and Newfoundland-Labrador, and the First
Nations. In both conflicts, there are transnationalization processes at work in the
environmental, political, economic, and cultural spheres. For example,

> confidential power contracts, concluded by the Quebec government with
> several multinational aluminum consortia, were first made public in Nor-
> . way and Australia, not in Canada;
> Hydro-Quebec, the publicly owned power utility, has set up an office in
> Brussels, headed by a vice president, to lobby both parliaments and the
> media in Europe;
> Cree Indians are putting pressure on the Canadian government and its
> diplomats by lobbying international organizations, including various
> United Nations bodies;
> the Department of National Defence and Labrador supporters lobbied
> NATO partners at the Brussels headquarters to gain support for the con-
> struction of a tactical training center;
> the Inuit Circumpolar Conference, a nongovernmental organization repre-
> senting the Inuit of Alaska, Canada, and Greenland, has proposed a
> transnational Inuit Regional Conservation Strategy for the Arctic [31] and
> has lobbied internationally for the demilitarization of the north; and
> representatives of the Labrador Innu, the Naskapi, and the Montagnais from
> Quebec have toured Europe on a number of occasions to lobby against
> military flight training over their homelands. In October 1992, represen-
> tatives of the Innu Nation were arrested after blocking a military base in
> the Netherlands in an act of civil disobedience to protest low-level flying
> by the Dutch in Canada.

These and other events show that the conflict arenas have extended well beyond the affected regions in Quebec and Labrador and even beyond the decision
centers in southern Canada.

The Protagonists in Action

Transnationalization affects many domains, including the economic, cultural, and
legal spheres. Although the focus here is on the international arena, these
processes and events are often mirrored on the domestic front. A three-stage se-
quence can be identified as proponents and opponents act and react, as the con-

flict unfolds. First, international linkages are developed as proponents promote the project abroad. In the cases discussed here, Hydro-Quebec sought to secure electric power contracts in New York and the New England states and signed confidential power contracts with multinational aluminum consortia. And the Department of National Defence lobbied NATO headquarters in Brussels to win a competition against Turkey for the siting of the proposed tactical training center. The project was promoted as a means for Canada to fulfill its NATO obligations, and Canada's competitive advantages over Turkey (such as the availability of empty space) were emphasized.

Second, indigenous peoples make direct attempts to stop the intrusion of large-scale technologies into their territories. In these cases, aboriginal people have

called for independent assessment by international bodies (for example, a delegation from the International Human Rights Federation visited Quebec and Labrador at the request of the Quebec Montagnais and submitted its report criticizing low-altitude flying in 1986);

prepared factual documentation of the perceived impacts, including self-assessments, and commissioned consultant studies;[32]

performed acts of civil disobedience in Canada and abroad (Innu protesters repeatedly occupied the Goose Bay airbase runway and, in 1992, penetrated a military airbase in Holland);

organized lobbying activities overseas (in the case of James Bay, representatives of the Grand Council of the Cree and supporters lobbied the state legislatures of New York, Massachusetts, and Vermont; in the case of the military flying dispute, the Innu and Cree lobbied the European Parliament, the Innu Nations lobbied Dutch, German, and British parliamentarians, and the Innu, Cree, and Montagnais have lobbied in United Nations forums);

run information campaigns abroad by linking their causes to highly symbolic events, such as the 500th anniversary of Columbus's landing, the 1992 Olympic Games, and the Amsterdam International Water Tribunal, by networking (for example, the Crees established contacts with several U.S. public-interest groups, such international organizations as Greenpeace, Friends of the Earth, and the Sierra Club, and prestigious national organizations abroad, such as the Audubon Society, and the Innu made contact with international human rights organizations and aboriginal support groups in Europe),[33] and by setting up protest marches and news conferences abroad, as well as meetings, such as those of the Innu-Montagnais delegations to Europe and their audience with the Pope;

participated in foreign legal and administrative procedures, as when representatives of the Grand Council of the Crees attended hearings of the New York State Standing Committee on Energy; and

formed alliances with supporter groups abroad (for example, the Cree allied themselves with environmental grassroots activists and organizations in the United States and Innu supporters allied themselves with U.S. groups opposed to military training in the southwestern states.

Third, project proponents respond directly to the initiatives of the opponents. For the James Bay project, Hydro-Quebec attempted to influence the media's discussion in Europe and the United States, and its lobbyists were active at state assemblies in New York and New England and at the European Parliament. For the flight training, Canada's Department of National Defence circulated a position paper called "Facts and Fallacies" in Canada and Europe to refute the opponents' arguments about low-altitude flight training. It has also organized tours to Goose Bay and selected Labrador communities for European journalists and parliamentarians. Another set of proponents, the Goose Bay–Happy Valley Town Council, has consulted with public relations experts to devise a campaign to promote the base and refute its critics. In addition, Canadian diplomats have attempted to abort, modify, or veto certain human rights and land-claims resolutions by international bodies, such as the International Human Rights Federation and the Centre for Transnational Corporations.

Two conclusions can be drawn from these examples: First, many of these events and activities must be seen as indicators of international networks, built up by the protagonists, and second, the protagonists' main interest lies in influencing the flow of information and its impact at the international level.

Thinking Locally, Acting Globally

Clearly, the interplay among marginalized groups in the north, southern domestic proponents (with substantial political empowerment), and foreign end-users has turned the conflicts over the James Bay hydroelectric power projects and low-level military flight training in Labrador and eastern Quebec into transnational, rather than purely Canadian, issues. When marginal groups lack power, believe that existing institutions and decisionmaking processes—such as the environmental assessment procedures and land-claim negotiations—are not sufficiently responsive, and feel that their rights are not recognized or protected, some try to gain bargaining power by seeking support in the international arena. The strategy is to "think locally" but "act globally."

It would be premature to draw definite conclusions about the effects of transnationalization on the outcomes of the two conflicts before the final decisions are made. However, it is clear that the protagonists are interested in influencing opinion abroad that might lend support to their own causes and weaken those of their opponents. Of course, the outcomes may be concrete and substantial, such as cancellation, modification, or postponement of the project, or more indirect and contextual, such as changes in the general or specific context of policies, activities, and so forth. Once networks are built up by the protagonists, pressure can be increased by information or disinformation campaigns aimed at forcing the opponent to react, preferably in the desired direction. The most striking example of such a reaction in the James Bay controversy was the cancellation of an important contract by the New York Power Authority in early 1992. However, this action resulted not only because of pressure from the Cree and their allies but also because of slumping energy demand caused by conscious demand-side management, energy conservation strategies, and the recession.

The decision to cancel Component 2 of the Goose Bay project, the NATO tactical training center, was a direct consequence of radically changed strategic relations in the world and not the result of opponents' lobbying abroad. But pressures from the Innu and Inuit, although very different in nature, did place the Department of National Defence and its performance of the environmental assessment under much public scrutiny. This scrutiny may well have contributed to the decision to design impact avoidance criteria for the selection of flight paths (however controversial these may be).

The visits of Innu delegations to the Netherlands and Germany did not result in the two NATO partners pulling out of low-level flight training in Canada: It is considered to be strategically necessary and cannot be carried out domestically because of opposition from their own residents. At best, sensitivity to the concerns of the Innu and acceptance of the need for impact avoidance measures, such as flight restrictions, may have grown. (If the outcome of the environmental assessment is increased flying restrictions, the three NATO partners may well decide to withdraw.) This is just one example of an opponent generating indirect, contextual impacts: The use of information campaigns at home and abroad can make the proponents more willing to listen and compromise because of real or perceived pressure. These two Canadian examples are by no means unique, as the transnationalization of disputes over tropical deforestation, whaling, and the ivory trade shows. All of these issues compete for public attention in a world flooded with information from diverse and opposing sources. The extent to which the protagonists are successful in influencing the outcome of each conflict depends on a constellation of factors and varies from case to case. One trend is clear, however: Interest groups that do not necessarily share the same agenda—for example, aboriginal peoples and environmentalists—will continue to seek more effective strategies and wider, albeit often temporary, coalitions in an effort to level what they consider to be very uneven political playing fields.

PAUL WAPNER

12

Politics Beyond the State: Environmental Activism and World Civic Politics

Interest in transnational activist groups such as Greenpeace, European Nuclear Disarmament (END), and Amnesty International has been surging.... This work is important, especially insofar as it establishes the increasing influence of transnational nongovernmental organizations (NGOs) on states. Nonetheless, for all its insight, it misses a different but related dimension of activist work—the attempt by activists to shape public affairs by working within and across societies themselves.

Recent studies neglect the societal dimension of activists' efforts in part because they subscribe to a narrow understanding of politics. They see politics as a practice associated solely with government and thus understand activist efforts exclusively in terms of their influence upon government. Seen from this perspective, transnational activists are solely global pressure groups seeking to change states' policies or create conditions in the international system that enhance or diminish interstate cooperation. Other efforts directed toward societies at large are ignored or devalued because they are not considered to be genuinely political in character....

Excerpted from Paul Wapner, "Politics Beyond the State: Environmental Activism and World Civic Politics," *World Politics* 47 (April 1995):311–340. © 1995 The Johns Hopkins University Press.

This article focuses on activist society-oriented activities and demonstrates that activist organizations are not simply transnational pressure groups, but rather are political actors in their own right. The main argument is that the best way to think about transnational activist societal efforts is through the concept of "world civic politics." When activists work to change conditions without directly pressuring states, their activities take place in the civil dimension of world collective life or what is sometimes called global civil society.[4] Civil society is that arena of social engagement which exists above the individual yet below the state.[5] It is a complex network of economic, social, and cultural practices based on friendship, family, the market, and voluntary affiliation.[6] Although the concept arose in the analysis of domestic societies, it is beginning to make sense on a global level. The interpenetration of markets, the intermeshing of symbolic meaning systems, and the proliferation of transnational collective endeavors signal the formation of a thin, but nevertheless present, public sphere where private individuals and groups interact for common purposes. Global civil society as such is that slice of associational life which exists above the individual and below the state, but also across national boundaries. When transnational activists direct their efforts beyond the state, they are politicizing global civil society.

. . . In the following I analyze the character of world civic politics by focusing on one relatively new sector of this activity, transnational environmental activist groups (TEAGs). . . . This article demonstrates that, while TEAGs direct much effort toward state policies, their political activity does not stop there but extends into global civil society. In the following, I describe and analyze this type of activity and, in doing so, make explicit the dynamics and significance of world civic politics.

. . .

Disseminating an Ecological Sensibility

Few images capture the environmental age as well as the sight of Greenpeace activists positioning themselves between harpoons and whales in an effort to stop the slaughter of endangered sea mammals. Since 1972, with the formal organization of Greenpeace into a transnational environmental activist group, Greenpeace has emblazoned a host of such images onto the minds of people around the world. Greenpeace activists have climbed aboard whaling ships, parachuted from the top of smokestacks, plugged up industrial discharge pipes, and floated a hot air balloon into a nuclear test site. These direct actions are media stunts, exciting images orchestrated to convey a critical perspective toward environmental issues. Numerous other organizations, including the Sea Shepherds Conservation Society, EarthFirst! and Rainforest Action Network, engage in similar efforts. The dramatic aspect attracts journalists and television crews to specific actions and makes it possible for the groups themselves to distribute their own media presentations. Greenpeace, for example, has its own media facilities; within hours it can provide photographs to newspapers and circulate scripted video news spots to television stations in eighty-eight countries.[32] The overall intent is to use international mass communications to expose antiecological practices and thereby inspire audiences to change their views and behavior vis-à-vis the environment.[33]

Direct action is based on two strategies. The first is simply to bring what are often hidden instances of environmental abuse to the attention of a wide audience: harpooners kill whales on the high seas; researchers abuse Antarctica; significant species extinction takes place in the heart of the rain forest; and nuclear weapons are tested in the most deserted areas of the planet. Through television, radio, newspapers, and magazines transnational activist groups bring these hidden spots of the globe into people's everyday lives, thus enabling vast numbers of people to "bear witness" to environmental abuse.[34] Second, TEAGs engage in dangerous and dramatic actions that underline how serious they consider certain environmental threats to be. That activists take personal risks to draw attention to environmental issues highlights their indignation and the degree of their commitment to protecting the planet. Taken together, these two strategies aim to change the way vast numbers of people see the world—by dislodging traditional understandings of environmental degradation and substituting new interpretive frames. This was put particularly well by Robert Hunter, a founding member of Greenpeace, who participated in the group's early antiwhaling expeditions. For Hunter, the purpose of the effort was to overturn fundamental images about whaling: where the predominant view was of brave men battling vicious and numerous monsters of the deep, Greenpeace documented something different. As Hunter put it:

> Soon, images would be going out into hundreds of millions of minds around the world, a completely new set of basic images about whaling. Instead of small boats and giant whales, giant boats and small whales; instead of courage killing whales, courage saving whales; David had become Goliath, Goliath was now David; if the mythology of Moby Dick and Captain Ahab had dominated human consciousness about Leviathan for over a century, a whole new age was in the making.[35]

Raising awareness through media stunts is not primarily about changing governmental policies, although this may of course happen as state officials bear witness or are pressured by constituents to codify into law shifts in public opinion or widespread sentiment. But this is only one dimension of TEAG direct action efforts. The new age envisioned by Hunter is more than passing environmental legislation or adopting new environmental policies. Additionally, it involves convincing all actors—from governments to corporations, private organizations, and ordinary citizens—to make decisions and act in deference to environmental awareness. Smitten with such ideas, governments will, activists hope, take measures to protect the environment. When the ideas have more resonance outside government, they will shift the standards of good conduct and persuade people to act differently even though governments are not requiring them to do so. In short, TEAGs work to disseminate an ecological sensibility to shift the governing ideas that animate societies, whether institutionalized within government or not, and count on this to reverberate throughout various institutions and collectivities.

The challenge for students of international relations is to apprehend the effects of these efforts and their political significance. As already mentioned, scholars have traditionally focused on state policy and used this as the criterion for endowing NGOs with political significance. Such a focus, however, misses the broader changes initiated by NGOs beyond state behavior. To get at this dimension of change requires a more sociological orientation toward world affairs.[36] One such orientation is a so-called fluid approach.

The fluid approach has been used in the study of domestic social movements but can be adopted to analyze TEAGs.[37] It gauges the significance of activist groups by attending to cultural expressions that signal cognitive, affective, and evaluative shifts in societies. Observers are attuned to the quickening of actions and to changes in meaning and perceive that something new is happening in a wide variety of places. When analyzing the peace movement, for instance, a fluid approach recognizes that activists aim not only to convince governments to cease making war but also to create more peaceful societies. This entails propagating expressions of nonviolence, processes of conflict resolution, and, according to some, practices that are more cooperative than competitive. A fluid approach looks throughout society and interprets shifts in such expressions as a measure of the success of the peace movement.[38] Similarly, a fluid approach acknowledges that feminist groups aim at more than simply enacting legislation to protect women against gender discrimination. Additionally, they work to change patriarchal practices and degrading representations of women throughout society. Thus, as Joseph Gusfield notes, the successes of the feminist movement can be seen "where the housewife finds a new label for discontents, secretaries decide not to serve coffee and husbands are warier about using past habits of dominance."[39] A fluid approach, in other words, interprets activist efforts by noticing and analyzing, in the words of Herbert Blumer, a "cultural drift," "societal mood," or "public orientation" felt and expressed by people in diverse ways.[40] It focuses on changes in lifestyle, art, consumer habits, fashion, and so forth and sees these, as well as shifts in laws and policies, as consequences of activist efforts.

Applied to the international arena, a fluid approach enables one to appreciate, however imperfectly, changes initiated by transnational activists that occur independently of state policies. With regard to TEAGs, it allows one to observe how an environmental sensibility infiltrates deliberations at the individual, organizational, corporate, governmental, and interstate levels to shape world collective life.

Consider the following. In 1970 one in ten Canadians said the environment was worthy of being on the national agenda; twenty years later one in three felt not only that it should be on the agenda but that it was the most pressing issue facing Canada.[41] In 1981, 45 percent of those polled in a U.S. survey said that protecting the environment was so important that "requirements and standards cannot be too high and continuing environmental improvements must be made regardless of cost"; in 1990, 74 percent supported the statement.[42] This general trend is supported around the world. In a recent Gallup poll majorities in twenty countries gave priority to safeguarding the environment even at the cost of slowing economic growth; additionally, 71 percent of the people in sixteen countries, including India, Mexico, South Korea, and Brazil, said they were willing to pay higher prices for products if it would help to protect the environment.[43]

These figures suggest a significant shift in awareness and concern about the environment over the past two decades. It is also worth noting that people have translated this sentiment into changes in behavior. In the 1960s the U.S. Navy and Air Force used whales for target practice. Twenty-five years later an international effort costing $5 million was mounted to save three whales trapped in the ice in Alaska.[44] Two decades ago corporations produced products with little regard for their environmental impact. Today it is incumbent upon corporations to reduce negative environmental impact at the production, packaging, and distribution phases of industry.[45] When multilateral development banks and other aid institutions were established after the Second World War, environmental impact assessments were unheard of; today they are commonplace.[46] Finally, twenty years ago recycling as a concept barely existed. Today recycling is mandatory in many municipalities around the world, and in some areas voluntary recycling is a profit-making industry. (Between 1960 and 1990 the amount of municipal solid waste recovered by recycling in the United States more than quintupled.)[47] In each of these instances people are voluntarily modifying their behavior in part because of the messages publicized by activists. If one looked solely at state behavior to account for this change, one would miss a tremendous amount of significant world political action.

A final, if controversial, example of the dissemination of an ecological sensibility is the now greatly reduced practice of killing harp seal pups in northern Canada. Throughout the 1960s the annual Canadian seal hunt took place without attracting much public attention or concern. In the late 1960s and throughout the 1970s and 1980s the International Fund for Animals, Greenpeace, the Sea Shepherds Conservation Society, and a host of smaller preservation groups saw this—in hindsight inaccurately, according to many—as a threat to the continued existence of harp seals in Canada. They brought the practice to the attention of the world, using, among other means, direct action. As a result, people around the globe, but especially in Europe, changed their buying habits and stopped purchasing products made out of the pelts. As a consequence, the market for such merchandise all but dried up with the price per skin plummeting.[48] Then, in 1983, the European Economic Community (EEC) actually banned the importation of seal pelts.[49] It is significant that the EEC did so only after consumer demand had already dropped dramatically.[50] Governmental policy, that is, may have simply been an afterthought and ultimately unnecessary. People acted in response to the messages propagated by activist groups.[51]

When Greenpeace and other TEAGs undertake direct action or follow other strategies to promote an ecological sensibility, these are the types of changes they are seeking. At times, governments respond with policy measures and changed behavior with respect to environmental issues. The failure of governments to respond, however, does not necessarily mean that the efforts of activists have been in vain. Rather, they influence understandings of good conduct throughout societies at large. They help set the boundaries of what is considered acceptable behavior.[52]

When people change their buying habits, voluntarily recycle garbage, boycott certain products, and work to preserve species, it is not necessarily because governments are breathing down their necks. Rather, they are acting out of a belief that the environmental problems involved are severe, and they wish to contribute to alleviating them. They are being "stung," as it were, by an ecological sensibility. This sting is a type of governance. It represents a mechanism of authority that can shape widespread human behavior.

Multinational Corporate Politics

In 1991 the multinational McDonald's Corporation decided to stop producing its traditional clamshell hamburger box and switch to paper packaging in an attempt to cut back on the use of disposable foam and plastic. In 1990 Uniroyal Chemical Company, the sole manufacturer of the apple-ripening agent Alar, ceased to produce and market the chemical both in the United States and abroad. Alar, the trade name for daminozide, was used on most kinds of red apples and, according to some, found to cause cancer in laboratory animals. Finally, in 1990 Starkist and Chicken of the Sea, the two largest tuna companies, announced that they would cease purchasing tuna caught by setting nets on dolphins or by any use of drift nets; a year later Bumble Bee Tuna followed suit. Such action has contributed to protecting dolphin populations around the world.

In each of these instances environmental activist groups—both domestic and transnational—played an important role in convincing corporations to alter their practices. To be sure, each case raises controversial issues concerning the ecological wisdom of activist pressures, but it also nevertheless demonstrates the effects of TEAG efforts. In the case of McDonald's, the corporation decided to abandon its foam and plastic containers in response to prodding by a host of environmental groups. These organizations, which included the Citizens Clearinghouse for Hazardous Waste, Earth Action Network, and Kids against Pollution, organized a "send-back" campaign in which people mailed McDonald's packaging to the national headquarters. Additionally, Earth Action Network actually broke windows and scattered supplies at a McDonald's restaurant in San Francisco to protest the company's environmental policies. The Environmental Defense Fund (EDF) played a mediating role by organizing a six-month, joint task force to study ways to reduce solid waste in McDonald's eleven thousand restaurants worldwide. The task force provided McDonald's with feasible responses to activist demands.[53] What is clear from most reports on the change is that officials at McDonald's did not believe it necessarily made ecological or economic sense to stop using clamshell packaging but that they bent to activist pressure.[54]

Uniroyal Chemical Company ceased producing Alar after groups such as Ralph Nader's Public Interest Research Group (PIRG) and the Natural Resources Defense Council (NRDC) organized a massive public outcry about the use of the product on apples in the U.S. and abroad. In 1989 NRDC produced a study that found that Alar created cancer risks 240 times greater than those declared safe by the U.S. Environmental Protection Agency (EPA).[55] This was publicized on CBS's *60 Minutes* and led to critical stories in numerous newspapers and magazines. Moreover, activists pressured supermarket chains to stop selling apples grown with Alar and pressured schools to stop serving Alar-sprayed apples. The effects were dramatic. The demand for apples in general shrank significantly because of the scare, lowering prices well below the break-even level.[56] This led to a loss of $135 million for Washington State apple growers alone.[57] Effects such as these and pressure by activist groups convinced Uniroyal to cease production of the substance not only in the U.S. but overseas as well. Like McDonald's, Uniroyal changed its practices not for economic reasons nor to increase business nor because it genuinely felt Alar was harmful. Rather, it capitulated to activist pressure. In fact, there is evidence from nonindustry sources suggesting that Alar did not pose the level of threat publicized by activists.[58]

Finally, in the case of dolphin-free tuna, Earth Island Institute (EII) and other organizations launched an international campaign in 1985 to stop all drift-net and purse seine fishing by tuna fleets. For unknown reasons, tuna in the Eastern Tropical Pacific Ocean swim under schools of dolphins. For years tuna fleets have set their nets on dolphins or entangled dolphins in drift nets as a way to catch tuna. While some fleets still use these strategies, the three largest tuna companies have ceased doing so. TEAGs were at the heart of this change. Activists waged a boycott against all canned tuna, demonstrated at stockholders' meetings, and rallied on the docks of the Tuna Boat Association in San Diego. Furthermore, EII assisted in the production of the film *Where Have All the Dolphins Gone?* which was shown throughout the United States and abroad; it promoted the idea of "dolphin-safe" tuna labels to market environmentally sensitive brands; and it enlisted Heinz, the parent company of Starkist, to take an active role in stopping the slaughter of dolphins by all tuna companies. Its efforts, along with those of Greenpeace, Friends of the Earth, and others, were crucial to promoting dolphin-safe tuna fishing.[59] One result of these efforts is that dolphin kills associated with tuna fishing in 1993 numbered fewer than 5,000. This represents one-third the mortality rate of 1992, when 15,470 dolphins died in nets, and less than one-twentieth of the number in 1989, when over 100,000 dolphins died at the hands of tuna fleets.[60] These numbers represent the effects of activist efforts. Although governments did eventually adopt domestic dolphin conservation policies and negotiated partial international standards to reduce dolphin kills, the first such actions came into force only in late 1992 with the United Nations moratorium on drift nets. Moreover, the first significant actions against purse seine fishing, which more directly affects dolphins, came in June 1994 with the United States International Dolphin Conservation Act.[61] As with the Canadian seal pup hunt, government action in the case of tuna fisheries largely codified changes that were already taking place.

In each instance, activist groups did not direct their efforts at governments. They did not target politicians; nor did they organize constituent pressuring. Rather, they focused on corporations themselves. Through protest, research, exposés, orchestrating public outcry, and organizing joint consultations, activists won corporate promises to bring their practices in line with environmental concerns. The levers of power in these instances were found in the economic realm of collective life rather than in the strictly governmental realm. Activists understand that the economic realm, while not the center of traditional notions of politics, nevertheless furnishes channels for effecting widespread changes in behavior; they recognize that the economic realm is a form of governance and can be manipulated to alter collective practices.

Perhaps the best example of how activist groups, especially transnational ones, enlist the economic dimensions of governance into their enterprises is the effort to establish environmental oversight of corporations. In September 1989 a coalition of environmental, investor, and church interests, known as the Coalition for Environmentally Responsible Economies (CERES), met in New York City to introduce a ten-point environmental code of conduct for corporations. One month later CERES, along with the Green Alliance, launched a similar effort in the United Kingdom. The aim was to establish criteria for auditing the environmental performance of large domestic and multinational industries. The code called on companies to, among other things, minimize the release of pollutants, conserve nonrenewable resources through efficient use and planning, utilize environmentally safe and sustainable energy sources, and consider demonstrated environmental commitment as a factor in appointing members to the board of directors. Fourteen environmental organizations, including TEAGs such as Friends of the Earth and the International Alliance for Sustainable Agriculture, publicize the CERES Principles (formerly known as the Valdez Principles, inspired by the Exxon *Valdez* oil spill) and enlist corporations to pledge compliance. What is significant from an international perspective is that signatories include at least one Fortune 500 company and a number of multinational corporations. Sun Company, General Motors, Polaroid, and a host of other MNCs have pledged compliance or are at least seriously considering doing so. Because these companies operate in numerous countries their actions have transnational effects.

The CERES Principles are valuable for a number of reasons. In the case of pension funds, the code is being used to build shareholder pressure on companies to improve their environmental performance. Investors can use it as a guide to determine which companies practice socially responsible investment. Environmentalists use the code as a measuring device to praise or criticize corporate behavior.

Finally, the Principles are used to alert college graduates on the job market about corporate compliance with the code and thus attempt to make environmental issues a factor in one's choice of a career. Taken together, these measures force some degree of corporate accountability by establishing mechanisms of governance to shape corporate behavior. To be sure, they have not turned businesses into champions of environmentalism, nor are they as effectual as mechanisms available to governments. At work, however, is activist discovery and manipulation of economic means of power.[62]

Via the CERES Principles and other forms of pressure, activists thus influence corporate behavior.[63] McDonald's, Uniroyal, and others have not been changing their behavior because governments are breathing down their necks. Rather, they are voluntarily adopting different ways of producing and distributing products. This is not to say that their actions are more environmentally sound than before they responded to activists or that their attempt to minimize environmental dangers is sincerely motivated. As mentioned, environmental activist groups do not have a monopoly on ecological wisdom, nor is corporate "greening" necessarily well intentioned.[64] Nonetheless, the multinational corporate politics of transnational groups are having an effect on the way industries do business. And to the degree that these enterprises are involved in issues of widespread public concern that cross state boundaries, activist pressure must be understood as a form of world politics.

Empowering Local Communities

For decades TEAGs have worked to conserve wildlife in the developing world. Typically, this has involved people in the First World working in the Third World to restore and guard the environment. First World TEAGs—ones headquartered in the North—believed that Third World people could not appreciate the value of wildlife or were simply too strapped by economic pressures to conserve nature. Consequently, environmental organizations developed, financed, and operated programs in the field with little local participation or input.

While such efforts saved a number of species from extinction and set in motion greater concern for Third World environmental protection, on the whole they were unsuccessful at actually preserving species and their habitats from degradation and destruction.[65] A key reason for this was that they attended more to the needs of plants and especially animals than to those of the nearby human communities. Many of the earth's most diverse and biologically rich areas are found in parts of the world where the poorest peoples draw their livelihood from the land. As demographic and economic constraints grow tighter, these people exploit otherwise renewable resources in an attempt merely to survive.[66] Ecological sustainability in these regions, then, must involve improving the quality of life of the rural poor through projects that integrate the management of natural resources with grassroots economic development.

Often after having supported numerous failed projects, a number of TEAGs have come to subscribe to this understanding and undertake appropriate actions. World Wildlife Fund (WWF) or World Wide Fund for Nature, as it is known outside English-speaking countries, is an example of such an organization. WWF is a conservation group dedicated to protecting endangered wildlife and wildlands worldwide. It originated in 1961 as a small organization in Switzerland, making grants to finance conservation efforts in various countries. Over the past thirty years it has grown into a full-scale global environmental organization with offices in over twenty countries. Within the past decade, WWF has established a wildlands and human needs program, a method of conservation to be applied to all WWF projects linking human economic well-being with environmental protection. It structures a game management system in Zambia, for example, which involves local residents in antipoaching and conservation efforts, and the channeling of revenues from tourism and safaris back into the neighboring communities that surround the preserves.[67] It informs a WWF-initiated Kilum Mountain project in the Cameroon that is developing nurseries for reforestation, reintroducing indigenous crops, and disseminating information about the long-term effects of environmentally harmful practices.[68] Finally, it is operative in a project in St. Lucia, where WWF has lent technical assistance to set up sanitary communal waste disposal sites, improved marketing of fish to reduce overfishing, and protected mangroves from being used for fuel by planting fast-growing fuel-wood trees.[69] WWF is not alone in these efforts. The New Forests Project, the Association for Research and Environmental Aid (AREA), the Ladakh Project, and others undertake similar actions.

In these kinds of efforts, TEAGs are not trying to galvanize public pressure aimed at changing governmental policy or directly lobbying state officials; indeed, their activity takes place far from the halls of congresses, parliaments, and executive offices. Rather, TEAGs work with ordinary people in diverse regions of the world to try to enhance local capability to carry out sustainable development projects. The guiding logic is that local people must be enlisted in protecting their own environments and that their efforts will then reverberate through wider circles of social interaction to affect broader aspects of world environmental affairs.[70]

Independent of the content of specific projects, the efforts of TEAGs almost always bring local people together.[71] They organize people into new forms of social interaction, and this makes for a more tightly woven web of associational life. To the degree that this is attentive to ecological issues, it partially fashions communities into ecologically sensitive social agents. This enables them more effectively to resist outside forces that press them to exploit their environments, and it helps them assume a more powerful role in determining affairs when interacting with outside institutions and processes. To paraphrase Michael Bratton, hands-on eco-development projects stimulate and release popular energies in support of community goals.[72] This strengthens a community's ability to determine its own affairs and influence events outside its immediate domain.

The dynamics of environmental destruction often do not originate at the local or state level. Poor people who wreck their environments are generally driven to do so by multiple external pressures. Embedded within regional, national, and ultimately global markets, living under political regimes riven by rivalries and controlled by leadership that is not popularly based, penetrated by MNCs, and often at the mercy of multilateral development banks, local people respond to the consumptive practices and development strategies of those living in distant cities or countries.[73] Once empowered, however, communities can respond to these pressures more successfully. For example, since 1985 tens of thousands of peasants, landless laborers, and tribal people have demonstrated against a series of dams in the Narmada Valley that critics believe will cause severe environmental and social damage. The Sardar Sarovar projects are intended to produce hydroelectric energy for the states of Gujarat, Madhya Pradesh, and Maharashtra and have been supported by the governments of these states, the Indian government, and until recently the World Bank. Resistance started locally, but since 1985 it has spread with the formation by local and transnational groups of an activist network that operates both inside India and abroad to thwart the project. While the final outcome has yet to be determined, local communities have already redefined the debate about the environmental efficacy of large dam projects, as well as those having to do with displacement and rehabitation. As a result, the Indian government, the World Bank, and other aid agencies now find themselves profoundly hesitant about future dam projects; indeed, in 1993 the Indian government withdrew its request for World Bank funding to support the Sardar Sarovar project.[74] Finally, local communities have served notice, through their insistence that they will drown before they let themselves be displaced, that they are better organized to resist other large-scale, external environmental and developmental designs.[75]

Local empowerment affects wider arenas of social life in a positive, less reactive fashion when communities reach out to actors in other regions, countries, and continents. Indeed, the solidification of connections between TEAGs and local communities itself elicits responses from regional, national, and international institutions and actors. This connection is initially facilitated when TEAGs that have offices in the developed world transfer money and resources to Third World communities. In 1989, for example, northern NGOs distributed $6.4 billion to developing countries, which is roughly 12 percent of all public and private development aid.[76] Much of this aid went to local NGOs and helped to empower local communities.[77]

This pattern is part of a broader shift in funding from First World governments. As local NGOs become better able to chart the economic and environmental destinies of local communities, First World donors look to them for expertise and capability. For instance, in 1975 donor governments channeled $100 million through local NGOs; in 1985 the figure had risen to $1.1 billion.[78] This represents a shift on the part of Official Development Assistance (ODA) countries. In 1975 they donated only 0.7 percent of their funding through Third World NGOs; in

1985 the figure rose to 3.6 percent.[79] This pattern is further accentuated when First World governments turn to transnational NGOs in the North for similar expertise. According to a 1989 OECD report, by the early 1980s virtually all First World countries adopted a system of co-financing projects implemented by their national NGOs. "Official contributions to NGOs' activities over the decades have been on an upward trend, amounting to $2.2 billion in 1987 and representing 5 percent of total ODA," according to the report.[80] While much of this was funneled through voluntary relief organizations such as Catholic Relief Services, overall there has been an upgrading in the status of NGOs concerned with development and environmental issues.[81]

Increased aid to local NGOs has obvious effects on local capability. It enhances the ability of communities to take a more active and effectual role in their economic and environmental destinies. The effects are not limited, however, to a more robust civil society. Many of the activities and certainly the funding directly challenge or at least intersect with state policies; thus, governments are concerned about who controls any foreign resources that come into the country. When funds go to NGOS, state activity can be frustrated. This is most clear in places like Kenya and Malaysia, where environmental NGOs are part of broader opposition groups. In these instances outside aid to local groups may be perceived as foreign intervention trying to diminish state power. At a lesser degree of challenge, outside support may simply minimize the control government exercises over its territory. Empowering local communities diminishes state authority by reinforcing local loyalties at the expense of national identity. At a minimum, this threatens government attempts at nation building. Put most broadly, TEAGs pose a challenge to state sovereignty and more generally redefine the realm of the state itself. Thus, while TEAGS may see themselves working outside the domain of the state and focusing on civil society per se, their actions in fact have a broader impact and interfere with state politics.

Nevertheless, it would be misleading to think about TEAGs as traditional interest groups. Rather, with their hands-on development/environmental efforts TEAGs attempt to work independent of governmental activity at the level of communities themselves. That their activities end up involving them in the political universe of the state is indicative of the porous boundary between local communities and the state or, more broadly, between the state and civil society. It does not mean that activist efforts in civil society gain political relevance only when they intersect state activities.[82]

The grassroots efforts of transnational environmental activists aim to engage people at the level at which they feel the most immediate effects—their own local environmental and economic conditions. At this level, TEAGs try to use activism itself, rooted in the actual experience of ordinary people, as a form of governance. It can alter the way people interact with each other and their environment, literally to change the way they live their lives. To the degree that such efforts have ramifications for wider arenas of social interaction—including states and other actors—they have world political significance.

World Civic Politics

The predominant way to think about NGOs in world affairs is as transnational interest groups. They are politically relevant insofar as they affect state policies and interstate behavior. In this article I have argued that TEAGs, a particular type of NGO, have political relevance beyond this. They work to shape the way vast numbers of people throughout the world act toward the environment using modes of governance that are part of global civil society.

Greenpeace, Sea Shepherds Conservation Society, and EarthFirst!, for example, work to disseminate an ecological sensibility. It is a sensibility not restricted to governments nor exclusively within their domain of control. Rather, it circulates throughout all areas of collective life. To the degree this sensibility sways people, it acts as a form of governance. It defines the boundaries of good conduct and thus animates how a host of actors—from governments to voluntary associations and ordinary citizens—think about and act in reference to the environment.

A similar dynamic is at work when TEAGs pressure multinational corporations. These business enterprises interact with states, to be sure, and state governments can restrict their activities to a significant degree. They are not monopolized by states, however, and thus their realm of operation is considerably beyond state control. Due to the reach of multinational corporations into environmental processes, encouraging them to become "green" is another instance of using the governing capacities outside formal government to shape widespread activities.

Finally, when TEAGs empower local communities, they are likewise not focused primarily on states. Rather, by working to improve people's day-to-day economic lives in ecologically sustainable ways, they bypass state apparatuses and activate governance that operates at the community level. As numerous communities procure sustainable development practices, the efforts of TEAGs take effect. Moreover, as changed practices at this level translate up through processes and mechanisms that are regional, national, and global in scope, the efforts by TEAGs influence the activities of larger collectivities, which in turn shape the character of public life.

I suggested that the best way to think about these activities is through the category of "world civic politics." When TEAGs work through transnational networks associated with cultural, social, and economic life, they are enlisting forms of governance that are civil as opposed to official or state constituted in character. Civil, in this regard, refers to the quality of interaction that takes place above the individual and below the state yet across national boundaries. The concept of world civic politics clarifies how the forms of governance in global civil society are distinct from the instrumentalities of state rule. . . .

PART THREE

The Prospects for International Environmental Cooperation

Ken Conca

Effective responses to global environmental problems clearly require international cooperation. But the barriers to such cooperation are substantial, and include uncertainty, mistrust, conflicting interests, different views of causality, complex linkages to other issues, and the myriad problems of coordinating the behavior of large numbers of actors.[1] Effective international cooperation will require both a series of international agreements that respond to specific, pressing environmental problems, and a more general commitment to reexamine and restructure existing international practices that are damaging the environment. In this section we take up the question of issue-specific international agreements; Part Four then turns to the related question of reforming existing practices and institutions.

Barriers notwithstanding, there have been some hopeful signs. International agreements of varying scope and effectiveness now exist on a number of important issues, including the international trade in endangered species, international shipments of toxic waste, ocean dumping, the Antarctic environment, whaling, nuclear safety, and the protection of regional seas.[2] Perhaps the most powerful example of international cooperation is provided by the international agreement on protecting the planet's ozone layer. The successful negotiation of the Montreal Protocol on Substances that Deplete the Ozone Layer in 1987, and its further strengthening in London in 1990, signaled what many hoped would be a new era of increased global environmental cooperation. Certainly that enthusiasm carried over into the 1992 Earth Summit, where governments attempted to hammer out agreements that would slow global warming, protect biological diversity, and reduce rates of deforestation. But effective cooperation on these and related global challenges has been elusive. It is too early to say that the Montreal Protocol is an isolated exception to the inability of governments to act collectively, but clearly it did not trigger a wave of effective new international agreements.

We begin with the question of whether the ozone accords represent a model for future cooperation. Richard Elliot Benedick, a key U.S. negotiator during the crafting of the agreement, provides a glimpse inside the negotiating process. In Benedick's view, skillful diplomacy backed by sound science overcame economic self-interest and brought about a treaty to control the emissions of chlorofluorocarbons (CFCs), the chief culprit in ozone depletion. According to Benedick, both the substance of the agreement and the process of negotiation provide useful models. In the first stage of negotiations, participants drafted a framework convention that provided a commitment to investigating the ozone problem without imposing any specific regulations or timetables for curtailing the production or consumption of CFCs. In subsequent meetings of the signatories to the framework convention, more specific regulations to control CFCs were adopted in the form of amendments or "protocols" to the original convention.[3]

The advantage of this "framework-protocol" method was its ability to gradually bring on board the necessary governments, without frightening them away with specific, costly regulations. More stringent regulations were negotiated incrementally, as the scientific evidence needed to support them became available. Also, countries with specific objections were offered inducements, or "side payments," to elicit their support. For example, a special monetary fund, promises of technology transfer, and a special phase-in time period were used to allay the fears of the developing countries that they would have to sacrifice future economic development to meet the provisions of the Montreal Protocol. The economic interests of various governments and their chemical industries were eventually overcome by gearing the initial convention mandates to the "lowest common denominator" and then allowing the mounting scientific evidence against CFCs to build pressure for tougher controls.

Writing in the late 1980s, Benedick spoke for many environmentalists, scholars, and diplomats when he suggested that the framework-protocol approach to the ozone issue could be a model for other global problems. Indeed, elements of the Montreal model can be seen in the treaties on climate and biodiversity signed at the Earth Summit. But as the international community grappled with more complex problems involving more actors, greater scientific uncertainty, more deeply entrenched interests, and potentially high costs of adjustment, the momentum for forming ambitious new international environmental regimes stalled in the post-UNCED 1990s.

Climate change negotiators, for example, face the challenge of putting together a much broader coalition of governments than that needed for the Montreal Protocol, and then convincing them to accept measures that make the costs of compliance with Montreal pale in comparison. Negotiators at Kyoto were hard-pressed to forge a consensus, even without trying to reconcile the interests of North and South. The negotiators of the Montreal Protocol were able to overcome this problem by, in essence, paying the South to forsake the use and production of CFCs. Because of the South's rather small current reliance on CFCs, this required the relatively small sum of a few hundred million dollars in a multilateral fund. It is difficult to envision a similar compromise on a problem as complex as climate change, where the activities needing restriction are far more central to both Northern and Southern economies, and where the adjustment costs are far greater.[4] Not surprisingly, the face-saving compromise hammered out on climate at Kyoto remains a far cry from the elimination of CFCs and other ozone-depleting substances as negotiated in the Montreal process.

Moreover, Ruth Greenspan Bell, writing in the context of Kyoto, raises a more fundamental question: Do international environmental treaties really work? Even the most carefully crafted treaties, successfully balancing conflicting interests and dealing with problems of cost and uncertainty, are only as good as their implementation. As Bell points out, "The implementation record for many existing agreements has been mixed at best. . . . Countries signing on to these regimes must have capacity and political will to carry them out." If we understand the problem of implementation to be not only technical and administrative but also political, then Bell's discussion of the U.S. case on climate change makes clear that implementation capacity can by no means be taken for granted.

Even if this complex maze of competing interests can be negotiated, the problem of scientific uncertainty remains. Instead of having the strong support of the scientific community behind them, climate change negotiators face a potentially dizzying variety of scientific theories. Although climate scientists are converging on a consensus that human activities will increase global temperatures, there is still a wide variety of opinion as to the amount of temperature change we can expect, how quickly it is likely to occur, and how it will affect different regions of the planet.

This leads to the question of the role of scientific knowledge in fostering or inhibiting international agreements. Is scientific consensus required for international cooperation to occur? Can the sheer power of scientific knowledge spur cooperative action? Sheila Jasanoff argues that while knowledge plays an important role, science alone is an inadequate compass to guide global action. People can examine the same scientific information and come up with dramatically different interpretations of the cause(s) of a particular natural phenomenon. They also might disagree strongly over the best course of action to remedy the situation even when they agree that a problem exists. Science is inevitably politicized, given the high stakes and great uncertainty surrounding environmental change. And Jasanoff makes the provocative claim that too much scientific information can paralyze efforts to achieve cooperation. Returning again to the climate change example, every new finding regarding the role of some feedback mechanism involving cloud cover or the oceans, every new theory about the influence of solar flares or volcanoes, can lead to calls for more research in lieu of moving toward more specific action.

Under such circumstances knowledge alone is no substitute for the political will to act, and science requires some value orientation and set of agreed-upon social goals in order to know which questions to ask.

Finally, even if the politics of science, uncertainty, and technical complexity can be addressed so that new knowledge facilitates rather than inhibits effective international cooperation, there remains the task of crafting agreements that are seen by all sides as reasonably fair, effective, and in their interest. Again, the climate change example illustrates the substantial barriers. In an essay by Anil Agarwal and Sunita Narain of India's Centre for Science and Environment, we see an example of how different groups can look at the same scientific data—in this case, estimates of how much different countries contribute to the problem of global warming—and come up with radically different interpretations. According to Agarwal and Narain, it is highly misleading to look at the statistics on ozone-depleting emissions in terms of national contributions. Even if it is true that China, India, and Brazil are now three of the most significant sources of carbon dioxide (the leading cause of ozone depletion), two important points are ignored by such data. Gross national figures make no distinction between the "luxury emissions" of the rich and the "survival emissions" of the poor. The data also mask the fact that, given their low level of emissions per capita, densely populated countries such as India are using up much less than their "fair share" of the earth's ability to absorb pollutants. Thus, a task seemingly as neutral as compiling a list of greenhouse-gas emissions on a country-by-country basis is an intensely political act; it can skew our thinking toward proposed solutions that others see as patently unfair.[5]

Given these diverse barriers, it may seem that the prospects for international cooperation on environmental problems are limited. But perhaps there is more than one way to judge progress. Instead of using the signing of formal treaties as the standard of success, perhaps the key indicators are a broad global awareness of the problem, environmental learning, and the beginnings of broader sociocultural change. In this context, some observers see the 1992 U.N. Conference on Environment and Development (UNCED) as an important step in the institutionalization of global environmental governance. Among its consequences, they point to the creation of a Sustainable Development Commission within the United Nations; new financing mechanisms, such as the World Bank's Global Environmental Facility; forums for continued interactions between diplomats, scientists, and environmental activists; and a solidified global network of environmental groups that will continue to press for change. These accomplishments could create enough momentum to produce more tangible action by governments in the future. In the words of UNCED Secretary-General Maurice Strong, "The Earth Summit is not an end in itself, but a new beginning."[6]

Others have presented a more skeptical view: While numerous "institutions for the earth" have been created at and since UNCED, the historic gathering of world leaders failed to push the environment to the top of the international agenda in any sustained fashion. It may be years before UNCED's true legacy is apparent; the conference remains open to multiple assessments. To illustrate this diversity of opinion, we conclude this section with short excerpts from the views of a wide group of commentators, including elite participants in the negotiating process, grassroots activists, scholars, and others. Their interpretations of UNCED's legacy reflect different political and environmental priorities as well as different views of what actually happened in Rio. These perspectives allow us to examine the relative utility of global summitry for achieving environmental rescue.

Thinking Critically

1. Do you share Benedick's relative optimism about the possibilities for international environmental cooperation? What are the principal barriers to governments' behaving as the relatively rational bargainers that he describes?

2. Bell's discussion of the implementation challenges for the problem of climate change focuses on the United States. Are the barriers she has identified in the U.S. case generalizable or unique to that country? How can we explain the fact that the United States has played a leading international role on ozone cooperation but is lagging behind other nations on climate issues? Can there be effective international action on climate with the United States playing this role? If not, what will it take to reduce U.S. resistance to strong global action on climate?

3. If total national contributions to climate change are indeed a simplistic and distorted measure of how different societies contribute to the problem, what would be a better measure? Can you imagine a measure that would deal fairly with issues of historical responsibility, apportionment of the Earth's buffering capacity, and the difference between luxury and survival emissions? What are the principal barriers to using such measures as a guide to international negotiations?

4. What role should science play in international environmental negotiations? Can it be a unifying force, or is it inevitably skewed toward the interests and values of a knowledge elite? Which is the greater barrier to cooperation—too much science or too little? If Jasanoff is correct in suggesting that science alone cannot guide us on questions that are fundamentally value-based, where is such guidance to be found?

5. In your judgment, which aspects of the Earth Summit will have lasting significance, and what will that significance be? Imagine that you are a journalist writing about the Summit's legacy from the vantage point of its thirtieth anniversary in the year 2022. What do you imagine the first paragraph of your story would say?

Additional Reading

International Environmental Regimes

Clapp, Jennifer, "Africa, NGOs, and the International Toxic Waste Trade," *Journal of Environment and Development* 3, no. 2 (Summer 1994):17–46.

Haas, Peter, Robert O. Keohane, and Marc A. Levy, *Institutions for the Earth: Sources of Effective International Environmental Protection* (Cambridge, MA: MIT Press, 1993).

Miller, Marian A. L., *The Third World in Global Environmental Politics* (Boulder, CO: Lynne Rienner, 1995).

Mitchell, Ronald B., *Intentional Oil Pollution at Sea: Environmental Policy and Treaty Compliance* (Cambridge, MA: MIT Press, 1994).

Rowlands, Ian H., *The Politics of Global Atmospheric Change* (Manchester, England: Manchester University Press, 1995).

Young, Oran R., *International Governance: Protecting the Environment in a Stateless Society* (Ithaca, NY: Cornell University Press, 1994).

Science and Uncertainty in International Diplomacy

Haas, Peter M., *Saving the Mediterranean: The Politics of International Environmental Cooperation* (New York: Columbia University Press, 1990).

Jasanoff, Sheila, *The Fifth Branch: Science Advisers as Policymakers* (Cambridge: Harvard University Press, 1990).

Litfin, Karen, *Ozone Discourses: Science and Politics in Global Environmental Cooperation* (New York: Columbia University Press, 1994).

Susskind, Lawrence E., *Environmental Diplomacy: Negotiating More Effective Global Agreements* (New York: Oxford University Press, 1994).

Perspectives on UNCED

Chatterjee, Pratap, and Matthias Finger, *The Earth Brokers: Power, Politics and World Development* (London: Routledge, 1994).

Earth Summit '92: The United Nations Conference on Environment and Development (London: Regency Press, 1992).

Grubb, Michael, Matthias Koch, Abby Munson, Francis Sullivan, and Koy Thomson, *The Earth Summit Agreements: A Guide and Assessment* (London: Earthscan Publications, 1993), p. 46.

Haas, Peter M., Marc A. Levy, and Edward A. Parson, "Appraising the Earth Summit: How Should We Judge UNCED's Success? *Environment* 34, no. 8 (October 1992).

Internet Resources

The Ozone Secretariat, *http://www.unep.ch/ozone/treaties.htm*

Climate Change Convention Secretariat, *http://www.unfccc.de*

These two sites describe the international secretariats created by the international agreements on ozone and climate change, respectively. They contain the texts of the agreements, summaries of the secretariats' duties and activities, and other useful information on these issues.

Intergovernmental Panel on Climate Change (IPCC), *http://www.ipcc.ch*. The IPCC is an international group of scientists that publishes consensus documents on the state of climate change research, meant to provide a foundation for international cooperation.

Climate Action Network *http://www.igc.org/climate/AboutCAN.html#About-CAN*. A global network of NGOs seeking to promote action on climate change. Their on-line newsletter, *ECO,* monitors international climate diplomacy.

World Resources Institute, *http://www.wri.org*. This Washington-based environmental think tank is discussed in the essay by Agarwal and Narain.

Resources for the Future, *http://www.rff.org*. This U.S. research institute maintains a point-counterpoint discussion on climate change issues, entitled *Weathervane.*

Consortium for International Earth Science Information Network (CIESIN), *http://www.ciesin.org*. CIESIN is a nongovernmental organization specializing in environmental information services. This site contains a wealth of information, including the texts of major international environmental treaties, a global population database, and social indicators of development.

International Institute for Sustainable Development, *http://iisd1.iisd.ca/* and *http://www.iisd.ca*. This Canadian organization publishes the *Earth Negotiations Bulletin* and provides ongoing accounts of international environmental treaty negotiations.

RICHARD ELLIOT BENEDICK

13

Ozone Diplomacy

On September 16, 1987, representatives of countries from every region of the world reached an agreement unique in the annals of international diplomacy. In the Montreal Protocol on Substances that Deplete the Ozone Layer, nations agreed to significantly reduce production of chemicals that can destroy the stratospheric ozone layer (which protects life on earth from harmful ultraviolet radiation) and can also change global climate.

The protocol was not a response to an environmental disaster such as Chernobyl, but rather preventive action on a global scale. That action, based at the time not on measurable evidence of ozone depletion or increased radiation but rather on scientific hypotheses, required an unprecedented amount of foresight. The links between causes and effects were not obvious: a perfume spray in Paris helps to destroy an invisible gas 6 to 30 miles above the earth, and thereby contributes to deaths from skin cancer and extinction of species half a world and several generations away.

The ozone protocol was only possible through an intimate collaboration between scientists and policymakers. Based as it was on continually evolving theories of atmospheric processes, on state-of-the-art computer models simulating the results of intricate chemical and physical reactions for decades into the future, and on satellite-, land- and rocket-based monitoring of remote gases measured in

Reprinted with permission from *Issues in Science and Technology*, Benedick, "Ozone Diplomacy," Fall 1989, pp. 43–50. Copyright 1989 by the National Academy of Sciences, Washington, D.C.

parts per trillion, the ozone treaty could not have occurred at an earlier point in human history.

Another noteworthy aspect of the Montreal Protocol was the negotiators' decision not to take the timid path of controlling through "best available technology"—the traditional accommodation to economic interests. Instead, the treaty boldly established firm target dates for emissions reductions, even though the technologies for accomplishing these goals did not yet exist.

The ozone protocol sounded a death knell for an important part of the international chemical industry, with implications for billions of dollars in investment and hundreds of thousands of jobs in related industries such as food, transportation, plastics, electronics, cosmetics, and health care. Here, as in many other areas, international economic competition clashed with the need for international environmental cooperation, but in this case concerns about the environment eventually carried the day. . . .

Environmental Bombshells

In 1974, two theories were advanced that suggested potentially grave damage to the ozone layer. According to the first, chlorine in the atmosphere could continually destroy ozone for a period of decades: A single chlorine atom was capable, through a catalytic chain reaction, of eliminating tens of thousands of ozone molecules. The other theory postulated that man-made chlorofluorocarbons (CFCs) would break down in the presence of radiation in the stratosphere and release dangerously large quantities of chlorine.

These hypotheses were environmental bombshells. Production of CFCs had soared from 150,000 metric tons in 1960 to over 800,000 metric tons in 1974, reflecting their broad usefulness: CFCs are chemically stable and vaporize at low temperatures, which make them excellent coolants in refrigerators and air conditioners, and ideal as propellant gases in spray cans; they are good insulators; they are standard ingredients in the manufacture of such ubiquitous materials as styrofoam; and they are generally inexpensive to produce. The stability of CFCs means that, unlike other man-made gases, they are not chemically destroyed or rained out quickly in the lower atmosphere. Rather, they migrate slowly upward, remaining intact for decades. . . .

Theories about the relationship between the ozone layer, chlorine, and CFCs stimulated tremendous activity in scientific and industrial circles. Although the chemical industry vigorously denied the validity of any linkage between the state of the ozone layer and their growing sales of CFCs, the U.S. scientific community mounted a major research campaign that confirmed the fundamental validity of the chlorine-ozone hypotheses.

But although the theory was sound, making precise measurements of effects was not so easy—especially since growing concentrations of carbon dioxide and methane (originating at least in part from human activities) could greatly offset the projected chlorine impact, and nitrogen compounds could influence the reaction in either direction. Thus, in the years following the initial hypotheses, there were wide fluctuations in the predicted results of CFC emissions. Theoretical-model projections of global average ozone depletion 50 to 100 years in the future began at about 13 percent in 1974, increased to 19 percent in 1979, and dropped to less than 5 percent in 1982–83. For a time, these swings tended to diminish public concern over the urgency of the problem.

But consensus was soon to develop. In 1986, an assessment spearheaded by NASA and sponsored by the United Nations Environment Programme, the World Meteorological Organization, and other agencies concluded that continued CFC emissions at the 1980 rate would reduce global average ozone by about 9 percent by the latter half of the next century, with much larger seasonal and latitudinal decreases. New measurements also indicated that accumulations of CFCs in the atmosphere had nearly doubled between 1975 and 1985, even though production of these chemicals had stagnated over the same period, illustrating the potential long-term danger from these substances.

On the basis of these figures and of projections of continuing, though moderate, CFC emissions, the U.S. Environmental Protection Agency estimated that in the United States alone there could be over 150 million new cases of skin cancer among people currently alive and born by the year 2075, resulting in over 3 million deaths. EPA also projected 18 million additional eye cataract cases in the United States for the same population. Other possible results of CFC emissions included damage to the human immune system, serious impacts on agriculture and fisheries, increased formation of urban smog, and warming of the global climate.

The Great Atlantic Divide

As scientists analyzed the effects of CFCs on the ozone layer and the resultant implications for human health and the environment, the United States and the European Community (EC)—comprising 12 sovereign nations—emerged as the principal protagonists in the diplomatic process that culminated in the Montreal Protocol. Despite their shared political, economic, and environmental orientations, the United States and the European Community, which together accounted for 84 percent of world CFC output in 1974, differed over almost every issue at every step along the route to Montreal.

The U.S. Congress held formal hearings on the ozone layer soon after the theories were published, which led in 1977 to ozone protection legislation that banned use of CFCs as aerosol propellants in all but essential applications. This affected nearly $3 billion worth of sales in a wide range of household and cosmetic products, and rapidly reduced U.S. production of CFCs for aerosols by 95 percent. . . .

In contrast, European parliaments (except for the German Bundestag) showed scant interest in CFCs. The European Community delayed until 1980, and then enacted a 30 percent cutback in CFC aerosol use from 1976 levels and announced a decision not to increase production capacity.

These EC actions, however, were feeble compared to the U.S. regulation. With respect to the 30 percent aerosol reduction, European sales of CFCs for this purpose had, by 1980, already declined by over 28 percent from the 1976 peak year. Moreover, the European Community two years later defined "production capacity" in a manner that would enable current output to increase by over 60 percent. The capacity cap was therefore a painless move, supported by European industry, which gave the appearance of control while in reality permitting undiminished rates of expansion for at least two more decades.

Relative to gross national product, EC production of CFCs was over 50 percent higher than that of the United States. Aerosols, which had virtually disappeared in the U.S., still comprised during the 1980s over half of CFC sales within the European Community. The European Community was also the CFC supplier to the rest of the world, particularly the growing markets in developing countries. EC exports rose by 43 percent from 1976 to 1985 and averaged almost one-third of its production, whereas the United States consumed virtually all it produced.

These developments were reflected in growing differences in attitude between the chemical industries on the two sides of the Atlantic. Shaken by the force of public reaction in the 1970s over the threat to the ozone layer, American producers had quickly developed substitutes for CFCs in spray cans. U.S. chemical companies were also constantly aware of their vulnerability in the environmentally charged domestic atmosphere. . . . The threat of a patchwork of state laws . . . made U.S. industry not only resigned to but even publicly in favor of federal controls, which would at least be uniform and therefore less disruptive.

There was also resentment among American producers that their European rivals had escaped meaningful controls. A constant theme in the U.S. chemical industry during the 1980s was the need to have a "level playing field"—to avoid recurrence of unilateral U.S. regulatory action that was not followed by the other major producers.

In September 1986, the Alliance for Responsible CFC Policy, a coalition of about 500 U.S. producer and user companies, issued a pivotal statement. Following the obligatory reiteration of industry's position that CFCs posed no immediate threat to human health or the environment, the Alliance spokesman declared that "large future increases in . . . CFCs . . . would be unacceptable to future generations," and that it would be "inconsistent with [industry] goals . . . to ignore the potential for risk to those future generations." Thus, only three months before the protocol negotiations began, U.S. industry announced its support for new international controls on CFCs.

This unexpected policy change, which came after much soul-searching within U.S. industry, aroused consternation in Europe. The British and French had been suspicious all along that the United States was using an environmental scare to cloak commercial motivations. Now, some Europeans surmised (incorrectly) that the United States wanted CFC controls because they had substitute products on the shelf with which to enter the profitable EC export markets.

For its part, EC industry's primary objective was to preserve its dominance and to avoid the costs of switching to alternative products for as long as possible. Taking advantage of public indifference and political skepticism, European industrial leaders were able to persuade most EC governments that substitutes for CFCs were neither feasible nor necessary—despite the demonstrated U.S. success in marketing alternative spray propellants. Industry statements were echoed in official EC pronouncements that continually stressed the scientific uncertainties, the impossibility of finding effective substitutes, and the adverse effects of regulations on European living standards.

Self-Serving Positions

Although the United States and the European Community were the major CFC producers, the ozone problem threatened the entire world and therefore could be solved only by international agreement. Filling a catalytic role for such an agreement became the mission of a small and hitherto little publicized United Nations agency, the UN Environment Programme (UNEP). . . . The agency worked to inform governments and world public opinion about the danger to the ozone layer, it provided a nonpoliticized international forum for the negotiations, and it was a driving force behind the consensus that was eventually reached.

In January 1982, representatives of 24 countries met in Stockholm under UNEP auspices to decide on a "Global Framework Convention for the Protection of the Ozone Layer." The following year a group of countries, including the United States, Canada, the Nordic nations, and Switzerland, proposed a worldwide ban on "nonessential" uses of CFCs in spray cans, pointing out that the United States and others had already demonstrated that alternatives to CFC sprays were technically and economically feasible. In late 1984, the European Community countered with a proposal for alternative controls that would prohibit new additions to CFC production capacity.

Each side was backing a protocol that would require no new controls for itself, but considerable adjustment for the other. The United States had already imposed a ban on nonessential uses of CFCs, but U.S. chemical companies were operating at close to capacity and thus would suffer under a production cap. Their European counterparts, on the other hand, had substantial underutilized capacity and could expand CFC production at current rates for another 20 years before hitting the cap.

Despite these disagreements, by March 1985 the negotiators had drafted all elements of a protocol for CFC reductions except the crucial control provisions. Meeting in Vienna, all major producers except Japan signed an interim agreement—the Vienna Convention on Protection of the Ozone Layer—which promoted international monitoring, research, and exchange of data and provided the framework for eventual protocols to control ozone-modifying substances. Over strong objections from European industry representatives, the Vienna Conference passed a separate resolution that called upon UNEP to continue work on a CFC protocol with a target for adoption in 1987.

As formal negotiations began in December 1986, governments were divided into three camps. Despite growing internal strains, the European Community followed the European industry line and mirrored the views of the UK, France, and Italy. The European Community continued to advocate the kind of production capacity cap it had favored during the meetings leading up to the Vienna Convention. Because the scientific models showed there would be at least two decades before any significant ozone depletion would occur, EC negotiators felt there was time to delay production cuts and wait for more evidence. This perspective was initially shared by the USSR and Japan.

Opposing this view were the United States, Canada, Norway, Sweden, Finland, Switzerland, and New Zealand, all favoring stronger new controls. They argued that action needed to be taken well before critical levels of chlorine accumulated: The long atmospheric lifetimes of these compounds meant that future ozone depletion stemming from past and current production was inevitable, and the process could not suddenly be turned off like a faucet. . . .

Complicating the entire process was the fact that the European Community had to achieve internal consensus among its member countries before (and during) international negotiations, which tended to make it a difficult and inflexible negotiating partner. There were deep divisions within the European Community on the ozone issue. Germany, the Netherlands, Belgium, and Denmark were increasingly disposed toward strong CFC controls; but of these, only Germany was a major producer. The UK, supported by France and Italy—all large producers—resisted every step of the way. . . .

Deep Cuts

One of the central disputes of the negotiations was whether restrictions would be placed on the production or consumption of the substances covered by the agreement. This issue, though seemingly arcane, was one of the most important and most difficult to resolve.

The European Community pushed for controls on production, arguing that it was simpler to control output since there were only a small number of producing countries, whereas there were thousands of consuming industries and countless points of consumption. But the United States, Canada, and others who favored a consumption-related formula pointed out that controlling production would confer unusual advantages on the European Community while particularly prejudicing importing nations, including the developing countries. Since about a third of EC output was exported and there were no other exporters in the picture, a production limit essentially locked in the EC export markets. The only way the United States or others could supply those markets would be to decrease their domestic consumption.

The European Community, with no viable competitors, would thus have a virtual monopoly. If European domestic consumption should rise, the European Community could cut back its exports, leaving the current importing countries, with no recourse to other suppliers, to bear the brunt of CFC reductions. Because of this vulnerability, there would be incentives for importing countries to remain outside the treaty and build their own CFC facilities.

To meet the valid EC argument about controlling multiple consumption points, the United States and its allies came up with an ingenious solution: A limit would be placed on production plus imports minus exports to other Montreal Protocol signatories. This "adjusted production" formula eliminated any monopoly based on current export positions, in that producing countries could raise production for exports to protocol parties without having to cut their own domestic consumption. Only exports to nonparties would have to come out of domestic consumption, and this would be an added incentive for importing countries to join the protocol, lest they lose access to supplies. Additionally, an importing signatory whose traditional supplier raised prices excessively or refused to export could either produce on its own or turn to another producer country.

The single most contentious issue was the timing and extent of reductions. Again, the European Community and the United States were the principal opponents. The United States originally called for a freeze to be followed by three phases of progressively more stringent reductions, all the way up to a possible 95 percent cut. But even late into the negotiations, the European Community was reluctant to consider reductions beyond 10 to 20 percent.

The United States and others rejected this as inadequate. In fact, Germany, which had become increasingly concerned over the ozone problem, was already planning an independent 50 percent reduction and early in 1987 it made urgent appeals to the other EC members also to accept deep reductions. Meanwhile, new scientific research was demonstrating that all of the control strategies under consideration would result in some degree of ozone depletion, the extent of which would depend on the stringency of international regulation. These developments helped garner support for deep cuts. . . .

Ultimately, even the most reluctant parties—the European Community, Japan, and the Soviet Union—agreed to a 50 percent decrease. The treaty as signed stipulated an initial 20 percent reduction from the 1986 level of CFCs, followed by 30 percent. Halons were frozen at 1986 levels, pending further research. And one innovative provision—that these reductions were to be made on specific dates regardless of when the treaty should enter into force—removed any temptation to stall enactment of the protocol in the hopes of delaying cuts, and also provided industry with dates upon which to base its planning.

Negotiators at Montreal also faced the difficult task of encouraging developing countries to participate in the treaty. Per capita consumption of CFCs in those countries was tiny in comparison to that of the industrialized world, but their domestic consumption requirements—for refrigeration, for example—were growing, and CFC technology is relatively easy to obtain. The protocol thus had to meet their needs during a transition period while substitutes were being developed, and it had to discourage them from becoming major new sources of CFC emissions.

A formula was developed whereby developing countries would be permitted a 10-year grace period before they had to comply with the control provisions. During this time they could increase their consumption up to an annual level of 0.3 kilogram per capita—approximately one-third of the 1986 level prevailing in industrialized countries. It was felt that the realistic prospects of growth in CFC use to these levels in the developing countries was not great, as they would not want to invest in a technology that was environmentally detrimental and would soon be obsolete.

Basis for Optimism

. . .

The Montreal Protocol stands as a landmark—a symbol both of fundamental changes in the kinds of problems facing the modern world and of the way the international community can address those problems. . . . But the protocol may also have relevance for dealing with other common dangers, including national rivalries and war. The ozone treaty reflects a realization that nations must work together in the face of global threats, and that if some major actors do not participate, the efforts of others will be vitiated.

In the realm of international relations, there will always be uncertainties—political, economic, scientific, psychological. The protocol's greatest significance may be its demonstration that the international community is capable of undertaking complicated cooperative actions in the real world of ambiguity and imperfect knowledge. The Montreal Protocol can be a hopeful paradigm of an evolving global diplomacy, one wherein sovereign nations find ways to accept common responsibility for stewardship of the planet and for the security of generations to come.

new way of thinking, new pattern

RUTH GREENSPAN BELL

14

Do International Environmental Agreements Really Work?

The agreement in Kyoto on climate change has added one more set of requirements to the 900 or so international environmental agreements that countries around the world are struggling to meet. Research by the General Accounting Office indicates that the U.S. participates in or has a significant interest in more than 170 of these agreements. Few of the standing agreements, which cover matters as diverse as fisheries, biological resources, outer space, water and air pollution, address problems as global as greenhouse gas emissions in both its impacts and in the wide range of remedial measures that must be undertaken to get the problem under control.

However, the implementation record for many existing agreements has been mixed at best. Frustration with the rate of implementation has brought criticism of the international environmental regime, which is sometimes characterized as hopelessly idealistic or a form of antiquated central planning (e.g. A. Terry Rambo, *The Fallacy of Global Sustainable Development*, East-West Center, March 1997). No one to my knowledge has suggested entirely scrapping the system. The international agreement is currently the only tool we have to decide how to manage environmental problems that cross borders. Constructive criticism of the

Originally published in *Weathervane*, an on-line discussion forum of Resources for the Future (www.rff.org). Reprinted with permission.

agreements has focused on two general areas: devising sturdier agreements that can provide a stronger basis for concerted action on common problems, and support for strengthening local capacity to take on the challenges posed by international agreements.

Likewise, the success of any climate change agreements depends on getting a number of things right. Some can be addressed in the drafting phase; they include factors such as the clarity (or lack of clarity) of the agreement's provisions (for example, do the parties know what they are supposed to do to achieve the goals of the agreement?), reporting mechanisms, an effective secretariat, mechanisms at the international level to facilitate compliance, and the like. Apparent agreement on language may mask significant communication problems which even skillful negotiators don't fully recognize, rooted in differences in culture, familiarity and experience with environmental tools, and stages of economic and social development.

Ultimately, success depends on whether signatories are prepared to go home and institute measures to make the agreement happen. The difficulties of implementing the international regime mirror difficulties that many nations are having managing their domestic environmental requirements. Pollution is generally generated and controlled at a local or state level, facility by facility, household by household. Similarly, steps to preserve natural resources such as forests, water bodies and natural species require effective domestic activities. Countries signing on to these regimes must have capacity and political will to carry them out.

In preparation for Kyoto, and the prospect of a more demanding climate agreement, there were efforts to review successful agreements to identify elements that facilitate compliance and implementation. The 1987 Montreal Protocol to phase out substances that deplete the ozone layer has received the greatest scrutiny, since it is generally thought to be among the more effective international environmental agreements.

The Montreal Protocol implicitly recognized that there are few effective international ways to "enforce" agreements in the same sense that domestic environmental requirements are subject to enforcement procedures by a policing body or courts. Litigation has been an effective tool in the U.S. to push governments and facilities toward compliance but it plays a very small role internationally, and law suits requiring government agencies and others to implement laws ("mandatory duty" law suits) until recently have been a unique feature of the U.S. environmental scene. Other forms of confrontation have not proven productive. Montreal recognized the need for a carefully phased process and a consultative procedure.

Thus, the Protocol gave certain developing countries (the "Article 5" countries) additional time to meet the requirements of the agreement. The phasing approach recognizes and takes into account technical and economic constraints that restrict implementation. These countries are also provided financial and technical assistance, grace periods and decision making procedures that ease their transition. Progressive phase out and trade provisions encourage newly industrializing countries to move out of old technology. The Protocol also uses other trade-related restrictions.

Although these provisions have been relatively successful in achieving the goals of the Montreal Protocol, and climate negotiators appeared to be moving in that direction, there are obstacles that may make it difficult to incorporate analogous provisions into a climate accord. Among these is the apparent opposition of the U.S. Senate and among opponents of a climate treaty, who express suspicion that differential treatment will somehow allow those countries an unfair advantage. With respect to assistance, some developing countries feel that adequate support to implement the Montreal requirements has not been forthcoming from the international community.

Second, the Montreal regime has an Implementation Committee designed to provide maximum opportunities for compliance rather than punishment. The measures the Committee can use include technical and financial assistance, cautions and suspension. This Committee was successful in engineering solutions for the compliance problems of a number of "countries with economies in transition" of the former Soviet Bloc. The non-confrontation approach has eased the Protocol through difficult challenges to its capacity to accomplish the task of phasing out ozone-depleting substances, but the success of these measures is yet to be fully tested.

The techniques developed in the Montreal Protocol are appealing because they appear to have assisted a pragmatic, problem-solving approach to reporting and compliance problems under the Protocol. Drafters of climate change agreements must decide how transferable the provisions of the Montreal Protocol actually are, outside the specific dynamic of CFC reduction. The Protocol is designed to manage one environmental problem—the phase-out of specific, identified substances that are produced by a relatively small number of manufacturers, although they are then disbursed throughout the economy. The large, powerful companies that have given up manufacture of these products, and have developed substitutes for them, have a strong economic interest in making sure that others don't step into the breach. This fuels Protocol-related assistance efforts and creates a natural watchdog group.

Climate change arguably presents a different dynamic. Greenhouse gas emissions are a more unruly matter, released from innumerable sources of all sizes. They cannot be traced to an identifiable set of manufacturers and involve entire economies. Although it may occur in the future, climate change has not yet developed a dynamic in which a significant industry constituency sees economic advantage in greenhouse gas reduction and joins a "green" constituency to push for compliance with the terms of the agreement.

The second general area that warrants close attention by the international community if an international environmental agreement is to succeed is domestic capacity. Domestic efforts include both building capacity and building constituencies. Many countries are only beginning to develop the kind of mature environmental protection institutions that can manage the complex regulatory tasks associated with lowering greenhouse gas emissions. The concern is often expressed that the uneven success of international agreements is a failure of enforcement. Experience with the Montreal Protocol has shown that discussion and assistance can encourage more progress than classic enforcement in the sense of force and demands. Even at the domestic level, enforcement cannot be the primary means to make laws work, although the threat of enforcement can be a powerful tool in getting an individual or facility's attention. There must be some level of domestic commitment to the purpose and goals of any law for it to work.

There are various ways that domestic capacity can be increased. Assistance efforts such as those sponsored by the Global Environment Facility (GEF), international organizations and multilateral lending institutions, and national bodies such as the U.S. Agency for International Development are a few. Another is to encourage countries participating in the international environmental regime to pay greater attention to building domestic constituencies and interest groups as they prepare to negotiate, to find out what support they have and what they need to develop.

Although institutional capacity is not the obstacle for the U.S., domestic will and commitment currently seem to be. [EDITORS' NOTE: This essay was written on the eve of the December 1997 Kyoto conference.] Since implementation may be costly and may, over time, require lifestyle changes, the people who must absorb these changes must agree to them and constituencies in favor of an agreement must be developed. The U.S. public has recently begun a form of debate on these issues. The recent television advertisements threatening increased gasoline prices in service of a UN, rather than U.S., goal represents a crude way of playing on fears about an imagined loss of sovereignty, possible life style changes and the perennial fear—new taxes. More constructive efforts include newspaper series examining the issues. While some parts of the debate have been less than elegant, this give and take is a healthy and necessary part of building support for a treaty and achieving the result sought by the treaty.

There is no magic in international environmental agreements. They are only as good as the processes that produce them and the domestic will of those who return home to carry out their goals. Reaching agreement on a climate change agreement tests the resolve and creativity of the international negotiators and of their domestic partners who must carry these goals to fruition.

SHEILA JASANOFF

15

Skinning
Scientific Cats

Let me begin with the picture that unquestionably accounts for the birth of the modern environmental movement. The World Commission on Environment and Development has this to say in its influential work, *Our Common Future*:

> In the middle of the 20th century, we saw our planet from space for the first time. Historians may eventually find that this vision had a greater impact on thought than did the Copernican revolution of the 16th century. . . . From space we see a small and fragile ball, dominated not by human activity and edifice, but a pattern of clouds, greenery, oceans and soil. Humanity's inability to fit its activities into that pattern is changing boundary systems fundamentally.

The idea of the scientific revolution is never far from the minds of those who comment on the Apollo picture. Many environmentalists have argued that what the picture of the biosphere truly accomplished was a paradigm shift in our ways of thinking about how the world works: the "fourth discontinuity". It was a moment that displaced the human ego by making it conscious of the physical finiteness of the place it inhabits. The effect was on a par with the three great discontinuities of the past: the Copernican revolution, which displaced the earth from the centre of the human universe, the Darwinian revolution, which displaced human beings from the

Originally published in *New Statesman and Society*, 26 February 1993, pp. 29–30. Copyright © *New Statesman and Society*. Reprinted with permission.

pinnacle of the tree of creation, and the Freudian revolution, which exposed the unconscious, and told humankind that we are not the masters in our own house.

But the scientific paradigm of ecological interconnectedness does not, in fact, provide answers to questions about what we human beings are entitled to do with our environment. What science is, and how we apply it to our needs, is thus far from straightforward.

The first point I want to make is that scientific inquiry, contrary to expectation, does not always lead to the same explanation for the same observed phenomenon. Consider the seasonal flooding in the plains of northern India, where two competing theories obstinately occupy the field. On the one hand, there is a "mountain theory", preferred by environmental bureaucrats and developers, that holds that population pressure in the foothills of the Himalayas is causing deforestation and soil erosion, and that these effects in turn are responsible for the flooding below.

The contrasting "plains theory", upheld by environmental activists and indigenous people living in the hilly regions, ascribes the flooding to poor resource-management practices lower down. For them, it is the indiscriminate clearing of forests, the damming of rivers, and the resulting siltation of river beds that lead to uncontrollable floods. Uphill tree cutting adds little or nothing in the way of separate environmental stress. So who is to blame? The non-modernised primitive practices of ecologically unconscious indigenous peoples somewhere up in the mountains? Or a model of development dominated by centralised money-lenders, international financial and other institutions?

Controversies of this kind are familiar to many people, and science seems unable to provide satisfying answers. For in the complex systems under study, enough suggestive and even persuasive evidence can be found to sustain very different overall stories about what is *really* going on. Lacking ways of testing or falsification, neither theoretical position is able to deal a body blow to the other. Ideology and politics thus become the primary determinants of choosing among competing scientific accounts of felt reality.

A second point of almost equal importance is that when people reach scientific conclusions about the reasons for a particular natural phenomenon, their explanations are not always the same. To take one case, US public health experts have been convinced for many years that an important reason to reduce lead levels in the environment is the damage the metal causes even at lowest-dose levels to children's learning behavior. When Britain decided to phase out lead additives from petrol, almost ten years after the US, the reasons the British experts provided did not prominently include children's health, an issue regarded as hopelessly uncertain and divisive. Rather their decision was based on findings that lead was toxic, even at very low doses, that it was highly persistent in the environment, and that alternatives to many current uses of lead could be found without damaging the economy. So, in the end, both these countries chose to phase lead additives out of petrol, but the scientific pathways they took to get to these results were very different.

A third point that complicates our initially simplistic connection between science and action is that what compels people to act upon a perceived problem is not necessarily knowledge that is endorsed by science. An example of such an unscientific consensus are the factors that produced agreement on the Mediterranean Action Plan. Many countries signed on to the treaty because of a mistaken but compelling notion that pollution anywhere in the Mediterranean basin would be equally harmful to all of the coastal states.

By some accounts, UN Environment Programme experts, who participated in the treaty negotiations, apparently knew that the ecological paradigm as applied to the Mediterranean did not in fact drive everybody's pollution up on everybody else's shores. But they withheld this knowledge from the participants, on the theory that it was desirable for the right decision to be taken, in environmental terms, even on the basis of the wrong scientific reason.

In fourth place, just as too little science can sometimes aid decision-making, so too much science sometimes overwhelms the capacity to act. There are many reasons why this can be the case. More information may, to begin with, simply create more grounds for argument, especially when strong enough refereeing agencies cannot be found. Information, too, can outstrip the capacity of our societies to analyse, synthesise and apply to programmes of action. In our own recent past, environmental problems that have reached such a stalemate of knowledge include, prominently, the acid rain controversy, where no new study, however compelling, was likely to change how people believed on that issue. Unless great care is taken, there are signs that at least aspects of the climate-change problem are in danger today of being studied to death in this fashion.

Fifth, and finally, I'd like to mention those instances when states or interest groups agree that a problem exists, but cannot agree about how the problem should be conceptualised for purposes of scientific investigation. To decide what needs to be studied, one needs, in effect, to impose a kind of moral map on the issue in question. And this map may differ from country to country, or even from one scientific organisation to another.

Let's take the so-called problem of human cancer. Now there appears to be good scientific agreement that some fraction of human cancers are caused by environmental factors, such as diet, smoking, certain lifestyle choices *and* by exposure to chemicals. Yet if you look across the spectrum of research-rich nations, the emphasis has not, in fact, been equal on all of these possible areas of explanation. No other country, to my knowledge, can match the US in the richness, intensity, scope and variety of programmes for researching the health effects of industrial chemicals, including their carcinogenicity.

As a result, many have found it difficult to avoid the conclusion that chemicals occupy a different niche in the collective American consciousness of environmental hazards from the niche they occupy in any other country. When it comes to studying the causes of complex environmental problems, there is almost always more than one way to skin the scientific cat. And these choices are not themselves scientific. They're deeply social, cultural, and ethical.

A historical example of this was the mid-century study, funded by the Rockefeller Foundation, to study and solve the problem of world hunger. We all know the miraculous results of that voyage of discovery, the creation of those high-yielding grain varieties that ushered in the green revolution. But students of the green revolution have come in time to ask not merely what was achieved and scientifically celebrated, but also what was not studied, what went unexplored or under-explored, like the environmental consequences of the heavy use of pesticides and fertilisers, which were needed to make the green revolution take root and flourish. The individual life experiences, or even the collective local knowledge of the groups that science was going to help, whose problem of hunger science was going to solve, never figured in the scientific agenda setting.

You will recognise that the implicit hierarchy that the green revolution scientists established is the hierarchy that dominates our western scientific sensibility that some approaches to understanding nature are superior to others. In this hierarchy, not surprisingly, it is the basic physical and biological sciences that occupy the top of the ladder. The social sciences are relegated to some indeterminate middle position. Much lower down, usually disappearing from the frame of inquiry completely, are the unsystematised, or nonprofessionalised ways of knowing nature that are characteristic of the people often living closest to environmental problems.

If more international cooperation in science is necessary to do a better job of understanding and coping with environmental change, then we are not going to get much international cooperation unless we sit down together and address some very important prior questions: What is the problem we are trying to define? From whose point of view is it a problem? Why is it seen as scientific? What do we mean by science? And which areas of science are we going to privilege while we go about seeking solutions?

ANIL AGARWAL & SUNITA NARAIN

16

Global Warming in an Unequal World: A Case of Environmental Colonialism

The idea that developing countries like India and China must share the blame for heating up the Earth and destabilizing its climate—as espoused in a recent study published in the United States by the World Resources Institute in collaboration with the United Nations Environment Program—is an excellent example of environmental colonialism. India and China may account for more than one-third of the world's population, but are these two nations really responsible for flushing one-third of the muck and dirt into the world's air and oceans?

The report of the World Resources Institute (WRI), a Washington-based private research group, is based less on science than politically motivated mathematics. Its main intention seems to be to blame developing countries for global warming and to perpetuate the current global inequity in the use of the Earth's environment and its resources. . . .

The exercise of blaming developing countries has already begun. Until recently, it was widely accepted that developed countries of the West consume most of the world's fossil fuels and produce most of the carbon dioxide—the main agents of

Originally published in *Earth Island Journal* (Spring 1991):39–40. Reprinted with permission.

global warming. In recent years, however, Western nations have been carrying out a sustained propaganda campaign alleging that deforestation in developing countries, and the generation of methane through irrigated rice farming and the raising of cattle, is also contributing to global warming. This has shifted the onus onto developing countries.

Recently, the World Resources Institute and the United Nations Environment Program released the annual report, *World Resources 1990–91,* that stated for the first time that India, China and Brazil are among the top five countries responsible for the accumulation of these gases in the Earth's atmosphere.

Cooking the Figures

The figures used by the WRI to calculate the quantity of carbon dioxide and methane produced by each country are extremely questionable. Heavy emphasis has been placed on comparisons of carbon dioxide produced by deforestation and methane generated by rice fields and livestock to carbon dioxide produced by burning fossil fuels like oil and coal—an emphasis that tends to underplay the impact of the developed countries.

The methane issue raises further questions of justice and morality. Can we really equate the carbon dioxide contributions of gas guzzling automobiles in Europe and North America (or, for that matter, anywhere in the Third World) with the methane emissions of water buffalo and rice fields of subsistence farmers in West Bengal or Thailand? Do these people not have a right to live? No effort has been made to separate the "survival emissions" of the poor, from the "luxury emissions" of the rich.

Old Numbers; New Recipe

A study conducted by India's Centre for Science and Environment (CSE), which uses WRI's data for each country's gaseous emissions, concludes that developing countries are responsible for only 16 percent of the carbon dioxide accumulating in the Earth's atmosphere. The WRI report claims a Third World share of 48 percent. Similarly, developing countries were not found to be responsible for any excess methane accumulation, although WRI claims a Third World share of 56 percent.

This difference is explained by a simple fact: no country can be blamed for the gases accumulating in the Earth's atmosphere until each country's share in the Earth's cleansing ability has been apportioned on a fair and equitable basis. Since most of the cleansing is done by the oceans and troposphere, the Earth has to be treated as a common heritage of mankind. Good environmental management demands that all nations should learn to live within the Earth's ability to absorb these gaseous wastes.

Since there is no reason to believe that any human being in any part of the world is more or less important than another, CSE has apportioned the world's restoration ability to each country in proportion to its share of the world's population. Thus India, with 16 percent of the world's population, gets 16 percent of the Earth's natural air and ocean "sinks" for carbon dioxide and methane absorption. Describing these emissions as "permissible," CSE finds that India is producing carbon dioxide just equal to six percent of the world's natural sinks and methane equal to 14 of the natural sinks. How, then, can India be blamed for any of the excess carbon dioxide or methane that is accumulating in the Earth's atmosphere?

The same scenario is true for China, Pakistan, Sri Lanka, Egypt, Kenya, Nigeria, Tanzania, Zimbabwe and Chile. Meanwhile, almost all Western countries are emitting well beyond their "permissible shares" of the Earth's carbon dioxide and methane sinks. Clearly, it is Western wastes and willful over-consumption of the world's natural resources that are polluting the Earth and threatening the global environment.

What WRI has done instead is to calculate the percentage of India's total emissions of carbon dioxide and methane before they are absorbed and then hold India responsible for the same quantitative share of the gases actually accumulating in the Earth's atmosphere. This manner of calculating each nation's responsibility is extremely unfair and amounts to a scientific sleight of hand.

According to the WRI-UNEP calculations, the US, which produces 14.4 percent of the world's annual output of the carbon dioxide that is actually accumulating every year, becomes responsible for only 14.4 percent of the carbon dioxide that is actually accumulating every year. The CSE's analysis, however, indicates the United States, with only 4.73 percent of the world's population, emits as much as 26 percent of the carbon dioxide and 20 percent of the methane that is absorbed every year.

It is the production of carbon dioxide and methane by countries like the US and Japan—totally out of proportion to their population and that of the world's absorptive capacity—that is responsible for accumulation of excess, unabsorbed carbon dioxide and methane in the atmosphere. . . . Meanwhile India, with 3.4 times the population of the US, gets less than one fourth of the US' share of the planet's natural sink.

India and China account for less than 0.5 percent of net emissions to the atmosphere, while WRI claims they together contribute about 10 percent. The CSE analysis shows India to be the world's lowest per capita net emitter of greenhouse gases.

. . . Industrialized countries have together exceeded their permissible quotas of carbon dioxide by 2839 million tons of carbon equivalent—50 percent of excess global carbon dioxide emissions. The WRI-UNEP method of calculating pollution is extremely unfair because it favors the biggest polluters—i.e., the bigger the polluter, the larger the share of the sink it gets. . . .

Emissions & Omissions

CSE's method offers a better way of calculating each country's responsibility for global warming. Not only do developing countries get a fair share of the Earth's natural cleansing ability, but several industrialized countries also benefit. Using CSE's analysis, France's contribution to all greenhouse gases goes down by 43 percent, Japan's and Italy's by 36 percent, the United Kingdom's by 12 percent, and West Germany's by four percent.

On the other hand, Saudi Arabia's share goes up by 131 percent, Canada's by 110 percent, Australia's by 78 percent, and the US share jumps 53 percent. Since the US is the largest emitter of greenhouse gases, this increase overshadows that of all other countries.

The WRI-UNEP figures for methane and carbon dioxide emissions are based on just a handful of Western measurements of cattle and rice field emissions that have then been projected over the entire world. The existing data on deforestation rates are also extremely shaky. Brazil, a frequent target of WRI criticism for deforestation, has accused the organization of inflating its deforestation rates by 300 to 400 percent.

The entire WRI-UNEP study appears designed to bolster both foreign aid and domestic policy interests of Western nations whose governments would like to convince their environmentalists that their nations are not to blame and cannot do much locally unless they rope in the hapless Third World.

. . .

It is time for the Third World to ask the West: "Whose future generations are we seeking to protect—the Western World's or the Third World's?"

KEN CONCA AND GEOFFREY D. DABELKO

17

The Earth Summit: Reflections on an Ambiguous Event

For twelve days in June 1992, nearly ten thousand official delegates from 150 nations converged on Rio de Janeiro, Brazil for the United Nations Conference on Environment and Development (UNCED). At the same time, thousands of activists, organizers, and concerned citizens of the planet gathered for a parallel Global Forum held on the other side of the city. The entire spectacle, often referred to as the "Earth Summit," was covered by more than eight thousand journalists. Governments debated, and in most cases signed, an array of official documents: a set of general principles on environment and development known as the Rio Declaration; an eight-hundred-page "action plan" for the twenty-first century known as "Agenda 21"; international treaties on climate and biodiversity; an agreement to work toward an international treaty on desertification; and a nonbinding Statement of Forest Principles. Activist groups also generated declarations. For example, a coalition including Greenpeace International, the Forum of Brazilian NGOs, Friends of the Earth International, and the Third World Network sponsored a "10-point plan to save the Earth Summit," challenging governments to embrace legally binding limits on pollutant emissions, to confront the problem of the North's overconsumption, and to rein in harmful transnational economic practices.[1]

Half a decade later, the Earth Summit remains an ambiguous event. Was it a global town meeting or a closed-door reunion of political and economic elites? An important step toward institutionalizing global environmental governance or a failure of will? A watershed for a new era, a triumph of business as usual, or simply an irrelevant distraction? What follows is a sampling of the wide range of interpretations and meanings that have been attached to the conference. We present them as opposing viewpoints not to suggest that these are the only perspectives available but rather to show that the event has been interpreted in radically different ways.

On the power of UNCED's ideas:

In our opinion, as philosophers, the details of the treaties, and whether they were signed by all the parties to the negotiations, will fade in importance. Of lasting importance will be the monumentality of the event itself and the institutionalization of an idea. In June of 1992, in Rio de Janeiro, virtually all of the world's heads of state met for the first time—ever—not to create or dismantle military alliances, not to discuss currency and banking reform, and not to set up rules of world trade, but to try to agree to care for the planet's biosphere. And the idea that was ratified, however little agreement was achieved on how to implement it, is this: Environment and development are inextricably linked. Human economies are subsystems of natural economies. Hence, genuine economic development—sustainable development—cannot be achieved without safeguarding the environmental infrastructures in which human economies are embedded.[2]

—J. Baird Callicott and Fernando J. R. da Rocha,
professors of philosophy in the United States and Brazil, respectively

Even as the Earth Summit opened eyes to the need for new North-South discussions, it perpetuated myths about who is to blame for the problems and what steps to take. . . . By the end of the Earth Summit, many participants and journalists were articulating a simple equation to explain the complex relationship between environment and development: Poverty causes environmental degradation. They portrayed rich countries and wealthy people as environmentalists pressing for curbs on tropical deforestation to combat global climate change. They saw developing countries and poor people as fixated on survival and basic development issues—and if exploitation of natural resources contributed to those goals, so be it. . . . By accepting . . . myths about growth, aid, and the poor, negotiators at the Earth Summit conveniently avoided two of the central barriers to reversing environmental degradation across the planet: the widespread inequalities that characterize natural-resource ownership in much of the world and the environmentally destructive tendencies of large corporations in a deregulated world economy.[3]

—Robin Broad (American University) and
John Cavanagh (the Institute for Policy Studies, Washington, D.C.)

On whether UNCED marked a new era in global environmental politics:

In retrospect, there are two observations that stand out as to what happened in Rio. Firstly, this was not a conference about the environment at all; it concerned the world's economy and how the environment affects it. This in itself is a mammoth step forward as politicians come to understand that the issues do not just concern plants and animals, but life itself. Secondly, this was the first meeting of world leaders since the end of the Cold War. The old East-West agenda is dead, attention is now focused on North and South. Rio not only marked the beginning of a new era but a triumph for that small band of campaigners who set out at Stockholm.[4]

—Richard Sandbrook, executive director of the International Institute for
Environment and Development based in London

The Earth Summit showed that unless one deals with political reality, the most impressive statements, agendas, and manifestos will come to nothing. Unfortunately, it was precisely at the political level that the summit was least successful. Getting agreement, in principle, on protecting the environment, on saving human life, on increasing the share of global prosperity to the poorer peoples of the world is relatively simple. . . . The difficulty lies in achieving action. It is at this stage that one hears the global version of the old workplace argument, it is too expensive, it will cost jobs, the electorate would not stand for it. The message, despite grand speeches, appears to be "business as usual" for many governments and businesses.[5]

—Reg Green, International Federation of Chemical,
Energy, and General Workers' Unions

On UNCED as an exercise in global governance:

Where the Rio Conference took a quantum leap forward . . . was in recognizing that the interactions among sectors, and the intertwined nature of economic, social, and environmental trends warranted a new approach to defining and organizing tasks, both at the national level and internationally. . . . The Rio Conference has called for institutions that can expose policy and programme interactions in the planning stages, in order to anticipate and avoid conflicts that might arise later. It has also sought to open these processes to all affected constituencies and major groups, so as to better "ground-truth" the policies and increase the stake of those who can make them work.[6]

—Lee A. Kimball, senior associate at the
Washington, D.C.–based World Resources Institute

The best that can be said for the Earth Summit is that it made visible the vested interests standing in the way of the moral economies which local people, who daily face the consequences of environmental degradation, are seeking to re-establish. The spectacle of the great and the good at UNCED casting about for "solutions" that will keep their power and standards of living intact has confirmed the skepticism of those whose fate and livelihoods were being determined. The demands from many grassroots groups around the world are not for more "management"—a fashionable word at Rio—but for agrarian reform, local control over local resources, and power to veto developments and to run their own affairs. For them, the question is not *how* their environment should be managed—they have the experience of the past as their guide—but *who* will manage it and in *whose* interest.[7]

—The Ecologist

On the debate between the governments of North and South:

The Earth Summit has brought to a final resolution the age-old debate between economic development and protection of the environment. It used to be fashionable to argue in the developing countries that their priority should be economic development and that, if necessary, the environment should be sacrificed in order to achieve high economic growth. The sentiment was to get rich first and to clean up the environment later. Some leaders of the developing countries even accused the developed countries of using the environment as a weapon to retard their economic progress. Such rhetoric and mindset belong to the past. Today, developing countries understand the need to integrate environment into their development policies. At the same time, developed countries have become increasingly aware of the need to cut down on their wasteful consumption patterns. There is growing understanding between the environment community and the development community. They realise that they must seek mutual accommodation. The new wisdom is that we want economic progress but we also want to live in harmony with nature. To be sure, governments have to make hard choices and there are trade-offs between the two objectives. But, since the Earth Summit, it is no longer possible to talk about development without considering its impact on the environment.[8]

—Tommy Koh, Singaporean diplomat who chaired
the UNCED's Main Committee

Unlike what the term suggests, the global as it emerged in the discussions and debates around the UN Conference on Environment and Development . . . was not about universalism or about a planetary consciousness. The life of all people, including the poor of the Third World, or the life of the planet, are not at the center of concern in international negotiations on global environmental issues.

The "global" in the dominant discourse is the political space in which a particular dominant local seeks global control, and frees itself of local, national, and international restraints. . . . The seven most powerful countries, the G-7, dictate global affairs, but the interests that guide them remain narrow, local and parochial. . . . The North's slogan at UNCED and the other global negotiation fora seems to be: "What's yours is mine. What's mine is mine."[9]

—Vandana Shiva, scholar and activist in India

On the openness of the UNCED process:

The important, indeed vital, role which NGOs and social movements have to play in international negotiations has been broadened through the UNCED process. UN procedures will never be the same again.[10]

—Wangari Maathi, Greenbelt Movement, Kenya

[The summit] has attempted to involve otherwise powerless people of society in the process. But by observing the process we now know how undemocratic and untransparent the UN system is. Those of us who have watched the process have said that UNCED has failed. As youth we beg to differ. Multinational corporations, the United States, Japan, the World Bank, the International Monetary Fund have got away with what they always wanted, carving out a better and more comfortable future for themselves.[11]

—Wagaki Mwangi, International Youth Environment and
Development Network, Nairobi, Kenya

On the effectiveness of NGOs at UNCED:

Through the mass media, UNCED was able to focus attention on the emerging environmental and developmental problems in a manner that was inconceivable even a few years ago. . . . NGOs helped create a "civil society" at the discussions, they managed to keep a check on diplomats from their own and even other countries. They were often better informed and more articulate than government representatives, and better at obtaining and disseminating information than were the journalists themselves. They also engaged themselves in writing and speaking openly and forcefully on the issues involved, and lastly they were also more capable of creating the drama which makes good copy. For all these reasons, the eyes of the world became focused on the event, and therefore on the ideas behind the event.[12]

—Tariq Banuri, executive director, Sustainable
Development Policy Institute, Islamabad, Pakistan

Quite logically, the UNCED process sought to divide, co-opt, and weaken the green movement, a process for which the movement itself has some responsibility. On the one hand UNCED brought every possible NGO into the system of lobbying governments, while on the other it quietly promoted business to take over the solutions. Non-governmental organizations (NGOs) are now trapped in a farce: they have lent support to governments in return for some small concessions on language and thus legitimized the process of increased industrial development. The impact of the lobbying was minimal, while that of the compromise will be vast, as NGOs have come to legitimize a process that is in essence contrary to what many of them have been fighting for for years.[13]

—Matthias Finger, coauthor with Pratap Chatterjee of
The Earth Brokers: Power, Politics and World Development

On North-South cooperation among NGOs:

The UNCED process forged new and stronger links between Northern and Southern groups, between development and environmental activists. It would now be difficult for environmentalists to stick to wildlife issues or population, without simultaneously addressing international equity and global power structures. A major step forward has been the increasing involvement of Northern based environment groups like Greenpeace, WWF, and Friends of the Earth in economic issues such as terms of trade, debt, and aid.[14]

—Martin Khor, president, Third World Network

Negotiations between the NGOs at UNCED were certainly not as difficult as the official negotiations, but they were hardly easy, and it requires little imagination to foresee the depth of disputes had they been negotiating real policy and trying to take account of the full range of viewpoints and affected parties (for example by including NGOs from industry or trade unions).[15]

—Michael Grubb, Matthias Koch, Abby Munson,
Francis Sullivan, and Koy Thomson, scholars and
coauthors of *The Earth Summit Agreements: A Guide and Assessment*

On UNCED's legacy:

If historians in the 21st century have the fortunate task of explaining how global society was capable of solving the intertwined problems of environment and development, UNCED will undoubtedly figure prominently in their accounts. The conference has laid a foundation with which governments and other social actors will be able to pressure each other to maintain a high level of commitment to environmental protection and development; it established institutions and informal networks that will facilitate the striking of effective agreements; and it added momentum to the building of national capacity in weak governments. Moreover, it endorsed a tightly linked policy agenda that reflects the complex ecological and sociopolitical links among various human activities and between human activities and the environment. As governments are swayed by the array of international pressures that UNCED helped to reinforce, more comprehensive and holistic public policies for sustainable development will follow.[16]

—American scholars Peter M. Haas,
Marc A. Levy, and Edward A. Parson

The United Nations Conference on Environment and Development, the self-styled Earth Summit, finished where it began. After ten days of press conferences, tree-planting ceremonies and behind-the-scenes wheeling and dealing, the diplomats went home to their various other assignments and the politicians to their next round of international talks. Rio gave way to the Munich conference and the more familiar territory of GATT, G-7 power politics and interest rates. . . . Unwilling to question the desirability of economic growth, the market economy, or the development process itself, UNCED never had a chance of addressing the real problems of "environment and development". Its secretariat provided delegates with materials for a convention on biodiversity but not on free trade; on forests but not on logging; on climate but not on automobiles. Agenda 21—the Summit's "action plan"—featured clauses on "enabling the poor to achieve sustainable livelihoods" but none on enabling the rich to do so; a section on women but none on men. By such deliberate evasion of the central issues which economic expansion poses for human societies, UNCED condemned itself to irrelevance even before the first preparatory meeting got underway.[17]

—The Ecologist

Institutions as Though the Earth Mattered

Most efforts to promote international environmental cooperation have focused on issue-specific agreements for pressing environmental problems. But as more such agreements have come into force, it has become clear that their effectiveness can be limited by the environmentally destructive effects of more fundamental economic and political processes in the world system. Practices such as international trade, foreign investment, technology transfer, and development assistance, for example, can have effects that cut across issue-specific environmental concerns such as soils, forests, or water quality.

Oran Young has defined institutions as "social practices consisting of easily recognized roles coupled with clusters of rules or conventions governing relations among the occupants of these roles."[1] This definition of institutions is not synonymous with organizations, which are "material entities possessing physical locations (or seats), offices, personnel, equipment, and budgets."[2] Many institutions have a formal organizational base; others, such as language systems or the family, endure informally, being reproduced over time by the beliefs and practices of individuals and groups.

International trade, as codified in the General Agreement on Tariffs and Trade (GATT), World Trade Organization, and regional arrangements such as the European Union and the North American Free Trade Agreement (NAFTA), is an example of an institution—a set of established rules and roles—with important consequences for the global environment. Development assistance, as practiced by the World Bank and the various bilateral programs linking Northern donors and Southern recipients, is another. As the impact of international institutions such as trade and aid on the environment has become more apparent, pressures have mounted for international institutional reform. In this chapter we examine trade and aid as two central components of this broader debate.

The links between international trade and the global environment are a relatively new concern for environmentalists. Their attention has been engaged by the increasingly apparent environmental consequences of trade (see MacNeill, Winsemius, and Yakushiji in Part Two), the growing importance of trade in the world economy, and the recent flurry of efforts to rewrite the rules of the international trading game through agreements such as NAFTA and GATT. The growing controversies surrounding trade and the environment illustrate that the traditional claims made by neoclassical economists on behalf of free trade will no longer go unchallenged.

In an exchange between two leading voices in this debate, economists Jagdish Bhagwati and Herman Daly present their cases for and against free trade. Their essays reveal fundamentally different perspectives about the links between free trade and environmental externalities, about fairness in international trade competition, and about the appropriate way to view economic growth. Although the authors agree on the importance of protecting the environment and promoting prosperity, they disagree strongly on which institutional path to take in order to achieve those goals.

Bhagwati offers the traditional neoclassical defense of free trade. The fewer the restrictions on trade, the more efficient the international distribution of resources and the more the parties involved in trade will benefit from increased economic growth. While many environmentalists argue that increasing economic growth leads to proportionate increases in pollution, Bhagwati suggests that the link between growth rates and environmental degradation is hardly automatic. In fact, Bhagwati claims that economic growth actually increases the potential for environmental protection by providing the capital for poorer countries to pay for environmental protection programs.[3]

Bhagwati also argues that different environmental standards among countries should not be viewed as unfair trade advantages. Because one country's environmental values might not be universally held by other nations, we should hardly be surprised if different countries choose different paths to environmental protection or different balances between the environment and other values. Moreover, if firms do seek lower environmental standards to reduce their costs and boost their competitiveness, or if they attempt to relocate production to countries with lax standards, Bhagwati argues that governments can respond without resorting to protectionism—for example, by requiring that their businesses adhere to domestic environmental regulations when operating overseas.

Daly, in contrast, argues that the assumptions behind the neoclassical vision of free trade, comparative advantage, and gains from specialization are no longer valid. Now that capital is internationally mobile, it can easily move to those countries with less rigorous environmental, wage, or safety standards. The countries left behind will see increased unemployment and income inequality. Daly claims that the lower standards in the countries attracting capital are, in essence, a subsidy to the companies in those countries. To combat these unfair subsidies, governments with higher standards should be allowed to "level the playing field" by imposing tariffs on the products coming from those countries.

Daly's central argument, however, is his attack on the neoclassical claim that increased economic growth will redress the inequities and inefficiencies that can arise from unrestricted trade. As one of the founders of the idea of "steady-state economics," Daly argues that traditional neoclassical arguments in favor of increased economic growth and free trade must be seriously reevaluated if the economic growth created by trade increases material throughput in the world economy, thereby threatening to expand the economy beyond the "optimal scale" dictated by ecological realities.

Clearly, Daly and Bhagwati have different visions of the best course for the future. Bhagwati, in this article and other writings, has indicated a deep concern for the stability of the international trading system.[4] In his view, we should not risk trade wars by implementing protectionist measures to promote what are often subjective, culturally specific environmental goals. Instead, environmental goals should be accomplished with diplomacy and domestic legislation that minimize the impact on the trading system. Daly, on the other hand, goes far beyond advocating the incorporation of explicit environmental objectives into the rules of international trade. He argues instead that the best way for nations to stay within ecological limits is to move away from free trade and toward domestic production for national markets. While Daly's is the more radical vision for changing the institution of international trade, it should be noted that even Bhagwati's more limited set of prescriptions for environmental protection would require rewriting some aspects of the rules of international trade. We therefore conclude the discussion of trade and environment with an excerpt from a report by the International Institute for Sustainable Development (IISD), a Canadian NGO that monitors international environmental diplomacy. The IISD report outlines a set of principles for defining the environmental criteria that should be used in international trade practices.

The case of development assistance provides an interesting contrast to international trade in that a process of institutional reform for the purposes of environmental protection is already under way there. The World Bank, in particular, as the financially and intellectually dominant international organization on the development scene, has felt substantial pressure to change its lending practices. During the 1980s, the Bank's role in distributing tens of billions of dollars annually for development projects with devastating environmental impacts made it an obvious target of criticism from nongovernmental organizations (NGOs) in both the North and the South.[5] As a result, the Bank began to institute a series of internal reforms aimed at increasing the ecological soundness of its projects. The final two essays in this section present radically different assessments of the effectiveness of these changes, as well as of whether the Bank can be a force for environmental improvement and sustainability.

Bruce Rich offers a scathing indictment of the World Bank's purported environmental reforms. Writing in the early 1990s, almost a decade after the initial challenges to Bank environmental policy, he argues that the Bank is caught in a series of contradictions that limited the possibilities for true reform. These include bureaucratic pressures to measure success in terms of the number and size of loans made, the desire of both lenders and borrowers to keep money moving, a lack of Bank accountability to either lending or borrowing countries, and inherent contradictions between environmental protection and current global economic practices.

Others offer a more optimistic view. According to Mohamed T. El-Ashry, writing in 1993 as the Bank's Director of Environment:

> All Bank-financed projects are now categorized according to their potential environmental impact. Only projects that are unlikely to have adverse environmental effects—projects such as family planning, education, health and nutrition projects—are not subject to environmental scrutiny. All others must undergo either an environmental analysis or a full-blown environmental assessment depending on the potential significance of their environmental consequences.[6]

El-Ashry describes the Bank's response to its critics as a four-part strategy: comprehensive environmental assessment procedures for Bank-funded projects; exploitation of the "synergies between poverty reduction and environmental improvement"; assistance to member countries in the development of national environmental institutions and the building of domestic bureaucratic and administrative capacity; and grants and technical assistance made through the Global Environment Facility (GEF).

The chapter by Bank economists and consultants Wilfredo Cruz, Mohan Munasinghe, and Jeremy Warford illustrates both change and continuity in the Bank practices that Rich and others have found troubling. On the one hand, an increased attentiveness to the environmental impact of macroeconomic variables such as employment, trade relations, and currency values suggests that at least parts of the Bank have move beyond a narrow, project-centered understanding of environmental issues. On the other hand, the evidence of an enduring faith that "getting the prices right" will produce optimal outcomes reinforces the view that the Bank is first and foremost still a bank, and that it struggles with moving beyond economic variables and technical assessments. This chapter also provides clear evidence that the Bank's activities can have widely varying impacts in different local settings.

Despite the organizational and procedural changes within the Bank, even optimists acknowledge that change in the Bank's behavior has been slow and uneven. Like the reform of any large organization, reform in the Bank has collided with bureaucratic inertia and resistance. But reformers argue that the process of change is now irreversible. This optimism is in stark contrast with Rich's belief that the Bank is embedded in a set of institutional and political contradictions that inherently limit the possibilities of its reform. From this perspective the key to change is not to wait for the current reforms to take hold, but rather for concerned groups from both the North and the South to continue to press the Bank to become more open and democratic in its operations. Here, too, progress is difficult to measure, as witnessed by the widely varying opinions as to whether the Bank's new Inspection Panel constitutes such a democratic opening.[7]

International trade and development assistance are but two of the many international institutions that have a profound impact on the global environment. Indeed, one could view national sovereignty itself in institutional terms, as a long-standing set of roles and rules with profound environmental consequences. But the problems faced in reforming the prevailing trade and aid regimes are specific examples of a more general challenge of institutional change. One clear lesson is that implementing effective reforms will require careful attention to the internal workings of institutions. Failure to take into account the incentive structures of the actors involved can be devastating to reform efforts, as seen in the case of the World Bank. But we must also ask whether internal change of the sort advocated by reformers can be effective if Rich is correct in concluding that prevailing institutions reflect a larger, structural logic in which environmental concerns are marginalized.

Thinking Critically

1. Contrast the positions of Daly and Bhagwati on trade and the environment. Does the difference lie in the realm of theory, values, evidence, or all of the above? Do these two authors address each other's claims, or are they talking past one another? If these were the opening statements in an actual face-to-face debate, what would you expect each to say in rebuttal? What sort of evidence would be required to settle their central points of disagreement?

2. Do the seven principles on trade and the environment presented by the International Institute for Sustainable Development reconcile the conflicting positions of Bhagwati and Daly? Do they address the central concerns of each? What would be the principal barriers to institutionalizing these principles as international trade policy? As international environmental policy?

3. Do you share Rich's pessimism about the possibilities for change in a large, centralized institution such as the World Bank? Of the four "contradictions" Rich cites, which seem the least tractable? What would have to happen for each to change, and who would you expect to be the agents of such change?

4. Does the essay by Cruz, Munasinghe, and Warford reflect the sort of thinking that Rich criticized, or does it suggest changed thinking within at least portions of the Bank? How would Herman Daly respond to these au-

thors' emphasis on the environmentally positive aspects of liberalized trade in some of these country cases?

5. Contrast Cruz, Munasinghe, and Warford's essay with Nagpal's summary of the 2050 Project in Part Five. Does the largely technical discussion here complement or contradict the common human aspirations summarized by Nagpal?

Additional Reading

Trade and the Environment

Esty, Daniel C., *Greening the GATT: Trade, Environment and the Future* (Washington, DC: Institute for International Economics, 1994).

French, Hilary F., *Costly Tradeoffs: Reconciling Trade and the Environment,* Worldwatch Paper 113 (Washington, DC: Worldwatch Institute, 1993).

Mander, Jerry, and Edward Goldsmith, eds., *The Case Against the Global Economy and for a Turn to the Local* (San Francisco: Sierra Club Books, 1996).

Thompson, Peter, and Laura A. Strohm, "Trade and Environmental Quality: A Review of the Evidence," *Journal of Environment and Development* 5, no. 4 (December 1996):363–388.

Zaelke, Durwood, Paul Orbuch, and Robert F. Housman, eds., *Trade and the Environment: Law, Economics, and Policy* (Washington, DC: Island Press).

The World Bank

Le Prestre, Philippe G., *The World Bank and the Environmental Challenge* (Selinsgrove, PA: Susquehanna University Press, 1989).

Mason, Jocelyn, *Mainstreaming the Environment: The World Bank Group and the Environment since the Rio Earth Summit* (Washington, DC: World Bank, 1995).

Munasinghe, Mohan, and Wilfrido Cruz, *Economywide Policies and the Environment: Lessons from Experience* (Washington, DC: World Bank, 1995).

Nelson, Paul, *The World Bank and Nongovernmental Organizations: The Limits of Apolitical Development* (London: Macmillan, 1995).

Rich, Bruce, *Mortgaging the Earth: The World Bank, Environmental Impoverishment, and the Crisis of Development* (Boston: Beacon Press, 1994).

World Bank, *World Development Report 1992: Development and the Environment* (Washington, DC: World Bank, 1992).

Internet Resources

World Trade Organization (WTO), *http://www.wto.org*. This intergovernmental organization promotes trade liberalization and seeks to enforce principles and rules codified in the General Agreement on Tariffs and Trade.

Global Trade Watch, *http://www.citizen.org/pctrade/tradehome.html*. This site, maintained by the American NGO Public Citizen, casts a critical eye on international trade liberalization measures related to the GATT, WTO, and NAFTA.

Ecological Economics, *http://csf.colorado.edu/ecol-econ*. A discussion board on ecological economics, with the thoughts and writings of many leading thinkers in the field.

World Bank, *http://www.worldbank.org*. The World Bank's home page.

Global Environment Facility (GEF), *http://www.worldbank.org/html/gef/gef-text.htm*. This site describes the activities of the GEF, a funding instrument dedicated to global environmental problems and overseen by the World Bank, the U.N. Development Programme, and the U.N. Environment Programme.

Environmental Defense Fund (EDF), *http://www.edf.org*. EDF is an American environmental NGO that has been active in bringing pressure to bear on the World Bank and other multilateral development agencies. Bruce Rich, author of Chapter 21, led EDF's campaign.

Multinational Monitor, *http://essential.org/monitor*. This on-line publication "tracks corporate activity, especially in the Third World, focusing on the export of hazardous substances, worker health and safety, labor union issues, and the environment."

JAGDISH BHAGWATI

18

The Case for Free Trade

Economists are reconciled to the conflict of absolutes: that is why they invented the concept of tradeoffs. It should not surprise them, therefore, that the objective of environmental protection should at times run afoul of the goal of seeking maximum gains from trade. In fact, economists would be suspicious of any claims, such as those made by soothsaying politicians, that both causes would be only mutually beneficial. They are rightly disconcerted, however, by the passion and the ferocity, and hence often the lack of logic or facts, with which environmental groups have recently assailed both free trade and the General Agreement on Tariffs and Trade (GATT), the institution that oversees the world trading system.

The environmentalists' antipathy to trade is perhaps inevitable. Trade has been central to economic thinking since Adam Smith discovered the virtues of specialization and of the markets that naturally sustain it. Because markets do not normally exist for the pursuit of environmental protection, they must be specially created. Trade therefore suggests abstention from governmental intervention, whereas environmentalism suggests its necessity. Then again, trade is exploited and its virtues extolled by corporate and multinational interests, whereas environmental objectives are embraced typically by nonprofit organizations, which are generally wary of these interests. Trade is an ancient occupation, and its nurture is the objective of institutions crafted over many years of experience and reflection. Protection of the environment, on the other hand, is a recent preoccupation of national and international institutions that are nascent and still evolving.

Originally published in *Scientific American* (November 1993):42–49. Reprinted with permission.

Last year the environmentalists' hostility to trade exploded in outrage when an impartial GATT Dispute Settlement Panel ruled in favor of Mexico and free trade and against the U.S. and the welfare of the dolphin. The U.S. had placed an embargo on the import of Mexican tuna on the grounds that the fish had been caught in purse-seine nets, which kill dolphins cruelly and in greater numbers than U.S. law permits. The GATT panel ruled, in effect, that the U.S. could not suspend Mexico's trading rights by proscribing unilaterally the methods by which that country harvested tuna.

This decision spurred the conservationists' subsequent campaigns against free trade and GATT. GATT has no shortage of detractors, of course. In fact, some of its recent critics have feared its impotence and declared it "dead," referring to it as the General Agreement to Talk and Talk. But the environmentalist attacks, which presume instead GATT's omnipotence, are something else again.

An advertisement by a coalition of environmental groups in the *New York Times* on April 20, 1992, set a new standard for alarmist, even scurrilous, writing, calculated to appeal to one's instincts rather than one's intellect. It talks of "faceless GATT bureaucrats" mounting a "sneak attack on democracy." This veiled reference to Pearl Harbor provides an example of a common tactic in trade controversy: Japan-bashing. The innuendos have continued unabated and are manifest in the endless battles in Congress over the supplemental environmental accords for the North American Free Trade Agreement (NAFTA). The hostility is also intruding on the conclusion of the Uruguay Round of GATT talks, now in their seventh year, with the environmentalists opposing the establishment of the new Multilateral Trade Organization, which is meant to provide effective discipline and a necessary institutional structure for GATT. [Editors' note: The Uruguay Round of multilateral trade negotiations was concluded in early 1994, and the GATT agreement ratified by the U.S. Congress in December of that year.]

It is surely tragic that the proponents of two of the great causes of the 1990s, trade and the environment, should be locked in combat. The conflict is largely gratuitous. There are at times philosophical differences between the two that cannot be reconciled, as when some environmentalists assert nature's autonomy, whereas most economists see nature as a handmaiden to humankind. For the most part, however, the differences derive from misconceptions. It is necessary to dissect and dismiss the more egregious of these fallacies before addressing the genuine problems.

The fear is widespread among environmentalists that free trade increases economic growth and that growth harms the environment. That fear is misplaced. Growth enables governments to tax and to raise resources for a variety of objectives, including the abatement of pollution and the general protection of the environment. Without such revenues, little can be achieved, no matter how pure one's motives may be.

How do societies actually spend these additional revenues? It depends on how getting rich affects the desire for a better environment. Rich countries today have more groups worrying about environmental causes than do poor countries. Efficient policies, such as freer trade, should generally help environmentalism, not harm it.

If one wants to predict what growth will do to the environment, however, one must also consider how it will affect the production of pollution. Growth affects not only the demand for a good environment but also the supply of the pollution associated with growth. The net effect on the environment will therefore depend on the kind of economic growth. Gene M. Grossman and Alan B. Krueger of Princeton University found that in cities around the world sulfur dioxide pollution fell as per capita income rose. The only exception was in countries whose per capita incomes fell below $5,000. In short, environmentalists are in error when they fear that trade, through growth, will necessarily increase pollution.

Economic effects besides those attributable to rising incomes also help to protect the environment. For example, freer trade enables pollution-fighting technologies available elsewhere to be imported. Thus, trade in low-sulfur-content coal will enable the users of local high-sulfur-content coal to shift from the latter to the former.

Free trade can also lead to better environmental outcomes from a shift in the composition of production. An excellent example is provided by Robert C. Feenstra of the University of California at Davis. He has shown how the imposition of restraints on Japanese automobile exports to the U.S. during the 1980s shifted the composition of those exports from small to large cars, as the Japanese attempted to increase their revenues without increasing the number of units they sold. Yet the large cars were fuel inefficient. Thus, protective efforts by the U.S. effectively increased the average amount of pollution produced by imported cars, making it more likely that pollution from cars would increase rather than diminish in the U.S.

Although these erroneous objections to free trade are readily dismissed (but not so easily eliminated from public discourse), there are genuine conflicts between trade and the environment. To understand and solve them, economists draw a distinction between two kinds of environmental problems: those that are intrinsically domestic and those that are intrinsically transnational.

Should Brazil pollute a lake lying wholly within its borders, the problem would be intrinsically domestic. Should it pollute a river that flows into Argentina, the matter would take on an intrinsically transnational character. Perhaps the most important examples of transnational pollution are acid rain, created when sulfur dioxide emissions in one country precipitate into rain in another, and greenhouse gases, such as carbon dioxide, which contribute to global warming wherever they are emitted.

Why do intrinsically domestic environmental questions create international concern? The main reason is the belief that diversity in environmental standards may affect competitiveness. Businesses and labor unions worry that their rivals in other countries may gain an edge if their governments impose lower standards of environmental protection. They decry such differences as unfair. To level the playing field, these lobbies insist that foreign countries raise their standards up to domestic ones. In turn, environmental groups worry that if such "harmonization up" is not undertaken prior to freeing trade, pressures from uncompetitive businesses at home will force down domestic standards, reversing their hard-won victories. Finally, there is the fear, dramatized by H. Ross Perot in his criticisms of NAFTA, that factories will relocate to the countries whose environmental standards are lowest.

But if the competitiveness issue makes the environmentalists, the businesses and the unions into allies, the environmentalists are on their own in other ways. Two problem areas can be distinguished. First, some environmentalists are keen to impose their own ethical preferences on others, using trade sanctions to induce or coerce acceptance of such preferences. For instance, tuna fishing with purse-seine nets that kill dolphins is opposed by U.S. environmental groups, which consequently favor restraints on the importation of such tuna from Mexico and elsewhere. Second, other environmentalists fear that the rules of free trade, as embodied in GATT and strengthened in the Uruguay Round, will constrain their freedom to pursue even purely domestic environmental objectives, with GATT tribunals outlawing disputed regulation.

Environmentalists have cause for concern. Not all concerns are legitimate, however, and not all the solutions to legitimate concerns are sensible. Worry over competitiveness has thus led to the illegitimate demand that environmental standards abroad be treated as "social dumping." Offending countries are regarded as unfairly subsidizing their exporters through lax environmental requirements. Such implicit subsidies, the reasoning continues, ought to be offset by import duties.

Yet international differences in environmental standards are perfectly natural. Even if two countries share the same environmental objectives, the *specific* pollutions they would attack, and hence the industries they would hinder, will generally not be identical. Mexico has a greater social incentive than does the U.S. to spend an extra dollar preventing dysentery rather than reducing lead in gasoline.

Equally, a certain environmental good might be valued more highly by a poor country than by a rich one. Contrast, for instance, the value assigned to a lake with the cost of cleaning up effluents discharged into it by a pharmaceutical company. In India such a lake's water might be drunk by a malnourished population whose mortality would increase sharply with the rise in pollution. In the U.S. the water might be consumed by few people, all of whom have the means to protect themselves with privately purchased water filters. In this example, India would be the more likely to prefer clean water to the pharmaceutical company's profits.

The consequences of differing standards are clear: each country will have less of the industry whose pollution it fears relatively more than other countries do. Indeed, even if there were no international trade, we would be shrinking industries whose pollution we deter. This result follows from the policy of forcing polluters of all stripes to pay for the harm they cause. To object, then, to the effects our negative valuation of pollution has on a given industry is to be in contradiction: we would be refusing to face the consequences of our environmental preferences.

Nevertheless, there is sentiment for enacting legislation against social dumping. Senator David L. Boren of Oklahoma, the proponent of the International

Pollution Deterrence Act of 1991, demanded import duties on the grounds that "some U.S. manufacturers, such as the U.S. carbon and steel alloy industry, spend as much as 250 percent more on environmental controls as a percentage of gross domestic product than do other countries. . . . I see the unfair advantage enjoyed by other nations exploiting the environment and public health for economic gain when I look at many industries important to my own state." Similarly, Vice President Al Gore wrote in *Earth in the Balance: Ecology and the Human Spirit* that "just as government subsidies of a particular industry are sometimes considered unfair under the trade laws, weak and ineffectual enforcement of pollution control measures should also be included in the definition of unfair trading practices."

These demands betray lack of economic logic, and they ignore political reality as well. Remember that the so-called subsidy to foreign producers through lower standards is not given but only implied. According to Senator Boren, the subsidy would be calculated as "the cost that would have to be incurred by the manufacturer or producer of the foreign articles of merchandise to comply with environmental standards imposed on U.S. producers of the same class of merchandise." Anyone familiar with the way dumping calculations are made knows that the Environmental Protection Agency could come up with virtually any estimates it cared to produce. Cynical politics would inevitably dictate the calculations.

Still there may be political good sense in assuaging environmentalists' concerns about the relocation of factories to countries with lower standards. The governments of higher-standards countries could do so without encumbering free trade by insisting that their businesses accede to the higher standards when they go abroad. Such a policy lies entirely within the jurisdictional powers of a higher-standards country. Moreover, the governments of lower standards countries would be most unlikely to object to such an act of good citizenship by the foreign investors.

Environmentalists oppose free trade for yet another reason: they wish to use trade policy to impose their values on other communities and countries. Many environmentalists want to suspend the trading rights of countries that sanction the use of purse-seine nets in tuna fishing and of leg-hold traps in trapping. Such punishments seem an inappropriate use of state power, however. The values in question are not widely accepted, such as human rights, but idiosyncratic. One wonders when the opponents of purse-seine nets put the interests of the dolphin ahead of those of Mexico's people, who could prosper through more productive fishing. To borrow the campaign manifesto of President Bill Clinton: Should we not put people first?

Moreover, once such values intrude on free trade, the way is opened for an endless succession of demands. Environmentalists favor dolphins; Indians have their sacred cows. Animal-rights activists, who do not prefer one species over another, will object to our slaughterhouses.

The moral militancy of environmentalists in the industrialized world has begun to disillusion their closest counterparts in the undeveloped countries. These local environmentalists accuse the rich countries of "eco-imperialism," and they deny that the Western nations have a monopoly on virtue. The most radical of to-day's proenvironment magazines in India, *Down to Earth,* editorialized recently: "In the current world reality trade is used as an instrument entirely by Northern countries to discipline environmentally errant nations. Surely, if India or Kenya were to threaten to stop trade with the U.S., it would hardly affect the latter. But the fact of the matter is that it is the Northern countries that have the greatest [adverse] impact on the world's environment."

If many countries were to play this game, then repeated suspensions of trading rights would begin to undermine the openness of the trading system and the pre-dictability and stability of international markets. Some environmentalists assert that each country should be free to insist on the production methods of its trad-ing partners. Yet these environmentalists ignore the certain consequence of their policy: a Pandora's box of protectionism would open up. Rarely are production methods in an industry identical in different countries.

There are certainly better ways to indulge the environmentalists' propensity to export their ethical preferences. The U.S. environmental organizations can lobby in Mexico to persuade its government to adopt their views. Private boycotts can also be undertaken. In fact, boycotts can carry much clout in rich countries with big markets, on which the targeted poor countries often depend. The frequent and enormously expensive advertisements by environmental groups against GATT show also that their resources far exceed those of the cash-strapped coun-tries whose policies they oppose.

Cost-benefit analysis leads one to conclude that unilateral governmental sus-pension of others' trading rights is not an appropriate way to promote one's lesser ethical preferences. Such sanctions can, on the other hand, appropriately be in-voked multilaterally to defend universal moral values. In such cases—as in the censure of apartheid, as practiced until recently in South Africa—it is possible to secure widespread agreement for sanctions. With a large majority converted to the cause, GATT's waiver procedure can be used to suspend the offending coun-try's trading rights.

Environmentalists are also worried about the obstacles that the current and prospective GATT rules pose for environmental regulations aimed entirely at do-mestic production and consumption. In principle, GATT lets a country enforce any regulation that does not discriminate against or among foreign suppliers. One can, for example, require airbags in cars, provided that the rule applies to all automobile makers. GATT even permits rules that discriminate against trade for the purpose of safety and health.

GATT, however, recognizes three ways in which regulations may be set in gratu-itous restraint of trade; in following procedures aimed at avoiding such outcomes, GATT upsets the environmentalists. First, the true intention—and effect—of a regulation may be to protect not the environment but local business. Second, a country may impose more restrictions than necessary to achieve its stated envi-ronmental objective. Third, it may set standards that have no scientific basis.

The issue of intentions is illustrated by the recently settled "beer war" between Ontario and the U.S. Five years ago the Canadian province imposed a 10-cents-a-can tax on beer, ostensibly to discourage littering. The U.S. argued that the law in fact intended to discriminate against its beer suppliers, who used aluminum cans, whereas local beer companies used bottles. Ontario had omitted to tax the use of cans for juices and soups, a step that would have affected Ontario producers.

The second problem is generally tougher because it is impossible to find alternative restrictions that accomplish exactly the same environmental results as the original policy at lower cost. An adjudicating panel is then forced to evaluate, implicitly or explicitly, the tradeoffs between the cost in trade disruption and the cost in lesser fulfillment of the environmental objective. It is therefore likely that environmentalists and trade experts will differ on which weights the panel should assign to these divergent interests.

Environmentalists tend to be fearful about the use of scientific tests to determine whether trade in a product can be proscribed. The need to prove one's case is always an unwelcome burden to those who have the political power to take unilateral action. Yet the trade experts have the better of the argument. Imagine that U.S. growers sprayed apples with the pesticide Alar, whereas European growers did not, and that European consumers began to agitate against Alar as harmful. Should the European Community be allowed to end the importation of the U.S. apples without meeting *some* scientific test of its health concerns? Admittedly, even hard science is often not hard enough—different studies may reach different conclusions. But without the restraining hand of science, the itch to indulge one's fears—and to play on the fears of others—would be irresistible.

In all cases, the moderate environmentalists would like to see GATT adopt more transparent procedures for adjudicating disputes. They also desire greater legal standing to file briefs when environmental regulations are at issue. These goals seem both reasonable and feasible.

Not all environmental problems are local; some are truly global, such as the greenhouse effect and the depletion of the stratospheric ozone. They raise more issues that require cooperative, multilateral solutions. Such solutions must be both efficient and equitable. Still, it is easy to see that rich countries might use their economic power to reach protocols that maximize efficiency at the expense of poorer countries.

For instance, imagine that the drafters of a protocol were to ask Brazil to refrain from cutting down its rain forests while allowing industrialized countries to continue emitting carbon dioxide. They might justify this request on the grounds that it costs Brazil less to keep a tree alive, absorbing a unit of carbon dioxide every year, than it would cost the U.S. or Germany to save a unit by burning less oil. Such a trade-off would indeed be economically efficient. Yet if Brazil, a poorer country, were then left with the bill, the solution would assuredly be inequitable.

Before any group of countries imposes trade sanctions on a country that has not joined a multilateral protocol, it would be important to judge whether the protocol is indeed fair. Nonmembers targeted for trade sanctions should have the right to get an impartial hearing of their objections, requiring the strong to defend their actions even when they appear to be entirely virtuous.

The simultaneous pursuit of the two causes of free trade and a protected environment often raises problems, to be sure. But none of these conflicts is beyond resolution with goodwill and by imaginative institutional innovation. The aversion to free trade and GATT that many environmentalists display is unfounded, and it is time for them to shed it. Their admirable moral passion and certain intellectual vigor are better devoted to building bridges between the causes of trade and the environment.

HERMAN E. DALY

19

The Perils of Free Trade

No policy prescription commands greater consensus among economists than that of free trade based on international specialization according to comparative advantage. Free trade has long been presumed good unless proved otherwise. That presumption is the cornerstone of the existing General Agreement on Tariffs and Trade (GATT) and the proposed North American Free Trade Agreement (NAFTA). The proposals in the Uruguay Round of negotiations strengthen GATT's basic commitment to free trade and economic globalization. [Editors' note: NAFTA was approved in late 1993 and took effect January 1, 1994. The Uruguay Round of GATT negotiations concluded in early 1994.]

Yet that presumption should be reversed. The default position should favor domestic production for domestic markets. When convenient, balanced international trade should be used, but it should not be allowed to govern a country's affairs at the risk of environmental and social disaster. The domestic economy should be the dog and international trade its tail. GATT seeks to tie all the dogs' tails together so tightly that the international knot would wag the separate national dogs.

The wiser course was well expressed in the overlooked words of John Maynard Keynes: "I sympathize, therefore, with those who would minimize, rather than those who would maximize, economic entanglement between nations. Ideas, knowledge, art, hospitality, travel—these are the things which should of their nature be international. But let goods be homespun whenever it is reasonably and conveniently possible; and, above all, let finance be primarily national." Contrary

---

to Keynes, the defenders of the proposed Uruguay Round of changes to GATT not only want to downplay "homespun goods," they also want finance and all other services to become primarily international.

Economists and environmentalists are sometimes represented as being, respectively, for and against free trade, but that polarization does the argument a disservice. Rather the real debate is over what kinds of regulations are to be instituted and what goals are legitimate. The free traders seek to maximize profits and production without regard for considerations that represent hidden social and environmental costs. They argue that when growth has made people wealthy enough, they will have the funds to clean up the damage done by growth. Conversely, environmentalists and some economists, myself among them, suspect that growth is increasing environmental costs faster than benefits from production—thereby making us poorer, not richer.

A more accurate name than the persuasive label "free trade"—because who can be opposed to freedom?—is "deregulated international commerce." Deregulation is not always a good policy: recall the recent experience of the U.S. with the deregulation of the savings and loan institutions. As one who formerly taught the doctrine of free trade to college students, I have some sympathy for the free traders' view. Nevertheless, my major concern about my profession today is that our disciplinary preference for logically beautiful results over factually grounded policies has reached such lunatical proportions that we economists have become dangerous to the earth and its inhabitants.

The free trade position is grounded in the logic of comparative advantage, first explicitly formulated by the early 19th century British economist David Ricardo. He observed that countries with different technologies, customs and resources will incur different costs when they make the same products. One country may find it comparatively less costly to mine coal than to grow wheat, but in another country the opposite may be true. If nations specialize in the products for which they have a comparative advantage and trade freely to obtain others, everyone benefits.

The problem is not the logic of this argument. It is the relevance of Ricardo's critical but often forgotten assumption that factors of production (especially capital) are internationally immobile. In today's world, where billions of dollars can be transferred between nations at the speed of light, that essential condition is not met. Moreover, free traders encourage such foreign investment as a development strategy. In short, the free traders are using an argument that hinges on the impermeability of national boundaries to capital to support a policy aimed at making those same boundaries increasingly permeable to both capital and goods!

That fact alone invalidates the assumption that international trade will inevitably benefit all its partners. Furthermore, for trade to be mutually beneficial, the gains must not be offset by higher liabilities. After specialization, nations are no longer free *not* to trade, and that loss of independence can be a liability. Also, the cost of transporting goods internationally must not cancel out the profits.

Transport costs are energy intensive. Today, however, the cost of energy is frequently subsidized by governments through investment tax credits, federally subsidized research and military expenditures that ensure access to petroleum. The environmental costs of fossil-fuel burning also do not factor into the price of gasoline. To the extent that energy is subsidized, then, so too is trade. The full cost of energy, stripped of these obscuring subsidies, would therefore reduce the initial gains from long distance trade, whether international or interregional.

Free trade can also introduce new inefficiencies. Contrary to the implications of comparative advantage, more than half of all international trade involves the simultaneous import and export of essentially the same goods. For example, Americans import Danish sugar cookies, and Danes import American sugar cookies. Exchanging recipes would surely be more efficient. It would also be more in accord with Keynes's dictum that knowledge should be international and goods homespun (or in this case, homebaked).

Another important but seldom mentioned corollary of specialization is a reduction in the range of occupational choices. Uruguay has a clear comparative advantage in raising cattle and sheep. If it adhered strictly to the rule of specialization and trade, it would afford its citizens only the choice of being either cowboys or shepherds. Yet Uruguayans feel a need for their own legal, financial, medical, insurance and educational services, in addition to basic agriculture and industry. That diversity entails some loss of efficiency, but it is necessary for community and nationhood.

Uruguay is enriched by having a symphony orchestra of its own, even though it would be cost-effective to import better symphony concerts in exchange for wool, mutton, beef and leather. Individuals, too, must count the broader range of choices as a welfare gain: even those who are cowboys and shepherds are surely enriched by contact with countrymen who are not *vaqueros* or *pastores*. My point is that the community dimension of welfare is completely overlooked in the simplistic argument that if specialization and trade increase the per capita availability of commodities, they must be good.

Let us assume that even after those liabilities are subtracted from the gross returns on trade, positive net gains still exist. They must still offset deeper, more fundamental problems. The arguments for free trade run afoul of the three basic goals of all economic policies: the efficient *allocation* of resources, the fair *distribution* of resources and the maintenance of a sustainable *scale* of resource use. The first two are traditional goals of neoclassical economics. The third has only recently been recognized and is associated with the viewpoint of ecological, or steady-state, economics. It means that the input of raw materials and energy to an economy and the output of waste materials and heat must be within the regenerative and absorptive capacities of the ecosystem.

In neoclassical economics the efficient allocation of resources depends on the counting and internalization of all costs. Costs are internalized if they are directly paid by those entities responsible for them—as when, for example, a manufacturer pays for the disposal of its factory wastes and raises its prices to cover that expense. Costs are externalized if they are paid by someone else—as when the public suffers extra disease, stench and nuisance from uncollected wastes. Counting all costs is the very basis of efficiency.

Economists rightly urge nations to follow a domestiç program of internalizing costs into prices. They also wrongly urge nations to trade freely with other countries that do not internalize their costs (and consequently have lower prices). If a nation tries to follow both those policies, the conflict is clear: free competition between different cost-internalizing regimes is utterly unfair.

International trade increases competition, and competition reduces costs. But competition can reduce costs in two ways: by increasing efficiency or by lowering standards. A firm can save money by lowering its standards for pollution control, worker safety, wages, health care and so on—all choices that externalize some of its costs. Profit-maximizing firms in competition always have an incentive to externalize their costs to the degree that they can get away with it.

For precisely that reason, nations maintain large legal, administrative and auditing structures that bar reductions in the social and environmental standards of domestic industries. There are no analogous international bodies of law and administration; there are only national laws, which differ widely. Consequently, free international trade encourages industries to shift their production activities to the countries that have the lowest standards of cost internalization—hardly a move toward global efficiency.

Attaining cheapness by ignoring real costs is a sin against efficiency. Even GATT recognizes that requiring citizens of one country to compete against foreign prison labor would be carrying standards-lowering competition too far. GATT therefore allows the imposition of restrictions on such trade. Yet it makes no similar exception for child labor, for uninsured risky labor or for subsistence wage labor.

The most practical solution is to permit nations that internalize costs to levy compensating tariffs on trade with nations that do not. "Protectionism"—shielding an inefficient industry against more efficient foreign competitors—is a dirty word among economists. That is very different, however, from protecting an efficient national policy of full-cost pricing from standards-lowering international competition.

Such tariffs are also not without precedent. Free traders generally praise the fairness of "antidumping" tariffs that discourage countries from trading in goods at prices below their production costs. The only real difference is the decision to include the costs of environmental damage and community welfare in that reckoning.

This tariff policy does not imply the imposition of one country's environmental preferences or moral judgements on another country. Each country should set the rules of cost internalization in its own market. Whoever sells in a nation's market should play by that nation's rules or pay a tariff sufficient to remove the competitive advantage of lower standards. For instance, under the Marine Mammal Protection Act, all tuna sold in the U.S. (whether by U.S. or Mexican fishermen) must count the cost of limiting the kill of dolphin associated with catching tuna. Tuna sold in the Mexican market (whether by U.S. or Mexican fishermen) need not include that cost. No standards are being imposed through "environmental imperialism"; paying the costs of a nation's environmental standards is merely the price of admission to its market.

Indeed, free trade could be accused of reverse environmental imperialism. When firms produce under the most permissive standards and sell their products elsewhere without penalty, they press on countries with higher standards to lower them. In effect, unrestricted trade imposes lower standards.

Unrestricted international trade also raises problems of resource distribution. In the world of comparative advantage described by Ricardo, a nation's capital stays at home, and only goods are traded. If firms are free to relocate their capital internationally to wherever their production costs would be lowest, then the favored countries have not merely a comparative advantage but an absolute advantage. Capital will drain out of one country and into another, perhaps making what H. Ross Perot called "a giant sucking sound" as jobs and wealth move with it. This specialization will increase world production, but without any assurance that all the participating countries will benefit.

When capital flows abroad, the opportunity for new domestic employment diminishes, which drives down the price for domestic labor. Even if free trade and capital mobility raise wages in low-wage countries (and that tendency is thwarted by overpopulation and rapid population growth), they do so at the expense of labor in the high-wage countries. They thereby increase income inequality there. Most citizens are wage earners. In the U.S., 80 percent of the labor force is classified as "nonsupervisory employees." Their real wages have fallen 17 percent between 1973 and 1990, in significant part because of trade liberalization.

Nor does labor in low-wage countries necessarily gain from free trade. It is likely that NAFTA will ruin Mexican peasants when "inexpensive" U.S. corn (subsidized by depleting topsoil, aquifers, oil wells and the federal treasury) can be freely imported. Displaced peasants will bid down wages. Their land will be bought cheaply by agribusinesses to produce fancy vegetables and cut flowers for the U.S. market. Ironically, Mexico helps to keep U.S. corn "inexpensive" by exporting its own vanishing reserves of oil and genetic crop variants, which the U.S. needs to sustain its corn monoculture.

Neoclassical economists admit that overpopulation can spill over from one country to another in the form of cheap labor. They acknowledge that fact as an argument against free immigration. Yet capital can migrate toward abundant labor even more easily than labor can move toward capital. The legitimate case for restrictions on labor immigration is therefore easily extended to restrictions on capital emigration.

When confronted with such problems, neoclassical economists often answer that growth will solve them. The allocation problem of standards-lowering competition, they say, will be dealt with by universally "harmonizing" all standards upward. The distribution problem of falling wages in high-wage countries would only be temporary; the economists believe that growth will eventually raise wages worldwide to the former high-wage level and beyond.

Yet the goal of a sustainable scale of total resource use forces us to ask: What will happen if the entire population of the earth consumes resources at the rate of high-wage countries? Neoclassical economists generally ignore this question or give the facile response that there are no limits.

The steady-state economic paradigm suggests a different answer. The regenerative and assimilative capacities of the biosphere cannot support even the current levels of resource consumption, much less the manyfold increase required to generalize the higher standards worldwide. Still less can the ecosystem afford an ever growing population that is striving to consume more per capita. As a species, we already preempt about 40 percent of the landbased primary product of photosynthesis for human purposes. What happens to biodiversity if we double the human population, as we are projected to do over the next 30 to 50 years?

These limits put a brake on the ability of growth to wash away the problems of misallocation and maldistribution. In fact, free trade becomes a recipe for hastening the speed with which competition lowers standards for efficiency, distributive equity and ecological sustainability.

Notwithstanding those enormous problems, the appeal of bigger free trade blocs for corporations is obvious. The broader the free trade area, the less answerable a large and footloose corporation will be to any local or even national community. Spatial separation of the places that suffer the costs and enjoy the benefits becomes more feasible. The corporation will be able to buy labor in the low-wage markets and sell its products in the remaining high-wage, high-income markets. The larger the market, the longer a corporation will be able to avoid the logic of Henry Ford, who realized that he had to pay his workers enough for them to buy his cars. That is why transnational corporations like free trade and why workers and environmentalists do not.

In the view of steady-state economics, the economy is one open subsystem in a finite, nongrowing and materially closed ecosystem. An open system takes matter and energy from the environment as raw materials and returns them as waste. A closed system is one in which matter constantly circulates internally while only energy flows through. Whatever enters a system as input and exits as output is called throughput. Just as an organism survives by consuming nutrients and excreting wastes, so too an economy must to some degree both deplete and pollute the environment. A steady-state economy is one whose throughput remains constant at a level that neither depletes the environment beyond its regenerative capacity nor pollutes it beyond its absorptive capacity.

Most neoclassical economic analyses today rest on the assumption that the economy is the total system and nature is the subsystem. The economy is an isolated system involving only a circular flow of exchange value between firms and households. Neither matter nor energy enters or exits this system. The economy's growth is therefore unconstrained. Nature may be finite, but it is seen as just one sector of the economy, for which other sectors can substitute without limiting overall growth.

Although this vision of circular flow is useful for analyzing exchanges between producers and consumers, it is actively misleading for studying scale—the size of the economy relative to the environment. It is as if a biologist's vision of an animal contained a circulatory system but not a digestive tract or lungs. Such a beast would be independent of its environment, and its size would not matter. If it could move, it would be a perpetual motion machine.

Long ago the world was relatively empty of human beings and their belongings (man-made capital) and relatively full of other species and their habitats (natural capital). Years of economic growth have changed that basic pattern. As a result, the limiting factor on future economic growth has changed. If man-made and natural capital were good substitutes for one another, then natural capital could be totally replaced. The two are complementary, however, which means that the short supply of one imposes limits. What good are fishing boats without populations of fish? Or sawmills without forests? Once the number of fish that could be sold at market was primarily limited by the number of boats that could be built and manned; now it is limited by the number of fish in the sea.

As long as the scale of the human economy was very small relative to the ecosystem, no apparent sacrifice was involved in increasing it. The scale of the economy is now such that painless growth is no longer reasonable. If we see the economy as a subsystem of a finite, nongrowing ecosystem, then there must be a maximal scale for its throughput of matter and energy. More important, there must also be an optimal scale. Economic growth beyond that optimum would increase the environmental costs faster than it would the production benefits, thereby ushering in an antieconomic phase that impoverished rather than enriched.

One can find disturbing evidence that we have already passed that point and, like Alice in *Through the Looking Glass,* the faster we run the farther behind we fall. Thus the correlation between gross national product (GNP) and the index of sustainable economic welfare (which is based on personal consumption and adjusted for depletion of natural capital and other factors) has taken a negative turn in the U.S.

Like our planet, the economy may continue forever to develop qualitatively, but it cannot grow indefinitely and must eventually settle into a steady state in its physical dimensions. That condition need not be miserable, however. We economists need to make the elementary distinction between growth (a quantitative increase in size resulting from the accretion or assimilation of materials) and development (the qualitative evolution to a fuller, better or different state). Quantitative and qualitative changes follow different laws. Conflating the two, as we currently do in the GNP, has led to much confusion.

Development without growth is sustainable development. An economy that is steady in scale may still continue to develop a greater capacity to satisfy human wants by increasing the efficiency of its resource use, by improving social institutions and by clarifying its ethical priorities—but not by increasing the resource throughput.

In the light of the growth versus development distinction, let us return to the issue of international trade and consider two questions: What is the likely effect of free trade on growth? What is the likely effect of free trade on development?

Free trade is likely to stimulate the growth of throughput. It allows a country in effect to exceed its domestic regenerative and absorptive limits by "importing" those capacities from other countries. True, a country "exporting" some of its carrying capacity in return for imported products might have increased its throughput even more if it had made those products domestically. Overall, nevertheless, trade does postpone the day when countries must face up to living within their natural regenerative and absorptive capacities. That some countries still have excess carrying capacity is more indicative of a shortfall in their desired domestic growth than of any conscious decision to reserve that capacity for export.

By spatially separating the costs and benefits of environmental exploitation, international trade makes them harder to compare. It thereby increases the tendency for economies to overshoot their optimal scale. Furthermore, it forces countries to face tightening environmental constraints more simultaneously and less sequentially than would otherwise be the case. They have less opportunity to learn from one another's experiences with controlling throughput and less control over their local environment.

The standard arguments for free trade based on comparative advantage also depend on static promotions of efficiency. In other words, free trade in toxic wastes promotes static efficiency by allowing the disposal of wastes wherever it costs less according to today's prices and technologies. A more dynamic efficiency would be served by outlawing the export of toxins. That step would internalize the disposal costs of toxins to their place of origin—to both the firm that generated them and the nation under whose laws the firm operated. This policy creates an incentive to find technically superior ways of dealing with the toxins or of redesigning processes to avoid their production in the first place.

All these allocative, distributional and scale problems stemming from free trade ought to reverse the traditional default position favoring it. Measures to integrate national economies further should now be treated as a bad idea unless proved otherwise in specific cases. As Ronald Findley of Columbia University characterized it, comparative advantage may well be the "deepest and most beautiful result in all of economics." Nevertheless, in a full world of internationally mobile capital, our adherence to it for policy direction is a recipe for national disintegration.

20

Trade and Sustainable Development

. . .

Trade and Sustainable Development Principles

There are a number of good reasons why the gap between the trade and environment communities remains unbridged. First, the trade and environment debate misses the crucial truth that underlying its most difficult conflicts are disparities of development. The Rio bargain was based on the understanding that until global disparities could be lessened, progress on environmental issues of shared concern would be difficult. But this understanding has been scarce when environmentalists and free-traders argue their positions. The need is to expand the focus of the debate from trade and environment to trade, environment and development, or trade and sustainable development.

A trade and sustainable development debate not only brings into the picture the crucial issues of development—poverty, community, social well-being—but it also allows a framework for discussion and analysis that can move the debate for-

Excerpted from the Report to the Rio+5 Forum, Rio de Janeiro, Brazil, March 13–19, 1997. Reprinted with permission.

ward. Since before Rio the world's trade, environment and development communities have too often spoken past each other, in different languages, with different starting assumptions, but about problems of common interest which as a result are rarely addressed effectively. The common goal of sustainable development, which embraces the concerns of economy, environment and development, can allow productive discussion among the communities.

Such discussion must start from a common framework from which to view the issues—a starting set of principles for trade and sustainable development which all sides can agree on, and which can form the basis for common understanding of the problems we face, and the beginnings of dialogue on common approaches to address them. This section outlines such a set of principles, developed by an international Working Group drawn from the trade, environment and development communities world wide. The "Winnipeg Principles" represent a framework for addressing the interface between trade and sustainable development, in which it becomes evident that the trade, environment and development communities share a number of concerns and goals.

The Working Group identified seven principles, as follows:

Efficiency/Cost Internalization
Equity
Environmental Integrity
Subsidiarity
International Cooperation
Science and Precaution
Openness

Some readers will be tempted to emphasize one or two of these principles to the exclusion of others. This is a mistake; they are meant to be taken as an integrated framework for approaching the issues. "Cherry-picking" destroys the balance inherent in the principles, and may lead toward divisive conflict, rather than towards sustainable development.

1. Efficiency and Cost Internalization

Environmentalists, development specialists and trade economists share a common interest in promoting efficiency. More efficient production reduces the drain on scarce resources such as raw materials and energy, and limits the demands placed on the regenerative capacity of the environment. Efficient use of land, labour and capital is also the heart of development efforts to combat poverty and satisfy human needs.

Allowing the most efficient producers to provide the world's goods and services is the main rationale for an open trading system. Efficient resource use requires that the prices paid by producers for inputs, and by consumers for final goods and services, accurately reflect their full costs. In fact, most goods are not priced to reflect full costs (the magnitude of the distortion will vary from case to case), due to such factors as unpaid environmental costs and price-distorting trade barriers. This highlights an important distinction between the way we define efficiency here and the way it is traditionally defined: we will consider "costs" to include environmental and social costs, such as the damage to the stratospheric ozone layer caused by CFCs used in production, the costs inherent in the erosion of soil from arable land, and so on. If we use such a cradle-to-grave approach for calculating costs, the most efficient producer is also likely to be the one friendliest to society and the environment.

It should be noted that internalizing external environmental costs is not done solely through the use of economic instruments such as green taxes and effluent charges. Traditional forms of regulation, which cap emissions or specify advanced technologies, are also forms of cost internalization leading to greater efficiency.

2. Equity

Equity relates to the distribution both within and between generations of physical and natural capital, as well as knowledge and technology. Inequity and poverty contribute significantly to environmental degradation and political instability, particularly in developing countries. When basic needs are not met, the poor may have no choice but to live off whatever environmental resources are available. At the same time, past use of natural resources already limits the choices available to present generations, particularly in developing countries.

Many goods are traded at less than full-cost, if we figure in the environmental costs of production. This is partly an equity issue. In some cases, such as commodities, the structure of the markets makes internalization difficult. In many other cases and, indeed, in the commodities sectors as well, the producers and national regulating authorities lack the capacity to do so. Most developing countries lack the technical and administrative infrastructures necessary for concerted cost internalization, and do not have the finances to develop them.

Further, many are locked into a vicious circle of desperation production centred on commodity exports: poverty and debt force them to increase exports without internalized costs, leading to further environmental degradation. These exports face barriers in developed countries, from escalating tariffs and a barrage of non-tariff barriers, and face increased competition from other exporters following the same strategy. The resulting low revenues result in yet further increases in exports, and further environmental degradation.

3. Environmental Integrity

The principle of efficiency places strong emphasis on "getting the prices right"— on internalizing external environmental and social costs for traded goods. The principle of environmental integrity addresses those cases where cost internalization is either not possible or not appropriate as a policy tool. It requires respect for limits to the regenerative capacity of ecosystems such as fisheries and forests that are vulnerable to irreversible depletion; actions to avoid irreversible harm to plant and animal populations and species; and protection for valued areas such as designated parklands or sites of internationally recognized ecological, cultural or historical significance.

Many of these aspects of the environment have values which cannot be adequately captured by methods of cost internalization. Cost internalization is not useful in cases where the environmental losses in question are irreplaceable, as in the case of species extinction, since it is difficult to price something for which there is no substitute. Nor is it good at reflecting costs to future generations, since we have no way of knowing what value they will attach to environmental resources. Other policy instruments are thus needed, to deal with three types of cases:

> Actions which seriously damage the regenerative capacity of ecosystems such as fisheries and forests that are vulnerable to irreversible depletion.
> Actions which lead to irreplaceable losses, such as extinction of species and loss of biological diversity.
> Actions which threaten valued areas such as designated parklands or sites of internationally recognized ecological, cultural or historical significance.

4. Subsidiarity

In essence, subsidiarity represents no more than a general principle of good governance: decisions should be taken as close as possible to the affected public, at the lowest level of jurisdiction encompassing all those affected. It follows from the recognition that diversity and tolerance are among the attributes of a good society. In the context of trade and sustainable development, where issues of global dimension have significant and varied effects at the local level, it has particular relevance.

Decisions on appropriate standards and other environmental policy may vary from one jurisdiction to the next, for several legitimate reasons. First, environmental conditions may vary; different ecosystems respond differently to the same pollutants or pressures. Second, different jurisdictions may have different priorities; one country may have just enough resources to address severe water-related environmental problems, while another may not have such problems, or such resource constraints. Cultural and historical differences may also come into play in setting priorities.

Given the legitimacy of these differing bases for environmental policy, and given the rights of jurisdictions in many cases to decide for themselves what policy is best, the principle of subsidiarity has two important implications in the context of trade and sustainable development. First, harmonization of environmental standards is not necessarily desirable, though there may be an important role for harmonization of technical standards, procedural requirements, etc. Second, the policies of a jurisdiction which is internalizing costs as it sees them should not be "second-guessed" by the trade policies of a jurisdiction with different standards. It is wrong, for example, to unilaterally impose bans or eco-duties on imports because they were produced in ways which do not measure up to domestic standards. Instead, there must be an effort to construct an international structure of agreements and practices which equitably reflects legitimate differences in environmental conditions and priorities.

While subsidiarity implies a fair degree of discretion in the setting of environmental standards, it does not extend the argument for tolerance to cases where lower standards result in significant transborder effects. In such a case, since the appropriate level of jurisdiction includes all those affected, the matter becomes an international concern. This brings us once again to the need for a strong system of international cooperation in environmental management, and to the need for measures to address equity concerns. In general, the most effective solution for frictions over disparate standards will be to offer incentives for upward convergence, such as help in capacity-building, and technical and financial resource transfers. The responsibility of countries seeking higher environmental standards abroad to seek them multilaterally, shunning coercive measures, is matched by an obligation on the part of other countries to cooperate in such efforts.

5. International Cooperation

Sustainable development requires strengthening international systems of cooperation at all levels, encompassing environment, development and trade policies. The need for such cooperation on environmental matters is driven by the increasingly international character of many forms of environmental damage. The need for a rules-based cooperative system of trade is intensified by advances in information technology which make possible a much more global economy; in the end, the competition implied by more open markets and liberalization cannot succeed without cooperation. And the fundamental linkages between the environment and economic activity mean that strong cooperation must be fostered among international environmental and international trading regimes.

6. Science and Precaution

This principle involves a balanced approach to policy making, using science to inform decisions, but balancing it with precaution, recognizing the uncertainty inherent in the science of complex systems. Science is the basis for much of what we know about the environment. Since understanding ecological processes is central to valuing environmental damage, science is also a fundamental prerequisite for cost internalization measures. It therefore is an underpinning of environmental policy and should form the basis of any measures taken to protect the environment. Science must underlie any trade measures which seek to protect environment and health.

Our understanding of ecosystems, however, is still highly uncertain. They are characterized by thresholds—critical points beyond which all relationships change dramatically, triggered by events such as the extinction of a critical species in a food chain or an overloading of pollutants beyond the point of assimilative capacity. They are often unforgiving of errors in modeling and forecast. Many times, the resulting environmental damage cannot be easily reversed, if at all.

Inherent uncertainty, coupled with the reality of threshold effects and irreversibility, argues for a precautionary approach to rules and standards. There must be a margin of safety which prevents inevitable errors from having catastrophic effects. How wide the margin of safety should be will at times be controversial. Sanitary and phytosanitary standards have been consistently used in the past for reasons which have more to do with protecting domestic producers than with protecting human, plant and animal health. At the same time, it is obvious that there are circumstances in which a lack of scientific certainty should not be used as a justification for a lack of action to prevent potentially serious environmental or human health damage.

7. Openness

Openness . . . comprises two basic elements: first, timely, easy and full access to information for all those affected; and second, public participation in the decision-making process. Years of experience have shown that openness is essential for the formulation and implementation of effective environmental and development policies. Openness is also important in minimizing the risk that trade policies will be manipulated to favour inefficient producers. These truths are now reflected in the practice of multilateral development banks, and of many domestic systems of environmental and trade policy making.

. . .

BRUCE RICH

21

The Emperor's New Clothes: The World Bank and Environmental Reform

On October 24, 1989, an extraordinary hearing took place in the U.S. Congress. Two and a half years after the president of the World Bank, former congressman Barber Conable, had committed the Bank to sweeping environmental reforms, activists from its most important borrower and donor countries—India and the United States—testified about the Bank's systematic violation of its own environmental and social policies in the Sardar Sarovar dam project in north-central India. The activists objected that the Bank was continuing to finance the project despite five years of noncompliance by project authorities in preparing critical environmental studies and action plans, and in the absence of a resettlement plan for the 90,000 rural poor that the dam's 120-mile-long reservoir would displace. . . . Indeed, the Sardar Sarovar project is only one of literally scores of ongoing and proposed World Bank ecological debacles that have come to congressional and international attention over the past two years—debacles that have occurred despite a tenfold increase in Bank environmental staff and a proliferation of new environmental policies, action plans, and task forces. "[The Bank's] written assurances don't amount to a hill of beans; they don't exist for practical purposes," [New York Congressman James] Scheuer charged. "Where do the pressures come

Excerpted from *World Policy Journal* 7, no. 2 (Spring 1990):305–329. Reprinted with permission.

from," he asked, "pressing down on the World Bank to degrade its own procedures and to bring its own integrity into question?"

How has the Bank come to such an impasse, and where indeed do the pressures come from that have led it there?

The answers to these questions have important implications for the fate of the global environment in the 1990s and beyond. Since 1987 the World Bank has been at the forefront of the most important international development institutions—the multilateral development banks (MDBs) and the International Monetary Fund (IMF)—in initiating environmental reform of its lending policies. At the same time, after a period of relative stagnation, the importance of the MDBs and the IMF as international economic and political arbiters has begun to increase dramatically. In 1988 the World Bank's lending capacity was nearly doubled by a $75 billion capital increase, and together the four MDBs are now lending more than $32 billion annually for programs whose total cost is well over $100 billion. . . .

What led the World Bank to undertake environmental reform in the first place was largely the pressures from a coordinated campaign launched by nongovernmental organizations (NGOs) in the United States, Europe, and several developing nations. Starting in 1983, the "MDB Campaign" employed a variety of tactics to pressure the banks, including well-publicized case studies of World Bank-financed ecological disasters in Brazil, India, and Indonesia, congressional and parliamentary hearings in the United States and a number of European nations, and the mobilization of media attention in both the developed and developing world. In May 1987, World Bank President Barber Conable delivered a speech in Washington in which he publicly acknowledged that the Bank had been "part of the problem in the past," and announced that the Bank would mend its ways by greatly increasing its environmental staff and by increasing lending for environmentally beneficial projects.

Environmentalists were guardedly optimistic about Conable's new-found commitment to reform at the time. Now, three years later, it is apparent that the emperor's new clothes bear only faint traces of green. Instead of becoming a leading environmental lender, the Bank has become an arena where the political, practical, and theoretical difficulties of reconciling economic development with ecological sustainability are most glaring. The Bank continues to stress its commitment to the environment, but deep institutional and political contradictions prevent it from implementing reform in any meaningful way. Unless these contradictions are resolved, they will continue to inhibit real environmental change.

The Bank's Environmental Reforms: Appearance and Reality

The Bank's environmental reform program followed in large part the outlines of Conable's May 1987 speech. First, the Bank increased its environmental staff; by

1990, some 60 new positions—representing a tenfold increase—had been created. The Bank also launched a series of environmental issues papers and environmental action plans with the purpose of reviewing and addressing environmental problems in the most vulnerable developing countries. Conable also committed the Bank to financing environmental programs of various kinds, the most important of which was a plan to address tropical deforestation through unprecedented increases in forestry lending. Finally, Conable called for greater involvement of environmental and grass-roots NGOs in both borrowing and donor countries in the Bank's operations.

On the face of it, this program reflected much of what NGOs had pushed for. ... Beneath its self-proclaimed mission of banker to the poor, and behind its new green facade, the Bank is still essentially doing what it has always done: moving large amounts of money to Third World government agencies for capital-intensive projects or—an innovation of the 1980s—for free-market, export-oriented economic policy changes. Although ... Conable claimed that a third of Bank projects approved in fiscal year 1989 had "significant environmental components," NGOs now realize that this characterization includes mainly projects whose environmental impacts were so severe to begin with that the Bank felt compelled to incorporate some mitigating measures, as well as ostensibly environmental projects whose hasty design undermines prospects for implementation or, astoundingly, are positively destructive.... To their dismay, the NGOs are realizing that their very success in promoting conventional institutional changes has resulted in a proliferation of green rhetoric that hides a reality that is largely unchanged. The Washington-based NGOs that have led the campaign fear that they have inspired the creation of a new Orwellian dialect: greenspeak.

The basis for this fear can be well seen by taking a closer look at two of the most critical areas in the Bank's environmental reform program: the Tropical Forestry Action Plan (TFAP) and the Bank's record in dealing with forced resettlement caused by Bank projects....

The Tropical Forestry Action Plan.   Conable's May 1987 speech emphasized that the most important focus of the Bank's new environmental lending would be to contribute to a global program to support tropical forest conservation—the Tropical Forestry Action Plan. To that end he committed the Bank to increase its forestry lending 150 percent by 1989, and in September 1989 he announced a further tripling of forestry lending through the early 1990s.

... The TFAP sought to alleviate pressures causing deforestation in the Third World by mobilizing $8 billion from multilateral and bilateral aid agencies over a five-year period for a variety of forestry and agricultural activities that included the building of forestry and environmental institutions, supply of fuelwood needs, conservation of protected areas and vulnerable watershed regions, and support of forest management for industrial uses.

The World Bank's involvement in the TFAP is a revealing and shocking indicator of the gap between rhetoric and reality in the Bank's self-proclaimed greening.

Already by 1986, a number of Third World NGOs such as Friends of the Earth in Brazil and the Malaysia-based Asia-Pacific Peoples' Environmental Network (AP-PEN) were publishing urgent protests maintaining that the TFAP was basically a fraud. It had been prepared, they alleged, without any significant consultation or involvement of NGOs and local communities in tropical forest countries. Worse, it appeared mainly to be a plan to promote traditional, export-oriented timber industry investments camouflaged by small components for environmental purposes. Third World NGOs were particularly outraged because the plan seemed to blame the poor for the destruction of tropical forests while promoting investments to open up large areas of pristine forest for exploitation, rebaptizing such projects as "sustainable forestry."

WRI [EDITOR's NOTE: the World Resources Institute, a Washington-based environmental think-tank] attempted belatedly to address many of the criticisms, but following the Bank's commitment in 1987 to increased funding of the TFAP, the plan gathered seemingly unstoppable momentum to become the most ambitious environmental aid program ever conceived. By the end of 1989, 62 developing nations had requested forestry-sector aid under the TFAP and 21 nations had already completed forestry-sector reviews (pre-investment surveys), with the World Bank as the leader or a major participant in eight. The plan is well on track to mobilize billions of dollars for forestry projects in every country in the world with remaining tropical forests.

Environmentalists around the world now fear that an ecological Frankenstein has been unleashed. The World Rainforest Movement—a Malaysia-based coalition of mainly Third World NGOs—prepared a critique . . . of six completed national TFAP plans—for Peru, Guyana, Cameroon, Tanzania, Nepal, and Colombia. The study concluded that in most of these cases the forestry investments proposed would dramatically accelerate the rate of deforestation through increased logging; in no instance was it found that these investments would actually reduce deforestation. . . .

One of the first TFAP projects to be funded by the Bank (with a sizable contribution from West Germany) is a $23 million forestry and fisheries scheme for Guinea. Yet, as World Wildlife Fund International discovered in late 1989, the so-called "forest management and protection" component of the project actually amounts to a deforestation scheme: the Bank's money will help support the construction of 45 miles of roads in or around two humid forest reserves totalling 150,000 hectares, of which some 106,000 hectares are still pristine rainforest. Worse, hidden in the fine print of the "management and protection" section of the Bank's project document is its real thrust: two-thirds of the remaining 106,000 hectares of rainforest are to be opened for timber production. As a result of these findings, in late 1989 WWF [EDITOR's NOTE: World Wildlife Fund] mobilized eight national WWF organizations in North America and Europe to lobby the World Bank's executive board against the project. WWF's efforts were too late, however, and the project was approved in January, though minutes of the board meeting reveal the bewilderment of some of the Bank's executive directors.

They queried Bank staff on the WWF allegations, which were mostly repetitions of what the Bank's own project appraisal report had stated. The Bank staff replied that deforestation would proceed uncontrolled without the project and that with the project logging could be controlled within "sustainable" limits.

This rationale—that the environmental situation would be worse without Bank intervention—is a particularly specious one, and has been proffered in the past to justify a number of the worst Bank-financed environmental disasters, including rainforest colonization schemes in Brazil and Indonesia. On the contrary, it is often the large infusions of foreign exchange, rapid construction of infrastructure such as roads, and an international stamp of approval provided by the Bank that ensure that a government's environmentally destructive plans become a physical reality within the shortest time possible.

. . .

Forced Resettlement.   No single Bank activity has greater immediate social impact than the physical destruction or disruption of rural ecosystems caused by large infrastructure projects such as hydroelectric dams, power plants, and coal mines. The forced resettlement of populations that results from these projects occurs on an enormous scale: as of January [1990] an estimated 1.5 million people were being forcibly displaced by over 70 ongoing Bank projects, and proposed projects currently under consideration may displace another 1.5 million.

The World Bank policy on forced resettlement was established in 1980, predating most other Bank environmental directives. It is the most important of the Bank's environmental policies that deal with the social consequences of ecological destruction. Bank policy requires that when it finances a project that will forcibly displace populations, a resettlement and rehabilitation plan must be prepared and implemented by the borrower in a timely fashion, such that the affected population is at least put in a position where it is no worse off and preferably better off than before. . . .

If anything, since 1987 the situation has worsened. . . . NGOs in the North and South have brought to light more and more examples of the Bank's failure to remedy the plight of populations displaced by ongoing projects, some of which are destitute or on the brink of civil disorder. In Java, where some 20,000 people have been displaced by the Bank-financed Kedung Ombo dam, more than 5,000 "development refugees" still refused to move in early 1990, after the reservoir filled, because there had been no consultations with them regarding resettlement. Rather than ensure that a fair resettlement and rehabilitation plan was being implemented, for years the Bank accepted the Indonesian government's assertion that most of the people affected by the project were volunteering to become rainforest colonists in transmigration (resettlement) sites hundreds of miles away in Indonesia's outer islands. The Bank ignored evidence of coercion and intimidation by project authorities, as reported in numerous newspaper articles and in a letter of protest from a leading Indonesian NGO to the Bank's Jakarta office in 1987.

. . .

Since most of the projects that forcibly displace populations are in the energy sector—large dams and coal-fired power plants, for example—much forced resettlement could be avoided by investments in energy alternatives that are less disruptive environmentally. . . . The Bank again has made rhetorical commitments to increased energy efficiency and conservation investments, but the actual changes have been insignificant. For example, in 1988 and 1989, less than 2 percent of World Bank energy and industry loans were for projects that included end-use efficiency as a component; indeed, the proportion of conservation and efficiency loans in the Bank's energy-sector portfolio was actually higher in the mid-1980s than in more recent years. This gap between rhetoric and reality is one more example that points to deeper institutional problems at the Bank.

The Bank Beset By Contradictions

The Bank's efforts to respond to international pressures for environmental reform have exposed a whole series of contradictions that, when demands on the Bank and multilateral financial institutions were more modest, remained relatively dormant and unexposed. Some of these contradictions are largely internal, others result from conflicting pressures put on the Bank by donors and borrowers, and others appear to be rooted in the nature of the multilateral system itself—especially in its lack of accountability—as well as in current patterns of global economic development, which are often at odds with the requirements of global ecological sustainability.

Internal Contradictions.   The first order of Bank contradictions are internal in origin and include a number of classic bureaucratic syndromes, such as a longstanding lack of coordination between the Bank's operations staff, who identify and prepare loans, and its policy, planning and research divisions. The 1987 environmental reforms took place in the context of a larger Bank-wide reorganization that only exacerbated this dichotomy. About half of the new environment staff (approximately 30 positions) was placed in a newly created central Environment Department, but the quality control duties that this department's predecessor had exercised over operations were assigned to four new environmental assessment units that are hampered by limited budgets and staff.

Real power is concentrated even more than in the past in country directors and project officers who actually prepare loans and who have been granted greater autonomy and authority. Thus at times during the past three years the Environment Department has taken on the appearance of a vast paper mill, while the real business of the Bank continued as if on a separate planet called Operations. . . .

The Bank's environmental effectiveness has also been undermined in some cases by the Bank's senior management, which on occasion has overruled the recommendations of its environmental staff. . . . The lack of internal coordination that inhibits environmental effectiveness is compounded by pressures on operations staff to move money rapidly. Bank staff advance their careers by building up large loan portfolios and keeping them moving, not by slowing down the project pipeline to ensure environmental and social quality. Bank-lending priorities appear more understandable in this light. The bias toward large energy infrastructure projects, for instance, is not irrational given that efficiency and conservation loans are harder to prepare and move less money. Vested interests and government bureaucracies in borrowing countries prefer big dam projects for the same reasons. . . .

To some degree the Bank's internal contradictions are amenable to institutional reform. Already more budgetary and staff resources are being channelled into the environmental assessment divisions, which are best placed to influence operations. And with sufficient political will, greater progress could be made in integrating environmental studies and policies into country economic and sector work. But to change priorities from moving money quickly to emphasizing the environmental and social quality of projects requires more than greater political will on the part of senior management. Indeed, such efforts, though they would result in marginal improvements, would probably also have the effect of exacerbating the Bank's environmental schizophrenia. This is because of deeper problems that are linked to fundamentally contradictory pressures exerted on the Bank by its member countries.

Contradictory Pressure of Member Governments. The Bank is subject to a number of simultaneous and contradictory pressures from both its developed and Third World members—pressures that, with respect to the Bank's environmental performance, result not only in contradictory actions but in institutional paralysis.

The pressure to lend more money, for instance, is not only the consequence of the propensity of large bureaucracies to measure success in terms of their own growth and expansion. It also comes from the Bank's major donors, and especially from U.S. efforts to involve the Bank and other multilateral institutions in resolving the Third World debt crisis. . . .

In this regard, there has been a certain convergence of interest between the Bank and the U.S. government. The overall effect of this convergence, however, has been to exacerbate the Bank's tendency to ignore the environmental consequences of its lending. Some of the conditions associated with structural-adjustment loans—such as the reduction of domestic expenditures, currency devaluation, and the increase of exports—often have a negative impact on the environment. They prompt governments to reduce domestic conservation investments and they heighten pressures to exploit resources in an unsustainable fashion in order to increase exports. The Bank has recognized in theory the environmental implications of its adjustment lending, but the exclusion of substantive environmental analysis in its most important economic planning exercises, such as country strategy papers, bodes ill for practical attempts to incorporate environmental concerns into such lending in any systematic way. . . .

Of course borrower countries, too, bear much of the responsibility for the environmental quality of Bank-financed projects. The Bank encounters considerable
resistance from some borrowing nations to conditionality of any kind, and particularly to environmental conditionality, which is viewed as both an added cost and
as an imposition of the industrialized North's priorities on the South. . . . Not
surprisingly, the bigger borrowing nations such as Brazil, India, and Indonesia,
which have been subjected to international criticism by the MDB campaign, have
been the most vocal opponents of environmental conditionality.

The Bank is acutely sensitive to these pressures, and particularly with respect to
its larger borrowers, is reluctant to endanger its "dialogue with host countries" by
overly zealous insistence on environmental policies. . . . It is a mistake, however,
to assume that either the governments or the societies of developing nations are
monolithic. In many governments there are officials who advocate environmental
and social measures that equal or even exceed the Bank's standards. And in the
civil societies of these countries there can be found even stronger advocates
among environmental and social movements, and among disadvantaged minorities such as tribal peoples in India, who suffer a disproportionate share of the adverse effects of large projects and enjoy few of the benefits. Rarely, however, are
these advocates able to mount a serious enough challenge to the powerful vested
interests inside and outside the government who are often the chief beneficiaries
of these projects. . . .

Contradictions of the Multilateral System.   While the conflicting pressures of
member nations may sometimes hamper the Bank's environmental protection efforts, there is another explanation for its conduct that relates to the fundamental
character of the Bank and of the multilateral system generally. The Bank, like
other multilateral institutions, is not directly accountable to civil society within
borrower and donor countries, or even fully to the representatives of its member
nations. Moreover, the Bank heavily restricts access to information concerning
details of its activities. These practices make scrutiny of the World Bank and other
MDBs—which use *public* monies to lend for *public* purposes—extremely difficult, and place serious constraints on efforts to reform them.

The official avenue of accountability in the World Bank, other MDBs, and the
IMF lies with the board of executive directors for each of these institutions. The
World Bank's charter, for example, states that "all powers of the Bank are vested in
the Board of Governors" who are usually the finance ministers or central bank
presidents of each of the Bank's 152 member nations—and most of the powers of
the governors are delegated on a day-to-day basis to the Bank's 22 executive directors. The directors approve every loan and every major policy change.

Over the past decade, the executive directors—particularly those representing
the United States and a number of European nations—have come under increasing pressure by environmental groups in their countries not only to promote institutional reforms but also to monitor and review individual projects and lending programs of the Bank more closely. But the Bank's management withholds

from the executive board access to most of the documents produced by Bank staff in the identification and preparation of projects. Although a project may take over two years to prepare, the directors are given access to appraisal reports on average only two weeks before they are asked to approve a project. . . .

The lack of access to project documents has serious practical consequences. It means that the principal recourse for detailed information on projects are oral briefings by Bank staff. However, there is no assurance that these briefings will include any significant discussion of project risks and problems that can be found in the more candid documents in the project files—information that is obviously necessary for any critical assessment. These briefings often turn out to be little more than confidence-building sessions in which the directors nervously seek reassurances that the projects are under control, and the Bank staff gladly provides them. . . .

If there is a relative lack of Bank accountability to its directors, there is an almost total absence of accountability to the people affected by its projects and to the public in member countries. The Bank withholds all written documents prepared in the planning of projects from the public in both borrower and donor countries, despite the fact that the Bank has been insisting over the past three years that it recognizes the importance of involving local NGOs and community groups in its development activities. . . . Ultimately, the World Bank and other multilateral development institutions justify their lack of transparency and accountability on the grounds that the sole legitimate interlocutor with whom they deal is the nation-state. The Bank, in fact, restricts the channels of communication even further. According to its charter, "Each member shall deal with the Bank only through its treasury, central bank, stabilization fund or other similar fiscal agency, and the Bank shall deal with members only by or through the same agencies." This leaves little room for the substantive involvement of nongovernmental entities of any kind. . . .

The World Bank and other multilateral international institutions are caught in a double bind. The Bank has pledged to incorporate environmental with developmental concerns, but it is constrained to treat these as technical, apolitical matters. Its modus operandi is by definition only with sovereign governments and certain ministries within those governments, but the most crucial environmental challenges are political and social in nature, and call for planning and decision making that give much more legitimacy and empowerment to nongovernmental, civil society.

Contradictions of Global Economic Development. Finally, the World Bank's environmental quandaries are also a reflection of contradictions rooted in the Bank's attempts to reconcile ecological sustainability with global economic development. The most blatant of these contradictions relates to the very slogan that not only the World Bank but most international institutions and governments have adopted as the solution to the environmental dilemma: "sustainable development." The term was popularized by some NGOs in the early 1980s and received multilateral canonization in the 1987 Brundtland Report, the widely cited study by the U.N.'s World Commission on Environment and Development.

Sustainable development is a kind of mother-and-apple-pie formulation that everyone can agree on. The Brundtland Commission defines it as "meet[ing] the needs of the present without compromising the ability of future generations to meet their own needs." Critical to achieving sustainable development, the Commission argues, is the revival of economic growth in both the developing and the industrialized nations. Growth, it maintains, is essential to the alleviation of poverty, which intensifies pressures on the environment and as such is a major cause of environmental degradation in many Third World countries.

The World Bank and other multilateral institutions have enthusiastically embraced this aspect of sustainable development while virtually ignoring many of the Commission's other "strategic imperatives," such as the need to conserve and enhance the resource base and the need to change the quality of growth to one that is less material and energy intensive. The Bank's emphasis on expanding the export capacities of recipient countries thus may be consistent with its own conception of sustainable development, but it is clearly at odds with the requirements of ecological sustainability. . . .

What the World Bank and, for that matter, the Brundtland Commission fail to recognize is that fundamental political, economic, and social changes are required to cope effectively with the intensive use of natural resources that is responsible for so much environmental degradation. Unequal access to natural resources, for instance, must be overcome if per capita pressures on the environment are to be alleviated. Among other things, this means redressing skewed land distribution patterns that, by forcing populations to overwork the land, have resulted in deforestation, soil erosion, siltation of waterways, and other serious environmental problems. Similarly, the Third World and industrialized economies must shift to patterns of development that are less material and energy intensive in order to alleviate future burdens on the environment. These are matters that cannot be solved by economic or technical fixes, but require making difficult political decisions. The formulation and implementation of these decisions will require widespread public support and participation in both the North and South.

. . .

Beyond the Contradictions

When the World Bank announced its environmental reforms in 1987, nongovernmental groups seriously underestimated the barriers to their implementation. Yet while these barriers are formidable, they are not necessarily insurmountable. The Bank's institutional schizophrenia can be remedied, but only if it is forced to choose its identity. If the Bank is truly to be a vehicle of sustainable development, it must place greater emphasis on project quality over the quick disbursement of money. . . . Likewise, if the Bank is to be a democratic institution committed to greater involvement of local people in development planning, it cannot continue to bar the public from access to basic project information. Institutional tinkering is not sufficient for resolving these contradictions; instead, the Bank must be pressured to sort out conflicting priorities.

The growing green movements in the North and South can play a critical role in pushing the Bank to make some of these harder choices. NGOs, for instance, can and must press for stricter Bank observance of existing environmental policies, for more far-sighted Bank leadership in the formulation of debt-forgiveness strategies, for greater transparency and accountability on the part of the Bank, and for greater substantive participation in the Bank's deliberations of those affected by its projects in the Third World. . . .

WILFREDO CRUZ, MOHAN MUNASINGHE,
& JEREMY WARFORD

22

Greening Development:
Environmental Implications of
Economic Policies

Until recently, multilateral lending agencies and the development community at large have tended to address environmental concerns only at the relatively narrow project level. At the World Bank, for instance, the focus was on ensuring that particular development projects did not harm the environment rather than on the broader political and economic context in which environmental issues arise. The importance of that context is becoming increasingly clear, however, with the growing emphasis on sustainable development (as opposed to growth per se) and the far-reaching policy reforms that many developing countries have adopted in recent years.

The emphasis on sustainable development has encouraged a broader view of environmental concerns because it entails three closely related goals: economic efficiency, social stability, and environmental protection. At the same time, fundamental changes in economic policy have highlighted the role such policy plays in environmental outcomes. These changes include programs to address macroeconomic problems (international trade, government budgets, private investment,

Originally published in *Environment* 38, no. 5 (June 1996):6–11 and 31–38. Reprinted with permission of the World Bank.

wages, and income distribution) and broad sectoral issues (agricultural productivity, industrial protection, and energy use).[1] Although these programs are not intended to affect environmental quality, they can easily do so—for good or bad.

Because the linkages between economy-wide policies and the environment are not well understood, the World Bank recently conducted case studies related to this question in 11 developing countries. The results of those studies form the core of this article.[2] [EDITOR'S NOTE: Five of the eleven cases are included here; other cases focused on agricultural land use in Ghana, air quality in Mexico, water resource depletion in Morocco, industrial pollution in Poland, energy use in Sri Lanka, and wildlife management in Zimbabwe.] This highly empirical, country-specific approach was chosen because of the complexities and uncertainties involved: In the simpler cases, the direction of the environmental impact was fairly clear, but determining its magnitude required careful empirical analysis. In the more complex cases, however, even the direction of the impact was ambiguous beforehand.

. . . The case studies employ a variety of analytical methods to illustrate the different ways one may approach the environmental implications of economy-wide reforms. These methods range from simply tracing the links between economic incentives and resource use by means of direct observation to complex modeling of policies and their environmental effects. All the studies, however, required identifying key environmental concerns and relating them to important sectoral and macroeconomic reforms. The analysis underscores the difficulties of developing a general methodology for tracing the environmental effects of policy reform but also offers evidence that careful, case-specific empirical work can help in finding better ways to deal with these effects.

Establishing linkages between economy-wide policies and the environment has two main benefits: Focusing attention on the positive impacts of such policies (both economic and environmental) helps to build consensus for reform and improves cooperation among environmental and economic policymakers. Focusing attention on the potential negative impacts on the environment highlights the need to examine policies with great care.

The specific findings of the case studies may be summarized in five points:

Removal of price distortions, promotion of market incentives, and relaxation of other constraints will generally lead to both economic and environmental gains. For example, reforms that improve industrial or energy efficiency tend to reduce both economic waste and environmental pollution. Similarly, improving land tenure rights and access to financial and social services not only yields economic gains but also promotes better environmental stewardship.

Adverse side effects occur when economy-wide reforms are undertaken and other policy, market, or institutional imperfections remain unaddressed. Environmentally detrimental policy distortions include export promotion and trade liberalization that increase the profitability of exporting natural resources, particularly if those resources are underpriced or subsidized. Market failures occur where prices do not adequately reflect external effects such as pollution. Institutional constraints include poor accountability in state-owned enterprises, inadequately defined property rights, and weak financial intermediation, all of which lower the incentives for sustainable resource management. The remedy generally lies not in the reversal of the original reforms but in the implementation of additional measures (both economic and noneconomic) to remove the difficulties.

Measures aimed at restoring macroeconomic stability will generally yield environmental benefits because instability undermines sustainable resource use. Stability encourages decision makers at all levels to take a longer term view, and lower inflation rates give clearer price signals and lead to better investment decisions. These are essential prerequisites for environmental sustainability.

The stabilization process may also have adverse short-term impacts on the environment. While reductions in government spending are generally appropriate in developing countries, the cutbacks should be carefully targeted to avoid compromising environmental protection. It is also important that the cutbacks not increase poverty and unemployment, which will only aggravate existing pressures on fragile and open-access natural resources.

Economy-wide policies will have additional long-term effects on the environment through changes in employment and income distribution. On the positive side, the economic growth brought about by the reforms will lower the poverty rate and thus lessen poor people's need to exploit fragile natural resources simply to survive. On the negative side, this growth will increase the overall demand for natural resources. To accommodate this in an environmentally benign way, it will be necessary to increase efficiency and reduce waste by valuing these resources properly.

China

The study of China focuses on sustainable agriculture in the context of rapid evolution in the national economy. Dramatic changes have taken place in the relative prices of relevant farm inputs, including a reduction in the subsidies for chemical fertilizers and pesticides and increases in the price of energy and the opportunity cost of labor. Changes in other government policies have also affected environmental behavior via their influence on prices. Among these are the lifting of quotas for key agricultural products, substantial reductions in state intervention in product markets, and changes in government policies toward eco-farming and land tenure.

Looking at farm-level data from communities in Jiangsen Province, it is clear that a vast range of variables determine environmental behavior. This region has been experiencing rapid industrial development, and the opportunity cost of labor has increased significantly in recent years. This trend in labor cost discourages the application of crop and animal residues to the land, which is a labor intensive activity. Increases in commercial energy prices may also result in the diversion of biomass for fuel, thereby stimulating demand for chemical fertilizer. In assessing the environmental policy implications of changes in the prices of key inputs, the study makes it clear that "second best" problems abound.[3] For example, one major agricultural input, namely land, is still subject to state control and, in some communities, arbitrariness in its allocation. In such circumstances, the uncertainty about land tenure generated by this system has encouraged short-run profit maximization and exploitation of land at the expense of sustainable agricultural production.

Farmers' reactions to changes in strategic prices and other policy variables suggest how they might react to various reforms in the future. Based on the assumption that farmers are profit maximizers, models are being designed to simulate their reactions to various changes in input and output prices, where the options include crop switching, reducing the scale of operations, changing the mix of inputs, or going out of business. The environmental implications of these reactions, and therefore the need for possible remedial action, will be assessed subsequently.

Policies are rapidly evolving, but the relevance of this study, location-specific though it is, lies in its illustrating the leverage macro-level and sectoral policies exert on farmers' behavior and thus the environment. This study also suggests that while market liberalization is a necessary condition to encourage farmers to operate efficiently and thereby to ensure that neither producers nor consumers use resources wastefully, it is far from a sufficient condition for sound environmental management. Market reforms need to be accompanied by various forms of direct public intervention, such as education and training, to familiarize farmers with the latest techniques. However, where modern techniques and changes in the relative prices of key agricultural inputs yield unsatisfactory environmental by-products, the study suggests that the government should be prepared to step in and compensate for market failure. Above all, it demonstrates that policy reform in the environmental area, while urgent, has to parallel the overall trends in market liberalization in the Chinese economy.

Costa Rica

While the other case studies described in this article generally adopt a partial equilibrium approach in addressing the environmental consequences of economic policy, it is clear that general equilibrium effects are important.[4] Indeed, failure to protect the environment may have serious feedbacks that constrain economic development. To capture this whole-economy perspective, the Costa Rica case study used a computable general equilibrium (CGE) model.[5] The model pays special attention to deforestation, which is occurring rapidly in Costa Rica and which, together with soil erosion, has been identified as the country's main environmental problem. Even conservative estimates of the remaining forest cover indicate that Costa Rica's commercial forests will be exhausted within the next five years if current deforestation rates continue.

To evaluate how sectoral and economy-wide policies can help control deforestation, the model highlights the economic activities and factors affecting deforestation in Costa Rica. The model differs from standard approaches in two important respects. First, it can simulate the effect of introducing property rights to forest resources, thus allowing the private valuation of future returns to contribute to sustainable management. Second, it includes markets for logs and cleared land, reflecting the tendencies of loggers to strip forests and squatters to clear land for agricultural production when economic conditions favor these activities.

The simulations support the conventional view that establishing property rights tends to decrease deforestation because such fights allow economic agents to capture the benefits of reducing the damage to residual stands. At an interest rate of 10 percent, for instance, deforestation is reduced to 5 percent of its base level as both loggers and squatters internalize its costs. Significant reductions in deforestation occur even when the assumed logging damage is much lower. As in partial equilibrium models, the interest rate is a crucial variable: Higher rates promote deforestation while lower rates contribute to conservation.

Beyond augmenting the analysis of partial equilibrium models, the CGE model illustrates how the direct effects of forestry policies are modified by the indirect effects arising from intersectoral linkages. For example, partial equilibrium analysis predicts that an increase in the price of standing timber will reduce logging. The CGE model, however, shows that although deforestation from logging does decline, total deforestation increases because the contraction of the logging sector causes more land to be cleared for agriculture. The importance of these indirect effects is also apparent in the analysis of economy-wide policy changes, such as an increase in the wage rate. If the wage of unskilled labor is increased due to, say, minimum wage legislation, partial equilibrium models would predict less deforestation. The CGE model used in this study predicts the opposite, however: Although logging declines due to increased labor costs, this is more than offset by a shift from the industrial sector (where minimum wage legislation has the greatest impact) to agriculture. Each of these examples suggests the importance of promoting general economic growth while pursuing sectoral reforms.

. . .

Indonesia

Indonesia's experience with trade liberalization shows that while economic policy reforms can promote less pollution-intensive industrialization, the accompanying expansion of industrial activity points to the urgent need for regulation to complement the reforms. This case study first separated the industrial pollution in Indonesia into three components: the pollution intensity of output; its location relative to human populations and fragile ecosystems; and the increase in the absolute levels of pollutants due to the expansion of output. Using industrial data from 1975 to 1989, the likely impact of continuing reforms on the scale and structure of pollution was then projected to the year 2020.

Next, the sectoral characteristics of pollution-intensive activities were examined, using indicators of air, water, and toxic pollution per unit of output (i.e., pollution intensities). Materials-processing industries (food products, tobacco, pulp and paper, basic industrial chemicals, refined petroleum, and iron and steel) were generally found to score higher on these indicators than assembly-type industries (garments, furniture and fixtures, printing and publishing, metal products, office and computing machinery, and transport equipment). For example, almost 80 percent of the top polluters (based on suspended particulate emissions) were from materials-processing industries.

Lastly, the impact of liberalization on all three components of pollution and on the pollution characteristics of different industrial sectors was assessed. The analysis showed that liberalization in the 1980s promoted a surge in relatively clean assembly processes, reversing the 1970s pattern of more rapid growth in "dirty" materials-processing sectors. Projections indicate that basic processing industries' share in total industrial output will fall from 72 percent in 1993 to about 60 percent by 2020. In addition, liberalization efforts lowered the growth rate of the dirty sectors on the densely populated island of Java (relative to the growth rates elsewhere in the country), thereby reducing the health and productivity impact of pollution on population centers.

While reforms helped improve both the composition and the location of industrial production, growth has been so rapid that the scale effect dominates current and future trends in industrial pollution. Industry has responded very strongly to liberalization. The volume of manufacturing output doubled every six to seven years during the 1970s and 1980s, so that by 1990 manufacturing value added was about eight times its 1970 level in real terms. This accelerated growth, while clearly desirable for reducing poverty, has nevertheless undermined the positive impacts of liberalization on pollution intensity and industrial dispersion. Thus, efforts to augment the reform program with institutional support and regulation will clearly be required if Indonesia is to avoid severe pollution problems in the future.

. . .

The Philippines

The Philippines case study evaluates the policy determinants of the long-term changes in rural poverty and unemployment that have motivated increasing migration from the lowlands to the highlands. This has led to the conversion of forest lands to unsustainable agriculture, a key contributor to deforestation. While the government's inability to manage forest resources is an important direct cause of deforestation, there is increasing recognition that economic policies, both sectoral and economy-wide, also significantly contribute to the problem. These policies take the form of direct sectoral interventions through agricultural taxation, price controls, subsidies, and marketing restrictions. They could also work indirectly through exchange rate policies and industrial protection.

In general, these policies have tended to penalize lowland agriculture in favor of the industrial sector. On the one hand, this has resulted in the limited ability of the agricultural sector to productively employ a growing labor force. On the other hand, trade and exchange rate policies have made the industrial sector inefficient, and increasingly difficult economic conditions during the late 1970s and early 1980s further reduced its capacity to absorb surplus labor from the agricultural sector. The net result has been growing unemployment and worsening rural poverty, which provide the "push" for migration to forest lands. For the last two decades, deforestation in the Philippines has exceeded 150,000 hectares per year, often with devastating consequences: Between 1980 and 1987, for example, cultivated areas on land with slopes of 18–30 percent increased by more than 37,000 hectares annually.

Government interventions for key crops are evaluated to illustrate the role of commodity-specific policies in altering the incentives for lowland compared with upland agriculture. Policies on rice production, which dominates lowland agriculture, have been governed more by the goal of maintaining low prices for consumers than of assuring price incentives for producers. Corn and coconut production, which together make up the majority of agriculture on steep lands, have also experienced inappropriate government intervention. Corn cultivation has generally been encouraged while that of coconuts (a more environmentally stable crop) has been excessively taxed. Corn, for example, has received favorable protection while the copra export prohibition and the coconut levy kept producer prices more than 25 percent below world prices. The net effect of these policies has been to reduce the relative attractiveness of lowland agriculture and to encourage upland farming households to shift from coconut farming to more environmentally demanding corn production.

In addition to commodity-specific policies, trade and exchange rate policies have adversely affected lowland agriculture through an inherent bias in favor of urban consumers and the industrial sector. The agricultural sector was implicitly taxed (by having to pay above-market prices for inputs) by an average of about 20 percent for most of the 1970s and early 1980s. Because the industrial sector did not provide an alternative source of growth, poverty in general has worsened and rural incomes in particular have suffered.

The study used an econometric model to determine how migration patterns are affected by both economic and environmental factors, including income in lowland agriculture, accessibility of forests, and property rights in forest areas. Provincial migration levels from lowland to highland areas were obtained from 1990 census data. The particular framework utilized represents each migration decision as a choice among many discrete alternatives.

The results indicate the importance of economy-wide incentives in motivating upland migration: A lower incidence of poverty and higher incomes in forest areas lead to greater migration. Thus, improvements in lowland farm incomes would significantly reduce the influx into those areas. Accessibility and lack of effective property rights also encourage migration to forest areas. These results demonstrate that while forestry-specific conservation programs are needed, economy-wide policy reforms to improve lowland agricultural conditions are just as important in arresting deforestation in the Philippines.

. . .

Tunisia

In Tunisia, the government's goal of increasing self-sufficiency in livestock products and the affordability of these products for its citizens has led to a web of pricing and subsidy interventions in the livestock sector. The environmental consequence of these measures, namely the degradation of Tunisia's rangelands, has rarely been a central consideration, however. A variety of subsidies has promoted the intensification of livestock production in certain regions of Tunisia, while in other regions government policies have encouraged the maintenance of herd sizes that exceed the country's carrying capacity. Particularly during dry years, subsidized feed imports have provided a substitute for grazing and averted the large declines in animal numbers that usually stem from droughts. The failure of livestock numbers to respond to pasture conditions, however, has contributed to significant degradation of Tunisia's rangeland. This has direct effects on livestock production and longer term, indirect implications for the entire agricultural sector. While important efforts at pasture improvement and reforestation are under way, the positive impact of these and other measures is often undermined by subsidy and pricing policies that fail to consider or respond to environmental signals.

Livestock policies have had different environmental impacts in the northern, central, and southern regions of the country. In the north, government subsidies for feed, irrigation, and fertilizer have promoted the intensification of livestock production and its integration with growing feed crops. In the central part of the country, where similar policies have been pursued, sheep herds have increased without a commensurate increase in feed production. Rangelands here and in southern Tunisia appear to be deteriorating, a process that is exacerbated by the maintenance of large herds in drought years through subsidized feed imports and mild protection of domestic mutton production. (Following the liberalization of mutton prices in the late 1970s, it became profitable to feed sheep more concentrates, but this has not been sufficient to alleviate the pressure on Tunisia's central rangelands.) In addition, government policy encouraged the conversion of marginal lands from pastures to cereal (mainly barley) production. This not only fostered land degradation through the removal of permanent cover but also took some of the best pasture lands out of livestock production.

Thus, while subsidies may have had a beneficial effect in northern (and perhaps parts of central) Tunisia, their impact on rangelands overall has been negative. The failure of policies to distinguish between bioclimatic zones has contributed to the severe degradation of the country's range resources. The government's intention was to protect herders in the southern and central regions from wide income fluctuations. Although this short-term objective has been accomplished, no durable solution to the problems it creates for the relatively fragile ecosystem has been found. Moreover, the increased desertification and soil erosion will have a definite impact on the rest of the economy, lowering agricultural productivity and damaging some types of infrastructure (e.g., the siltation of reservoirs through increased erosion). The challenge is to introduce less environmentally destructive means to achieve the social objectives.

The sweeping policy changes introduced since structural reforms began in 1986 will ultimately have an important impact on the ways in which livestock activities affect rangeland. Although the interactions among the new policies make it difficult to predict their full impact, certain developments seem probable. First, raising producer prices for beef will probably encourage growth in the cattle herd after years of stagnation. This growth will initially be concentrated in the north, where feed resources are more abundant. Whether it will be possible to maintain fodder and barley production in the face of reduced subsidies for water and fertilizer is an open question, however. Second, in central Tunisia, the financial returns to sheep herding will probably decline with the elimination of subsidies on feed concentrates, and some shift to beef production can be expected. The impact of such a shift will depend on whether permanent cattle herds are maintained or the focus is on breeding calves (using seasonally available range resources) for sale to fattening operations in the north.

. . .

Summary

. . . While each study was relatively limited in scope (focusing on a particular environmental issue in a specific country), the connections between economy-wide policies and environmental concerns have far broader relevance. The issues of land degradation, deforestation, industrial pollution, energy efficiency, and water management are cropping up throughout the developing world, often at the same time. By determining the possible impacts of particular policies on the environment, these individual case studies can form a basis for the more comprehensive studies needed to address environment-development problems in actual situations.

PART FIVE

The Sustainable Development Debate

Clearly, effective responses to global environmental problems demand both international cooperation and institutional reform. As previous sections have indicated, these are substantial challenges. The prevailing structures and practices of the international system make attainment of these goals difficult, and they cannot be divorced from the larger political, economic, and cultural struggles that infuse world politics.

It would be a mistake, however, to study global environmental politics solely in terms of international treaties and institutional change. Perspectives on the essence of the global environmental problematique have changed in important ways. Few would argue that ideas alone have the power to change history. But there is no doubt that paradigms—bundles of fundamental ideas and beliefs—shape the strategies and goals of actors in important ways. They influence how actors understand their interests, how policies are formulated, how resources are allocated, and which actors and institutions are empowered to make the critical decisions that affect global environmental quality.[1]

One powerful but controversial new paradigm that emerged during the 1980s is the idea of sustainable development. As previously discussed, one of the central controversies at Stockholm was the debate over whether economic growth and development are inherently destructive to the environment. This question revealed sharp cleavages between governments of the industrialized North and the developing South, as well as sharp divisions between growth-oriented governments in general and nongovernmental actors concerned about the negative consequences of continually expanding economic activity.

The concept of sustainable development appeals to many people because it holds out the promise of reconciling these divergent views. Sustainable development approaches are predicated on the premises that poverty and economic stagnation are themselves environmentally destructive and that all forms of economic organization and activity are not equal in their environmental impact. If these premises are true, then it might be possible to design environment-friendly forms of production and exchange that simultaneously facilitate economic development, alleviate the pressures of poverty, and minimize environmental damage. Such forms of production and exchange might be aimed at "development without growth"—that is, improvement in the quality of people's lives without an increase in the aggregate level of economic activity.[2] Or they might be tailored to forms of economic growth that are more acceptable ecologically. Whatever the path advocated, reconciling the tension between ecology and economy is the central goal of sustainable development.

The most frequently cited definition of sustainable development is found in *Our Common Future*, an influential report published by the World Commission on Environment and Development. In 1983 the United Nations General Assembly charged the Commission—also known as the Brundtland Commission, after its chairperson, Norwegian Prime Minister Gro Harlem Brundtland—with devising a conceptual and practical "global agenda for change."[3] The Commission, which included representatives from twenty-two nations on five continents, conducted a series of hearings around the world before preparing its final report and presenting it to the General Assembly in 1987. The report had an enormous influence on the global environmental debate and played a key role in shaping the content and format of the 1992 Earth Summit.

According to the Brundtland Commission, sustainable development is "development that meets the needs of the present without compromising the ability of future generations to meet their own needs."[4] To meet the goal of achieving sustainable development, the Commission set forth a policy blueprint based on enhanced international cooperation, substantial changes in national policies, and a reoriented global economy. The report argues that the problem is not economic growth per se but the environmentally destructive character of many current activities and incentives. Economic growth remains vital, in the Commission's view, given the substantial impact of poverty on the environment. Thus the Commission combined its recommendations for ecologically sound forms of production and exchange with a call for renewed global growth to solve the problems of Third World poverty.

Some observers see the Commission's advocacy of these positions as inherently contradictory. The continued commitment to a basically unreformed global economic system is, in this view, the biggest impediment to true sustainability, rather than a prerequisite for managing environmental problems more effectively. In an editorial originally published in the British environmental journal *The Ecologist*, Larry Lohmann questions whether the Brundtland Commission has provided an agenda for change or simply a justification of business as usual. In Lohmann's view, the Brundtland proposals merely put a green face on current practices while perpetuating unequal relationships of power and wealth—both within individual countries and between the overdeveloped North and underdeveloped South.[5] Sustainable development, Lohmann asserts, is less threatening to powerful interests than other approaches to environmental policy.[6]

Sharachchandra Lélé provides a different but in some ways equally critical assessment of the concept of sustainable development. A comprehensive review of the burgeoning literature on sustainability leads Lélé to conclude that the concept lacks a clear, widely accepted definition. There are many different conceptions of sustainable development, not all of which endorse the Brundtland Commission's formulation. Lélé argues that because of the many frequently contradictory uses of the term, "sustainable development is in real danger of becoming a cliché . . . —a fashionable phrase that everyone pays homage to but nobody cares to define."

Like Lohmann, Lélé writes from the perspective of one who accepts the goal of meeting current needs without compromising the ability of future generations to meet their requirements. His quarrel is with several of the assumptions embedded in mainstream sustainable development thinking. These include a narrowly technical focus on the problem of poverty while ignoring its fundamentally sociopolitical roots; a neoclassical emphasis on economic growth as an end in itself, rather than a more precise specification of how to meet people's basic needs; and a lack of clarity about exactly what is to be sustained, for whom, and for how long. Definitions that begin instead with the ecological goal of sustaining the conditions for human life and well-being avoid some of these problems, in Lélé's view. But they suffer from an equally debilitating flaw: Too often, they stress the *ecological* conditions required for ecological sustainability but overlook the complex array of *social* conditions that are also required.

Lélé also worries that mainstream notions of sustainable development place an undue burden of structural and value adjustment on the South in order to facilitate the continuation of current consumption practices in the North. In his view, the problem of excessive Northern consumption poses fundamental challenges that are not being adequately addressed with the "managed-growth" model of sustainable development. The idea that the challenge lies primarily in the South is more a reflection of the power of some actors and institutions to set the global agenda than an accurate reflection of the true scope of the problem.

Lélé's concern for a *global* perspective on sustainability forces us to ask what sustainable societies might look like in both the North and the South. Here we face an irony: Although the focus tends to be on the South, the voices tend to be from the North. Rarely are the conceptualizations and concerns of people from the developing world heard or understood in the North. The World Resources Institute, a Northern NGO, initiated the 2050 Project to give voice to these perspectives and delineate common elements and divergence between how the North and South envision sustainability. The chapter

"Voices of the Developing World," by Tanvi Nagpal, provides insights into the common concerns manifested in different sociocultural contexts. People consulted by Nagpal in forty-seven countries identified strikingly common components of sustainability—education, basic necessities, communal responsibility, living in harmony, participation in governance—but differed, sometimes dramatically, in their conceptions of what these terms mean in practice.

And what of sustainability in the North? One vision is presented by the Swiss-based Business Council for Sustainable Development, which takes up the Brundtland Commission's challenge for sustainable economic growth in the next article. The business leaders on the Council endorse the Commission's notion of sustainability and identify quantitative economic growth as the means to address environmental challenges and achieve equitable development. They emphasize efficiency in the context of open markets to improve existing systemic structures such as free trade and a modern industrial economy. This private-sector perspective suggests that existing economic practices should be greened rather than more fundamentally questioned or restructured.

Alan Durning, in contrast, sees a far deeper crisis of Northern unsustainability rooted in "the consumer society" and less amenable to a technical solution. High rates of population growth in the developing world are often identified as a major impediment to sustainability: Increasing numbers of poor people cannot afford the luxury of environmental stewardship as they struggle for survival. Yet for Durning, this depiction misses the larger part of the story—the consumption habits of the smaller but wealthier populations in the North. In a book published by the Worldwatch Institute, a Washington-based environmental think tank, Durning turns a critical eye to the acquisitive definition of the good life that undergirds high levels of material consumption. The key questions he addresses are: How much is enough? Can the earth survive a world where more is always assumed to be better? Are technical fixes enough, when the dominant trend is for Madison Avenue and the World Bank to market this acquisitive logic to developing countries as the proper model for their own development?

In conclusion, we might well ask whether the idea of sustainable development can break the North-South stalemate on environment and development that emerged at Stockholm. To some extent, it already has; there is no question that the power of the concept—its vision of harmonizing environmental quality and economic well-being—has fundamentally altered the global debate. The next and more difficult step is to clarify whether and how that vision can be attained. Whether the debate on sustainable development moves to this higher level or stalemates at a "contradiction in terms" hinges on our ability to meet several challenges.[7] We must redirect our gaze to encompass the system as a whole and not just the South; we must clarify and reconcile the goals that underlie radically different visions of a sustainable society; and we must broaden our vision to engage the contested issues of power, wealth, and authority that underlie current environmental problems.

Thinking Critically

1. In your judgment, does "sustainable development" represent a powerful synthesis of the twin needs for environmental protection and economic development? Or is it a contradiction in terms? Is sustainability compatible with a wide array of definitions of "development" or does it narrowly limit what development can mean?

2. How do you think the members of the Brundtland Commission would respond to the criticisms voiced by Lohmann and Lélé?

3. In your view, does the Nagpal essay suggest a common framework for sustainability across the diverse societies of the global South? For North as well as South? Is a concept such as sustainability universal, or is it inherently contingent on culture?

4. Is the North's pathway to sustainability more likely to follow the course envisioned by Durning or by the Business Council on Sustainable Development?

5. Are you an overconsumer, according to Durning's indicators of consumption? How much control do you have over your consumption? What aspects of your life would have to change in order for you to change from overconsumer to sustainer? What are the structural barriers to the sort of change Durning advocates?

Additional Reading

Sustainability and Economic Theory

Costanza, Robert, ed., *Ecological Economics: The Science and Management of Sustainability* (New York: Columbia University Press, 1991).

Daly, Herman E., and John B. Cobb Jr., *For the Common Good: Redirecting the Economy Toward Community, the Environment, and a Sustainable Future* (Boston: Beacon Press, 1989).

Sustainability in the South

Blaikie, Piers, *The Political Economy of Soil Erosion in Developing Countries* (London: Longman, 1985).

The Ecologist, *Whose Common Future? Reclaiming the Commons* (Philadelphia: New Society Publishers, 1993).

Goodman, David, and Michael Redclift, eds., *Environment and Development in Latin America: The Politics of Sustainability* (Manchester, UK: Manchester University Press, 1991).

Redclift, Michael, *Sustainable Development: Exploring the Contradictions* (London: Methuen, 1987).

Sustainability in the North

Pirages, Dennis C., ed., *Building Sustainable Societies: A Blueprint for a Post-Industrial World* (Armonk, NY: M. E. Sharpe, 1996).
Sachs, Wolfgang, Reinhard Loske, and Manfred Linz, *Greening the North* (London: Zed Books, 1998).
Wackernagel, Mathis, and William Rees, *Our Ecological Footprint: Reducing Human Impact on the Earth*, (Philadelphia: New Society Publishers, 1995).

Internet Resources

United Nations Commission on Sustainable Development, *http://www.un.org/dpcsd/dsd/csd.htm*. Created in the wake of UNCED, the Commission is tasked with reviewing and promoting progress on sustainable development.
Norwegian Agenda 21, *http://www.grida.no/prog/norway/ungass/index.htm*. This site describes one government's activities toward the implementation of Agenda 21, the "action plan" endorsed by governments at UNCED.
United Nations Development Programme (UNDP), *http://www.undp.org*. UNDP's home page offers a wealth of information, reports, and indicators on "human development."
People and the Planet, *http://www.ecdpm.org/patp/index.html*. This is an on-line periodical publication sponsored by a combination of U.N. agencies, nongovernmental organizations, and the Swedish government. The contributors to *People and the Planet* seek to identify pathways "toward a sustainable future for healthy people living in a healthy world."
International Institute for Environment and Development, *http://www.iied.org*. This London-based nongovernmental organization seeks to promote sustainable patterns of world development, with particular attention to the global South.
Ecological Footprints of the Future, *http://www.ecdpm.org/patp/vol6/rees.html*. Professor William Rees of the University of British Columbia, Canada, discusses the concept of a society's "ecological footprint."
Tomorrow: Global Environment Business, *http://www.tomorrow-web.com*. An on-line publication about business and the environment, targeted at corporate leaders and business executives.

WORLD COMMISSION ON
ENVIRONMENT & DEVELOPMENT

23

Towards Sustainable Development

Sustainable development IS development that meets the needs of the present without compromising the ability of future generations to meet their own needs. It contains within it two key concepts:

- the concept of 'needs', in particular the essential needs of the world's poor, to which overriding priority should be given; and
- the idea of limitations imposed by the state of technology and social organization on the environment's ability to meet present and future needs.

Thus the goals of economic and social development must be defined in terms of sustainability in all countries—developed or developing, market-oriented or centrally planned. . . .

Development involves a progressive transformation of economy and society. A development path that is sustainable in a physical sense could theoretically be pursued even in a rigid social and political setting. But physical sustainability cannot be secured unless development policies pay attention to such considerations as changes in access to resources and in the distribution of costs and benefits. . . .

The Concept
of Sustainable Development

The satisfaction of human needs and aspirations is the major objective of development. The essential needs of vast numbers of people in developing countries—for food, clothing, shelter, jobs—are not being met, and beyond their basic needs these people have legitimate aspirations for an improved quality of life. A world in which poverty and inequity are endemic will always be prone to ecological and other crises. Sustainable development requires meeting the basic needs of all and extending to all the opportunity to satisfy their aspirations for a better life.

Living standards that go beyond the basic minimum are sustainable only if consumption standards everywhere have regard for long-term sustainability. Yet many of us live beyond the world's ecological means, for instance in our patterns of energy use. Perceived needs are socially and culturally determined, and sustainable development requires the promotion of values that encourage consumption standards that are within the bounds of the ecological possible and to which all can reasonably aspire.

Meeting essential needs depends in part on achieving full growth potential, and sustainable development clearly requires economic growth in places where such needs are not being met. Elsewhere, it can be consistent with economic growth, provided the content of growth reflects the broad principles of sustainability and non-exploitation of others. But growth by itself is not enough. High levels of productive activity and widespread poverty can coexist, and can endanger the environment. Hence sustainable development requires that societies meet human needs both by increasing productive potential and by ensuring equitable opportunities for all.

An expansion in numbers can increase the pressure on resources and slow the rise in living standards in areas where deprivation is widespread. Though the issue is not merely one of population size but of the distribution of resources, sustainable development can only be pursued if demographic developments are in harmony with the changing productive potential of the ecosystem.

A society may in many ways compromise its ability to meet the essential needs of its people in the future—by overexploiting resources, for example. The direction of technological developments may solve some immediate problems but lead to even greater ones. . . . At a minimum, sustainable development must not endanger the natural systems that support life on Earth: the atmosphere, the waters, the soils, and the living beings.

Growth has no set limits in terms of population or resource use beyond which lies ecological disaster. Different limits hold for the use of energy, materials, water, and land. Many of these will manifest themselves in the form of rising costs and diminishing returns, rather than in the form of any sudden loss of a resource base. The accumulation of knowledge and the development of technology can enhance the carrying capacity of the resource base. But ultimate limits there are, and sustainability requires that long before these are reached, the world must ensure equitable access to the constrained resource and reorient technological efforts to relieve the pressure.

Economic growth and development obviously involve changes in the physical ecosystem. Every ecosystem everywhere cannot be preserved intact. . . . In general, renewable resources like forests and fish stocks need not be depleted provided the rate of use is within the limits of regeneration and natural growth. But most renewable resources are part of a complex and interlinked ecosystem, and maximum sustainable yield must be defined after taking into account system-wide effects of exploitation.

As for non-renewable resources, like fossil fuels and minerals, their use reduces the stock available for future generations. But this does not mean that such resources should not be used. In general the rate of depletion should take into account the criticality of that resource, the availability of technologies for minimizing depletion, and the likelihood of substitutes being available. . . . Sustainable development requires that the rate of depletion of non-renewable resources should foreclose as few future options as possible.

Development tends to simplify ecosystems and to reduce their diversity of species. . . . The loss of plant and animal species can greatly limit the options of future generations; so sustainable development requires the conservation of plant and animal species.

So-called free goods like air and water are also resources. . . . Sustainable development requires that the adverse impacts on the quality of air, water, and other natural elements are minimized so as to sustain the ecosystem's overall integrity.

In essence, sustainable development is a process of change in which the exploitation of resources, the direction of investments, the orientation of technological development, and institutional change are all in harmony and enhance both current and future potential to meet human needs and aspirations.

Equity and the Common Interest

. . . How are individuals in the real world to be persuaded or made to act in the common interest? The answer lies partly in education, institutional development, and law enforcement. But many problems of resource depletion and environmental stress arise from disparities in economic and political power. An industry may get away with unacceptable levels of air and water pollution because the people who bear the brunt of it are poor and unable to complain effectively. . . .

Ecological interactions do not respect the boundaries of individual ownership and political jurisdiction. . . . Traditional social systems recognized some aspects of this interdependence and enforced community control over agricultural practices and traditional rights relating to water, forests, and land. This enforcement of the 'common interest' did not necessarily impede growth and expansion though it may have limited the acceptance and diffusion of technical innovations.

Local interdependence has, if anything, increased because of the technology used in modern agriculture and manufacturing. Yet with this surge of technical progress, the growing 'enclosure' of common lands, the erosion of common rights in forests and other resources, and the spread of commerce and production for the market, the responsibilities for decision making are being taken away from both groups and individuals. This shift is still under way in many developing countries.

It is not that there is one set of villains and another of victims. All would be better off if each person took into account the effect of his or her acts upon others. But each is unwilling to assume that others will behave in this socially desirable fashion, and hence all continue to pursue narrow self-interest. Communities or governments can compensate for this isolation through laws, education, taxes, subsidies, and other methods. . . . Most important, effective participation in decisionmaking processes by local communities can help them articulate and effectively enforce their common interest. . . .

The enforcement of common interest often suffers because areas of political jurisdictions and areas of impact do not coincide. . . . No supranational authority exists to resolve such issues, and the common interest can only be articulated through international cooperation.

In the same way, the ability of a government to control its national economy is reduced by growing international economic interactions. . . . If economic power and the benefits of trade were more equally distributed, common interests would be generally recognized. But the gains from trade are unequally distributed, and patterns of trade in, say, sugar affect not merely a local sugar-producing sector, but the economies and ecologies of the many developing countries that depend heavily on this product.

The search for common interest would be less difficult if all development and environment problems had solutions that would leave everyone better off. This is seldom the case, and there are usually winners and losers. Many problems arise from inequalities in access to resources. . . . 'Losers' in environment/development conflicts include those who suffer more than their fair share of the health, property, and ecosystem damage costs of pollution.

As a system approaches ecological limits, inequalities sharpen. Thus when a watershed deteriorates, poor farmers suffer more because they cannot afford the same anti-erosion measures as richer farmers. . . . Globally, wealthier nations are better placed financially and technologically to cope with the effects of possible climatic change.

Hence, our inability to promote the common interest in sustainable development is often a product of the relative neglect of economic and social justice within and amongst nations.

Strategic Imperatives

The world must quickly design strategies that will allow nations to move from their present, often destructive, processes of growth and development onto sustainable development paths. . . .

Critical objectives for environment and development policies that follow from the concept of sustainable development include:

- reviving growth;
- changing the quality of growth;
- meeting essential needs for jobs, food, energy, water, and sanitation;
- ensuring a sustainable level of population;
- conserving and enhancing the resource base;
- reorienting technology and managing risk; and
- merging environment and economics in decision making.

Reviving Growth

... Development that is sustainable has to address the problem of the large number of people who ... are unable to satisfy even the most basic of their needs. Poverty reduces people's capacity to use resources in a sustainable manner; it intensifies pressure on the environment. ... A necessary but not a sufficient condition for the elimination of absolute poverty is a relatively rapid rise in per capita incomes in the Third World. It is therefore essential that the stagnant or declining growth trends of ... [the 1980s] be reversed.

While attainable growth rates will vary, a certain minimum is needed to have any impact on absolute poverty. It seems unlikely that, taking developing countries as a whole, these objectives can be accomplished with per capita income growth of under 3 per cent. ...

Growth must be revived in developing countries because that is where the links between economic growth, the alleviation of poverty, and environmental conditions operate most directly. Yet developing countries are part of an interdependent world economy; their prospects also depend on the levels and patterns of growth in industrialized nations. The medium-term prospects for industrial countries are for growth of 3–4 per cent. ... Such growth rates could be environmentally sustainable if industrialized nations can continue the recent shifts in the content of their growth towards less material- and energy-intensive activities and the improvement of their efficiency in using materials and energy.

As industrialized nations use less materials and energy, however, they will provide smaller markets for commodities and minerals from the developing nations. Yet if developing nations focus their efforts upon eliminating poverty and satisfying essential human needs, then domestic demand will increase for both agricultural products and manufactured goods and some services. Hence the very logic of sustainable development implies an internal stimulus to Third World growth. ...

Changing the Quality of Growth

Sustainable development involves more than growth. It requires a change in the content of growth, to make it less material- and energy-intensive and more equitable in its impact. These changes are required in all countries as part of a package of measures to maintain the stock of ecological capital, to improve the distribution of income, and to reduce the degree of vulnerability to economic crises.

The process of economic development must be more soundly based upon the realities of the stock of capital that sustains it. . . . For example, income from forestry operations is conventionally measured in terms of the value of timber and other products extracted, minus the costs of extraction. The costs of regenerating the forest are not taken into account, unless money is actually spent on such work. Thus figuring profits from logging rarely takes full account of the losses in future revenue incurred through degradation of the forest. . . . In all countries, rich or poor, economic development must take full account in its measurements of growth of the improvement or deterioration in the stock of natural resources. . . .

Yet it is not enough to broaden the range of economic variables taken into account. Sustainability requires views of human needs and well-being that incorporate such non-economic variables as education and health enjoyed for their own sake, clean air and water, and the protection of natural beauty. . . .

Economic and social development can and should be mutually reinforcing. Money spent on education and health can raise human productivity. Economic development can accelerate social development by providing opportunities for underprivileged groups or by spreading education more rapidly.

Meeting Essential Human Needs

The satisfaction of human needs and aspirations is so obviously an objective of productive activity that it may appear redundant to assert its central role in the concept of sustainable development. All too often poverty is such that people cannot satisfy their needs for survival and well-being even if goods and services are available. At the same time, the demands of those not in poverty may have major environmental consequences.

The principal development challenge is to meet the needs and aspirations of an expanding developing world population. The most basic of all needs is for a livelihood: that is, employment. Between 1985 and 2000 the labour force in developing countries will increase by nearly 900 million, and new livelihood opportunities will have to be generated for 60 million persons every year.[5] . . .

More food is required not merely to feed more people but to attack undernourishment. . . . Though the focus at present is necessarily on staple foods, the projections given above also highlight the need for a high rate of growth of protein availability. In Africa, the task is particularly challenging given the recent declining per capita food production and the current constraints on growth. In Asia and Latin America, the required growth rates in calorie and protein consumption seem to be more readily attainable. But increased food production should not be based on ecologically unsound production policies and compromise long-term prospects for food security.

Energy is another essential human need, one that cannot be universally met unless energy consumption patterns change. The most urgent problem is the requirements of poor Third World households, which depend mainly on fuelwood. By the turn of the century, 3 billion people may live in areas where wood is cut faster than it grows or where fuelwood is extremely scarce.[7] Corrective action would both reduce the drudgery of collecting wood over long distances and preserve the ecological base. . . .

The linked basic needs of housing, water supply, sanitation, and health care are also environmentally important. Deficiencies in these areas are often visible manifestations of environmental stress. In the Third World, the failure to meet these key needs is one of the major causes of many communicable diseases such as malaria, gastro-intestinal infestations, cholera, and typhoid. . . .

Ensuring a Sustainable Level of Population

The sustainability of development is intimately linked to the dynamics of population growth. The issue, however, is not simply one of global population size. A child born in a country where levels of material and energy use are high places a greater burden on the Earth's resources than a child born in a poorer country. . . .

In industrial countries, the overall rate of population growth is under 1 per cent, and several countries have reached or are approaching zero population growth. The total population of the industrialized world could increase from its current 1.2 billion to about 1.4 billion in the year 2025.[8]

The greater part of global population increase will take place in developing countries, where the 1985 population of 3.7 billion may increase to 6.8 billion by 2025.[9] The Third World does not have the option of migration to 'new' lands, and the time available for adjustment is much less than industrial countries had. Hence the challenge now is to quickly lower population growth rates, especially in regions such as Africa, where these rates are increasing.

Birth rates declined in industrial countries largely because of economic and social development. Rising levels of income and urbanization and the changing role of women all played important roles. Similar processes are now at work in developing countries. These should be recognized and encouraged. Population policies should be integrated with other economic and social development programmes—female education, health care, and the expansion of the livelihood base of the poor. . . .

Developing-country cities are growing much faster than the capacity of authorities to cope. Shortages of housing, water, sanitation, and mass transit are widespread. A growing proportion of city-dwellers live in slums and shanty towns, many of them exposed to air and water pollution and to industrial and natural hazards. Further deterioration is likely, given that most urban growth will take place in the largest cities. Thus more manageable cities may be the principal gain from slower rates of population growth. . . .

Conserving and Enhancing
the Resource Base

... Pressure on resources increases when people lack alternatives. Development policies must widen people's options for earning a sustainable livelihood, particularly for resource-poor households and in areas under ecological stress. . . .

The conservation of agricultural resources is an urgent task because in many parts of the world cultivation has already been extended to marginal lands, and fishery and forestry resources have been overexploited. These resources must be conserved and enhanced to meet the needs of growing populations. Land use in agriculture and forestry should be based on a scientific assessment of land capacity, and the annual depletion of topsoil, fish stock, or forest resources must not exceed the rate of regeneration.

The pressures on agricultural land from crop and livestock production can be partly relieved by increasing productivity. But shortsighted, short-term improvements in productivity can create different forms of ecological stress, such as the loss of genetic diversity in standing crops, salinization and alkalization of irrigated lands, nitrate pollution of ground-water, and pesticide residues in food. Ecologically more benign alternatives are available. Future increases in productivity, in both developed and developing countries, should be based on the better controlled application of water and agrochemicals, as well as on more extensive use of organic manures and non-chemical means of pest control. These alternatives can be promoted only by an agricultural policy based on ecological realities. . . .

The ultimate limits to global development are perhaps determined by the availability of energy resources and by the biosphere's capacity to absorb the by-products of energy use.[11] These energy limits may be approached far sooner than the limits imposed by other material resources. First, there are the supply problems: the depletion of oil reserves, the high cost and environmental impact of coal mining, and the hazards of nuclear technology. Second, there are emission problems, most notably acid pollution and carbon dioxide build-up leading to global warming.

Some of these problems can be met by increased use of renewable energy sources. But the exploitation of renewable sources such as fuelwood and hydropower also entails ecological problems. Hence sustainability requires a clear focus on conserving and efficiently using energy.

Industrialized countries must recognize that their energy consumption is polluting the biosphere and eating into scarce fossil fuel supplies. Recent improvements in energy efficiency and a shift towards less energy-intensive sectors have helped limit consumption. But the process must be accelerated to reduce per capita consumption and encourage a shift to non-polluting sources and technologies. The simple duplication in the developing world of industrial countries' energy use patterns is neither feasible nor desirable. . . .

The prevention and reduction of air and water pollution will remain a critical task of resource conservation. Air and water quality come under pressure from such activities as fertilizer and pesticide use, urban sewage, fossil fuel burning, the use of certain chemicals, and various other industrial activities. Each of these is expected to increase the pollution load on the biosphere substantially, particularly in developing countries, Cleaning up after the event is an expensive solution. Hence all countries need to anticipate and prevent these pollution problems. . . .

Reorienting Technology and Managing Risk

The fulfillment of all these tasks will require the reorientation of technology—the key link between humans and nature. First, the capacity for technological innovation needs to be greatly enhanced in developing countries. . . . Second, the orientation of technology development must be changed to pay greater attention to environmental factors.

The technologies of industrial countries are not always suited or easily adaptable to the socio-economic and environmental conditions of developing countries. To compound the problem, the bulk of world research and development addresses few of the pressing issues facing these countries. . . . Not enough is being done to adapt recent innovations in materials technology, energy conservation, information technology, and biotechnology to the needs of developing countries. . . .

In all countries, the processes of generating alternative technologies, upgrading traditional ones, and selecting and adapting imported technologies should be informed by environmental resource concerns. Most technological research by commercial organizations is devoted to product and process innovations that have market value. Technologies are needed that produce 'social goods', such as improved air quality or increased product life, or that resolve problems normally outside the cost calculus of individual enterprises, such as the external costs of pollution or waste disposal.

The role of public policy is to ensure, through incentives and disincentives, that commercial organizations find it worthwhile to take fuller account of environmental factors in the technologies they develop. . . .

Merging Environment and Economics in Decision Making

The common theme throughout this strategy for sustainable development is the need to integrate economic and ecological considerations in decision making. They are, after all, integrated in the workings of the real world. This will require a change in attitudes and objectives and in institutional arrangements at every level.

Economic and ecological concerns are not necessarily in opposition. For example, policies that conserve the quality of agricultural land and protect forests improve the long-term prospects for agricultural development. . . . But the compatibility of environmental and economic objectives is often lost in the pursuit of individual or group gains, with little regard for the impacts on others, with a blind faith in science's ability to find solutions, and in ignorance of the distant consequences of today's decisions. Institutional rigidities add to this myopia. . . .

Intersectoral connections create patterns of economic and ecological interdependence rarely reflected in the ways in which policy is made. Sectoral organizations tend to pursue sectoral objectives and to treat their impacts on other sectors as side effects, taken into account only if compelled to do so. . . . Many of the environment and development problems that confront us have their roots in this sectoral fragmentation of responsibility. Sustainable development requires that such fragmentation be overcome.

Sustainability requires the enforcement of wider responsibilities for the impacts of decisions. This requires changes in the legal and institutional frameworks that will enforce the common interest. Some necessary changes in the legal framework start from the proposition that an environment adequate for health and well-being is essential for all human beings—including future generations. . . .

The law alone cannot enforce the common interest. It principally needs community knowledge and support, which entails greater public participation in the decisions that affect the environment. This is best secured by decentralizing the management of resources upon which local communities depend, and giving these communities an effective say over the use of these resources. . . .

Changes are also required in the attitudes and procedures of both public and private-sector enterprises. Moreover, environmental regulation must move beyond the usual menu of safety regulations, zoning laws, and pollution control enactments; environmental objectives must be built into taxation, prior approval procedures for investment and technology choice, foreign trade incentives, and all components of development policy.

The integration of economic and ecological factors into the law and into decision-making systems within countries has to be matched at the international level. The growth in fuel and material use dictates that direct physical linkages between ecosystems of different countries will increase. Economic interactions through trade, finance, investment, and travel will also grow and heighten economic and ecological interdependence. Hence in the future, even more so than now, sustainable development requires the unification of economics and ecology in international relations. . . .

Conclusion

In its broadest sense, the strategy for sustainable development aims to promote harmony among human beings and between humanity and nature. In the specific context of the development and environment crises of the 1980s, which current national and international political and economic institutions have not and perhaps cannot overcome, the pursuit of sustainable development requires:

- a political system that secures effective citizen participation in decision-making,
- an economic system that is able to generate surpluses and technical knowledge on a self-reliant and sustained basis,
- a social system that provides for solutions for the tensions arising from disharmonious development,
- a production system that respects the obligation to preserve the ecological base for development,
- a technological system that can search continuously for new solutions,
- an international system that fosters sustainable patterns of trade and finance, and
- an administrative system that is flexible and has the capacity for self-correction.

These requirements are more in the nature of goals that should underlie national and international action on development. What matters is the sincerity with which these goals are pursued and the effectiveness with which departures from them are corrected.

LARRY LOHMANN

24

Whose Common Future?

Never underestimate the ability of modern elites to work out ways of coming through a crisis with their power intact.

From the days of the American populists through the Depression, postwar reconstruction, the end of colonialism and the age of 'development', our contemporary leaders and their institutions have sought to turn pressures for change to their advantage. The New Deal, the Marshall Plan, Bretton Woods, multilateral lending—all in their turn have taken challenges to the system and transformed them into ways of defusing popular initiatives and developing the economic and political domains of the powerful.

Now comes the global environmental crisis. Once again those in high places are making solemn noises about "grave threats to our common security and the very survival of our planet". Once again their proposed solutions leave the main causes of the trouble untouched. As ordinary people try to reclaim local lands, forests and waters from the depredations of business and the state, and work to build democratic movements to preserve the planet's health, those in power continue to occupy themselves with damage control and the containment of threats to the way power is currently distributed and held. The difference is important to keep in mind when listening to the calls to arms from the new statesmen and women of 'environmentalism'.

Excerpted from *The Ecologist* 20, no. 3 (May-June 1990):82–84. Used by permission of Larry Lohmann.

Political Management
of the Crisis

Two of the most prominent of these, former Norwegian Prime Minister Gro Harlem Brundtland and Canadian businessman Maurice Strong, . . . Secretary General of the 1992 United Nations Conference on Environment and Development (UNCED), were in Vancouver in March [1990] to reiterate the message that we all share a 'common future' in environmental preservation and 'sustainable development'. Their speeches at the 'Globe 90' conference and 'green' trade fair gave valuable clues about how the more progressive global elites are organizing themselves for the political management of the environment crisis.

The first instinct of those in high places when faced with a problem is to avoid analyzing its causes if doing so would put the current power structure in an unfavourable light. In Vancouver, Brundtland averted her gaze from the destruction brought about through economic growth, technology transfer and capital flows from North to South and vice versa, and instead rounded up the usual suspects of 'poverty', 'population growth' and 'underdevelopment', without exploring the origins of any of them. She spoke of global warming, a declining resource base, pollution, overexploitation of resources and a 'crushing debt burden' for the South, but omitted mentioning who or what might be responsible. Environmental problems, she implied, were mainly to be found in the South. Admittedly the North had made some mistakes, she said, but luckily it knows the answers now and can prevent the South from making the same errors as it toddles along behind the North on the path to sustainable development.

Whose Security?

The stress of a crisis also tends to drive those in power to the use of vague code words that can rally other members of the elite. In Vancouver the word was 'security'. Brundtland and Strong warned of the "new (environmental) threats to our security" and dwelt on the ideas of a 'global concept of security', a 'safe future' and a new 'security alliance' with an obsessiveness worthy of Richard Nixon.

What was all this talk of 'security' about? In the rural societies where most of the world's people live, security generally means land, family, village and freedom from outside interference. Had the ex-Prime Minister of Norway and the Chairman of Strovest Holdings, Inc. suddenly become land reform activists and virulent opponents of the development projects and market economy expansion which uproot villagers from their farms, communities and livelihoods? Or were they perhaps hinting at another kind of security, the security that First World privilege wants against the economic and political chaos that would follow environmental collapse? In the atmosphere of Globe 90, where everyone was constantly assured that all humanity had 'common security' interests, it was not always easy to keep in mind the distinction between the first, which entails devolution of power, and the second, which requires the reverse.

A third instinct of crisis managers in high places is to seek the 'solution' that requires the least change to the existing power structure. Here Brundtland and Strong, as befits two contenders for the UN Secretary-Generalship, repeated a formula to be found partly in UN General Assembly documents relating to UNCED. This is:

1. reverse the financial flows currently coursing from South to North, using debt relief, new lending, and new infusions of aid possibly augmented by taxes on fossil fuels and transfers from military budgets;
2. transfer technology, particularly 'green' technology, from North to South; and
3. boost economic growth, particularly in the South.

This scheme has obvious attractions for the world's powerful. For one thing, a resumption of net North-South capital flows would provide a bonanza for Northern export industries. Funds from the West and Japan would be sent on a quick round trip through a few institutions in other parts of the world before being returned, somewhat depleted by payoffs to elites along the way, to the coffers of Northern firms. Third World income freed up by debt relief would add immensely to corporate profits. Buoyed up by a fresh flow of funds, Southern leaders would become more receptive to the advice of Northern-dominated institutions and more dependent on Northern technology and aid. Injections of remedial technology, in addition, might well provide an incentive for the South to follow the strategy of dealing with the effects rather than the causes of environmental degradation. That would mean more money for both polluting and pollution-correcting industries.

The scheme also shores up the present industrial and financial system by suggesting that the solution to the environmental crisis lies within that system. . . . It implies that environmental issues are technological and financial and not matters of social equity and distribution of power—discussion of which would call much of the system into question. The scheme invokes and reinforces the superstitions that it is lack of capital that leads to environmental crisis; that capital flows are going to 'expand the resource base', replace soil fertility and restore water tables and tropical forests lost to commercial exploitation; that poverty will be somehow relieved rather than exacerbated by economic growth; and that capital flows 'naturally' in large quantities from North to South.[1]

Weighing Up the Costs

Admittedly, the UNCED plan has costs for those in power. Bankers may not be overjoyed at the prospect of debt relief, but since the alternatives seem to be either continued insupportable and destabilizing South-North net financial transfers or the perpetuation of the process of servicing Third World debts with new loans, they may agree in the end. Northern countries will also have to spend massively on 'green' technology now in order to be in a position to put pressure on the South to do the same later.[2] But this is not necessarily a bad thing for industry, which can 'clean up' the mess it itself makes around the world, perhaps in the process creating new problems which will require further business solutions. As one of Globe 90's organizers put it, "a solution to most environmental issues is a business opportunity".[3] Another obstacle to the UNCED scheme is that it may stir resistance among its Southern 'beneficiaries'. . . .

Perhaps a bigger problem for the UNCED scheme is that it does not actually address the environmental crisis in either North or South. By tailoring solutions not to the problems but to the interests of those who created them, the plan is in fact likely to make things worse. . . . The UNCED plan will reinforce Southern dependence on environmentally destructive models of development imposed by the North and increase the power of Southern elites over their societies. It will promote technology most of which, like the tree-planting machine on display at Globe 90, has only a spurious claim to being 'green' and which will have to be paid for eventually by cashing in resources. It does not examine the effects of importing large amounts of capital into the South and endorses the continuing devastating economization of the natural and social heritage of both North and South. It is, however, probably as far as elites can go at present without challenging their own position. As for the future, there is always the hope that, as the brochure of one Japanese organization present at Globe 90 put it, the problems of global warming, ozone depletion, acid rain, desertification and tropical forest destruction can someday be solved "through technological innovations".[4]

The 'New' Alliance

A fourth tendency among elite crisis managers is to identify the executors of the solution with the existing power structure. . . .

The technical fixes of the UNCED agenda are to be promoted and implemented by a 'new global partnership' or environmental quadruple alliance consisting of industry, government, scientists and non-governmental organizations—"the most important security alliance we have ever entered into on this planet" according to Strong. . . .

Seasoned observers . . . may wonder what is supposed to distinguish the new environmental alliance from the familiar sort of elite ententes that helped land the world in its current environmental mess—the old-boy networks and clubs typified by the military-industrial complex, the World Bank's web of clients, consultants and contractors, the Trilateral Commission, and so on.

Co-opting the NGOs

The answer is non-governmental organizations (NGOs). . . . Why the interest in NGOs? One reason is that they might be used to push business and government in a slightly less destructive direction. Another is that official or corporate environmental initiatives need credibility. Establishment political strategists have not failed to note the growing role of NGOs in recent popular movements from Latin America to South and Southeast Asia and Eastern and Central Europe. . . . 'New alliance' leaders are thus courting and manipulating NGOs, particularly tame NGO umbrella groups, groups with establishment links, and groups with jet-set ambitions, in the hope of being able to use their names to say that UNCED initiatives have the backing of environmentalists, youth, trade unions, women's groups, the socially concerned and "all the nations and peoples of the world".

These manoeuvres, however, cannot conceal the fact that grassroots NGO 'participation' in UNCED and other 'new alliance' activities, to say nothing of the participation of ordinary people, is a fraud. . . . It is governments who decide who is allowed to say what, just as it is governments who will be signing agreements. . . . NGOs are expected to carry governments' message to the people and help them stay in power.[5]

A Common Interest?

Outside official meetings, of course, it is business whose voice will inevitably carry above that of all others in the 'new alliance'. If Globe 90 is any indication, it is not likely to be a voice urging environmental and political sanity. Nor are grassroots-oriented environmental activists likely to be excited about joining a coalition carrying the industry agenda. . . .

Many environmentalists, nevertheless, will feel that joining the 'new global alliance' can do no harm if it presents an opportunity for nudging business and government in a more 'green' direction. Such a conclusion is questionable. It is one thing to pressure business and government into changing their ways with all the means at one's disposal. It is quite another to pledge allegiance in advance to a new elite coalition with a predetermined or unknown agenda which one will have little power to change.

Any alliance which tells us that we *must* seek consensus, that no opposition is to be brooked to Brundtland as Our Common Leader, or that there is a perfect potential community of interest between, say, a UN bureaucrat and a Sri Lankan subsistence fisherman, is one that deserves suspicion at the outset. Consensus-seeking is neither good nor necessary in itself—it may, after all, function merely to conceal exploitation—but only when it is agreed by all parties after full discussion to be possible and fruitful.

This is not to denigrate the ambitious professionals associated with the UNCED, but merely to state a fact. To seek genuine solutions it is necessary to accept, respect and explore differences, to face causes, and to understand the workings of power. It may well be that parties with wildly divergent interests can come to agreements on the crisis confronting the planet. Come the millennium, we may all even be able to form one grand coalition. But until then, it is best to remember the lesson of history: that no matter how warmly it seems to have embraced the slogans of the rebels, the Empire always strikes back.

SHARACHCHANDRA M. LÉLÉ

25

Sustainable Development: A Critical Review

Introduction

The last few years have seen a dramatic transformation in the environment-development debate. The question being asked is no longer "Do development and environmental concerns contradict each other?" but "How can sustainable development be achieved?" All of a sudden the phrase Sustainable Development (SD) has become pervasive. . . . It appears to have gained the broad-based support that earlier development concepts such as "ecodevelopment" lacked, and is poised to become the developmental paradigm of the 1990s.

But murmurs of disenchantment are also being heard. "What *is* SD?" is being asked increasingly frequently without, however, clear answers forthcoming. SD is in real danger of becoming a cliché like appropriate technology—a fashionable phrase that everyone pays homage to but nobody cares to define. . . . Agencies such as the World Bank, the Asian Development Bank and the Organization for Economic Cooperation and Development have been quick to adopt the new rhetoric. The absence of a clear theoretical and analytical framework, however, makes it difficult to determine whether the new policies will indeed foster an environmentally sound and socially meaningful form of development. . . .

Originally published in *World Development* 19, 6 (June 1991):607–621. Reprinted with permission from Elsevier Science Ltd., Pergamon Imprint, Oxford, England.

The persuasive power of SD (and hence the political strength of the SD move-ment) stems from the underlying claim that new insights into physical and social phenomena force one to concur with the operational conclusions of the SD plat-form almost regardless of one's fundamental ethical persuasions and priorities. I argue that while these new insights are important, the argument is not inexorable, and that the issues are more complex than is made out to be. Hence . . . many of the policy prescriptions being suggested in the name of SD stem from subjective (rather than consensual) ideas about goals and means, and worse, are often inad-equate and even counterproductive. . . .

Interpreting Sustainable Development

The manner in which the phrase "sustainable development" is used and inter-preted varies so much that while O'Riordan (1985) called SD a "contradiction in terms," Redclift suggests that it may be just "another development truism" (Redclift, 1987, p. 1). These interpretational problems, though ultimately concep-tual, have some semantic roots. Most people use the phrase "sustainable develop-ment" interchangeably with "ecologically sustainable or environmentally sound development" (Tolba, 1984a). This interpretation is characterized by: (a) "sustain-ability" being understood as "ecological sustainability"; and (b) a conceptualiza-tion of SD as a process of change that has (ecological) sustainability added to its list of objectives.

In contrast, sustainable development is sometimes interpreted as "sustained growth," "sustained change," or simply "successful" development. Let us examine how these latter interpretations originate and why they are less useful than the former one. . . .

Contradictions and Trivialities

Taken literally, sustainable development would simply mean "development that can be continued—either indefinitely or for the implicit time period of concern". But what is development? Theorists and practitioners have both been grappling with the word and the concept for at least the past four decades. . . . Some equate development with GNP growth, others include any number of socially desirable phenomena in their conceptualization. The point to be noted is that development is *a process of directed change*. Definitions of development thus embody both (a) the objectives of this process, and (b) the means of achieving these objectives.

Unfortunately, a distinction between objectives and means is often not made in the development rhetoric. This has led to "sustainable development" frequently being interpreted as simply a process of change that can be continued forever. . . . This interpretation is either impossible or trivial. When development is taken to be synonymous with growth in material consumption—which it often is even today—SD would be "sustaining the growth in material consumption" (presumably indefinitely). But such an idea contradicts the general recognition that "*ultimate* limits [to usable resources] exist"[4] (WCED, p. 45, emphasis added). At best, it could be argued that growth in the per capita consumption of certain basic goods is necessary in certain regions of the world in the short term. To use "sustainable development" synonymously with "sustain[ing] growth performance" (Idachaba, 1987) or to cite the high rates of growth in agricultural production in South Asia as an example of SD is therefore a misleading usage, or at best a short-term and localized notion that goes against the long-term global perspective of SD.

One could finesse this contradiction by conceptualizing development as simply a process of socio-economic change. But one cannot carry on a meaningful discussion unless one states what the objectives of such change are and why one should worry about continuing the process of change indefinitely.

. . .

Sustainability

. . . The concept of sustainability originated in the context of renewable resources such as forests or fisheries, and has subsequently been adopted as a broad slogan by the environmental movement. Most proponents of sustainability therefore take it to mean "the existence of the ecological conditions necessary to support human life at a specified level of well-being through future generations," what I call *ecological sustainability*. . . .

Since ecological sustainability emphasizes the constraints and opportunities that nature presents to human activities, ecologists and physical scientists frequently dominate its discussion. But what they actually focus on are the ecological conditions for ecological sustainability—the biophysical "laws" or patterns that determine environmental responses to human activities and humans' ability to use the environment. The major contribution of the environment-development debate is, I believe, the realization that in addition to or in conjunction with these ecological conditions, there are social conditions that influence the ecological sustainability or unsustainability of the people-nature interaction. To give a stylized example, one could say that soil erosion undermining the agricultural basis for human society is a case of ecological (un)sustainability. It could be caused by farming on marginal lands without adequate soil conservation measures—the ecological cause. But the phenomenon of marginalization of peasants may have social roots, which would then be the social causes of ecological unsustainability.

. . .

The Concept of
Sustainable Development
Evolution of Objectives

The term sustainable development came into prominence in 1980, when the International Union for the Conservation of Nature and Natural Resources (IUCN) presented the World Conservation Strategy (WCS) with "the overall aim of achieving sustainable development through the conservation of living resources" (IUCN, 1980). Critics acknowledged that "By identifying Sustainable Development as the basic goal of society, the WCS was able to make a profound contribution toward reconciling the interests of the development community with those of the environmental movement" (Khosla, 1987). They pointed out, however, that the strategy restricted itself to living resources, focussed primarily on the necessity of maintaining genetic diversity, habits and ecological processes. . . . It was also unable to deal adequately with sensitive or controversial issues—those relating to the international economic and political order, war and armament, population and urbanization (Khosla, 1987). . . .

The United Nations Environment Program (UNEP) was at the forefront of the effort to articulate and popularize the concept. UNEP's concept of SD was said to encompass

  (i)   help for the very poor, because they are left with no options but to destroy their environment;
 (ii)   the idea of self-reliant development, within natural resource constraints;
(iii)   the idea of cost-effective development using nontraditional economic criteria;
 (iv)   the great issues of health control [sic], appropriate technology, food self-reliance, clean water and shelter for all; and
  (v)   the notion that people-centered initiatives are needed (Tolba, 1984a).

This statement epitomizes the mixing of goals and means, or more precisely, of fundamental objectives and operational ones, that has burdened much of the SD literature. While providing food, water, good health and shelter have traditionally been the fundamental objectives of most development models (including UNEP's), it is not clear whether self-reliance, cost-effectiveness, appropriateness of technology and people-centeredness are additional objectives or the operational requirements for achieving the traditional ones. . . .

In contrast to the aforementioned, the currently popular definition of SD—the one adopted by the World Commission on Environment and Development (WCED)—is quite brief:

Sustainable development is development that meets the needs of the present without compromising the ability of future generations to meet their own needs (WCED, 1987; p. 43).

The constraint of "not compromising the ability of future generations to meet their needs" is (presumably) considered by the Commission to be equivalent to the requirement of some level of ecological and social sustainability.[5]

While the WCED's statement of the fundamental objectives of SD is brief, the Commission is much more elaborate about (what are essentially) the operational objectives of SD. It states that "the critical objectives which follow from the concept of SD" are:

(1) reviving growth;
(2) changing the quality of growth;
(3) meeting essential needs for jobs, food, energy, water, and sanitation;
(4) ensuring a sustainable level of population;
(5) conserving and enhancing the resource base;
(6) reorienting technology and managing risk;
(7) merging environment and economics in decision making; and
(8) reorienting international economic relations (WCED, 1987, p. 49).

Most organizations and agencies actively promoting the concept of SD subscribe to some or all of these objectives with, however, the notable addition of a ninth operational goal, viz.,

(9) making development more participatory.[6]

This formulation can therefore be said to represent the mainstream of SD thinking. This "mainstream" includes international environmental agencies such as UNEP, IUCN and the World Wildlife Fund (WWF), developmental agencies including the World Bank, the US Agency for International Development, the Canadian and Swedish international development agencies, research and dissemination organizations such as the World Resources Institute, the International Institute for Environment and Development, the Worldwatch Institute (1984–88), and activist organizations and groups such as the Global Tomorrow Coalition.

. . .

The Premises of SD

The perception in mainstream SD thinking of the environment-society link is based upon the following premises:

(i) *Environmental degradation:*
 • Environmental degradation is already affecting millions in the Third

World, and is likely to severely reduce human well-being all across the globe within the next few generations.
- Environmental degradation is very often caused by poverty, because the poor have no option but to exploit resources for short-term survival.
- The interlinked nature of most environmental problems is such that environmental degradation ultimately affects everybody, although poorer individuals/nations may suffer more and sooner than richer ones.

(ii) *Traditional development objectives:*
- These are: providing basic needs and increasing the productivity of all resources (human, natural and economic) in developing countries, and maintaining the standard of living in the developed countries.
- These objectives do not necessarily conflict with the objective of ecological sustainability. In fact, achieving sustainable patterns of resource use is necessary for achieving these objectives permanently.
- It can be shown that, even for individual actors, environmentally sound methods are "profitable" in the long run, and often in the short run too.

(iii) *Process:*
- The process of development must be participatory to succeed even in the short run).

Given these premises, the need for a process of development that achieves the traditional objectives, results in ecologically sustainable patterns of resource use, and is implemented in a participatory manner is obvious.

Most of the SD literature is devoted to showing that this process is also feasible and can be made attractive to the actors involved. SD has become a bundle of neat fixes: technological changes that make industrial production processes less polluting and less resource intensive and yet more productive and profitable, economic policy changes that incorporate environmental considerations and yet achieve greater economic growth, procedural changes that use local non-governmental organizations (NGOs) so as to ensure grassroots participation, agriculture that is less harmful, less resource intensive and yet more productive, and so on. In short, SD is a "metafix" that will unite everybody from the profit-minded industrialist and risk-minimizing subsistence farmer to the equity-seeking social worker, the pollution-concerned or wildlife-loving First Worlder, the growth-maximizing policy maker, the goal-oriented bureaucrat, and therefore, the vote-counting politician.

Weaknesses

The major impact of the SD movement is the rejection of the notion that environmental conservation necessarily constrains development or that development necessarily means environmental pollution—certainly not an insignificant gain.

Where the SD movement has faltered is in its inability to develop a set of concepts, criteria and policies that are coherent or consistent—both externally (with physical and social reality) and internally (with each other). The mainstream formulation of SD suffers from significant weaknesses in:

- its characterization of the problems of poverty and environmental degradation;
- its conceptualization of the objectives of development, sustainability and participation; and
- the strategy it has adopted in the face of incomplete knowledge and uncertainty.

Poverty and Environmental Degradation: An Incomplete Characterization

The fundamental premise of mainstream SD thinking is the two-way link between poverty and environmental degradation. . . .

In fact, however, even a cursory examination of the vast amount of research that has been done on the links between social and environmental phenomena suggests that both poverty and environmental degradation have deep and complex causes. . . .

To say that mainstream SD thinking has completely ignored [this complexity] would be unfair. But . . . inadequate technical know-how and managerial capabilities, common property resource management, and pricing and subsidy policies have been the major themes addressed, and the solutions suggested have been essentially techno-economic ones. . . . Deeper socio-political changes (such as land reform) or changes in cultural values (such as overconsumption in the North) are either ignored or paid lip-service. . . .

Conceptual Weaknesses

Removal of poverty (the traditional developmental objective), sustainability and participation are really the three fundamental objectives of the SD paradigm. Unfortunately, the manner in which these objectives are conceptualized and operationalized leaves much to be desired. On the one hand, economic growth is being adopted as a major operational objective that is consistent with both removal of poverty and sustainability. On the other hand, the concepts of sustainability and participation are poorly articulated, making it difficult to determine whether a particular development project actually promotes a particular form of sustainability, or what kind of participation will lead to what kind of social (and consequently, environmental) outcome.

The Role of Economic Growth. By the mid-1970s, it had seemed that the economic growth and trickle-down theory of development had been firmly rejected, and the "basic needs approach" (Streeten, 1979) had taken root in development circles. Yet economic growth continues to feature in today's debate on SD. In fact, "reviving [economic] growth" heads WCED's list of operational objectives quoted earlier. Two arguments are implicit in this adoption of economic growth as an operational objective. The first, a somewhat defensive one, is that there is no fundamental contradiction between economic growth and sustainability, because growth in economic activity may occur simultaneously with either an improvement or a deterioration in environmental quality. Thus, "governments concerned with long-term sustainability need not seek to limit growth in economic output so long as they stabilize aggregate natural resource consumption" (Goodland and Ledec, 1987). But one could turn this argument around and suggest that, if economic growth is not correlated with environmental sustainability, there is no reason to have economic growth as an operational objective of SD.[8]

The second argument in favor of economic growth is more positive. The basic premise of SD is that poverty is largely responsible for environmental degradation. Therefore, removal of poverty (i.e., development) is necessary for environmental sustainability. This, it is argued, implies that economic growth is absolutely necessary for SD. The only thing that needs to be done is to "change the quality of [this] growth" (WCED, 1987, pp. 52–54) to ensure that it does not lead to environmental destruction. In drawing such an inference, however, there is the implicit belief that economic growth is necessary (if not sufficient) for the removal of poverty. But was it not the fact that economic growth per se could not ensure the removal of poverty that led to the adoption of the basic needs approach in the 1970s?

Thus, if economic growth by itself leads to neither environmental sustainability nor removal of poverty, it is clearly a "non-objective" for SD. The converse is a possibility worth exploring, viz., whether successful implementation of policies for poverty removal, long-term employment generation, environmental restoration and rural development will lead to growth in GNP, and, more important, to increases in investment, employment and income generation. This seems more than likely in developing countries, but not so certain in developed ones. In any case, economic growth may be the fallout of SD, but not its prime mover.

Sustainability. The World Conservation Strategy was probably the first attempt to carry the concept of sustainability beyond simple renewable resource systems. It suggested three ecological principles for ecological sustainability (see the nomenclature developed above), viz., "maintenance of essential ecological processes and life-support systems, the preservation of genetic diversity, and the sustainable utilization of species and resources" (IUCN, 1980). This definition, though a useful starting point, is clearly recursive as it invokes "sustainability" in resource use without defining it. Many subsequent attempts to discuss the notion are disturbingly muddled. There is a very real danger of the term becoming a meaningless cliché, unless a concerted effort is made to add precision and content to the discussion. . . .

Any discussion of sustainability must first answer the questions "What is to be sustained? For whom? How long?" The value of the concept (like that of SD), however, lies in its ability to generate an operational consensus between groups with fundamentally different answers to these questions, i.e., those concerned either about the survival of future human generations, or about the survival of wildlife, or human health, or the satisfaction of immediate subsistence needs (food, fuel, fodder) with a low degree of risk. It is therefore vital to identify those aspects of sustainability that do actually cater to such diverse interests, and those that involve tradeoffs.

Differentiating between ecological and social sustainability could be a first step toward clarifying some of the discussion. Further, in the case of ecological sustainability, a distinction needs to be made between renewable resources, nonrenewable resources, and environmental processes that are crucial to human life, as well as to life at large. The few researchers who have begun to explore the idea of ecological sustainability emphasize its multidimensional and complex nature. . . .

In the rush to derive ecological principles of (ecological) sustainability, we cannot afford to lose sight of the social conditions that determine which of these principles are socially acceptable, and to what extent. Sociologists, eco-Marxists and political ecologists are pointing out the crucial role of socioeconomic structures and institutions in the pattern and extent of environmental degradation globally. Neoclassical economists, whose theories have perhaps had the greatest influence in development policy making in the past and who therefore bear the responsibility for its social and environmental failures, however, have been very slow in modifying their theories and prescriptions. The SD movement will have to formulate a clear agenda for research in what is being called "ecological economics" and press for its adoption by the mainstream of economics in order to ensure the possibility of real changes in policy making.

Social sustainability is a more nebulous concept than ecological sustainability. Brown et al. (1987), in a somewhat techno-economic vein, state that sustainability implies "the existence and operation of an infrastructure (transportation and communication), services (health, education, and culture), and government (agreements, laws, and enforcement)." Tisdell (1988) talks about "the sustainability of political and social structures" and Norgaard (1988) argues for cultural sustainability, which includes value and belief systems. Detailed analyses of the concept, however, seem to be nonexistent.[9] Perhaps achieving desired social situations is itself so difficult that discussing their maintainability is not very useful; perhaps goals are even more dynamic in a social context than in an ecological one, so that maintainability is not such an important attribute of social institutions/structures. There is, however, no contradiction between the social and ecological sustainability; rather, they can complement and inform each other.

Participation. A notable feature of . . . some of the earlier SD literature was the emphasis placed on equity and social justice. . . . Subsequently, however, the mainstream appears to have quietly dropped these terms (suggesting at least a deemphasizing of these objectives), and has instead focused on "local participation."

There are, however, three problems with this shift. First, by using the terms equity, participation and decentralization interchangeably, it is being suggested that participation and decentralization are equivalent, and that they can somehow substitute for equity and social justice. . . .

Second, the manner in which participation is being operationalized shows up the narrow-minded, quick-fix and deceptive approach adopted by the mainstream promoters of SD. . . . Mainstream SD literature blithely assumes and insists that "involvement of local NGOs" in project implementation will ensure project success (Maniates, 1990; he dubs this the "NGOization" of SD).

Third, there is an assumption that participation or at least equity and social justice will necessarily reinforce ecological sustainability. Attempts to test such assumptions rigorously have been rare. But preliminary results seem to suggest that equity in resource access may not lead to sustainable resource use unless new institutions for resource management are carefully built and nurtured. . . . This should not be misconstrued as an argument against the need for equity, but rather as a word of caution against the tendency to believe that social equity automatically ensures environmental sustainability (or vice-versa).

. . .

Concluding Remarks: Dilemmas and Agendas

The proponents of SD are faced with a dilemma that affects any program of political action and social change: the dilemma between the urge to take strong stands on fundamental concerns and the need to gain wide political acceptance and support. . . . SD is being packaged as the inevitable outcome of objective scientific analysis, virtually an historical necessity, that does not contradict the deep-rooted normative notion of development as economic growth. In other words, SD is an attempt to have one's cake and eat it too.

It may be argued that this is indeed possible, that the things that are wrong and need to be changed are quite obvious, and there are many ways of fixing them without significantly conflicting with either age-old power structures or the modern drive for a higher material standard of living. . . . If, by using the politically correct jargon of economic growth and development and by packaging SD in the manner mentioned above, it were possible to achieve even 50% success in implementing this bundle of "conceptually imprecise" policies, the net reduction achieved in environmental degradation and poverty would be unprecedented.

I believe, however, that (analogous to the arguments in SD) in the long run there is no contradiction between better articulation of the terms, concepts, analytical methods and policy-making principles, and gaining political strength and broad social acceptance—especially at the grassroots. In fact, such clarification and articulation is necessary if SD is to avoid either being dismissed as another development fad or being coopted by forces opposed to changes in status quo. More specifically, proponents and analysts of SD need to:

(a) clearly reject the attempts (and temptation) to focus on economic growth as means to poverty removal and/or environmental sustainability;

(b) recognize the internal inconsistencies and inadequacies in the theory and practice of neoclassical economics, particularly as it relates to environmental and distributional issues; in economic analyses, move away from arcane mathematical models toward exploring empirical questions such as limits to the substitution of capital for resources, impacts of different sustainability policies on different economic systems, etc.;

(c) accept the existence of structural, technological and cultural causes of poverty and environmental degradation; develop methodologies for estimating relative importance of and interaction between these causes in specific situations; and explore political, institutional and educational solutions to them;

(d) understand the multiple dimensions of sustainability, and attempt to develop measures, criteria and principles for them; and

(e) explore what patterns and levels of source demand and use would be compatible with different forms or levels of ecological and social sustainability, and with different notions of equity and social justice.

There are, fortunately, some signs that a debate on these lines has now begun.

In a sense, if SD is to be really "sustained" as a development paradigm, two apparently divergent efforts are called for: making SD more precise in its conceptual underpinnings, while allowing more flexibility and diversity of approaches in developing strategies that might lead to a society living in harmony with the environment and with itself.

References

Brown, B. J., M. Hanson, D. Liverman, and R. Merideth, Jr. "Global Sustainability: Toward Definition," *Environmental Management,* Vol. 11, No. 6 (1987), pp. 713–719.

Brown, L. R., *Building a Sustainable Society* (New York: W. W. Norton, 1981).

Chambers, R., *Sustainable Livelihoods: An Opportunity for the World Commission on Environment and Development* (Brighton, UK: Institute of Development Studies, University of Sussex, 1986).

Daly, H., *Economics, Ecology, Ethics: Essays Toward a Steady-State Economy* (San Francisco: W. H. Freeman, 1980).

Goodland, R., and G. Ledec, "Neoclassical Economics and Principles of Sustainable Development," *Ecological Modelling,* Vol. 38 (1987), pp. 19–46.

Idachaba, F. S., "Sustainability Issues in Agriculture Development," in T. J. Davis and I. A. Schirmer (Eds.), *Sustainability Issues in Agricultural Development* (Washington, DC: World Bank, 1987), pp. 18–53.

IUCN, *World Conservation Strategy: Living Resource Conservation for Sustainable Development* (Gland, Switzerland: International Union for Conservation of Nature and Natural Resources, United Nations Environment Program and World Wildlife Fund, 1980).

Khosla, A., "Alternative Strategies in Achieving Sustainable Development," in P. Jacobs and D. A. Munro (Eds.), *Conservation with Equity: Strategies for Sustainable Development* (Cambridge, England: International Union for Conservation of Nature and Natural Resources, 1987), pp. 191–208.

Maniates, M., "Organizing for Rural Energy Development: Local Organizations, Improved Cookstoves, and the State in Gujarat, India," Ph.D. thesis (Berkeley: Energy & Resources Group, University of California, 1990).

Norgaard, R. B., "Sustainable Development: A Coevolutionary View," *Futures*, Vol. 20, No. 6 (1988), pp. 606–620.

———, "Three Dilemmas of Environmental Accounting," *Ecological Economics*, Vol. 1, No. 4 (1989), pp. 303–314.

O'Riordan, T., "Future Directions in Environmental Policy," *Journal of Environment and Planning*, Vol. 17 (1985), pp. 1431–1446.

Peskin, H. M., "National Income Accounts and the Environment," *Natural Resources Journal*, Vol. 21 (1981), pp. 511–537.

Redclift, M., *Sustainable Development: Exploring the Contradictions* (New York: Methuen, 1987).

Repetto, R., *World Enough and Time* (New Haven, CT: Yale University Press, 1986a).

Riddell, R., *Ecodevelopment* (New York: St. Martin's Press, 1981).

Sachs, I., *Environment and Development—A New Rationale for Domestic Policy Formulation and International Cooperation Strategies* (Ottawa: Environment Canada and Canadian International Development Agency, 1977).

Streeten, P., "Basic Needs: Premises and Promises," *Journal of Policy Modelling*, Vol. 1 (1979), pp. 136–146.

Tisdell, C., "Sustainable Development: Differing Perspectives of Ecologists and Economists, and Relevance to LDCs," *World Development*, Vol. 16, No. 3 (1988), pp. 373–384.

Tolba, M. K., "The Premises for Building a Sustainable Society. Address to the World Commission on Environment and Development," October 1984 (Nairobi: United Nations Environment Programme, 1984).

World Commission on Environment and Development, *Our Common Future* (New York: Oxford University Press, 1987).

Worldwatch Institute, *State of the World* (New York: Norton, various years).

TANVI NAGPAL

26

Voices from the Developing World: Progress Toward Sustainable Development

Few would contest that we have an obligation to future generations: not to leave them an impoverished Earth and fragmented societies. In its simplest interpretation, sustainability is about this concern for intergenerational equity. Intellectuals and government decision makers are not alone in their concern about a long-term sustainable future. Small-scale farmers, community activists, leaders of women's groups and nongovernmental organizations (NGOs), and parents around the world are equally committed to leaving our children a world worth inheriting.

Much has been written about sustainability, what the term means, and what a sustainable future might entail. Global policy studies of the conditions required for sustainability abound, as do grassroots initiatives to improve the lives of common people by investing in their present and future. How do the recommendations of top-down analyses mesh with the bottom-up experience of leaders and

Originally published in *Environment* 37, no. 8 (October 1995):10–15 and 30–35. Reprinted with permission of the Helen Dwight Reid Educational Foundation. Published by Heldref Publications, 1319 Eighteenth St. N.W., Washington, D.C. 20036–1802. © 1995.

activists? What have we in the West learned that must be shared with the East, and what can the proverbial "South" teach the "North"? Are the philosophical and methodological differences between the two irreconcilable? Most importantly, does a single definition of sustainability exist, and should we be searching for a globally acceptable plan for the future?

The 2050 Project was developed to explore the common elements—and the deep cleavages—in people's views of a sustainable future, to design innovative, integrated strategies for achieving sustainability in the next century.[1] Eighty-eight individuals in 47 countries were asked to submit essays on their visions of a sustainable world, and 19 interviews were conducted in 14 countries. The majority of those surveyed were from developing countries. This bias was intentional: The views of the industrialized world are already well known through a rich literature of Western visions. Sustainable development strategies cannot be based solely on these known views, both because they will be incomplete and because they will be rejected as "culture-bound" by the majority of the world's people. Those who were surveyed were asked to "imagine and describe a sustainable future, ideal yet plausible, that you desire for your grandchildren." The exercises yielded a varied set of responses: coherent visions of the future, immediate strategies to be implemented, and nostalgic commentaries on the link between the past and the future.

Envisioning sustainability is not about imagining utopias—perfect worlds without resource constraints and hard choices. Rather, it is about making decisions about the world we desire and, therefore, what should be sustained. Although the interviews and essays were as varied as the respondents themselves, many voiced common concerns. What was overwhelmingly evident was a desire to emphasize basic needs—ensuring food, shelter, clean water, health care, and education to all. An extension of this sentiment was a desire to protect basic values as well—to respect nature rather than dominate it and to use the wisdom of indigenous groups, elders, and tribal leaders to reexamine current structures of government and sources of knowledge.

The visions exercise of the 2050 Project did not bring us closer to a universally accepted definition of sustainability. Quite the opposite: The survey strengthens the belief that we should not be seeking a blueprint for a sustainable future because none exists. Instead, we should try to listen more carefully to one another, to learn from those whose knowledge we have long ignored. A sustainable future should be built on common aspirations and enriched with the diversity of cultures, languages, and belief systems. We face hard choices about our relationships with our communities and the Earth, but by working together, we can and must secure a sustainable future for our children.

Defining Sustainable Development

The term sustainable development was introduced in the 1987 report *Our Common Future*. There, the World Commission on Environment and Development (the Brundtland Commission) defined sustainable development as "development that meets the needs of the present generation without compromising the ability of future generations to meet their own needs."[2] Although this definition places needed focus on the importance of long-term planning, as a policy tool it is vague, providing no specifics about which needs and desires must be met and fulfilled and how.

Nonetheless, this definition has been adopted by several high-profile groups, including the Switzerland-based Business Council on Sustainable Development, a group of powerful business executives; the United Nations Commission on Sustainable Development, created to supervise and evaluate the achievement of the goals set by the Rio conference in 1992; and the President's Council on Sustainable Development, a U.S. group with representatives from environmental groups, industry, and local communities to formulate a strategy for sustainable development in the United States.[3] Indeed, the influential groups mentioned above are not alone in pondering sustainability. Sustainable development is a buzzword in even the smallest African countries, and commissions are being formed around the world to devise national and regional plans for the future.

Thousands of small grassroots NGOs are grappling with these questions, and many indigenous leaders and grassroots activists are presenting their own priorities for the future. At times, the variety of agendas come together fortuitously, but more often than not there are major disconnects in the manner in which people define and understand sustainable development. However, in the years since it was first introduced, the Brundtland Commission's definition has been dissected and reconstructed dozens of times. Moreover, it has been criticized on grounds that it is culturally bankrupt, dodges the issue of development without growth and redistribution, and pays little attention to human dignity, including the relationship that people have with the environment. Individuals and groups in less industrialized countries have led the protest, although they have many sympathizers in the West.

Those in developing countries argue that Western proponents of sustainable development "just don't get it." They point out that the debates on sustainability closely mirror those on development. By using terms of economic growth and efficiency, important issues are ignored: the urgency of nurturing human life and ecosystem health and the primacy of people, their communities, and the environment they depend on for their livelihood.[4]

In the project's survey, respondents echoed the same discontent. Some contributors gave scathing critiques of the Western influence on the definition of sustainability. For example, Saneh Charmarik (Thailand) asserted that "the whole issue of sustainability is fundamentally cultural and any effective solution to the current impasse requires nothing short of a shift in worldview."[5] Others argued that the predominant paradigms of our time are based on knowledge that has come exclusively from industrial societies, and they are angry that the West seems to have once again dominated the development of a new paradigm. To many, Western dominance implies that such issues as economic growth are paramount, and the environment is only superficially inserted into development plans. Those who challenge this domination are asking a fundamental question: Is the West ready to listen to those whose lives reflect a different set of values and priorities? As one contributor, Arshad Zaman (Pakistan), argues, perhaps our first task should be to explore whether a "global society can be created around a plural system of values, voluntarily." A consensus on that question may need to be reached before the hard work of sustainable development can truly begin.

Living in Harmony

What are the main features of a sustainable system, and how does it present itself? Both essays and interviews reflect a longing for peaceful coexistence within communities and nature. Contributors, whether from Africa, Asia, or the Americas, voiced deep concern about the fragmentation of their communities and their growing detachment from the environment. Their concern stems in part from a somewhat idealized reconstruction of the past and in part from heartfelt anxiety about the lack of alternatives to the modern existence that has alienated them from the environment.

Communal Responsibility

Contributors from Africa offered many clear and compelling insights into how they see their communities changing. Families and communities remain the primary units of production in African society. For centuries, Africans have depended on extended families for economic and emotional support. Sometimes these ties have been blamed for holding back individuals. Now, with increasing urbanization and emphasis on nuclear families and individual achievements, many Africans are wondering what will replace old social structures and obligations. By highlighting the primacy of families and communities in their cultures, African contributors presented deep dilemmas about the battle between individual and communal achievement. Margaret Maringa (Kenya) outlined her ideas on the foundations of a sustainable future: empowerment of women, acknowledgment of the importance of religion, deep understanding of ethnicity, and management of natural resources through family holdings and communal responsibility. However, drawing on the customs, practices, and wisdom of her Agikuyu ancestors, she also idealized communities of the past:

> Obligations rather than individual rights were advocated. Each age-set institution had an unwritten code of conduct. In this manner, the entire community was mobilized towards a common, positive standard with the least amount of supervision and waste. There were no policemen or prisons. The hoarding and misuse of resources was uncommon even in times of natural disaster.

Respondents often suggested that communal responsibility was essential for properly caring for natural resources. In a sustainable system, collective responsibility would ensure this care even if the structure and character of communities change. For example, Okyeame Ampadu-Agyei (Ghana) included communal management of resources in his definition of a sustainable system. He stated that in a desirable system, the inherited knowledge on resource management, which has been developed and refined over several generations, will not be disrupted but improved upon. Joseph Bedouma (Togo) echoes this sentiment, envisioning that traditional skills now forgotten by his children will be relearned by his grandchildren as they become protectors and builders of their environment and community. He feels humans have the power to destroy and protect the environment and hopes that his grandchildren will recognize this power.

Others surveyed pondered the contradictions of communities, their traditional hierarchies, and the knowledge systems they represent. We live in an era in which innovation, not experience, is revered; technological changes are accepted even when they do not improve the quality of human life or when they do more harm than good. This presents a significant dilemma for communities that are struggling to survive: Should they attempt to make progress using tried and tested methods and advice from the elders, or should they bypass traditional methods and follow the dictates of modern Western society? V. B. Mbaya (Kenya) admits that "there are pros and cons for either choice, as well as case studies that demonstrate the folly of naively choosing one over the other."

Education

Visions of sustainable communities varied, and family profiles, living arrangements, and social hierarchies differed substantially. However, a common element in many contributors' statements was a belief that communities need the ability to provide education and employment for their children, so that they do not have to leave for opportunities elsewhere. Schooling was seen by many as a basic human right, so they consider compulsory, universal primary education essential. Education is perceived as the single greatest equalizer of status and income, and a society that cannot assure it to all its members is neither desirable nor sustainable.

There was one universal caveat to this emphasis on education: It must contain the best the West has to offer while retaining elements of a location's unique culture. This is a challenge to those thinking about sustainability. Many acknowledge that wisdom comes not just from school books but also from traditional knowledge and customs, such as folk tales. It was widely felt that institutionalized schooling will become the norm. From Africa to Asia to South and Central America, participants voiced suggestions for reforming universities and combining culturally relevant material with technical education, as well as concern for the loss of civic learning. Several strategies were offered to retain cultural histories: schooling in native languages and graduate education in selected African tongues, combining the wisdom of traditional healers with the expertise of modern medicine, and establishing regional universities and centers of excellence that will stress integrated plans for development.

Welcoming Change

There is no prototypical African or Asian definition of a sustainable future. The visions heard were individual accounts of desires tempered by current reality, and the similarity that emerged from respondents came from present shared experiences. In fact, both the similarities and differences among contributors merely highlighted how we are all to some extent shackled to the present: Our visions of distant futures hinge on solutions to current problems. Therefore, it was no surprise that Asian and South American contributors were more worried about changing patterns of energy use than were Africans; that South Americans spoke of simplifying consumption while African interviewees desired more consumer goods; and that concerns about population growth were clearly expressed by Asian authors, less so by Africans, and very little by South Americans. It is no revelation that Africans stressed agricultural practices and food security, or that South Americans spoke so eloquently about democracy, personal freedom, and safety.

Basic Necessities

African contributors spoke about the importance of fulfilling basic needs, especially food. The majority of Africans depend directly on the natural resource base for sustenance; more than 80 percent still grow their own food. Several contributors presented detailed strategies for improving food security. Many of these hinge on an appreciation of farmers' preexisting knowledge and increased freedom from centrally controlled pricing and marketing of crops. Pesticide-free production and the use of natural fertilizers were recommended, as well as improved farming techniques and investment in a "dry revolution" (nonirrigated agriculture). One can almost imagine a continent self-sufficient in food production, with a safe water supply, and a roof over everyone's head.

Among those interviewed, there was a strong desire for more equitable opportunities, especially for sustainable livelihoods and fair salaries. Toum Mohammed, a teacher from Tanzania, hoped that her grandchildren "will be paid enough money to buy the things they need and still have enough left over to save." Albert Makina, a Zimbabwean teacher, concurred:

> My children will be educated and secure in their jobs. They will be doctors and engineers. They will not be teachers like me, because it does not pay well. . . . Farming is difficult and tiresome, and the financial rewards are poor. My parents are farmers and I think all of us should do better than our parents.

Sometimes this means bringing the city to the village. Chief Darboe of the Gambia is hopeful that the oil reserves off the Gambian coast will bring in wealth that will transform his villages into small cities. The trappings of a modern city—automobiles, televisions, VCRs—will all be available to villagers, and he hopes this will keep them in their ancestral homes. The disjuncture between this image and others of traditional idyllic pastoral villages is clear. Can communities survive the onslaught of modernization and retain the essence that has kept them alive for thousands of years? It appears as though this is strongly desired but difficult to achieve. Yet there are optimists such as Alfred Ayeah-Tefuh (Cameroon):

> Customs and traditions will change. It is my vision that the cumbersome traditions will disappear, while only the strongest and best will remain. Do I worry about the loss of these traditions by the year 2050? No, I think that in order for a tree to grow up strong and tall it most lose some of its branches. This is the law of nature.

Participation in Governance

In some instances, the entire discussion of sustainability focused on the issue of human rights. People must have the rights and resources to make decisions about their environment and livelihood. Coming from a family of herders in Inner Mongolia, Urna Chahartogche's primary concern was the abrogation of the basic rights of herdsmen in her land. She remarks:

> Sustainability must have its foundation. Culture, arts, economy, and freedom make up this foundation. The most important thing among them is freedom! Only after this foundation has been prepared can we talk about protecting the environment. It is senseless to talk about sustainability, not having created the most fundamental conditions for it.

Indeed, there was remarkable consensus that a sustainable society must be democratic, with multiple fora for negotiation. Democracy is not solely about the creation of a set of institutions but about much improved collective capacity to resolve common problems. In other words, sustainable societies should have the mechanisms to ensure that conflicts are resolved peacefully.

Describing a sustainable Cameroon, Christopher Atang envisions a democratically elected president and parliament that will work with people to not only speed up growth but also distribute its rewards more fairly. Graciela Diaz de Hasson (Argentina) refers to this as "economic democracy: greater participation of all social layers in the accumulation and distribution of the social product." Yet, this is by no means a universally accepted precondition of sustainability. Critics point out that several civilizations characterized by extreme inequities have been sustained for long periods. Giap Van Dang (Thailand) believes that the poor will always be among us. In a desirable future, he contends, they will not be abandoned by society, and their basic needs may be met.

A majority of contributors also emphasized the importance of responsible leadership and expressed a longing for increased authority at the local level. Respondents as diverse as a small farmer in Senegal and a fisherman on the Atlantic coast of Central America demanded that state and local governments stop imposing programs and dictating solutions to rural communities.

Both economies and the environment will gain from these sorts of changes. For example, Viviane Brachet-Marquez (Mexico) maintained that even our best efforts to protect human and biological resources will be wasted if ordinary people are not involved in the discussion of sustainability and governing elites continue to act as free, unchecked, and unaccountable agents, exercising their own will. Respondents pointed out that environmental conservation is not just a matter of technical, scientific, or sectoral debate. Therefore, stakeholders from both the private and public sectors should come together to make decisions about their collective well-being. Vernon Masayesva, speaking for the Hopi people of the Colorado Plateau, believes that sustainability at the local level depends on cooperation among federal, state, local, and tribal governments. Clearly, the ability of people to organize and express themselves at all levels is a fundamental precondition of sustainable systems.

No visions hinged on democracy in quite the same way as those of the Central and South American respondents. Again, this is evidence of how views of the future are unavoidably influenced by the present. From Haiti to Brazil, people called for popular participation and responsive leadership, equal participation of ethnic and linguistic minorities, access to information, and freedom of expression. The political and economic hegemony of the few was repeatedly challenged, not just because of the heartfelt desire for personal freedom and safety but also because contributors felt that pluralism would prevent future abuse of natural resources.

For example, Marta Echavarria Uribe (Colombia) wrote:

We have to relearn our capacity to disagree with respect, to give other people the treatment they deserve as fellow human beings—not based on social positions or income—and to live in some sort of harmony. For Colombian society to improve itself in the long term requires that all citizens adopt the principle of basic human and civil rights, which are essential for peace.

What was most surprising (and perhaps inspiring) was the breadth of change that contributors imagined, much of which touched on long-standing laws and traditions. Joseph Palacio (Belize) suggested resource abuse in the small nations of the Atlantic coast can only be prevented by the creation of a United Nations–protected sanctuary. For peace and security to be achieved in South Asia, ethnic and linguistic groups must have autonomy, as S. Sathananthan (Sri Lanka) wrote; therefore, governments and electorates should review their inherited colonial borders and consider redefining sovereignty. Uri Marinov and Deborah Sandler (Israel) suggested that in view of the population pressures and resource scarcities in Israel, the famous Law of Return may have to be amended or revoked. Anna Tibaijuka (Tanzania) believes we need a Marshall Plan for Africa. This recommendation must be held up against Ruth Bamela Engo-Tjega's (Cameroon) image of an Africa rejuvenated by its inner strengths, not external assistance. And in the fiftieth year of the United Nations, maybe it is time to revolutionize international governance as Eduardo Viola (Brazil) suggested, and make representation proportional to population.

The Role of Indigenous Groups

Nowhere is the chasm between the developing and industrialized worlds more clear than in the discussion of the role of indigenous groups. Indigenous people and their spokespersons contend that Western societies place human beings in a position of dominance over nature, making the search for sustainability fruitless. In contrast, they feel that sustainability is not about prosperity but about living a life of dignity in harmony with nature. Although the lives of indigenous people have always been tied to the Earth, their knowledge and experience with sustainable practices have systematically been ignored by the West. Some argue that even attaching words as seemingly contradictory as "sustainable" and "development" reflects the industrialized world's inability to give priority to the environment.

Many of the survey respondents expressed deep concern for the survival of indigenous knowledge and culture. Those who have lived with and studied these groups are often convinced that modernization is forcing the extinction of indigenous languages and cultures and leading to the permanent loss of knowledge and practices that have allowed indigenous peoples to live in consonance with their environments for centuries. Respect for indigenous knowledge and the creation of mechanisms that will ensure its possessors equal participation in policymaking was a familiar refrain in the 2050 Project.

Many feel modern science has devalued traditional knowledge. Jorge Terena (Ecuador) faults both the insular world of modern scientists and technologists and the system that profits by appropriating communal knowledge and granting "intellectual property rights" to its usurpers. He believes that among the indigenous people, by contrast, collective wisdom is derived from group knowledge of natural laws that are pertinent for the group's sustenance and survival. This collective memory works for everyone's benefit, not solely for the interests of individual leaders and entrepreneurs.

Indigenous peoples see a natural link between their lives and environmental protection. Pauline E. Tangiora, a Maori woman from New Zealand, stated that "the instinct to preserve is present in all people but the indigenous live it. It is not a question of dedication because that would imply choice. For us, it is not a choice. It is a responsibility." Tangiora and others suggest that their relationship with the environment is a spiritual one, where nature provides more than physical sustenance. In a sustainable system, there is no place for a biotechnology firm that fells a tree for the extraction of a single medicine; instead, there must be appreciation for the complex life of the tree—that it is a giver of shade and decorative flowers and a home to birds and animals as well as a source of medicine. Coexistence with nature is the crux of a desirable future. The symbiosis she describes stands in contrast to the Western perception of the environment as an enabler of human activity; thus, humans have a responsibility to preserve it.

In sharp contrast to this indigenous view of the primacy of the environment is the argument that sustainability is about "a systematic shift in economic development patterns" and that there are no inherent inconsistencies between the object of the market system and the goals of sustainability as long as "markets internalize environmental costs."[6] While many essayists would agree that "getting prices right" is certainly a component of the transition to a sustainable future, they appear to be increasingly disenchanted with the exclusive focus on economic growth and market instruments. Moreover, many felt we are facing an important choice: economic growth or harmony with nature. In German I. Andrade's (Colombia) words:

> From the perspective of minority groups it is clear that the concept of sustainability should include an ethical component. . . . In this region (the Amazon), it is clear that the only uses of nature that do not lead to losses in biodiversity are precisely those which can be interpreted as being antithetical to 'development.' Further, there are no known successful experiences of development which have not implied a loss of cultural diversity.

If economic growth must come at the expense of the Earth's ecosystem, as many contend it does, such growth is nonsustainable. Equating development with growth and growth with increases in wealth are at the heart of the struggle between development and sustainability. Indigenous leaders and grassroots activists, representing the priorities of people in the nonindustrialized world, argue for development with an emphasis not on growth but on a restructuring of economies and consumption patterns.[7]

Frugality in the consumption of nature is not antithetical to a system that ensures human survival and the satisfaction of basic needs instead of wealth and prosperity for all. Margaret Maringa (Kenya) asserted that in her desired future, "no person has more or less than he or she needs for basic survival." The suggestion that progress implies an increase in consumption was attacked not only by non-Western essayists but also squarely by two community activists from North America. Florence Robinson (United States) pointed to "classism" and the "excessive consumption of resources or materialism" as the two worst problems of America in the 20th century. She and Alex Steffen (United States) hoped for a future in which "luxury" will become a pejorative term.

Overemphasis on consumption was also addressed by Sixto Roxas (Philippines):

> We must not only de-materialize consumption and production, we must, as in the far distant past, resacralize everything: nature, community, consumption, production, governance, science, and technology. Which also means that everything is repersonal-

ized: the earth is our mother, the tree is our brother, as are the birds and all the fish and the deer. Every forest is a sacred grove, and every cow is a sacred cow, all lambs must be worthy of sacrifice, and all water is holy water. . . . In time, perhaps, the Asia which the West converted to a non-sustainable lifestyle will re-pay the West by teaching it the ways of sustainability.

The debate on the nonsustainability of growth and increased consumption illustrates the ideological divide between groups that appear to be equally concerned about the well-being of future generations. What is clear is that while the nonindustrialized world has learned a great deal about Western paradigms and priorities, the industrialized world has systematically ignored the unique and valuable knowledge of the developing world. Without such learning, a universal definition of sustainability, empty of ecological content and rife with cultural biases, can only lead to strategies, programs, and policies that project a false consensus.

Building Consensus

Global or even continent-wide formulas for sustainability may be an elusive goal for many reasons. First, as contributors have illustrated, there are many paths to a sustainable future, each determined by individualized priorities of what is desired and therefore worthy of sustaining. Second, the future is constrained by physical resources that are often finite or whose availability is difficult to determine. Third, the problems we face are multidimensional and interlinked, and no region can achieve sustainability in isolation. Hence, a desirable and sustainable future will be the result of many policy changes, some small and at the local level, others international and far-reaching. These will impact individuals, families, communities, businesses, and governments alike. We are only now taking the first steps toward understanding the complexity of the task that lies ahead.

Despite acceptance of the Brundtland definition of sustainable development, deep ideological divides must be overcome to progress toward sustainability. Desires for the future both unite and divide us. Accepting that our futures are inextricably linked could give us the humility to make compromises. Compromises around sustainability, however defined, should be based on open dialogues and partnerships among people in different nations and among diverse economic, linguistic, ethnic, and religious groups. If policy-makers could share power with those whom their policies most readily impact, they may not only design better strategies but also see them succeed more often. Broader policy instruments—impressive conventions and treaties—will have little bearing if ordinary people have no authority to see them implemented.

There are millions of positive images of the future. Our responsibility is not to choose among them—that belongs to future generations. Our responsibility is to leave them social and natural resources that will allow them to make these images a reality.

27

The Business of
Sustainable Development

Sustainable Development

During the first great wave of environmental concern in the late 1960s and early 1970s, most of the problems seemed local: the products of individual pipes and smokestacks. The answers appeared to lie in regulating these pollution sources.

When the environment reemerged on the political agenda in the 1980s, the main concerns had become international: acid rain, depletion of the ozone layer, and global warming. Analysts sought causes not in pipes and stacks but in the nature of human activities. One report after another concluded that much of what we do, many of our attempts to make "progress," are simply unsustainable. We cannot continue in our present methods of using energy, managing forests, farming, protecting plant and animal species, managing urban growth, and producing industrial goods. We certainly cannot continue to reproduce our species at the present rate.

Energy provides a striking example of present unsustainability. Most energy today is produced from fossil fuels: coal, oil, and gas. In the mid-1980s, the world

Excerpted from *Changing Course: A Global Business Perspective on Development and the Environment*, by Stephan Schmidheiny, with the Business Council for Sustainable Development (Cambridge, MA: MIT Press, 1992). © 1992 MIT Press.

was burning the equivalent of 10 billion metric tons of coal per year, with people in industrial nations using much more than those of the developing world. At these rates, by 2025 the expected global population of more than 8 billion would be using the equivalent of 14 billion metric tons of coal. But if all the world used energy at industrial-country levels, by 2025 the equivalent of 55 billion metric tons would be burned. Present levels of fossil fuel use may be warming the globe; a more than fivefold increase is unthinkable. Fossil fuels must be used more efficiently while alternatives are being developed if economic development is to be achieved without radically changing the global climate.[7]

Given such widespread evidence of unsustainability, it is not surprising that the concept of "sustainable development" has come to dominate the environment/development debate. In 1987, the World Commission on Environment and Development, appointed three years earlier by the U.N. General Assembly and headed by Norwegian Prime Minister Gro Harlem Brundtland, made sustainable development the theme of its entire report, *Our Common Future*. It defined the concept simply as a form of development or progress that "meets the needs of the present without compromising the ability of future generations to meet their own needs."[8]

The phrase itself can be misleading, as the word development might suggest that it is a chore for "developing" nations only. But development is more than growth, or quantitative change. It is primarily a change in quality. More than a decade ago, the influential World Conservation Strategy, compiled by the United Nations and organizations representing governments and private bodies, defined development as "the modification of the biosphere and the application of human, financial, living and non-living resources to satisfy human needs and improve the quality of human life."[9]

Thus all nations are, or would wish to be, developing. And sustainable development will require the greatest changes in the wealthiest nations, which consume the most resources, release the most pollution, and have the greatest capacity to make the necessary changes. These nations must also respond to the criticism from many leaders in the poor parts of the world that industrial countries risk reversing the relationship between production and the satisfaction of needs. They charge that increased production in wealthy nations no longer serves primarily to satisfy needs; rather, the creation of needs serves to increase production.

. . .

The Business Challenge

The requirement for clean, equitable economic growth remains the biggest single difficulty within the larger challenge of sustainable development.

Proving that such growth is possible is certainly the greatest test for business and industry, which must devise strategies to maximize added value while minimizing resource and energy use. Given the large technological and productive capacity of business, any progress toward sustainable development requires its active leadership.

Open, prospering markets are a powerful force for creating equity of opportunity among nations and people. Yet for there to be equal opportunity, there must first be opportunity itself. Open, competitive markets create the most opportunities for the most people. It is often the nations where markets most closely approach the ideal of "free," open, and competitive that have the least poverty and the greatest opportunity to escape from that poverty.

The World Commission listed as the first prerequisite for sustainable development a political system in which people can effectively participate in decision making. But freedom to participate in political decisions and freedom to participate in markets are inseparable over the long run. The citizens of Central Europe, having achieved political freedom, are now building market freedom. The Asian nations that achieved thriving market economies under authoritarian regimes are now moving toward more democratic governments.

Yet no market can be called "free" in which the decisions of a few can cause misuse of resources and pollution that threaten the present and future of the many. Today, for instance, the earth's atmosphere is providing the valuable service of acting as a dump for these pollutants; those enjoying this service rarely pay a reasonable price for it.

"Eco-efficiency"

The present limits to growth are not so much those imposed by resources, such as oil and other minerals, as was argued by the 1972 Club of Rome report *The Limits to Growth*.[19] In many cases they arise more from a scarcity of "sinks," or systems that can safely absorb wastes. The atmosphere, many bodies of water, and large areas of soil are reaching their own absorptive limits as regards wastes of all kinds.

Business has begun to respond to this truth. It is moving from a position of limiting pollution and cleaning up waste to comply with government regulations toward one of avoiding pollution and waste both in the interests of corporate citizenship and of being more efficient and competitive. The economies of the industrial countries have grown while the resources and energy needed to produce each unit of growth have declined. Chemical companies in industrial nations have doubled output since 1970 while more than halving energy consumption per unit of production.[20]

Industry is moving toward "demanufacturing" and remanufacturing"—that is, recycling the materials in their products and thus limiting the use of raw materials and of energy to convert those raw materials. That this is technically feasible is encouraging; that it can be done profitably is more encouraging. It is the more competitive and successful companies that are at the forefront of what we call "eco-efficiency."

But eco-efficiency is not achieved by technological change alone. It is achieved only by profound changes in the goals and assumptions that drive corporate activities, and change in the daily practices and tools used to reach them. This means a break with business-as-usual mentalities and conventional wisdom that sidelines environmental and human concerns.

A growing number of leading companies are adopting and publicly committing themselves to sustainable development strategies. They are expanding their concepts of who has a stake in their operations beyond employees and stockholders to include neighbors, public interest groups (including environmental organizations), customers, suppliers, governments, and the general public. They are communicating more openly with these new stakeholders. They are coming to realize that "the degree to which a company is viewed as being a positive or negative participant in solving sustainability issues will determine, to a very great degree, their long-term business viability," in the words of Ben Woodhouse, director of Global Environmental Issues at Dow Chemical.

The Challenge of Time

As the World Commission noted, sustainable development requires forms of progress that meet the needs of the present without compromising the ability of future generations to meet their own needs. In the late twentieth century, we are failing in the first clause of that definition by not meeting the basic needs of more than 1 billion people. We have not even begun to come to grips with the second clause: the needs of future generations. Some argue that we have no responsibility for the future, as we cannot know its needs. This is partly true, but it takes no great leap of reason to assume that our offspring will require breathable air, drinkable water, productive soils and oceans, a predictable climate, and abundant plant and animal species on the planet they will share.

Yet it is a hard thing to demand of political leaders, especially those who rely on the votes of the living to achieve and remain in high office, that they ask those alive today to bear costs for the sake of those not yet born, and not yet voting. It is equally hard to ask anyone in business, providing goods and services to the living, to change their ways for the sake of those not yet born, and not yet acting in the marketplace. The painful truth is that the present is a relatively comfortable place for those who have reached positions of mainstream political or business leadership.

This is the crux of the problem of sustainable development, and perhaps the main reason why there has been great acceptance of it in principle, but less concrete actions to put it into practice: many of those with the power to effect the necessary changes have the least motivation to alter the status quo that gave them that power.

When politicians, industrialists, and environmentalists run out of practical advice, they often take refuge in appeals for a new vision, new values, a new commitment, and a new ethic. Such calls often ring hollow and rhetorical. But given that sustainable development requires a practical concern for the needs of people in the future, then it does ultimately require a new shared vision and a collective ethic based on equality of opportunity not only among people and nations, but also between this generation and those to come. Sustainability will require new technology, new approaches to trade to spread the technology and the goods necessary for survival, and new ways of meeting needs through markets. Business leadership will be required, and expected, in all these areas.

However, sustainable development will ultimately be achieved only through cooperation among people and all their various organizations, including business and governments. And leaders elected to decision-making and executive offices retain a fundamental obligation to inform and educate their constituencies about the urgent necessity and the reasons for changing course.

We believe that the best aspects of the human propensity to buy, sell, and produce can be an engine of change. Business has helped to create much of what is valuable in the world today. It will play its part in ensuring the planet's future. . . .

ALAN DURNING

28

How Much Is Enough?

The Conundrum of Consumption

For Sidney Quarrier of Essex, Connecticut, Earth Day 1990 was Judgment Day—the day of ecological reckoning. While tens of millions of people around the world were marching and celebrating in the streets, Sidney was sitting at his kitchen table with a yellow legal pad and a pocket calculator. The task he set himself was to tally up the burden he and his family had placed on the planet since Earth Day 1970.[1]

Early that spring morning he began tabulating everything that had gone into their house—oil for heating, nuclear-generated electricity, water for showers and watering the lawn, cans of paint, appliances, square footage of carpet, furniture, clothes, food, and thousands of other things—and everything that had come out—garbage pails of junk mail and packaging, newspapers and magazines by the cubic meter, polluted water, and smoke from the furnace. He listed the resources they had tapped to move them around by car and airplane, from fuel and lubricants to tires and replacement parts. "I worked on that list most of the day," Sid remembers. "I dug out wads of old receipts, weighed trash cans and the daily mail, excavated the basement and shed, and used triangulation techniques I hadn't practiced since graduate school to estimate the materials we used in the roofing job."[2]

Manufacturing and delivering each of the objects on his list, Sid knew, had required additional resources he was unable to count. National statistics suggested,

Excerpted from *How Much Is Enough? The Consumer Society and the Future of the Earth* (New York: W. W. Norton, 1992). Reprinted with permission of the Worldwatch Institute.

for example, that he should double the energy he used in his house and car to allow for what businesses and government used to provide him with goods and services. He visualized a global industrial network of factories making things for him, freighters and trucks transporting them, stores selling them, and office buildings supervising the process. He wondered how much steel and concrete his state needed for the roads, bridges, and parking garages he used. He wondered about resources used by the hospital that cared for him, the air force jets and police cars that protected him, the television stations that entertained him, and the veterinary office that cured his dog.

As his list grew, Sid was haunted by an imaginary mountain of discarded televisions, car parts, and barrels of oil—all piling up toward the sky on his lot. "It was a sober revisiting of that period. . . . It's only when you put together all the years of incremental consumption that you realize the totality." That totality hit him like the ton of paper packaging he had hauled out with the trash over the years: "The question is," Sid said, "Can the earth survive the impact of Sid, and can the Sids of the future change?"[3]

That *is* the question. Sidney Quarrier and his family are no gluttons. "During those years, we lived in a three-bedroom house on two-and-a-half acres in the country, about 35 miles from my job in Hartford," Sidney recounts. "But we have never been rich," he insists. "What frightened me was that our consumption was typical of the people here in Connecticut."[4]

Sid's class—the American middle class—is the group that, more than any other, defines and embodies the contemporary international vision of the good life. Yet the way the Quarriers lived for those 20 years is among the world's premier environmental problems, and may be the most difficult to solve.

Only population growth rivals high consumption as a cause of ecological decline, and at least population growth is now viewed as a problem by many governments and citizens of the world. Consumption, in contrast, is almost universally seen as good—indeed, increasing it is the primary goal of national economic policy. The consumption levels exemplified in the two decades Sid Quarrier reviewed are the highest achieved by any civilization in human history. They manifest the full flowering of a new form of human society: the consumer society.

This new manner of living was born in the United States, and the words of an American best capture its spirit. In the age of U.S. affluence that began after World War II, retailing analyst Victor Lebow declared: "Our enormously productive economy . . . demands that we make consumption our way of life, that we convert the buying and use of goods into rituals, that we seek our spiritual satisfaction, our ego satisfaction, in consumption. . . . We need things consumed, burned up, worn out, replaced, and discarded at an ever increasing rate." Most citizens of western nations have responded to Lebow's call, and the rest of the world appears intent on following.[5]

In industrial lands, consumption now permeates social values. Opinion surveys in the world's two largest economies—Japan and the United States—show that people increasingly measure success by the amount they consume. The Japanese speak of the "new three sacred treasures": color television, air conditioning, and the automobile. One-fourth of Poles deem "Dynasty," which portrays the life-style of the richest Americans, their favorite television program, and villagers in the heart of Africa follow "Dallas," the television series that portrays American oil tycoons. In Taiwan, a billboard demands "Why Aren't You a Millionaire Yet?" A *Business Week* correspondent beams: "The American Dream is alive and well . . . in Mexico." Indeed, the words "consumer" and "person" have become virtual synonyms.[6]

The life-style made in the United States is emulated by those who can afford it around the world, but many cannot. The economic fault lines that fracture the globe defy comprehension. The world has 202 billionaires and more than 3 million millionaires. It also has 100 million homeless people who live on roadsides, in garbage dumps, and under bridges. The value of luxury goods sales worldwide—high-fashion clothing, top-of-the-line autos, and the other trappings of wealth—exceeds the gross national products of two-thirds of the world's countries. Indeed, the world's average income, about $5,000 a year, is below the U.S. poverty line.[7]

The gaping divide in material consumption between the fortunate and unfortunate stands out starkly in their impacts on the natural world. The soaring consumption lines that track the rise of the consumer society are, from another perspective, surging indicators of environmental harm. The consumer society's exploitation of resources threatens to exhaust, poison, or unalterably disfigure forests, soils, water, and air. We, its members, are responsible for a disproportionate share of all the global environmental challenges facing humanity. . . .

Ironically, high consumption is a mixed blessing in human terms too. People living in the nineties are on average four-and-a-half times richer than their great-grandparents were at the turn of the century, but they are not four-and-a-half times happier. Psychological evidence shows that the relationship between consumption and personal happiness is weak. Worse, two primary sources of human fulfillment—social relations and leisure—appear to have withered or stagnated in the rush to riches. Thus many of us in the consumer society have a sense that our world of plenty is somehow hollow—that, hoodwinked by a consumerist culture, we have been fruitlessly attempting to satisfy with material things what are essentially social, psychological, and spiritual needs.[8]

Of course, the opposite of overconsumption—destitution—is no solution to either environmental or human problems. It is infinitely worse for people and bad for the natural world too. Dispossessed peasants slash-and-burn their way into the rain forests of Latin America, hungry nomads turn their herds out onto fragile African rangeland, reducing it to desert, and small farmers in India and the Philippines cultivate steep slopes, exposing them to the erosive powers of rain. Perhaps half the world's billion-plus absolute poor are caught in a downward spiral of ecological and economic impoverishment. In desperation, they knowingly abuse the land, salvaging the present by savaging the future.[9]

If environmental destruction results when people have either too little or too much, we are left to wonder, How much is enough? What level of consumption can the earth support? When does having more cease to add appreciably to human satisfaction? Is it possible for all the world's people to live comfortably without bringing on the decline of the planet's natural health? Is there a level of living above poverty and subsistence but below the consumer life-style—a level of sufficiency? Could all the world's people have central heating? Refrigerators? Clothes dryers? Automobiles? Air conditioning? Heated swimming pools? Airplanes? Second homes?

Many of these questions cannot be answered definitively, but for each of us in the consumer society, asking is essential nonetheless. Unless we see that more is not always better, our efforts to forestall ecological decline will be overwhelmed by our appetites. Unless we ask, we will likely fail to see the forces around us that stimulate those appetites, such as relentless advertising, proliferating shopping centers, and social pressures to "keep up with the Joneses." We may overlook forces that make consumption more destructive than it need be, such as subsidies to mines, paper mills, and other industries with high environmental impacts. And we may not act on opportunities to improve our lives while consuming less, such as working fewer hours to spend more time with family and friends.

Still, the difficulty of transforming the consumer society into a sustainable one can scarcely be overestimated. We consumers enjoy a life-style that almost everybody else aspires to, and why shouldn't they? Who would just as soon not have an automobile, a big house on a big lot, and complete control over indoor temperature throughout the year? The momentum of centuries of economic history and the material cravings of 5.5 billion people lie on the side of increasing consumption.

We may be, therefore, in a conundrum—a problem admitting of no satisfactory solution. Limiting the consumer life-style to those who have already attained it is not politically possible, morally defensible, or ecologically sufficient. And extending that life-style to all would simply hasten the ruin of the biosphere. The global environment cannot support 1.1 billion of us living like American consumers, much less 5.5 billion people, or a future population of at least 8 billion. On the other hand, reducing the consumption levels of the consumer society, and tempering material aspirations elsewhere, though morally acceptable, is a quixotic proposal. It bucks the trend of centuries. Yet it may be the only option.

If the life-supporting ecosystems of the planet are to survive for future generations, the consumer society will have to dramatically curtail its use of resources— partly by shifting to high-quality, low-input durable goods and partly by seeking fulfillment through leisure, human relationships, and other nonmaterial avenues. We in the consumer society will have to live a technologically sophisticated version of the life-style currently practiced lower on the economic ladder. Scientific advances, better laws, restructured industries, new treaties, environmental taxes, grassroots campaigns—all can help us get there. But ultimately, sustaining the environment that sustains humanity will require that we change our values.

The Consumer Society

The world has three broad ecological classes: the consumers, the middle income, and the poor. These groups, ideally defined by their per capita consumption of natural resources, emissions of pollution, and disruption of habitats, can be distinguished in practice through two proxy measures: their average annual incomes and their life-styles (see Table 28.1).

The world's poor—some 1.1 billion people—includes all households that earn less than $700 a year per family member. They are mostly rural Africans, Indians, and other South Asians. They eat almost exclusively grains, root crops, beans, and other legumes, and they drink mostly unclean water. They live in huts and shanties, they travel by foot, and most of their possessions are constructed of stone, wood, and other substances available from the local environment. This poorest fifth of the world's people earns just 2 percent of world income.[10]

The 3.3 billion people in the world's middle-income class earn between $700 and $7,500 per family member and live mostly in Latin America, the Middle East, China, and East Asia. This class also includes the low-income families of the former Soviet bloc and of western industrial nations. With notable exceptions, they eat a diet based on grains and water, and lodge in moderate buildings with electricity for lights, radios, and, increasingly, refrigerators and clothes washers. (In Chinese cities, for example, two-thirds of households now have washing machines and one-fifth have refrigerators.) They travel by bus, railway, and bicycle, and maintain a modest stock of durable goods. Collectively, they claim 33 percent of world income.[11]

The consumer class—the 1.1 billion members of the global consumer society—includes all households whose income per family member is above $7,500. Though that threshold puts the lowest ranks of the consumer class scarcely above the U.S. poverty line, they—rather, we—still enjoy a life-style unknown in earlier ages. We dine on meat and processed, packaged foods, and imbibe soft drinks and other beverages from disposable containers. We spend most of our time in climate-controlled buildings equipped with refrigerators, clothes washers and dry-

Table 28.1   World Consumption Classes, 1992

Category of Consumption	Consumers (1.1 billion)	Middle (3.3 billion)	Poor (1.1 billion)
Diet	meat, packaged food, soft drinks	grain, clean water	insufficient grain, unsafe water
Transport	private cars	bicycles, buses	walking
Materials	throwaways	durables	local biomass

SOURCE: Worldwatch Institute

ers, abundant hot water, dishwashers, microwave ovens, and a plethora of other electric-powered gadgets. We travel in private automobiles and airplanes, and surround ourselves with a profusion of short-lived, throwaway goods. The consumer class takes home 64 percent of world income—32 times as much as the poor.[12]

The consumer class counts among its members most North Americans, West Europeans, Japanese, Australians, and the citizens of Hong Kong, Singapore, and the oil sheikdoms of the Middle East. Perhaps half the people of Eastern Europe and the Commonwealth of Independent States are in the consumer class, as are about one-fifth of the people in Latin America, South Africa, and the newly industrializing countries of Asia, such as South Korea.[13]

. . .

A Culture of Permanence

. . . The future of life on earth depends on whether we among the richest fifth of the world's people, having fully met our material needs, can turn to nonmaterial sources of fulfillment. Whether we—who have defined the tangible goals of world development—can now craft a new way of life at once simpler and more satisfying. Having invented the automobile and the airplane, can we return to bicycles, buses, and trains? Having pioneered sprawl and malls, can we recreate human-scale settlements where commerce is an adjunct to civic life rather than its purpose? Having introduced the high-fat, junk-food diet, can we instead nourish ourselves on wholesome fare that is locally produced? Having devised disposable plastics, packaging without end, and instantaneous obsolescence, can we design objects that endure and a materials economy that takes care of things?

If our grandchildren are to inherit a planet as bounteous and beautiful as we have enjoyed, we in the consumer class must—without surrendering the quest for advanced, clean technology—eat, travel, and use energy and materials more like those on the middle rung of the world's economic ladder. If we can learn to do so, we might find ourselves happier as well, for in the consumer society, affluence has brought us to a strange pass. Who would have predicted a century ago that the richest civilizations in history would be made up of polluted tracts of suburban development dominated by the private automobile, shopping malls, and a throwaway economy? Surely, this is not the ultimate fulfillment of our destiny.

In the final analysis, accepting and living by sufficiency rather than excess offers a return to what is, culturally speaking, the human home: to the ancient order of family, community, good work, and good life; to a reverence for skill, creativity, and creation; to a daily cadence slow enough to let us watch a sunset and stroll by the water's edge; to communities worth spending a lifetime in; and to local places pregnant with the memories of generations. Perhaps Henry David Thoreau had it right when he scribbled in his notebook beside Walden Pond, "A man is rich in proportion to the things he can afford to let alone."[14]

PART SIX

From Ecological Conflict to Environmental Security?

Chris J. Calwell, Ecos Consulting

As seen in the previous section, the concept of sustainability has emerged as a powerful new paradigm shaping the interpretations, goals, and behavior of a broad range of actors on the global environmental stage. But the global environmental debate of the past two decades has engaged not only economic issues of welfare, production, and livelihood but also political questions of international conflict, violence, and geopolitics. It is not surprising that paradigms focused on the conflictual dimensions of environmental problems also have begun to emerge.

One attempt to grapple with these intensely political themes is the emerging paradigm of "environmental security." Like sustainability, environmental security offers a potentially powerful but also controversial new way to think about the social dimensions of environmental problems. The environmental security paradigm rests on a series of claims: that environmental change is an important source of social conflict; that many societies face graver dangers from environmental change than from traditional military threats; and that security policies must be redefined to take account of these new realities.

The essay by Thomas Homer-Dixon addresses the connection between environmental change and violent conflict. Homer-Dixon argues that environmental change is becoming an increasingly important source of social instability, civil strife, and violence within and between societies. The growing scarcity of renewable resources—principally water, fish stocks, forests, and fertile land—already promotes such conflict, and it is likely to cause a surge in violence in the future. Homer-Dixon stresses that political and economic institutions remain central to determining specific patterns of conflict. But he also argues that "environmental scarcity" is driven by environmental change, population growth, and the unequal social distribution of natural resources—is an increasingly important factor.

Given such conflict potential, proponents of environmental security have argued that there is an urgent, compelling need to "redefine" the concept of security.[1] Environmental threats must become central concerns of the security policies of states. In the second chapter of this part, the United Nations Development Programme (UNDP) proposes that security issues be viewed within the broader category of "human security," the definition of which encompasses environmental as well as other specific concerns. The UNDP's seven components of human security, enumerated in the 1994 edition of its influential annual *Human Development Report*, hold up human well-being as what

281

should be "secured" or provided to individuals and societies. Just as economic considerations have become increasingly important in security policy deliberations, so too must environmental concerns be raised to the level of "high politics." The UNDP's call for redefining security, and others like it, also stress that cooperation, and not defensive preparation for conflict, is the most effective way to address nonmilitary threats. Current military means are deemed inadequate to counter the new threats of environmental degradation, violent crime, economic inequities, food shortages, and infectious diseases.

The arguments for redefining security make clear that environmental security is more than an effort to reconceptualize the nature of the present and future threats that societies face. It is also a political agenda aimed at mobilizing the state and society toward a new set of goals and at redirecting resources and energies away from exclusively military concerns. Some proponents argue that only by framing the environmental problematique in security terms can the necessary level of governmental attention and social mobilization be ensured.[3] Others argue that security institutions could contribute directly to environmental protection, given their financial resources, monitoring and intelligence-gathering capabilities, and scientific and technological expertise.[4]

Thus, although the origins of the environmental security paradigm can be traced at least to the early post–World War II period,[5] it is surely no accident that the idea of rethinking security policy in ecological terms has flourished in the post–Cold War era. Policymakers, military institutions, and entire societies have begun to reconsider the character of the threats they face. Many proponents of environmental security are driven by the belief that the end of the Cold War has opened a window of opportunity for fundamental changes in security policies and a reordering of social priorities.

Among the many controversies surrounding the paradigm of environmental security, two are central. First, is there enough strong evidence to support the claim that ecological change is, or will be, a major new source of conflict? Although a growing body of research points to specific cases in which environmental change seems to have played a role in promoting or exacerbating social conflict, many questions remain. Why does environmental stress produce such conflict in some cases but not in others? Is it possible that environmental problems are a *symptom* of conflict-prone social systems rather than a root cause of conflict? Observers who pose these questions are indicating their doubt that environmental change is an important, independent source of conflict. A second set of questions involves the more nebulous concept of "security." Are the advantages of linking environmental problems to security concerns worth the risk of militarizing a society's responses to environmental problems?

The essay by Daniel Deudney raises both sets of questions. Deudney is skeptical that environmental change precipitates acute conflict, at least in the form of war; he argues that environmental problems have little in common with the traditional security problem of interstate violence.[6] Deudney is also wary of evoking the powerful concept of security in order to mobilize society: "For environmentalists to dress their programs in the bloodsoaked garments of the war system betrays their core values and creates confusion about the real tasks at hand." Others have voiced stronger criticisms, suggesting that the powerful association between the concept of security and the use of military force creates the danger of turning environmental problems into sources of military tension and conflict.[7] Matthias Finger argues that "the military must be addressed as a cause and not a cure of global environmental problems." In Finger's view, worldwide militarization wastes scarce resources that could be deployed in the struggle against environmental degradation and is itself a source of massive amounts of pollution.[8] These critics share Deudney's view that the conflictual mind-set and the military tools of security institutions are poorly suited to the global environmental problematique.

The environmental security debate is further complicated by the way in which it intersects the North-South axis in world politics. The focus of ecological conflict research tends to be on the economically less-developed regions of the planet; most analysts emphasize these regions when identifying likely sites of future environmentally induced conflicts. There are many reasons for this focus on the South: its limited financial and technological resources, high population growth rates, preexisting political instability, and the day-to-day struggles for survival that engulf large segments of its population. However, even if it is plausible to claim that the South will be the site of environmental conflicts, this concern cannot be divorced from the broader pattern of North-South relations. The essay by Egyptian diplomat Somaya Saad reflects the deep suspicion with which many Southern governments view the North's concern for "security" in the South, environmental or otherwise. She sees the rhetoric of environmental security as an excuse to continue the North's long-standing practice of military and economic intervention. She also suggests that the extensive focus on the South is a way for the North to deny its own overwhelming responsibility for the deteriorating state of the planet. Saad's concerns emphasize the importance of history and context. In a world where many people feel their security threatened by other people, calls for changes in security policies may seem like a way to break the cycle of violence, suspicion, and zero-sum thinking; but given the purposes that security policies have served in the past, such calls also raise deep suspicions about ulterior motives.

Social science may lack the tools to tell us exactly when and where environmental problems will produce violence. Nevertheless, the capacity of environmental change to disrupt people's lives, erode standards of living, and threaten established interests tells us that the possibility of widespread violent conflict must be taken seriously. Research that helps us understand when and where such conflict is likely to occur could be an important tool for conflict avoidance, international confidence building, and nonviolent conflict resolution. But the paradigm of environmental security remains controversial because it links plausible claims about conflict to the symbolically powerful and highly charged concept of security. At best, linking environment and security could be a way to build trust among nations and make security a cooperative, global endeavor, while at the same time steering resources and public energy toward the resolution of environmental problems; but at worst, tying environmental concerns to militarized approaches to social conflict could itself be a recipe for greater violence in the future.

Thinking Critically

1. Can you think of examples that run counter to the Homer-Dixon argument—that is, cases where the conditions for environmentally induced violent conflict seem to exist but violence does not occur? What social institutions or other conditions are likely to influence whether violence occurs? Is the connection between environment and conflict solely a problem for the developing world?

2. Must security be redefined in the post–Cold War world? Can it be? Does the UNDP identify the correct set of threats? Are they new?

3. Which seems more likely: the "greening" of security policy or the militarization of environmental policy? Are Deudney's concerns about the mismatched tools of traditional security institutions well founded? Can we generalize across countries in answering this question?

4. Is environmental security an idea with more appeal in the North than the South? Are Saad's fears of Northern intent legitimate? Does the broader definition of security enunciated by the UNDP speak convincingly to the problems of the South?

Additional Reading

Environment and Violent Conflict

Baechler, Günther, "Environmental Transformation and Violence: A Synthesis," *Environmental Change and Security Project Report* 4 (1998).

Environmental Change and Security Project Report (Washington, DC: Woodrow Wilson International Center for Scholars, annual).

Gleditsch, Nils Petter, *Conflict and the Environment* (Dordrecht, The Netherlands: Academic Publishers, 1997).

Westing, Arthur H., ed., *Environmental Hazards of War* (London: Sage Publications, 1990).

Redefining Security

Brown, Lester, *Redefining National Security,* Worldwatch Paper 14 (Washington, DC: Worldwatch Institute, 1977).

Conca, Ken, "The Environment-Security Trap," *Dissent*, Summer 1998.

Dabelko, Geoffrey D., and P. J. Simmons, "Environment and Security: Core Ideas and U.S. Government Initiatives," *The SAIS Review* 17 (Winter-Spring 1997):127–146.

Finger, Matthias, "The Military, the Nation State and the Environment," *The Ecologist* 21, no. 5 (September-October 1991):220–225.

Käkönen, Jyrki, ed., *Green Security or Militarized Environment* (Aldershot, UK: Dartmouth, 1994).

Mathews, Jessica Tuchman, "Redefining Security," *Foreign Affairs* 67 (1989):162–177.

Myers, Norman, *Ultimate Security: The Environmental Basis of Political Stability* (New York: W. W. Norton, 1993).

Internet Resources

Project on Environment, Population, and Security, *http://utl2.library.utoronto. ca/www/pcs/eps.htm.* This site summarizes research activities based at the University of Toronto and described in the essay by Thomas Homer-Dixon. The site provides information on case studies and offers an extensive bibliography.

Environment and Conflicts Project, *http://www.fsk.ethz.ch.* This Swiss project produced forty in-depth case studies on environmental transformation and violence. The Web site contains information about these cases as well as many useful links to related sites.

Environmental Change and Security Project, *http://www.ecsp.si.edu.* This project of the Washington-based Woodrow Wilson Center is an information clearinghouse for issues related to environment, population, and security. Its reports include meeting summaries, book reviews, an extensive bibliography, and other useful information.

Global Environmental Change and Human Security Project, *http://steve. geog.uvic.ca/GECHS/index.html.* A project of the International Human Dimensions Program on Global Environmental Change, this site provides information on a wide array of research, publications, and activities related to environmental and human security.

Center for Environmental Security, *http://w3.pnl.gov.2080/ces*. This center was established by one of the U.S. national science laboratories "to debate and evaluate environmental issues that impact [U.S.] national security."

Office of the U.S. Deputy Undersecretary of Defense for Environmental Security, *http://www.acq.osd.mil/ens*. This site describes the activities of the central environmental node at the Pentagon.

Canadian Department of National Defence, Environment Division, *http://www.dnd.caladmieldge/dge2e.htm*. This site describes the environment-related activities of the Canadian armed forces.

Nautilus Institute for Security and Sustainable Development, *http://www.nautilus.org*. This California-based NGO is "a policy-oriented research and consulting organization focusing on emerging environmental, energy, and security issues, primarily in the Asia-Pacific region."

THOMAS F. HOMER-DIXON

29

Environmental Scarcities and Violent Conflict: Evidence from Cases

Within the next fifty years, the planet's human population will probably pass nine billion, and global economic output may quintuple. Largely as a result, scarcities of renewable resources will increase sharply. The total area of high-quality agricultural land will drop, as will the extent of forests and the number of species they sustain. Coming generations will also see the widespread depletion and degradation of aquifers, rivers, and other water resources; the decline of many fisheries; and perhaps significant climate change.

If such "environmental scarcities" become severe, could they precipitate violent civil or international conflict? I have previously surveyed the issues and evidence surrounding this question and proposed an agenda for further research.[1] Here I report the results of an international research project guided by this agenda.[2] . . .

In brief, our research showed that environmental scarcities are already contributing to violent conflicts in many parts of the developing world. These conflicts are probably the early signs of an upsurge of violence in the coming decades that will be induced or aggravated by scarcity. The violence will usually be sub-

Abridged article reprinted from *International Security* 19, no. 1 (1994):5–40 by permission of MIT Press, Cambridge, Massachusetts. © 1994 The President and Fellows of Harvard College and the Massachusetts Institute of Technology.

national, persistent, and diffuse. Poor societies will be particularly affected since they are less able to buffer themselves from environmental scarcities and the social crises they cause. These societies are, in fact, already suffering acute hardship from shortages of water, forests, and especially fertile land.

Social conflict is not always a bad thing: mass mobilization and civil strife can produce opportunities for beneficial change in the distribution of land and wealth and in processes of governance. But fast-moving, unpredictable, and complex environmental problems can overwhelm efforts at constructive social reform. Moreover, scarcity can sharply increase demands on key institutions, such as the state, while it simultaneously reduces their capacity to meet those demands. These pressures increase the chance that the state will either fragment or become more authoritarian. The negative effects of severe environmental scarcity are therefore likely to outweigh the positive.

General Findings

Our research was intended to provide a foundation for further work. We therefore focused on two key preliminary questions: does environmental scarcity cause violent conflict? And, if it does, how does it operate?

The research was structured as I proposed in my previous article. Six types of environmental change were identified as plausible causes of violent inter-group conflict:

- greenhouse-induced climate change;
- stratospheric ozone depletion;
- degradation and loss of good agricultural land;
- degradation and removal of forests;
- depletion and pollution of fresh water supplies; and
- depletion of fisheries.

We used three hypotheses to link these changes with violent conflict. First, we suggested that decreasing supplies of physically controllable environmental resources, such as clean water and good agricultural land, would provoke interstate "simple-scarcity" conflicts or resource wars. Second, we hypothesized that large population movements caused by environmental stress would induce "group-identity" conflicts, especially ethnic clashes. And third, we suggested that severe environmental scarcity would simultaneously increase economic deprivation and disrupt key social institutions, which in turn would cause "deprivation" conflicts such as civil strife and insurgency. . . .

Resource Depletion and Degradation

Of the major environmental changes facing humankind, degradation and depletion of agricultural land, forests, water, and fish will contribute more to social turmoil in coming decades than will climate change or ozone depletion.

When analysts and policymakers in developed countries consider the social impacts of large-scale environmental change, they focus undue attention on climate change and stratospheric ozone depletion.[4] But vast populations in the developing world are already suffering from shortages of good land, water, forests, and fish; in contrast, the social effects of climate change and ozone depletion will probably not be seen till well into the next century. If these atmospheric problems do eventually have an impact, they will most likely operate not as individual environmental stresses, but in interaction with other, long-present resource, demographic, and economic pressures that have gradually eroded the buffering capacity of some societies.

Mexico, for example, is vulnerable to such interactions. People are already leaving the state of Oaxaca because of drought and soil erosion. Researchers estimate that future global warming could decrease Mexican rainfed maize production up to 40 percent. This change could in turn interact with ongoing land degradation, free trade (because Mexico's comparative advantage is in water-intensive fruits and vegetables), and the privatization of communal peasant lands to cause grave internal conflict.[5]

Environmental Scarcity

Environmental change is only one of three main sources of scarcity of renewable resources; the others are population growth and unequal social distribution of resources. The concept "environmental scarcity" encompasses all three sources.

Analysts often usefully characterize environmental problems as resource scarcities. Resources can be roughly divided into two groups: non-renewables, like oil and iron ore, and renewables, like fresh water, forests, fertile soils, and the earth's ozone layer. The latter category includes renewable "goods" such as fisheries and timber, and renewable "services" such as regional hydrological cycles and a benign climate.

The commonly used term "environmental change" refers to a human-induced decline in the quantity or quality of a renewable resource that occurs faster than it is renewed by natural processes. But this concept limits the scope of environment-conflict research. Environmental change is only one of three main sources of renewable-resource scarcity. The second, population growth, reduces a resource's per-capita availability by dividing it among more and more people.[6] The third, unequal resource distribution, concentrates a resource in the hands of a few people and subjects the rest to greater scarcity.[7] The property rights that govern resource distribution often change as a result of large-scale development projects or new technologies that alter the relative values of resources.

In other words, reduction in the quantity or quality of a resource shrinks the resource pie, while population growth divides the pie into smaller slices for each individual, and unequal resource distribution means that some groups get disproportionately large slices.[8] Unfortunately, analysts often study resource depletion and population growth in isolation from the political economy of resource distribution.[9] The term "environmental scarcity," however, allows these three distinct sources of scarcity to be incorporated into one analysis. Empirical evidence suggests, in fact, that the first two sources are most pernicious when they interact with unequal resource distribution.

We must also recognize that resource scarcity is, in part, subjective; it is determined not just by absolute physical limits, but also by preferences, beliefs, and norms. This is illustrated by a debate about the role of population growth and resource scarcity as causes of the conflict between the Sandinista government and the Miskito Indians in Nicaragua.[10] Bernard Nietschmann argues that the Nicaraguan state's need for resources to sustain the country's economic and agricultural development caused environmental degradation to spread from the Pacific to the Atlantic coast of the country. As this happened, indigenous Miskitos in the east came into conflict with the central government. Sergio Diaz-Briquets responds that the Sandinistas expropriated Miskito lands because of ideology, not scarcity. The Atlantic coastal region was largely ignored by the Nicaraguan state under Somoza. Following the revolution, the Sandinistas had ample newly expropriated land to distribute to their followers; but the new government— guided by Marxism—saw the Miskitos as a backward people with a competing worldview and a precapitalist mode of production, whose land rightfully belonged to a state that was removing impediments to the historical progress of the working class.

The gap between the two views can be bridged by noting that scarcity is partly subjective. Marxist ideology encouraged the Sandinistas to adopt a strategy of state-directed industrialization and resource-use; this led them to perceive resources as more scarce than had the Somoza regime.

Interaction of Sources
of Environmental Scarcity

The three sources of environmental scarcity often interact, and two patterns of interaction are particularly common: "resource capture" and "ecological marginalization." . . .

A fall in the quality and quantity of renewable resources can combine with population growth to encourage powerful groups within a society to shift resource distribution in their favor. This can produce dire environmental scarcity for poorer and weaker groups whose claims to resources are opposed by these powerful elites. I call this type of interaction "resource capture." Unequal resource access can combine with population growth to cause migrations to regions that are ecologically fragile, such as steep upland slopes, areas at risk of desertification, and tropical rain forests. High population densities in these areas, combined with a lack of knowledge and capital to protect local resources, cause severe environmental damage and chronic poverty. This process is often called "ecological marginalization."[11]

. . .

Hypothesis 1: Simple-Scarcity
Conflicts Between States

There is little empirical support for the first hypothesis that environmental scarcity causes simple-scarcity conflicts between states. Scarcities of renewable resources such as forests and croplands do not often cause resource wars between states. This finding is intriguing because resource wars have been common since the beginning of the state system. For instance, during World War II, Japan sought to secure oil, minerals, and other resources in China and Southeast Asia, and the 1991 Gulf War was at least partly motivated by the desire for oil.

However, we must distinguish between non-renewable resources such as oil, and renewable resources. Arthur Westing has compiled a list of twelve conflicts in the twentieth century involving resources, beginning with World War I and concluding with the Falklands/Malvinas War.[28] Access to oil or minerals was at issue in ten of these conflicts. Just five conflicts involved renewable resources, and only two of these—the 1969 Soccer War between El Salvador and Honduras, and the Anglo-Icelandic Cod War of 1972–73—concerned neither oil nor minerals (cropland was a factor in the former case, and fish in the latter). However, the Soccer War was not a simple-scarcity conflict between states; rather it arose from the ecological marginalization of Salvadorean peasants and their consequent migration into Honduras.[29] It is evidence in support, therefore, of our second and third hypotheses (below), but not for the first. And, since the Cod War, despite its name, involved very little violence, it hardly qualifies as a resource war.

States have fought more over non-renewable than renewable resources for two reasons, I believe. First, petroleum and mineral resources can be more directly converted into state power than can agricultural land, fish, and forests. Oil and coal fuel factories and armies, and ores are vital for tanks and naval ships. In contrast, although captured forests and cropland may eventually generate wealth that can be harnessed by the state for its own ends, this outcome is more remote in time and less certain. Second, the very countries that are most dependent on renewable resources, and which are therefore most motivated to seize resources from their neighbors, also tend to be poor, which lessens their capability for aggression.

Our research suggests that the renewable resource most likely to stimulate interstate resource war is river water.[30] Water is a critical resource for personal and national survival; furthermore, since river water flows from one area to another, one country's access can be affected by another's actions. Conflict is most probable when a downstream riparian is highly dependent on river water and is strong in comparison to upstream riparians. Downstream riparians often fear that their upstream neighbors will use water as a means of coercion. This situation is particularly dangerous if the downstream country also believes it has the military power to rectify the situation. The relationships between South Africa and Lesotho and between Egypt and Ethiopia have this character.[31] . . .

However, our review of the historical and contemporary evidence shows that conflict and turmoil related to river water are more often internal than international. The huge dams that are often built to deal with general water scarcity are especially disruptive. Relocating large numbers of upstream people generates turmoil among the relocatees and clashes with local groups in areas where the relocatees are resettled. The people affected are often members of ethnic or minority groups outside the power hierarchy of their society, and the result is frequently rebellion by these groups and repression by the state. Water developments can also induce conflict over water and irrigable land among a country's downstream users, as we saw in the Senegal River basin.[33]

Hypothesis 2: Population Movement and Group-Identity Conflicts

There is substantial evidence to support the hypothesis that environmental scarcity causes large population movement, which in turn causes group-identity conflicts. But we must be sensitive to contextual factors unique to each socio-ecological system. These are the system's particular physical, political, economic, and cultural features that affect the strength of the linkages between scarcity, population movement, and conflict.

For example, experts emphasize the importance of both "push" and "pull" factors in decisions of potential migrants.[34] These factors help distinguish migrants from refugees: while migrants are motivated by a combination of push and pull, refugees are motivated mainly by push. Environmental scarcity is more likely to produce migrants than refugees, because it usually develops gradually, which means that the push effect is not sharp and sudden and that pull factors can therefore clearly enter into potential migrants' calculations.

Migrants are often people who have been weak and marginal in their home society and, depending on context, they may remain weak in the receiving society. This limits their ability to organize and to make demands. States play a critical role here: migrants often need the backing of a state (either of the receiving society or an external one) before they have sufficient power to cause conflict, and this backing depends on the region's politics. Without it, migration is less likely to produce violence than silent misery and death, which rarely destabilizes states.[35] We must remember too that migration does not always produce bad results. It can act as a safety valve by reducing conflict in the sending area. Depending on the economic context, it can ease labor shortages in the receiving society, as it sometimes has, for instance, in Malaysia. Countries as different as Canada, Thailand, and Malawi show the astonishing capacity of some societies to absorb migrants without conflict.

. . .

Hypothesis 3: Economic Deprivation, Institutional Disruption, and Civil Strife

Empirical evidence partially supports the third hypothesis that environmental scarcity simultaneously increases economic deprivation and disrupts key social institutions, which in turn causes "deprivation" conflicts such as civil strife and insurgency. Environmental scarcity does produce economic deprivation, and this deprivation does cause civil strife. But more research is needed on the effects of scarcity on social institutions.

Resource degradation and depletion often affect economic productivity in poor countries and thereby contribute to deprivation. For example, erosion in upland Indonesia annually costs the country's agricultural economy nearly half a billion dollars in discounted future income.[45] The Magat watershed on the northern Filipino island of Luzon—a watershed representative of many in the Philippines—suffers gross erosion rates averaging 219 tons per hectare per year; if the lost nutrients were replaced by fertilizer, the annual cost would be over $100 per hectare.[46] Dryland degradation in Burkina Faso reduces the country's annual gross domestic product by nearly 9 percent annually because of fuelwood loss and lower yields of millet, sorghum, and livestock.[47] . . .

I originally hypothesized that scarcity would undermine a variety of social institutions. Our research suggests, however, that one institution in particular—the state—is most important. Although more study is needed, the multiple effects of environmental scarcity, including large population movements and economic decline, appear likely to weaken sharply the capacity and legitimacy of the state in some poor countries.

First, environmental scarcity increases financial and political demands on governments. For example, to mitigate the social effects of loss of water, soil, and forest, governments must spend huge sums on industry and infrastructure such as new dams, irrigation systems, fertilizer plants, and reforestation programs. Furthermore, this resource loss can reduce the incomes of elites directly dependent on resource extraction; these elites usually turn to the state for compensation. Scarcity also expands marginal groups that need help from government by producing rural poverty and by displacing people into cities where they demand food, shelter, transport, energy, and employment. In response to swelling urban populations, governments introduce subsidies that drain revenues, distort prices, and cause misallocations of capital, which in turn hinders economic productivity. Such large-scale state intervention in the marketplace can concentrate political and economic power in the hands of a small number of cronies and monopolistic interests, at the expense of other elite segments and rural agricultural populations.

Simultaneously, if resource scarcity affects the economy's general productivity, revenues to local and national governments will decline. This hurts elites that benefit from state largesse and reduces the state's capacity to meet the increased demands arising from environmental scarcity. A widening gap between state capacity and demands on the state, along with the misguided economic interventions such a gap often provokes, aggravates popular and elite grievances, increases rivalry between elite factions, and erodes the state's legitimacy.

Key contextual factors affect whether lower economic productivity and state weakening lead to deprivation conflicts. Civil strife is a function of both the level of grievance motivating challenger groups and the opportunities available to these groups to act on their grievances. The likelihood of civil strife is greatest when multiple pressures at different levels in society interact to increase grievance and opportunity simultaneously. Our third hypothesis says that environmental scarcity will change both variables, by contributing to economic crisis and by weakening institutions such as the state. But numerous other factors also influence grievance and opportunity.

. . .

A Combined Model

There are important links between the processes identified in the second and third hypotheses. For example, although population movement is sometimes caused directly by scarcity, more often it arises from the greater poverty caused by this scarcity. Similarly, the weakening of the state increases the likelihood not only of deprivation conflicts, but of group-identity conflicts.

It is useful, therefore, to bring the hypotheses together into one model of environment-conflict linkages. . . . Decreases in the quality and quantity of renewable resources, population growth, and unequal resource access act singly or in various combinations to increase the scarcity, for certain population groups, of cropland, water, forests, and fish. This can reduce economic productivity, both for the local groups experiencing the scarcity and for the larger regional and national economies. The affected people may migrate or be expelled to new lands. Migrating groups often trigger ethnic conflicts when they move to new areas, while decreases in wealth can cause deprivation conflicts such as insurgency and rural rebellion. In developing countries, the migrations and productivity losses may eventually weaken the state which in turn decreases central control over ethnic rivalries and increases opportunities for insurgents and elites challenging state authority. . . .

South Africa and Haiti illustrate this combined model. In South Africa, apartheid concentrated millions of blacks in some of the country's least productive and most ecologically sensitive territories, where population densities were worsened by high natural birth rates. In 1980, rural areas of the Ciskei homeland had 82 people per square kilometer, whereas the surrounding Cape province had a rural density of 2. Homeland residents had little capital and few resource-management skills and were subject to corrupt and abusive local governments. Sustainable development in such a situation was impossible, and wide areas were completely stripped of trees for fuelwood, grazed down to bare dirt, and eroded of top soil. A 1980 report concluded that nearly 50 percent of Ciskei's land was moderately or severely eroded, and nearly 40 percent of its pasturage was overgrazed.[70]

This loss of resources, combined with a lack of alternative employment and the social trauma caused by apartheid, created a subsistence crisis in the homelands. Thousands of people have migrated to South African cities, which are as yet incapable of adequately integrating and employing these migrants. The result is the rapid growth of squatter settlements and illegal townships that are rife with discord and that threaten the country's move to democratic stability.[71]

In Haiti, the irreversible loss of forests and soil in rural areas deepens an economic crisis that spawns social strife, internal migration, and an exodus of "boat people." When first colonized by the Spanish in the late fifteenth century and the French in the seventeenth century, Haiti was treasured for abundant forests. Since then, Haiti has become one of the world's most dramatic examples of environmental despoliation. Less than two percent of the country remains forested, and the last timber is being felled at four percent per year.[72] As trees disappear, erosion follows, worsened by the steepness of the land and by harsh storms. The United Nations estimates that at least 50 percent of the country is affected by topsoil loss that leaves land "unreclaimable at the farm level."[73] So much soil washes off the slopes that the streets of Port-au-Prince have to be cleared with bulldozers in the rainy season.

Unequal land distribution was not a main cause of this catastrophe. Haiti gained independence in 1804 following a revolt of slaves and ex-slaves against the French colonial regime. Over a period of decades, the old plantation system associated with slavery was dismantled, and land was widely distributed in small parcels.[74] As a result, Haiti's agricultural structure, unique to Latin America, has 73 percent of cropland in private farms of less than 4 hectares.[75]

But inheritance customs and population growth have combined to produce scarcity, as in Bangladesh. Land has been subdivided into smaller portions with each generation. Eventually the plots cannot properly support their cultivators, fallow periods are neglected, and greater poverty prevents investment in soil conservation. The poorest people leave for steeper hillsides, where they clear the forest and begin farming anew, only to exhaust the land in a few years.[76] Many peasants try to supplement their falling incomes by scavenging wood for charcoal production, which contributes to further deforestation.

These processes might have been prevented had a stable central government invested in agriculture, industrial development, and reforestation. Instead, since independence Haiti has endured a ceaseless struggle for power between black and mulatto classes, and the ruling regimes have been solely interested in expropriating any surplus wealth the economy generated. Today, over 60 percent of the population is still engaged in agriculture, yet capital is unavailable for agricultural improvement, and the terms of exchange for crop production favor urban regions.[77] The population growth rate has actually increased, from 1.7 percent in the mid-1970s to over 2 percent today: the UN estimates that the current population of 6.75 million will grow to over 13 million by 2025.[78] As the land erodes and the population grows, incomes shrink: agricultural output per capita has decreased 10 percent in the last decade.[79]

Analysts agree that rising rural poverty has caused ever-increasing rural-rural and rural-urban migration. In search of work, agricultural workers move from subsistence hillside farms to rice farms in the valleys. From there, they go to cities, especially to Port-au-Prince, which now has a population of over a million. Wealthier farmers and traders, and even those with slimmer resources, try to flee by boat. . . .

Implications for International Security

Environmental scarcity has insidious and cumulative social impacts, such as population movement, economic decline, and the weakening of states. These can contribute to diffuse and persistent sub-national violence. The rate and extent of such conflicts will increase as scarcities worsen.

This sub-national violence will not be as conspicuous or dramatic as inter-state resource wars, but it will have serious repercussions for the security interests of both the developed and the developing worlds. Countries under such stress may fragment as their states become enfeebled and peripheral regions are seized by renegade authorities and warlords. Governments of countries as different as the Philippines and Peru have lost control over outer territories; although both these cases are complicated, it is nonetheless clear that environmental stress has contributed to their fragmentation. Fragmentation of any sizeable country will produce large outflows of refugees; it will also hinder the country from effectively negotiating and implementing international agreements on collective security, global environmental protection, and other matters.

Alternatively, a state might keep scarcity-induced civil strife from causing its progressive enfeeblement and fragmentation by becoming a "hard" regime that is authoritarian, intolerant of opposition, and militarized. Such regimes are more prone to launch military attacks against neighboring countries to divert attention from internal grievances. If a number of developing countries evolve in this direction, they could eventually threaten the military and economic interests of rich countries.

A state's ability to become a hard regime in response to environmentally induced turmoil depends, I believe, on two factors. First, the state must have sufficient remaining capacity—despite the debilitating effects of scarcity—to mobilize or seize resources for its own ends; this is a function of the internal organizational coherence of the state and its autonomy from outside pressures. Second, there must remain enough surplus wealth in the country's ecological-economic system to allow the state, once it seizes this wealth, to pursue its authoritarian course. Consequently, the countries with the highest probability of becoming "hard" regimes, and potential threats to their neighbors, are large, relatively wealthy developing countries that are dependent on a declining environmental base and that have a history of state strength. Candidates include Indonesia and, perhaps, Nigeria.

. . .

Conclusions

Our research shows that environmental scarcity causes violent conflict. This conflict tends to be persistent, diffuse, and sub-national. Its frequency will probably jump sharply in the next decades as scarcities rapidly worsen in many parts of the world. Of immediate concern are scarcities of cropland, water, forests, and fish, whereas atmospheric changes such as global warming will probably not have a major effect for several decades, and then mainly by interacting with already existing scarcities.

The degradation and depletion of environmental resources is only one source of environmental scarcity; two other important sources are population growth and unequal resource distribution. Scarcity often has its harshest social impact when these factors interact. As environmental scarcity becomes more severe, some societies will have a progressively lower capacity to adapt. Of particular concern is the decreasing capacity of the state to create markets and other institutions that promote adaptation. The impact of environmental scarcity on state capacity deserves further research.

Countries experiencing chronic internal conflict because of environmental stress will probably either fragment or become more authoritarian. Fragmenting countries will be the source of large out-migrations, and they will be unable to effectively negotiate or implement international agreements on security, trade and environmental protection. Authoritarian regimes may be inclined to launch attacks against other countries to divert popular attention from internal stresses. Any of these outcomes could seriously disrupt international security. The social impacts of environmental scarcity therefore deserve concerted attention from security scholars.

30

New Dimensions of Human Security

Fifty years ago, Albert Einstein summed up the discovery of atomic energy with characteristic simplicity: "Everything changed." He went on to predict: "We shall require a substantially new manner of thinking if mankind is to survive." Although nuclear explosions devastated Nagasaki and Hiroshima, humankind has survived its first critical test of preventing worldwide nuclear devastation. But five decades later, we need another profound transition in thinking—from nuclear security to human security.

The concept of security has for too long been interpreted narrowly: as security of territory from external aggression, or as protection of national interests in foreign policy, or as global security from the threat of a nuclear holocaust. It has been related more to nation-states than to people. The superpowers were locked in an ideological struggle—fighting a cold war all over the world. The developing nations, having won their independence only recently, were sensitive to any real or perceived threats to their fragile national identities. Forgotten were the legitimate concerns of ordinary people who sought security in their daily lives. For many of them, security symbolized protection from the threat of disease, hunger, unemployment, crime, social conflict, political repression, and environmental hazards.

With the dark shadows of the cold war receding, one can now see that many conflicts are within nations rather than between nations.

For most people, a feeling of insecurity arises more from worries about daily life than from the dread of a cataclysmic world event. Will they and their families have enough to eat? Will they lose their jobs? Will their streets and neighborhoods be safe from crime? Will they be tortured by a repressive state? Will they become a victim of violence because of their gender? Will their religion or ethnic origin target them for persecution?

In the final analysis, human security is a child who did not die, a disease that did not spread, a job that was not cut, an ethnic tension that did not explode in violence, a dissident who was not silenced. Human security is not a concern with weapons—it is a concern with human life and dignity.

The idea of human security, though simple, is likely to revolutionize society in the twenty-first century. A consideration of the basic concept of human security must focus on four of its essential characteristics:

- Human security is a *universal* concern. It is relevant to people everywhere, in rich nations and poor. There are many threats that are common to all people—such as unemployment, drugs, crime, pollution, and human rights violations. Their intensity may differ from one part of the world to another, but all these threats to human security are real and growing.
- The components of human security are *interdependent*. When the security of people is endangered anywhere in the world, all nations are likely to get involved. Famine, disease, pollution, drug trafficking, terrorism, ethnic disputes, and social disintegration are no longer isolated events that are confined within national borders. Their consequences travel the globe.
- Human security is *easier to ensure through early prevention* than later intervention. It is less costly to meet these threats upstream than downstream. For example, the direct and indirect cost of HIV/AIDS (human immunodeficiency virus/acquired immune deficiency syndrome) was roughly $240 billion during the 1980s. Even a few billion dollars invested in primary health care and family planning education could have helped contain the spread of this deadly disease.
- Human security is *people-centered*. It is concerned with how people live and breathe in a society, how freely they exercise their many choices, how much access they have to market and social opportunities—and whether they live in conflict or in peace.

Several analysts have attempted rigorous definitions of human security. But like other fundamental concepts, such as human freedom, human security is more easily identified through its absence than its presence. And most people instinctively understand what security means.

Nevertheless, it may be useful to have a more explicit definition. Human security can be said to have two main aspects. It means, first, safety from such chronic threats as hunger, disease and repression. And second, it means protection from sudden and hurtful disruptions in the patterns of daily life—whether in homes, in jobs or in communities. Such threats can exist at all levels of national income and development

The loss of human security can be a slow, silent process—or an abrupt, loud emergency. It can be human-made—due to wrong policy choices. It can stem from the forces of nature. Or it can be a combination of both—as is often the case when environmental degradation leads to a natural disaster, followed by human tragedy.

In defining security, it is important that human security not be equated with human development. Human development is a broader concept—defined in previous [UN] *Human Development Reports* as a process of widening the range of people's choices. Human security means that people can exercise these choices safely and freely—and that they can be relatively confident that the opportunities they have today are not totally lost tomorrow.

There is, of course, a link between human security and human development: progress in one area enhances the chances of progress in the other. But failure in one area also heightens the risk of failure in the other, and history is replete with examples.

Failed or limited human development leads to a backlog of human deprivation—poverty, hunger, disease, or persisting disparities between ethnic communities or between regions. This backlog in access to power and economic opportunities can lead to violence.

When people perceive threats to their immediate security, they often become less tolerant, as the anti-foreigner feelings and violence in Europe show. Or, where people see the basis of their livelihood erode—such as their access to water—political conflict can ensue, as in parts of Central Asia and the Arab states. Oppression and perceptions of injustice can also lead to violent protest against authoritarianism, as in Myanmar and Zaire [Congo].

Ensuring human security does not mean taking away from people the responsibility and opportunity for mastering their lives. To the contrary, when people are insecure, they become a burden on society.

The concept of human security stresses that people should be able to take care of themselves: all people should have the opportunity to meet their most essential needs and to earn their own living. This will set them free and help ensure that they can make a full contribution to development—their own development and that of their communities, their countries, and the world. Human security is a critical ingredient of participatory development.

Human security is therefore not a defensive concept—the way territorial or military security is. Instead, human security is an integrative concept. . . . It is embedded in a notion of solidarity among people. It cannot be brought about through force, with armies standing against armies. It can happen only if we agree that development must involve all people.

. . .

Components of Human Security

It is now time to make a transition from the narrow concept of national security to the all-encompassing concept of human security.

People in rich nations seek security from the threat of crime and drug wars in their streets, the spread of deadly diseases like HIV/AIDS, soil degradation, rising levels of pollution, the fear of losing their jobs, and many other anxieties that emerge as the social fabric disintegrates. People in poor nations demand liberation from the continuing threat of hunger, disease, and poverty, while also facing the same problems that threaten industrial countries.

At the global level, human security no longer means carefully constructed safeguards against the threat of a nuclear holocaust—a likelihood greatly reduced by the end of the cold war. Instead, it means responding to the threat of global poverty traveling across international borders in the form of drugs, HIV/AIDS, climate change, illegal migration, and terrorism. The prospect of collective suicide through an impulsive resort to nuclear weapons was always exaggerated. But the threat of global poverty affecting all human lives—in rich nations and in poor— is real and persistent. And there are no global safeguards against these real threats to human security.

The concept of security must thus change urgently in two basic ways:

- From an exclusive stress on territorial security to a much greater stress on people's security;
- From security through armaments to security through sustainable human development.

The list of threats to human security is long, but most can be considered under seven main categories:

- Economic security
- Food security
- Health security
- Environmental security
- Personal security
- Community security
- Political security

. . .

Environmental Security

Human beings rely on a healthy physical environment, curiously assuming that whatever damage they inflict on the earth, it will eventually recover. This clearly is not the case, for intensive industrialization and rapid population growth have put the planet under intolerable strain. . . .

In developing countries, one of the greatest environmental threats is to water. Today, the world's supply of water per capita is only one-third of what it was in 1970. Water scarcity is increasingly becoming a factor in ethnic strife and political tension. In 1990, about 1.3 billion people in the developing world lacked access to clean water. And much water pollution is the result of poor sanitation: nearly 2 billion people lack access to safe sanitation.

But people in developing countries have also been putting pressure on the land. Some 8 million to 10 million acres of forest land are lost each year—areas the size of Austria. And deforestation combined with overgrazing and poor conservation methods is accelerating desertification. In sub-Saharan Africa alone in the past 50 years, 65 million hectares of productive land turned to desert.

Even irrigated land is under threat—from salt residues. Salinization damage affects 25% of the irrigated land in Central Asia, and 20% in Pakistan.

In industrial countries, one of the major environmental threats is air pollution. Los Angeles produces 3,400 tons of pollutants each year, and London 1,200 tons. Harmful to health, this pollution also damages the natural environment. The deterioration of Europe's forests from air pollution causes economic losses of $35 billion a year. And the estimated annual loss of agricultural production due to air pollution is $1.5 billion in Sweden, $1.8 billion in Italy, $2.7 billion in Poland, and $4.7 billion in Germany. . . .

Many environmental threats are chronic and long-lasting. Others take on a more sudden and violent character. Bhopal and Chernobyl are the more obvious sudden environmental catastrophes. Many chronic "natural" disasters in recent years have also been provoked by human beings. Deforestation has led to more intense droughts and floods. And population growth has moved people into areas prone to cyclones, earthquakes, or floods—areas always considered dangerous and previously uninhabited. Poverty and land shortages are doing the same— driving people onto much more marginal territory and increasing their exposure to natural hazards. The result: disasters are more significant and more frequent. During 1967–91, disasters hit three billion people—80% of them in Asia. More than seven million people died, and two million were injured.

Most developing countries have plans to cope with natural emergencies— Bangladesh, for example, has an elaborate warning system for cyclones arriving in the Bay of Bengal. Sometimes the scale is beyond national resources and calls for international action. Responses however, are often slow, inadequate and uncoordinated. Current humanitarian efforts, particularly in the UN system, are seriously underfunded. And many of the most vulnerable people perish before any international help arrives.

. . .

Environmental Degradation

Most forms of environmental degradation have their strongest impact locally. But other effects tend to migrate. Polluted air drifts inexorably across national frontiers, with sulfur dioxide emissions in one country falling as acid rain in another. About 60 percent of Europe's commercial forests suffer damaging levels of sulfur deposition. In Sweden, about 20,000 of the country's 90,000 lakes are acidified to some degree; in Canada, 48,000 are acidic. And the source of the problem in these instances is not only within the country.

The emission of chlorofluorocarbons also has an international, indeed a truly global, effect, as the gases released in individual countries attack the ozone layer. . . . The production of greenhouse gases also has a global impact. . . . Biological diversity is more threatened now than at any time in the past. Tropical deforestation is the main culprit, but the destruction of wetlands, coral reefs, and temperate forests also figures heavily. Germany and the Netherlands lost nearly 60 percent of their wetlands between 1950 and 1980. And a recent analysis of tropical forest habitats, which contain between 50 and 90 percent of the world's species, concluded that, at current rates of loss, up to 15 percent of the earth's species could disappear over the next 25 years. Today, only 45 percent of the world's temperate rainforests remain.

The trends of the past 20 years show an accelerated destruction of coastal marine habitats, increases in coastal pollution, and in many areas, a shrinking of the marine fish catch. In 1990, the global fish catch declined for the first time in 13 years—a result of overfishing, coastal habitat destruction and water pollution. . . .

As habitats are fragmented, altered, or destroyed, they lose their ability to provide ecosystem services—water purification, soil regeneration, watershed protection, temperature regulation, nutrient and waste recycling, and atmospheric maintenance. All these changes threaten global human security.

DANIEL DEUDNEY

31

The Case Against Linking Environmental Degradation and National Security

Introduction

... Environmental issues are likely to become an increasingly important dimension of political life at all levels—locally, inside states, as well as internationally. How institutions respond to these emerging constraints is likely to shape politics in a profound manner. Because state and interstate conflict are such central features of both world politics and geopolitical theory, there is a strong tendency for people to think about environmental problems in terms of national security and to assume that environmental conflicts will fit into the established patterns of interstate conflict.

The aim of this essay is to cast doubt upon this tendency to link environmental degradation and national security. Specifically, I make three claims. First, it is analytically misleading to think of environmental degradation as a national security threat, because the traditional focus of national security—interstate violence—has little in common with either environmental problems or solutions. Second,

© *Millennium: Journal of International Studies.* This article first appeared in *Millennium* 19, no. 3 (Winter 1990):461–476 and is reproduced with the permission of the publisher.

the effort to harness the emotive power of nationalism to help mobilise environmental awareness and action may prove counterproductive by undermining globalist political sensibility. And third, environmental degradation is not very likely to cause interstate wars.

The Weak Analytical Links Between Environmental Degradation and National Security

One striking feature of the growing discussion of environmental issues in the United States is the attempt by many liberals, progressives and environmentalists to employ language traditionally associated with violence and war to understand environmental problems and to motivate action. Lester Brown, Jessica Tuchman Matthews, Michael Renner and others have proposed 'redefining national security' to encompass resource and environmental threats.[2] More broadly, Richard Ullman and others have proposed 'redefining security' to encompass a wide array of threats, ranging from earthquakes to environmental degradation.[3] Hal Harvey has proposed the concept of 'natural security',[4] and US Senator Albert Gore has spoken extensively in favour of thinking of the environment as a national security issue.[5] During the renewed Cold War tensions of the late 1970s and early 1980s, such concepts were advanced to prevent an excessive focus on military threats. As the Cold War winds down, such links are increasingly popular among national security experts and organisations looking for new missions. . . .

Historically, conceptual ferment of this sort has often accompanied important changes in politics.[7] New phrases are coined and old terms are appropriated for new purposes. Epochal developments like the emergence of capitalism, the growth of democracy and the end of slavery were accompanied by shifting, borrowing and expanding political language. The wide-ranging contemporary conceptual ferment in the language used to understand and act upon environmental problems is therefore both a natural and an encouraging development.

But not all neologisms and linkages are equally plausible or useful. Until this recent flurry of reconceptualising, the concept of 'national security' (as opposed to national interest or well-being) has been centred upon *organised violence*.[8] As is obvious to common sense and as Hobbes argued with such force, security from violence is a primal human need, because loss of life prevents the enjoyment of all other goods. Of course, various resource factors, such as access to fuels and ores, were understood as contributing to states' capacities to wage war and achieve security from violence.

Before either 'expanding' the concept of 'national security' to encompass both environmental and violence threats, or 're-defining' 'national security' or 'security' to refer mainly to environmental threats, it is worth examining just how much the national pursuit of security from violence has in common with environmental problems and their solutions.

Military violence and environmental degradation are linked directly in at least three major ways. First, the pursuit of national-security-from-violence through military means consumes resources (fiscal, organisational and leadership) that could be spent on environmental restoration. Since approximately one trillion US dollars is spent worldwide on military activities, substantial resources are involved. However, this relationship is not unique to environmental concerns, and unfortunately there is no guarantee that the world would spend money saved from military expenditures on environmental restoration. Nor is it clear that the world cannot afford environmental restoration without cutting military expenditures.

Second, war is directly destructive of the environment. In ancient times, the military destruction of olive groves in Mediterranean lands contributed to the long-lasting destruction of the lands' carrying capacities. More recently, the United States' bombardment and use of defoliants in Indochina caused significant environmental damage. Further, extensive use of nuclear weapons could have significant impacts on the global environment, including altered weather (i.e., 'nuclear winter') and further depletion of the ozone layer. Awareness of these environmental effects has played an important role in mobilising popular resistance to the arms race and in generally de-legitimising use of nuclear explosives as weapons.

Third, preparation for war causes pollution and consumes significant quantities of resources. In both the United States and the Soviet Union, significant quantities of radioactive waste have been produced as a by-product of the nuclear arms race, and several significant releases of radiation have occurred—perhaps most disastrously when a waste dump at a Soviet nuclear weapons facility exploded and burned, spreading radioactive materials over a large area near the Urals. Military activities have also produced significant quantities of toxic wastes.

In short, war and the preparation for war are clearly environmental threats and consume resources that could be used to ameliorate environmental degradation. In effect, these environmental impacts mean that the war system has costs beyond the intentional loss of life and destruction. Nevertheless, most of the world's environmental degradation is not caused by war and the preparation for war. Completely eliminating the direct environmental effects of the war system would leave most environmental degradation unaffected. Most of the causes and most of the cures of environmental degradation must be found outside the domain of the traditional national security system related to violence.

The war system is a definite but limited environmental threat, but in what ways is environmental degradation a threat to 'national security'? Making such an identification can be useful if the two phenomena—security from violence and security from environmental threats—are similar. Unfortunately, they have little in common, making such linkages largely useless for analytical and conceptual purposes. Four major dissimilarities . . . deserve mention.

First, environmental degradation and violence are very different types of threats. Both violence and environmental degradation may kill people and may reduce human well-being, but not all threats to life and property are threats to security. Disease, old age, crime and accidents routinely destroy life and property, but we do not think of them as 'national security' threats or even threats to 'security'. (Crime is a partial exception, but crime is a 'security' threat at the individual level, because crime involves violence.) And when an earthquake or hurricane strikes with great force, we speak about 'natural disasters' or designate 'national disaster areas', but we do not speak about such events threatening 'national security'. If everything that causes a decline in human well-being is labelled a 'security' threat, the term loses any analytical usefulness and becomes a loose synonym of 'bad'.

Second, the scope and source of threats to environmental well-being and national-security-from-violence are very different. There is nothing about the problem of environmental degradation which is particularly 'national' in character. Since environmental threats are often oblivious of the borders of the nation-state, they rarely afflict just one nation-state. Nevertheless, this said, it would be misleading to call most environmental problems 'international'. Many perpetrators and victims are within the borders of one nation-state. Individuals, families, communities, other species and future generations are harmed. A complete collapse of the biosphere would surely destroy 'nations' as well as everything else, but there is nothing distinctively national about either the causes, the harms or the solutions that warrants us giving such privileged billing to the 'national' grouping.

A third misfit between environmental well-being and national-security-from-violence stems from the differing degrees of *intention* involved. Violent threats involve a high degree of intentional behaviour. Organisations are mobilised, weapons procured and wars waged with relatively definite aims in mind. Environmental degradation, on the other hand, is largely unintentional, the side-effects of many other activities. No one really sets out with the aim of harming the environment (with the so far limited exception of environmental modification for military purposes).

Fourth, organisations that provide protection from violence differ greatly from those in environmental protection. National-security-from-violence is conventionally pursued by organisations with three distinctive features. First, military organisations are secretive, extremely hierarchical and centralised, and normally deploy vastly expensive, highly specialised and advanced technologies. Second, citizens typically delegate the goal of achieving national security to remote and highly specialised organisations that are far removed from the experience of civil society. And third, the specialised professional group staffing these national security organisations are trained in the arts of killing and destroying.

In contrast, responding to the environmental problem requires almost exactly opposite approaches and organisations. Certain aspects of virtually all mundane activities—for example, house construction, farming techniques, sewage treatment, factory design and land use planning—must be reformed. The routine everyday behaviour of practically everyone must be altered. This requires behaviour modification in situ. The professional ethos of environmental restoration is husbandmanship—more respectful cultivation and protection of plants, animals and the land.

In short, national-security-from-violence and environmental habitability have little in common. Given these differences, the rising fashion of linking them risks creating a conceptual muddle rather than a paradigm or world view shift—a *de-definition* rather than a *re-definition* of security. If we begin to speak about all the forces and events that threaten life, property and well-being (on a large-scale) as threats to our national security, we shall soon drain the term of any meaning. All large-scale evils will become threats to national security. To speak meaningfully about actual problems, we shall have to invent new words to fill the job previously performed by the old spoiled ones.

The Risks in Harnessing the Rhetorical and Emotional Appeals of National Security for Environmental Restoration

Confronted with these arguments, the advocate of treating environmental degradation as a national security problem might retort:

> Yes, some semantic innovation without much analytical basis is occurring, but it has a sound goal—to get people to react as urgently and effectively to the environmental problem as they have to the national-security-from-violence problem. If people took the environmental problem as seriously as, say, an attack by a foreign power, think of all that could be done to solve the problems!

In other words, the aim of these new links is not primarily descriptive, but polemical. It is not a claim about fact, but a rhetorical device designed to stimulate action. Like William James, these environmentalists hope to find a 'moral equivalent to war' to channel the energies behind war into constructive directions. . . .

At first glance, the most attractive feature of linking fears about environmental threats with national security mentalities is the sense of urgency engendered, and the corresponding willingness to accept great personal sacrifice. If in fact the basic habitability of the planet is being undermined, then it stands to reason that some crisis mentality is needed. Unfortunately, it may be difficult to engender a sense of urgency and a willingness to sacrifice for extended periods of time. . . . A second apparently valuable similarity between the national security mentality and the environmental problem is the tendency to use worse case scenarios as the basis for planning. However, the extreme conservatism of military organisations in responding to potential threats is not unique to them. The insurance industry is built around preparations for the worst possibilities, and many fields of engineering, such as aeronautical design and nuclear power plant regulation, routinely employ extremely conservative planning assumptions. These can serve as useful models for improved environmental policies.

Third, the conventional national security mentality and its organisations are deeply committed to zero-sum thinking. 'Our' gain is 'their' loss. Trust between national security organisations is extremely low. The prevailing assumption is that everyone is a potential enemy, and that agreements mean little unless congruent with immediate interests. If the Pentagon had been put in charge of negotiating an ozone layer protocol, we might still be stockpiling chlorofluorocarbons as a bargaining chip.

Fourth, conventional national security organisations have short time horizons. The pervasive tendency for national security organisations to discount the future and pursue very near-term objectives is a poor model for environmental problem solving.

Finally, and perhaps most importantly, is the fact that the 'nation' is not an empty vessel or blank slate waiting to be filled or scripted, but is instead profoundly linked to war and 'us vs. them' thinking. The tendency for people to identify themselves with various tribal and kin groupings is as old as humanity. In the last century and a half, however, this sentiment of nationalism, amplified and manipulated by mass media propaganda techniques, has been an integral part of totalitarianism and militarism. Nationalism means a sense of 'us vs. them', of the insider vs. the outsider, of the compatriot vs. the alien. The stronger the nationalism, the stronger this cleavage, and the weaker the transnational bonds. Nationalism reinforces militarism, fosters prejudice and discrimination, and feeds the quest for 'sovereign' autonomy. . . .

Thus, thinking of national security as an environmental problem risks undercutting both the globalist and common fate understanding of the situation and the sense of world community that may be necessary to solve the problem. In short, it seems doubtful that the environment can be wrapped in national flags without undercutting the 'whole earth' sensibility at the core of environmental awareness.

If pollution comes to be seen widely as a national security problem, there is also a danger that the citizens of one country will feel much more threatened by the pollution from other countries than by the pollution created by their fellow citizens. This could increase international tensions and make international accords more difficult to achieve, while diverting attention from internal cleanup. Citizens of the United States, for example, could become much more concerned about deforestation in Brazil than in reversing the centuries of North American deforestation. Taken to an absurd extreme—as national security threats sometimes are—seeing environmental degradation in a neighboring country as a national security threat could trigger various types of interventions, a new imperialism of the strong against the weak.

Instead of linking 'national security' to the environmental problem, environmentalists should emphasise that the environmental crisis calls into question the national grouping and its privileged status in world politics. The environmental crisis is not a threat to national security, but it does challenge the utility of thinking in 'national' terms. . . .

Environmental Degradation and Interstate War

Many people are drawn to calling environmental degradation a national security problem, in part because they expect this phenomenon to stimulate interstate conflict and even violence. States often fight over what they value, particularly if related to 'security'. If states begin to be much more concerned with resources and environmental degradation, particularly if they think environmental decay is a threat to their 'national security', then states may well fight resource and pollution wars. . . . In general, I argue that interstate violence is not likely to result from environmental degradation, because of several deeply rooted features of the contemporary world order—both material and institutional—and because of the character of environmental and resource interests.

Few ideas seem more intuitively sound than the notion that states will begin fighting each other as the world runs out of usable natural resources. The popular metaphor of a lifeboat adrift at sea with declining supplies of clean water and rations suggests there will be fewer and fewer opportunities for positive-sum gains between actors. . . .

There are, however, three strong reasons for concluding that the familiar scenarios of resource war are of diminishing plausibility for the foreseeable future. First, the robust character of the world trade system means that states no longer experience resource dependency as a major threat to their military security and political autonomy. During the 1930s, the world trading system had collapsed, driving states to pursue autarkic economies. In contrast, the resource needs of contemporary states are routinely met without territorial control of the resource source, as Ronnie Lipschutz has recently shown.[17]

Second, the prospects for resource wars are diminished, since states find it increasingly difficult to exploit foreign resources through territorial conquest. Although the invention of nuclear explosives has made it easy and cheap to annihilate humans and infrastructure in extensive areas, the spread of small arms and national consciousness has made it very costly for an invader, even one equipped with advanced technology, to subdue a resisting population—as France discovered in Indochina and Algeria, the United States in Vietnam and the Soviet Union in Afghanistan. . . .

Third, the world is entering what H. E. Goeller and Alvin M. Weinberg have called the 'age of substitutability', in which industrial civilisation is increasingly capable of taking earth materials such as iron, aluminum, silicon and hydrocarbons (which are ubiquitous and plentiful) and fashioning them into virtually everything needed.[19] The most striking manifestation of this trend is that prices for virtually every raw material have been stagnant or falling for the last several decades, despite the continued growth in world output. In contrast to the expectations voiced by many during the 1970s—that resource scarcity would drive up commodity prices to the benefit of Third World raw material suppliers—prices have fallen, with disastrous consequences for Third World development.

In a second scenario, increased interstate violence results from internal turmoil caused by declining living standards. . . . Faced with declining living standards, groups at all levels of affluence can be expected to resist this trend by pushing the deprivation upon other groups. Class relations would be increasingly 'zero-sum games', producing class war and revolutionary upheavals. Faced with these pressures, liberal democracy and free-market systems would increasingly be replaced by authoritarian systems capable of maintaining minimum order.[20]

The international system consequences of these domestic changes may be increased conflict and war. If authoritarian regimes are more war-prone because of their lack of democratic control and if revolutionary regimes are more war-prone because of their ideological fervour and lack of socialisation into international norms and processes, then a world political system containing more such states is likely to be an increasingly violent one. The historical record from previous economic depressions supports the general proposition that widespread economic stagnation and unmet economic expectations contribute to international conflict.

Although initially compelling, this scenario has flaws as well. First, the pessimistic interpretation of the relationship between environmental sustainability and economic growth is arguably based on unsound economic theory. Wealth formation is not so much a product of cheap natural resource availability as of capital formation via savings and more efficient ways of producing. The fact that so many resource-poor countries, like Japan, are very wealthy, while many countries with more extensive resource endowments are poor, suggests that there is no clear and direct relationship between abundant resource availability and national wealth. Environmental constraints require an end to economic growth based on increasing raw material through-puts, rather than an end to growth in the output of goods and services.

Second, even if economic decline does occur, interstate conflict may be dampened, not stoked. . . . How societies respond to economic decline may in large measure depend upon the rate at which such declines occur. An offsetting factor here is the possibility that as people get poorer, they will be less willing to spend increasingly scarce resources for military capabilities. In this regard, the experience of economic depressions over the last two centuries may not be relevant, because such depressions were characterised by under-utilised production capacity and falling resource prices. In the 1930s, increased military spending had a stimulative effect, but in a world in which economic growth had been retarded by environmental constraints, military spending would exacerbate the problem. . . .

Environmental degradation in a country or region could become so extreme that the basic social and economic fabric comes apart. Should some areas of the world suffer this fate, the impact of this outcome on international order may not, however, be very great. If a particular country, even a large one like Brazil, were tragically to disintegrate, among the first casualties would be the capacity of the industrial and governmental structure to wage and sustain interstate conventional war. As Bernard Brodie observed in the modern era, 'the predisposing factors to military aggression are full bellies, not empty ones'.[22] The poor and wretched of the earth may be able to deny an outside aggressor an easy conquest, but they are themselves a minimal threat to outside states. Offensive war today requires complex organisational skills, specialised industrial products and surplus wealth.

In today's world everything is connected, but not everything is tightly coupled. Regional disasters of great severity may occur, with scarcely a ripple in the rest of the world. After all, Idi Amin drew Uganda back into savage darkness, the Khmer Rouge murdered an estimated two million Cambodians and the Sahara has advanced across the Sahel without the economies and political systems of the rest of the world being much perturbed. Indeed, many of the world's citizens did not even notice.

A fourth possible route from environmental degradation to interstate conflict and violence involves pollution across state borders. It is easy to envision situations in which country A dumps an intolerable amount of pollution on a neighboring country B (which is upstream and upwind), causing country B to attempt to pressure and coerce country A into eliminating its offending pollution. We can envision such conflict of interest leading to armed conflict.

Fortunately for interstate peace, strongly asymmetrical and significant environmental degradation between neighboring countries is relatively rare. Probably more typical is the situation in which activities in country A harm parts of country A and country B, and in which activities in country B also harm parts of both countries. This creates complex sets of winners and losers, and thus establishes a complex array of potential intrastate and interstate coalitions. In general, the more such interactions are occurring, the less likely it is that a persistent, significant and highly asymmetrical pollution 'exchange' will result. The very multitude of interdependency in the contemporary world, particularly among the industrialised countries, makes it unlikely that intense cleavages of environmental harm will match interstate borders, and at the same time not be compensated and complicated by other military, economic or cultural interactions. Resolving such conflicts will be a complex and messy affair, but the conflicts are unlikely to lead to war.

Finally, there are conflict potentials related to the global commons. Many countries contribute to environmental degradation, and many countries are harmed, but since the impacts are widely distributed, no one country has an incentive to act alone to solve the problem. Solutions require collective action, and with collective action comes the possibility of the 'free rider'. . . .

It is difficult to judge this scenario, because we lack examples of this phenomenon on a large scale. 'Free-rider' problems may generate severe conflict, but it is doubtful that states would find military instruments useful for coercion and compliance. . . .

Conclusion

The degradation of the natural environment upon which human well-being depends is a challenge of far-reaching significance for human societies everywhere.

But this challenge has little to do with the national-security-from-violence problem that continues to plague human political life. Not only is there little in common between the causes and solutions of these two problems, but the nationalist and militarist mindsets closely associated with 'national security' thinking directly conflict with the core of the environmentalist world view. Harnessing these sentiments for a 'war on pollution' is a dangerous and probably self-defeating enterprise. And fortunately, the prospects for resource and pollution wars are not as great as often conjured by environmentalists.

The pervasive recourse to national security paradigms to conceptualise the environmental problem represents a profound and disturbing failure of imagination and political awareness. If the nation-state enjoys a more prominent status in world politics than its competence and accomplishments warrant, then it makes little sense to emphasise the links between it and the emerging problem of the global habitability.[23] Nationalist sentiment and the war system have a long-established logic and staying power that are likely to defy any rhetorically conjured 're-direction' toward benign ends. The movement to preserve the habitability of the planet for future generations must directly challenge the tribal power of nationalism and the chronic militarisation of public discourse. Environmental degradation is not a threat to national security. Rather, environmentalism is a threat to 'national security' mindsets and institutions. For environmentalists to dress their programmes in the bloodsoaked garments of the war system betrays their core values and creates confusion about the real tasks at hand.

SOMAYA SAAD

32

For Whose Benefit? Redefining Security

...

The Quest for a Redefinition of Security

Today, the North is preoccupied by environmental threats. Indeed, since the Stockholm Conference of 1972, a very different approach to the environment has become evident.

Twenty years ago, the emphasis was on ending the pollution that the industrialized North had been inflicting on the nations of the South. The goals were clean air and water and arable land—the requisites of a decent life; and the modality was international cooperation.

Today, however, the North has seized hold of environmental issues by using them to cloak its own security concerns. The new ideology—or, to some, religion—of the environment allows its proponents to ignore nationalities and national boundaries.

Earth Rights or National Rights?

For some, a parallel meeting of non-government organizations at the . . . [1992] United Nations Conference on Environment and Development could be the forum for redefining security and sovereignty. The aim is to exert pressure on the participating national governments.

Originally published in *Eco-Decisions*, September 1991, pp. 59–60. Reprinted with permission.

314

The call for such a meeting is highly revealing. For those making it, the cause of the environment is to be used as a tool that can efface national boundaries and uproot national affiliations. They appeal instead to wider concepts: the sovereignty of the earth, the Global Commons, humanity or universal rights.

That approach could undermine national solidarity, stir up local conflicts, put individuals at odds with their governments, and cause governments to be judged without due consideration for the particular conditions that they face.

Such an approach might distort the issue. After all, it is the comparatively weaker states—who also happen to be developing nations—that have the bulk of the world's remaining natural resources. And it is these same countries that have relatively clean environments. Now these nations are being told to limit their military expenditures for the sake of development.

The Tilt Toward the "Haves"

Even in the boundary-free global utopia that some imagine lies ahead, a form of administration would still be required. Very likely, that "administration" would cover not territory but rather particular aspects of human activity.

Of these, most important is the domain of development. Within this area falls the entire range of environmental concerns: population, migration, poverty, the use of resources, patterns of production and consumption, and finally pollution. All these are shaped by the asymmetry in the global distribution of power.

That imbalance has political and military aspects. As a result, certain nations, cultures and lifestyles exert dominance over others. If those not favoured by the current arrangement try to redress the balance, their efforts are met with resistance which can escalate into conflict.

In consequence, the present division of power is likely to be maintained. The balance—whether military, economic or technological—is tilted in favour of the nations of the North, who now are seeking international cooperation in their bid to put their own house in order. Outside the North, there are strict limits on the amount of permitted national or regional power.

Redefining the Environment

Some nations are redefining the environment as a territory-free, non-geographical issue in which supranational institutions may intervene. They seek to mediate when necessary between other nations, and to force them to follow particular policies. Apparently their aim is to impose the economic and political norms and lifestyles of the North on the rest of the world, instead of allowing other nations to develop their own norms. The outcome will be a still greater tilt in favour of those that already hold economic and political power.

This trend will produce a new division of labour between nations. The powerful will gain more power, while the weak will lose what little power they have.

What Kind of Future?

Such a development naturally arouses questions. For instance, what does the brave talk of global security mean? Security, after all, implies the protection of a particular territory by one group against another. We need to know who will define the new concept of security. And herein lies the danger.

There are indications that now that the Cold War is ended, the larger countries consider the environment as a major field of security concern. Defined in those terms, the environment will present an ugly face particularly to the developing world.

In the new order taking shape, who or what will be sacrificed? There are several possible scenarios.

One is that weak nations will be subjugated to powerful ones. Some analysts point to the inadequacy of a world order based on state sovereignty. According to these thinkers, the passing of the Cold War may mark the passing of the nation states created by the earlier great wars of this century, replacing them with an order having a new basis. The tool used will be the economic leverage which the North exerts over the rest of the world.

Another possibility is an increase in tensions within and between nations. Environmental concerns could provoke disagreements that would exacerbate internal problems. Further, if sovereignty, regional and international legal standards and instruments are all swept away, the new so-called environmental rights could serve as a pretext for more conflicts.

Still another outcome might be the imposition of the norms, cultures and lifestyles of powerful nations on the others. Evidence for such a development is provided by the move to attach conditions to international assistance, and the banding together of the powerful nations in such groupings as the Enterprise of the Americas (starting with the United States, Canada and Mexico) and Europe 1992. Nations that refuse to accept this domination might be subjected to restrictions that could endanger their growth and even their survival.

It would be highly ironic if the move to protect the environment ended up thus destroying some cultures and peoples. Are the interests of humanity to be sacrificed to the interests of the earth?

PART SEVEN

Ecological Justice

Some of the main controversies surrounding the paradigms of sustainable development and ecological security involve questions of justice. Critics have raised concerns that these paradigms can blur questions of fairness, power, and distribution. Worse yet, environmental arguments might be used to justify measures that worsen social inequality, promote authoritarian measures, or otherwise concentrate power in the hands of elites. Thus, questions of justice are raised not only by the unequal effects of pollution and ecosystem destruction but also by the socially unequal effects of environmental policy responses.

Concerns about the relationship between environmental protection and social equity have been voiced since the Stockholm Conference first placed the environment on the international agenda.[1] As the pace of environmental degradation has accelerated and policy responses to environmental problems have grown more complex and ambitious, the question of how various forms of environmental change affect different social groups has become increasingly central to environmental debates.

Today the link between ecology and justice is being articulated by a diverse array of voices: people of color in cities throughout the United States challenging the "environmental racism" of concentrating toxic facilities in minority communities; rural women in India protesting the impact of deforestation on their lives and communities; Green party activists in Europe drawing links between militarism, patriarchy, and environmental destruction; Third World activists arguing that the North seeks to solve its environmental problems at the expense of the South, particularly in ways that harm the poorest of the poor; indigenous peoples of both the North and South organizing to reclaim their lands and their traditions as an alternative to the ecological onslaught of modernity.[2]

Given this diversity, is it possible to identify a single paradigm of ecological justice based on a common set of core arguments? While there are many different visions of an ecologically just world, a number of common themes lie at the heart of the ecological justice paradigm: first, the close linkage between violence against nature and violence against human beings; second, the linkage between the power to control nature and the power to control people; third, the observation that not all people or groups are affected equally by environmental problems or by the responses to those problems; fourth, the pursuit of solutions that are both ecologically sound *and* socially just, because neither can endure in the absence of the other; and fifth, the need for a fundamental transformation of politics, economics, and society.

Because the call for ecological justice often comes from groups that lack the power to set policy, these arguments are often presented as a critique of prevailing policies and institutions. One common theme among the selections in this section, however, is that ecological justice also contains an alternative vision for society and for the relationship between people and nature.

The paradigm can be used to analyze questions of ecology and justice at many different social levels. The question of justice among nations, with a particular focus on North-South inequality, was a central dispute at Stockholm in 1972 (see the selection by Castro in Part One). As the comments by Malaysian Prime Minister Mahathir Mohamad at the 1992 Earth Summit make clear, the issue was not fully resolved in the two decades between Stockholm and Rio. Despite the promise that "sustainable development" can merge the conflicting concerns of North and South with regard to environment and development, distributional issues remain central to the North-South environmental debate. Mohamad stresses that the question of justice applies not only to who should pay the costs of environmental protection in poor societies but also to who holds decisionmaking power and who bears historical responsibility for the planet's predicament.

Although the North-South gap is a central concern of the ecological justice literature, it would be wrong to conclude that the paradigm pertains only to debates between governments of the North and South. The concept of ecological justice also addresses the links among ecology, justice, and power within societies. Power is distributed unequally not only among nations but also in social divisions based on race, class, gender, ethnicity, and region. The selection by Gita Sen illustrates one such division, in this case that of gender. Sen's work shows some of the complex ways in which the construction of gender roles in society empowers men and disempowers women. In this essay, Sen's particular focus is on the population debate. Failure to grasp the link between gender and power—a link that operates at the interpersonal level of the household as well as at the national or international level—produces a flawed understanding of the forces driving population growth. The common result is an unjust and ineffective response to the urgent problem of rapid population growth.

Sen's focus on the links among gender, ecology, and power are the concern of a rapidly growing body of thought that is often referred to as *ecofeminism*.[3] Karen Warren summarizes the central tenets of ecofeminist perspectives:

> Ecological feminism is the position that there are important connections—histori-
> cal, symbolic, theoretical—between the domination of women and the domina-

tion of nonhuman nature. . . . Any feminist theory with any environmental ethic which fails to take seriously the interconnected dominations of women and nature is simply inadequate.[4]

Some ecofeminists see an inherent difference in how men and women relate to and interact with nature, and explain environmentally destructive societies as a consequence of male dominance. Other ecofeminists have pointed out that gender is in many important ways a socially constructed set of roles and rules and not a biological fact. These "social" ecofeminists tend to see patriarchy and environmental destruction as stemming from a common source: the hierarchical concentration of power in society.[5]

The chapter following Sen's focuses on indigenous peoples, linking questions of justice at the local and global levels. The Coordinating Body for the Indigenous Peoples' Organizations of the Amazon Basin (COICA) published two letters in 1989 arguing that the future of the Amazon and the fate of its indigenous occupants are inherently linked. The rampant quest for modernization, colonization, territorial occupation, and economic development of the Amazon has damaged natural ecosystems and destroyed indigenous communities. The destruction has been driven by governments of the Amazon Basin countries, which have excluded indigenous communities from decision-making about the region. Much of the destructive activity has been funded by external sources, including multinational corporations and multilateral development agencies such as the World Bank. Decisions about the fate of the Amazon forest and its people, whether made at the national or the international level, have excluded those who are most directly affected by such decisions.[6]

COICA addressed the first letter to the multilateral development banks that fund so many projects and policies threatening indigenous peoples. The second letter is addressed to the international environmental movement, which is also taken to task for its lack of attention to indigenous concerns. While acknowledging the efforts of environmentalists and the potential for common cause between the environmental and indigenous peoples' movements, the letter points out that governments, international organizations, and Northern environmental groups have struck bargains that leave out the people most directly and immediately affected. The members of COICA defend an alternative vision: Given the long history of sustainable interaction between indigenous peoples and the region's ecology, they argue, the best way to ensure an ecologically sound future is to restore and protect the land rights and lifestyles of indigenous peoples.

The struggles of indigenous peoples bear much in common with the movement against "environmental racism" that has flourished in the United States in the 1990s.[7] This movement has both urban and rural components: the struggle of urban communities of color against the practice of locating toxic facilities in the inner city, and the struggle of rural communities to combat the health and safety risks of environmentally unsound agricultural practices (in particular the heavy use of toxic agricultural chemicals)—risks borne disproportionately by low-paid agricultural workers. In both the North American and the South American case the goal is not merely to change environmental outcomes but also to return greater decisionmaking power to the community. And in both cases the notion that current practices are inherently unjust has been an important weapon in the struggle.

Advocates of ecological justice have played a crucial role in pointing out that environmental problems often cause greater harm to the poor and powerless than to other groups. Perhaps their greatest contribution, however, has been to show that "solutions" to environmental problems also can be unjust, both locally and globally—and that such outcomes may not be solutions at all. This idea is evident in Sen's concern that some environmentalists fail to see the centrality of gender relations and reproductive rights in matters of population growth, and in COICA's rejection of environment-development dialogues that exclude indigenous peoples.

The final essay in this part, by Nancy Peluso, raises the same concerns in an even more provocative fashion. Peluso argues that international environmental organizations, detached from the reality of local resource struggles, have participated in environmental preservation efforts that demonize local people and bolster oppressive, authoritarian regimes. Using wildlife conservation efforts in Kenya as an example, Peluso argues that the result—"coercing conservation"—pits the environment against social justice considerations, precluding an outcome that is both socially and ecologically sustainable.

Together, these chapters reject the Stockholm-era claim that effective environmental protection requires increasingly authoritarian governance. By showing that some forms of environmental protection can be unfair or even coercive, the environmental justice paradigm suggests that true sustainability will require responses to environmental problems that are both ecologically effective and socially just.

Thinking Critically

1. After reading the essays in this section, are you persuaded that the environment is a social justice issue? Must there be social justice in order for there to be environmental protection? Are there trade-offs between these two values?

2. Do you accept Mahathir Mohamad's suggestion that some types of global environmental protection impose an unfair burden on the global

South? Does this mean that the resistance of many governments of the South to particular forms of international environmental protection has the effect of promoting social justice?

3. Can you identify other environmental issues that confront the sort of broad and deep differences of perspective that Sen describes on the population issue? How can such differences be overcome? Must they be overcome in order to promote global environmental protection? In order to promote global social justice?

4. Contrast the picture of international environmental NGOs drawn by Peluso with the essay by Wapner in Part Two. How can we account for the dramatically different interpretations of these two observers?

Additional Reading

North-South Dimensions of Environmental Justice

Crosby, Alfred W., *Ecological Imperialism: The Biological Expansion of Europe, 900–1900* (London: Cambridge University Press, 1986).

Grove, Richard, *Green Imperialism: Colonial Expansion, Tropical Island Edens and the Origins of Environmentalism, 1600–1800* (London: Cambridge University Press, 1995).

Sachs, Wolfgang, ed., *Global Ecology: A New Arena of Political Conflict* (London: Zed Books, 1993).

Shiva, Vandana, *Ecology and the Politics of Survival* (Newbury Park, CA: Sage Publications, 1991).

Ecology, Race, and Gender

Biehl, Janet, *Rethinking Ecofeminist Politics* (Boston: South End Press, 1991).

Bullard, Robert D., *Dumping in Dixie: Race, Class, and Environmental Quality,* 2d ed.(Boulder, CO: Westview Press, 1994).

Diamond, Irene, and Gloria Femen Orenstein, eds., *Reweaving the World: The Emergence of Ecofeminism* (San Francisco: Sierra Club Books, 1990).

Merchant, Carolyn, *Ecological Revolutions: Nature, Gender and Science in New England* (Chapel Hill, NC: University of North Carolina Press, 1989).

Forest Peoples and the Struggle for Environmental Justice

Cronon, William, *Changes in the Land: Indians, Colonists, and the Ecology of New England* (New York: Hill and Wang, 1983).

Guha, Ramachandra, *The Unquiet Woods: Ecological Change and Peasant Resistance in the Himalayas* (Berkeley: University of California Press, 1989).

Hecht, Susanna, and Alexander Cockburn, *The Fate of the Forest: Developers, Destroyers, and Defenders of the Amazon* (New York: HarperCollins, 1990).

Peluso, Nancy Lee, *Rich Forests, Poor People: Resource Control and Resistance in Java* (Berkeley: University of California Press, 1992).

Internet Resources

Cultural Survival, *kumo.swcp.com./xines/indigenous/347.html*. This NGO promotes awareness of and advocacy for indigenous peoples worldwide.

EcoJustice Network, *http://www.igc.apc.org/envjustice*. The EcoJustice Network "addresses environmental issues facing communities of color in the United States." Activities include on-line services, informational resources, and training for activists and organizations.

Women's Environment and Development Organization (WEDO), *gopher://gopher.igc.apc.org:70/11/orgs/wedo*. WEDO aims "to foster women's leadership and advocacy skills to transform women's concerns about the environment, development, population, and gender equity into actions, programs, and policies in countries around the world."

Indigenous Environmental Network, *http://www.alphacdc.com/ien*. A coalition of grassroots indigenous groups seeking "to protect the sacredness of Mother Earth from contamination and exploitation by strengthening, maintaining, and respecting the traditional teachings and the natural laws." Provides information on a wide range of environmental problems facing indigenous communities.

Oneworld, *http://www.oneworld.org*. This site plugs in to a network of more than 120 social justice organizations worldwide.

Serviço Brasileiro de Justiça e Paz (SEJUP), *http://www.oneworld.org/sejup*. This site provides an example of how groups advocating social justice are using the Internet to raise international awareness about various forms of injustice. SEJUP monitors events in Brazil and distributes information on a wide range of issues related to the environment, human rights, and economic and social justice.

MAHATHIR MOHAMAD

33

Statement to the U.N. Conference on Environment & Development

It is claimed that one of the causes of environmental degradation is the size of the population of some developing countries. We dispute this assumption.

However, we note that rich developed communities tend to have low birth rates. If we want to reduce population growth then we must help poor communities to become developed. Yet we hear from the rich, proposals which would result in stopping the development of poor countries in order to reduce population. You may be able to reduce pollution but you will end up with massive overpopulation in the poorest developing countries.

We know that the 25 per cent of the world population who are rich consume 85 per cent of its wealth and produce 90 per cent of its waste. Mathematically speaking, if the rich reduce their wasteful consumption by 25 per cent, worldwide pollution will be reduced by 22.5 per cent. But if the poor 75 per cent reduce consumption totally and disappear from this earth altogether the reduction in pollution will only be by 10 per cent.

It is what the rich do that counts, not what the poor do, however much they do it. That is why it is imperative that the rich change their life-styles. A change in the life-styles of the poor only, apart from being unfair, is quite unproductive environment-wise. But the rich talk of the sovereignty of the consumers and their

---

Originally published in *Environmental Policy and Law* 22, 4 (1992):232. Reprinted with permission.

right to their life-styles. The rich will not accept a progressive and meaningful cutback in their emissions of carbon dioxide and other greenhouse gases because it will be a cost to them and retard their progress. Yet they expect the poor people of the developing countries to stifle even their minute growth as if it will cost them nothing.

The other issue before us is bio-diversity. The poor countries have been told to preserve their forests and other genetic resources on the off-chance that at some future date something is discovered which might prove useful to humanity. This is the same as telling these poor countries that they must continue to be poor because their forests and other resources are more precious than themselves. Still they are not rejecting the value of bio-diversity, at least not totally.

Denying them their own resources will impoverish them and retard their development. Surely, if something is discovered in their forests, they should be entitled to some returns.

But now we are told that the rich will not agree to compensate the poor for their sacrifices. The rich argue that the diversity of genes stored and safeguarded by the poor are of no value until the rich, through their superior intelligence, release the potential within. It is an intellectual property and must be copy-righted and protected.

Developing countries which met in Kuala Lumpur in April have agreed on a plan to reafforest the whole world. A Fund for this Greening of the World was proposed. But the North are resisting this proposal. Perhaps it is considered to be yet another attempt by the developing countries to squeeze the rich using the environmental issue. The rich North can only see the chiseling ways of the South and is determined that they will not be squeezed. Yet the North demands a forest convention.

Obviously the North wants to have a direct say in the management of forests in the poor South at next to no cost to themselves. The pittance they offer is much less than the loss of earnings by the poor countries and yet it is made out as a generous concession.

We will accept the Global Environmental Facility, and we will accept that it be administered by the OECD dominated World Bank. But can we not have a little say; can we not have more transparency in the administration of this Fund? Surely, this does not amount to the South squeezing the North.

The poor is not asking for charity. When the rich chopped down their own forests, built their poison-belching factories and scoured the world for cheap resources, the poor said nothing. Indeed, they paid for the development of the rich. Now the rich claim a right to regulate the development of the poor countries. And yet any suggestion that the rich compensate the poor adequately is regarded as outrageous. As colonies we were exploited. Now as independent nations we are to be equally exploited.

Malaysia was disillusioned about these inequities long before we reached Rio. In a world that has been won for democracy, we find powerful nations laying down terms even for participating in a democratic process. We find scant regard for the principles of fairness and equity. We find that even the Rio Declaration and Agenda 21 have been watered down upon insistence from the powerful and the rich.

Notwithstanding all these, we still have high expectations of this conference and we would consider this Conference on the Environment and Development a success if there emerged a better understanding of the enormity of the problems we face and the need for us to cooperate on an equitable basis. Malaysia will do what can reasonably be expected of it for the environment.

GITA SEN[1]

34

Women, Poverty & Population: Issues for the Concerned Environmentalist

Introduction

Differences in perceptions regarding the linkages between population and environment became particularly acute during the preparatory build-up to the UN Conference on Environment and Development, variously known as the Earth Summit and Rio 92. Disagreement between Southern and Northern countries on the extent of attention to be given to population received considerable publicity. At the non-governmental level too, the issue of population has been, of late, a subject of considerable debate among environmentalists (especially those from the North), feminists and population lobbyists.

The basis of these differences often appears baffling; the apparent lack of willingness to compromise, or to acknowledge the obvious merits of opposing views seems to indicate a lack of analytical rigour. The debate appears, to some at least, to be based on passionately held but ultimately ephemeral differences. I wish to argue that, although the positions taken in the policy debate have been exagger-

Originally published in Wendy Harcourt, ed., *Feminist Perspectives on Sustainable Development* (London: Zed Books, 1994). Reprinted with permission of Zed Books Ltd.

ated at times, some of the oppositions have deeper roots. They arise from conceptual and possibly paradigmatic differences rather than from disagreements regarding the 'truth-value' of particular scientific propositions. These shape the protagonists' perceptions of problems, the analytical methods used, and weights assigned to different linkages and relationships. In particular, varying views regarding development strategies, the linkages between poverty and population growth, and the role of gender relations in shaping those links colour the positions taken in the debate.

This chapter is an attempt to examine the different perspectives on these issues held by environmental scientists and environmental activists[2] on one hand, and women's health researchers and feminist activists on the other. Its motivation is twofold: first, to identify the positions taken by these two broad groupings within the larger discourses on development and on population; secondly to propose a possible basis for greater mutual understanding.[3]

Gender in the Population Field

In the history of population policy, women have been viewed typically in one of three ways. The narrowest of these is the view of women as principal 'targets' of family planning programmes; of women's bodies as the site of reproduction, and therefore as the necessary locus of contraceptive technology, and reproductive manipulation. The early history of population programmes is replete with examples of such views; but even more recently, the 'objectification' of women's bodies as fit objects for reproductive re-engineering, independent of a recognition of women as social subjects, continues apace. (Hubbard, 1990)

A second view of women which gained currency after the Bucharest Population Conference in 1983 was women as potential decision-makers whose capabilities in managing childcare, children's health in particular, could be enhanced through greater education. Women began to be viewed as social subjects in this case, but the attention given to women's education has not spun off (in the population policy literature) into a fuller consideration of the conditions under which the education of girls takes hold in a society, and therefore the extent to which education is embedded within larger social processes and structures. While this view represented a step away from objectification, women were still perceived as a means to a demographic end, with their own health and reproductive needs becoming thereby incidental to the process.

A third view which grew in the 1980s focused on maternal mortality as an important health justification for family planning. This view, which was at the core of the Safe Motherhood Initiative, attempted to claim a health justification for family planning on the basis of rates of maternal mortality. In practice, the initiative has received relatively little funding or support.

Conceptual Approaches

Economic theories of fertility are closely associated with the 'new' household economics. Premised on the belief that children are a source of both costs and benefits to their parents, such theories argue that parents determine their 'optimum' number of children based on a balancing of costs and benefits at the margin. As a description of differences between societies where children are viewed as a source of both present and future streams of income vs. those where children are essentially a cost to parents (balanced by a measure of psychological satisfaction but not by a significant flow of money income), the theory has an appealing simplicity. It purports to explain why the former societies may be more pro-natalist than the latter. It also suggests that shifting children away from child labour (a source of parental income) towards schooling (a parental cost) might work to reduce fertility.

Such theories have been criticized on a number of grounds. (Folbre, 1988) The main criticism centres on the assumption that actual fertility is the result of choices made by a homogenous household unit innocent of power and authority relations based on gender and age. Once such relations are acknowledged, and there is enough anthropological and historical evidence of their existence, the basis of decision-making within households has to be rethought in terms of differential short-term gains and losses for different members, as well as strategic choices by dominant members which will protect and ensure their continued dominance. For example, if the costs of child-raising increase, ceteris paribus, there may be little impact on fertility if the increased costs are largely borne by subordinate members of the household (such as younger women) who do not have much say in household decision-making.

Traditionally, in many societies the costs of high fertility in terms of women's health and work-burdens are rarely acknowledged as such, as long as the benefits in terms of access to a larger pool of subordinate children's labour or the social prestige inherent in being the father of many sons continue to accrue to men. Such authority relations are further cemented by ideologies which link woman's own personal status within the authoritarian household to her fertility. Newer game-theoretic models of household behaviour (Sen, 1987) provide more interesting and complex theories that take better account of the differential distribution of types of assets as well as gains and losses within the household. These have not thus far, however, generated adequate explanations of fertility outcomes.[4]

Against the Stream: Gender Relations and Reproductive Rights

Many of the influential approaches to theory and policy within the population field have been less than able or equipped to deal with the complexity and pervasiveness of gender relations in households and the economies and societies within which they function. Both feminist researchers and activists within women's health movements have been attempting to change the terms of the debate and to expand its scope. An important part of this challenge is the critique of population policy and of family-planning programmes as being biased (in gender, class and race terms) in their basic objectives and in the methods that they predominantly use.

The definition of a social objective of population limitations[5] which does not recognize that there may be costs to limiting family size that are differential across social classes and income groups, has long been criticized.[6] In particular, such costs are likely to be less than transparent in non-democratic polities or even within democratic states where the costs are disproportionately visited on groups that are marginal on ethnic or racial bases and therefore do not have sufficient voice.[7]

Population policy has also been criticized by some as being a substitute for rather than complementary to economic development strategies that are broad-based in their allocation of both benefits and costs. For example, if impoverished peasants were persuaded or coerced to limit family size on the premise that their poverty is a result of high fertility, independent of the possible causal impact of skewed land-holding patterns, commercialization processes, or unequal access to development resources, then it is questionable whether smaller families would make them more or less poor.

The critique becomes more complicated once the gender dimension is introduced. Critics of population policy on class grounds have sometimes been as gender blind as the policy itself. Having many children may be an economic imperative for a poor family in certain circumstances, but the costs of bearing and rearing children are still borne disproportionately by the women of the household. Gender concerns cannot be subsumed under a notion of homogeneous national or global concerns. For feminist critics of population policy, development strategies that otherwise ignore or exploit poor women, while making them the main target of population programmes, are highly questionable. But they do not believe that the interests of poor women in the area of reproduction are identical to those of poor men.

In general terms, the feminist critique agrees with many other critics that population control cannot be made a surrogate for directly addressing the crisis of economic survival that many poor women face. Reducing population growth is not a sufficient condition for raising livelihoods or meeting basic needs.[8] In particular, the critique qualifies the argument that reducing fertility reduces the health risks of poor women and therefore meets an important basic need. This would be true provided the means used to reduce fertility did not themselves increase the health hazards that women face, or were considerably and knowably less than the risks of childbearing. If family-planning programmes are to do this, critics argue, they will have to function differently in the future than they have in the past.

The most trenchant criticism questions the objectives (population control rather than, and often at the expense of, women's health and dignity), the strategies (family planning gaining dominance over primary and preventive health care in the budgets and priorities of departments), the methods (use of individual incentives and disincentives for both 'target' populations and programme personnel, targets and quotas for field personnel, overt coercion, the prevalence of 'camps' and absence of medical care either beforehand or afterwards, inadequate monitoring of side-effects), and the birth-control methods (a narrow range of birth prevention methods, technology that has not been adequately tested for safety, or which has not passed regulatory controls in Northern countries) advocated and supplied through population programmes. A now extensive debate around the 'quality of care' has focused particularly on the implications of alternative programme methods and birth-control techniques for the quality of family programme services. (Bruce, 1989) More broad-ranging evaluations of population policy objectives and strategies have found them guilty of biases of class, race/ethnicity and gender. (Hartmann, 1987)

Viewed as a development strategy, the critics see population policies as usually falling within a class of strategies that are 'top-down' in orientation, and largely unconcerned with (and often violating) the basic human rights needs of target populations. Even the developmentalist concern with improving child health and women's education has received little real support from population programmes despite the extensive research and policy debate it has generated.

The critical perspective argues that ignoring co-requisites, such as economic and social justice and women's reproductive health and rights, also makes the overt target of population policies (a change in birth rates) difficult to achieve. Where birth rates do fall (or rise as the case may be) despite this, the achievement is often predicated on highly coercive methods, and is antithetical to women's health and human dignity. The women's health advocates argue for a different approach to population policy—one that makes women's health and other basic needs more central to policy and programme focus, and by doing so increases human welfare, transforms oppressive gender relations, and reduces population growth rates. (Germain and Ordway, 1989)

Around the world there is a growing emergence of positive statements about what human rights in the area of reproduction might encompass. (Petchesky and Weiner, 1990) Many of these statements are culturally and contextually specific, but they usually share a common critique of existing population programmes, and a common understanding of alternative principles. Many of them prioritize the perspective of poor women, although they recognize that the reproductive rights of all women in most societies are less than satisfactory. Their attempt to recast population policies and programmes is also, therefore, a struggle to redefine development itself to be more responsive to the needs of the majority.

Enter the Environmentalists

Environmentalist concern with population growth pre-dates the public debate sparked by the UN Conference on Environment and Development (UNCED). Probably some of the most influential early documents were the Club of Rome's *Limits to Growth* and Ehrlich and Ehrlich's *The Population Bomb*. (Ehrlich, 1969) The interest in global and local carrying capacity, vis-à-vis growing human population sizes and densities, stimulated the production of considerable literature, both scientific and popular. Unfortunately, the popular and activist literature has tended to ignore some of the important anthropological debates about carrying capacity, as well as to disregard the inconclusiveness of empirical evidence linking environmental change to population growth.[9] It tends, furthermore, to treat the population-environment linkages as simple mathematical ones, linking numbers of people to their environments through technology.

But the argument of both developmentalists in the population field and women's health and rights advocates has been precisely that population is not just an issue of numbers, but of complex social relationships which govern birth, death and migration. People's interactions with their environments can be only partially captured by simple mathematical relationships which fail to take the distribution of resources, incomes and consumption into account; such mathematical relationships by themselves may therefore be inadequate as predictors of outcomes or as guides to policy.[10]

Furthermore, from a policy point of view, more precise modelling of population-environment interactions has not, thus far, provided much better guidance about appropriate population policy programmes. Ignoring the wide disparities in the growth rates of consumption between rich and poor within developing countries and hence their relative environmental impacts, as well as the critiques of women's health advocates outlined in previous sections, leads to single-minded policy prescriptions directed once more simply to increasing family-planning funding and effort. The leap from over-aggregated population-environmental relations to policy prescriptions favouring increased family planning becomes an implicit choice of politics, of a particular approach to population policy, to environmental policy, and to development. Because it glosses over so many fundamental issues of power, gender and class relations, and of distribution, and because it ignores the historical experience of population programmes, it has come to be viewed by many as a retrograde step in the population-development discourse.

Population Actors

The preceding discussion suggests that important actors in the population field are as follows.

First come those population specialists who traditionally have focused on the size and growth of populations, on age structures, migration and population composition. In general, they enter the development discourse primarily through their concern with what impact population growth might have on rates of economic growth. In addition, population projections are mapped onto planning needs in areas such as food production, energy, and other infrastructures, as well as health, education, and so on. These mappings can be said to belong to a class of simple mathematical planning models which usually ignore problems of distribution (based as they tend to be on per capita needs and availabilities), as well as the social and institutional aspects of making a plan actually work.

The second group are the developmentalists who focus less on the impact of demographic change, and more on the prerequisites of sustained decline in mortality and fertility rates. In particular they stress the importance of improving health and women's education. They thus represent a major revision of traditional population approaches, but all too often stop short of addressing the problem of sustainability or of livelihoods.

A third group, the fundamentalists, has become increasingly important in the population field during the 1980s, gaining political legitimacy through their links to mainstream political organizations. Their primary interest is not the size or growth of populations, but rather control over reproduction and a conservative concern to preserve traditional family structures and gender rules. The moral overtones of the US abortion debate notwithstanding, their interest in procreation appears to derive largely from an opposition to changing gender relations in society.

The fourth group are the Northern environmentalists. At the risk of oversimplification, one might argue that many of these individuals and groups focus mainly on the links between economic growth and ecological sustainability on the one hand, and the size and growth of population on the other.

The fifth important group of actors are the women's health groups which have evolved either out of the feminist movement or out of other social movements or population organizations. Their understanding of the population problem is distinctive in that they define it as primarily a question of reproductive rights and reproductive health, in the context of livelihoods, basic needs and political participation. They often acknowledge that economic growth and ecological sustainability are concerns, but believe these ought to be viewed in the context of reproductive rights and health. In particular, many of them give priority to the needs and priorities of poor women in defining issues, problems and strategies.

Each of these sets of population actors has a view of the population question that is consistent with a particular view of development; as such they tend to overlap with particular sets of development actors, and find a niche within a particular set of development ideas. For example, population specialists are attracted to problems of economic growth, developmentalists to basic needs issues, and women's health activists to the problems of livelihoods, basic needs and political empowerment. Many Northern environmentalists, on the other hand, tend to view population solely through the lens of ecological sustainability, and this accounts for a considerable amount of the dissonance between their views and those of grassroots groups in the South.

Towards More Synergy Between Environmentalists and Feminists

Despite the dissonance provoked by the population-environment debate, there is much in common between feminists and environmentalists in their visions of society and in the methods they use. Both groups (or at least their more progressive

wings) have a healthy critical stance towards ecologically profligate and inequitable patterns of economic growth, and have been attempting to change
mainstream perceptions in this regard. Both use methods that rely on grassroots
mobilization and participation, and are therefore sensitive to the importance of
political openness and involvement. As such, both believe in the power of widespread knowledge and in the rights of people to be informed and to participate in
decisions affecting their lives and those of nations and the planet. Indeed, there
are many feminists within environmental movements (North and South) and environmentalists within feminist movements.

Greater mutual understanding on the population question can result from a
greater recognition that the core problem is that of development within which
population is inextricably meshed. Privileging the perspective of poor women can
help ground this recognition in the realities of the lives and livelihoods of many
within the South.

Economic growth and ecological sustainability must be such as to secure livelihoods, basic needs, political participation and women's reproductive rights, not
work against them. Thus, environmental sustainability must be conceptualized so
as to support and sustain livelihoods and basic needs, and not in ways that automatically counterpose 'nature' against the survival needs of the most vulnerable. Where
trade-offs among these different goals exist or are inevitable, the costs and burdens
must not fall on the poorest and most vulnerable, and all people must have a voice
in negotiating resolutions through open and genuinely participatory political
processes. Furthermore, environmental strategies that enhance livelihoods and fulfill needs can probably help lay the basis for reduced rates of mortality and fertility.

Population and family-planning programmes should be framed in the context of
health and livelihood agendas, should give serious consideration to women's health
advocates, and be supportive of women's reproductive health and rights. This has to
be more than lip service; it requires reorienting international assistance and national
policy, reshaping programmes and rethinking research questions and methodologies. Using the language of welfare, gender equity or health, while continuing advocacy for family planning as it is at present practised will not meet the need.

Reproductive health strategies are likely to succeed in improving women's
health and making it possible for them to make socially viable fertility decisions if
they are set in the context of an overall supportive health and development
agenda. Where general health and social development are poorly funded or given
low priority, as has happened in the development agendas of many major development agencies and countries during the last decade, reproductive rights and
health are unlikely to get the funding or attention they need. Reproductive health
programmes are also likely to be more efficacious when general health and development are served. A poor female agricultural wage-labourer, ill-nourished and
anaemic, is likely to respond better to reproductive health care if her nutritional
status and overall health improve at the same time.

The mainstream Northern environmental movement needs to focus more
sharply on gender relations and women's needs in framing its own strategies, as

well as on the issues raised by minority groups. These issues (such as those raised by native peoples and African Americans in the US) tend to link environmental issues with livelihoods and basic needs concerns in much the same way as do the people's organizations in the South.[11] Greater sensitivity to the one, therefore, might bring greater awareness of the other.

Wide discussion and acknowledgement of these principles could help to bridge some of the current gaps between feminists and environmentalists, and make it possible to build coalitions that can move both agendas forward.

References

Bruce, J. (1989) 'Fundamental Elements of the Quality of Care: A Simple Framework'. The Population Council, Programmes Division Working Papers No. 1, May, New York.

Caldwell, J., and P. Caldwell (1987) 'The Cultural Context of High Fertility in Sub-Saharan Africa', in *Population and Development Review,* 13:3, September, pp 409–38.

Ehrlich, P. (1969) *The Population Bomb.* Ballantine Books, New York.

Folbre, N. (1988) 'The Black Four of Hearts: Towards a New Paradigm of Household Economics', in J. Bruce and D. Dwyer (eds.), *A Home Divided: Women and Income in the Third World.* Stanford University Press, Stanford.

Germain, A., and J. Ordway (1989) *Population Control and Women's Health: Balancing the Scales.* International Women's Health Coalition, New York.

Hartmann, B. (1987) *Reproductive Rights and Wrongs: The Global Politics of Control and Contraceptive Choice.* Harper and Row, New York.

Hubbard, R. (1990) *The Politics of Women's Biology.* Rutgers University Press, New Brunswick.

Little, P. (1992) 'The Social Causes of Land Degradation in Dry Regions' (manuscript). Institute of Development Anthropology, Binghamton.

Mamdani, M. (1974) *The Myth of Population Control.* Monthly Review Press, New York.

Petchesky, R., and J. Weiner (1990) *Global Feminist Perspectives on Reproductive Rights and Reproductive Health.* Report on the Special Sessions at the Fourth International Interdisciplinary Congress on Women, Hunter College, New York, NY.

Scott, J. (n.d.) 'Norplant: Its Impact on Poor Women and Women of Color'. National Black Women's Health Project Public Policy/Education Office, Washington, DC.

Sen, A. K. (1987) 'Gender and Cooperative Conflicts'. Discussion Paper No. 1342. Harvard Institute of Economic Research, Cambridge.

Shaw, R. P. (1989) 'Population Growth: Is It Ruining the Environment?', in *Populi,* 16:2, pp. 21–9.

35

Two Agendas on Amazon Development

For Bilateral and Multilateral Funders

(This document is addressed to the World Bank, the Inter-American Development Bank, the US Agency International Development, and the European Economic Community.)

We, the Indigenous Peoples, have been an integral part of the Amazon Biosphere for millennia. We have used and cared for the resources of that biosphere with a great deal of respect, because it is our home, and because we know that our survival and that of our future generations depends on it. Our accumulated knowledge about the ecology of our home, our models for living with the peculiarities of the Amazon Biosphere, our reverence and respect for the tropical forest and its other inhabitants, both plant and animal, are the keys to guaranteeing the future of the Amazon Basin, not only for our peoples, but also for all of humanity.

What COICA Wants

1. The most effective defense of the Amazonian Biosphere is the recognition and defense of the territories of the region's Indigenous Peoples and the promo-

Originally published in *Cultural Survival Quarterly* 13, 4 (1989):75–78. Reprinted with permission.

tion of their models for living within that Biosphere and for managing its resources in a sustainable way. The international funders of Amazonian development should educate themselves about the Indigenous Peoples' relationship with their environment, and formulate new concepts of Amazonian development together with new criteria for supporting Amazonian development projects which would be compatible with the Indigenous Peoples' principles of respect and care for the world around them, as well as with their concern for the survival and well-being of their future generations.

2. The international funders must recognize the rights of Indigenous Peoples as those are being defined within the Working Group on Indigenous Peoples, established by the UN Human Rights Commission. These rights should form the basis of the institution's policy towards the Indigenous Peoples and their territories who live in those areas where the funder is supporting development work. The funders should consult directly with the organizations of the Indigenous Peoples throughout the process of establishing this policy and should distribute that policy widely among governments and the organizations of Indigenous Peoples.

3. There can be no development projects in indigenous areas without the informed consent of the Indigenous Peoples affected. The funders must make every effort, through field research conducted by personnel of the funding institution, to verify the existence of an indigenous population, or the possible negative impact on an indigenous population, in areas where they are considering the implementation of a project. If either is the case, the funder must openly recognize the existence of this population or the negative impact on them, and then should establish as a condition for further funding the project

- that the government responsible for implementing the project also recognize the existence of the population and/or the negative impact;
- that the affected population be informed of the plans and impact of the plans; and
- that the affected population consent to the implementation of the plans.

These conditions should be monitored by both the funder and the organization which represents the affected population.

4. If the indigenous population has given its informed consent to the implementation of a development project within its territory, the project must be designed in such a way that it respects the territories of the population as they define them, their economy and their social organization, according to the institutional policy as described in Point One. There should be special components of the project which lend support directly to the indigenous population for their own needs and for the development proposals which they may have. The organization which represents the affected population should participate in the design of the project.

5.   The international funders should enter into a direct relation of collaboration and mutual respect with the organizations of Indigenous Peoples, through their representatives. This relation should establish the basis for:

- *consultations* on all aspects of projects implemented in areas with an indigenous population or which have an impact on an indigenous population;
- *participation* of representatives of Indigenous Peoples in the planning, implementation, and evaluation of projects;
- *exchange* of information of mutual interest on plans, projects, activities, and needs of both.

. . .

Indigenous Peoples' Alternatives for Amazonian Development

An important task of the Coordinating Body is to present to the international community the alternatives which we indigenous peoples offer for living with the Amazonian Biosphere, caring for it and developing within it. This is one of our important contributions to a better life for humankind. The following represent, in general terms, our program for the defense of the Amazonian Biosphere.

1.   The best defense of the Amazonian Biosphere is the defense of the territories recognized as homeland by Indigenous Peoples, and their promotion of our models for living within that biosphere and for managing its resources. This implies:

- education for the national and international communities regarding the Indigenous Peoples' concept of the unity between people and territory, and regarding our models for managing and caring for our environment.
- work with national governments, environmental organizations, and international institutions which fund Amazon development to develop new concepts and models for occupying and using the Amazon Basin in keeping with our long-term perspective (future generations), our respect for the interdependence between humankind and our environments, and our need to improve the well-being of the entire community; further work with the same institutions to translate these new concepts into concrete programs for developing and caring for the Amazon Basin and its inhabitants.
- work with national governments, environmental organizations, and international funders to reorganize the occupation of supposedly empty Amazonian territories by combining indigenous territories, with forest, wildlife, and extractive reserves in favor of the indigenous and other cur-

rent inhabitants; by discouraging the "conquest and colonization" of our homeland; and by recuperating those vast areas devastated by state policies of conquest and colonization.

- research on the natural resources and traditional crops used by Indigenous Peoples, on the traditional systems for utilizing and conserving resources, and on models for the extraction of renewable resources.
- evaluation and systematization of the development projects implemented by Indigenous Peoples which attempt to combine the demands of the market with a respect for indigenous principles of development.

2.   The defense of the Amazon Biosphere/Indigenous territories must go hand-in-hand with the recognition of and respect for the territorial, political, cultural, economic, and human rights of the Indigenous Peoples. This implies:

- continued participation and support for the UN process for establishing an international instrument recognizing the rights of Indigenous Peoples.
- education for the national and international communities regarding the rights of Indigenous Peoples.
- establishment of mechanisms at both the national and international level for defending the rights of Indigenous Peoples in cases of violations of or conflicts over those rights.

3.   The right of self-determination for Indigenous Peoples within their environment/territory is fundamental for guaranteeing the well-being of the indigenous population and of the Amazonian Biosphere. This implies:

- respect for our autonomous forms of community, ethnic, and regional government.
- indigenous control over the economic activities within the indigenous territories, including the extraction of mineral reserves.
- respect for indigenous customary law and the indigenous norms for social control.

4.   Concrete Proposals for International Cooperation: For many decades now, most of our peoples have been experimenting with ways to participate in the encroaching market economies of our respective countries while trying to survive as peoples intimately linked to the Amazonian forest. We have done this despite the hostility shown us by the frontier society and despite the fact that, within the context of the market economy, we are desperately poor. For these reasons, we have organized ourselves in new ways and developed and managed a variety of small programs to improve our health, education, and economy. . . . It is these small scale, locally controlled initiatives which should be the cornerstone of future Amazonian development.

. . .

To the Community of Concerned Environmentalists

We, the Indigenous Peoples, have been an integral part of the Amazonian Biosphere for millennia. We use and care for the resources of that biosphere with respect, because it is our home, and because we know that our survival and that of our future generations depend on it. Our accumulated knowledge about the ecology of our forest home, our models for living within the Amazonian Biosphere, our reverence and respect for the tropical forest and its other inhabitants, both plant and animal, are the keys to guaranteeing the future of the Amazon Basin. A guarantee not only for our peoples, but also for all of humanity. Our experience, especially during the past 100 years, has taught us that when politicians and developers take charge of our Amazon, they are capable of destroying it because of their shortsightedness, their ignorance and their greed.

We are pleased and encouraged to see the interest and concern expressed by the environmentalist community for the future of our homeland. We are gratified by the efforts you have made in your country to educate your peoples about our homeland and the threat it now faces as well as the efforts you have made in South America to defend the Amazonian rain forests and to encourage proper management of their resources. We greatly appreciate and fully support the efforts some of you are making to lobby the US Congress, the World Bank, USAID, and the InterAmerican Development Bank on behalf of the Amazonian Biosphere and its inhabitants. We recognize that through these efforts, the community of environmentalists has become an important political actor in determining the future of the Amazon Basin.

We are keenly aware that you share with us a common perception of the dangers which face our homeland. While we may differ about the methods to be used, we do share a fundamental concern for encouraging the long-term conservation and the intelligent use of the Amazonian rain forest. We have the same conservation goals.

Our Concerns

We are concerned that you have left us, the Indigenous Peoples, out of your vision of the Amazonian Biosphere. The focus of concern of the environmental community has typically been the preservation of the tropical forest and its plant and animal inhabitants. You have shown little interest in its human inhabitants who are also part of that biosphere.

We are concerned about the "debt for nature swaps" which put your organizations in a position of negotiating with our governments for the future of our homelands. We know of specific examples of such swaps which have shown the most brazen disregard for the rights of the indigenous inhabitants and which are resulting in the ultimate destruction of the very forests which they were meant to preserve.

We are concerned that you have left us Indigenous Peoples and our organizations out of the political process which is determining the future of our homeland. While we appreciate your efforts on our behalf, we want to make it clear that we never delegated any power of representation to the environmentalist community nor to any individual or organization within that community.

We are concerned about the violence and ecological destruction of our homeland caused by the increasing production and trafficking of cocaine, most of which is consumed here in the US.

What We Want

We want you, the environmental community, to recognize that the most effective defense of the Amazonian Biosphere is the recognition of our ownership rights over our territories and the promotion of our models for living within that biosphere.

We want you, the environmental community, to recognize that we Indigenous Peoples are an important and integral part of the Amazonian Biosphere.

We want you, the environmental community, to recognize and promote our rights as Indigenous Peoples as we have been defining those rights within the UN Working Group for Indigenous Peoples.

We want to represent ourselves and our interests directly in all negotiations concerning the future of our Amazonian homeland.

What We Propose

We propose that you work directly with our organizations on all your programs and campaigns which affect our homelands.

We propose that you swap "debt for indigenous stewardship" which would allow your organizations to help return areas of the Amazonian rain forest to our care and control.

We propose establishing a permanent dialogue with you to develop and implement new models for using the rain forest based on the list of alternatives presented with this document.

We propose joining hands with those members of the worldwide environmentalist community who:

- recognize our historical role as caretakers of the Amazon Basin.
- support our efforts to reclaim and defend our traditional territories.
- accept our organizations as legitimate and equal partners.

We propose reaching out to other Amazonian peoples such as the rubber tappers, the Brazil-nut gatherers, and others whose livelihood depends on the nondestructive extractive activities, many of whom are of indigenous origin.

We propose that you consider allying yourselves with us, the Indigenous Peoples of the Amazon, in defense of our Amazonian homeland.

NANCY LEE PELUSO

36

Coercing Conservation

The flurry of ecological awareness and action in the late 1980s has led to a prolif-eration of international environmental agreements among nation-states. . . . Such agreements assume that each nation-state, including those which have only re-cently emerged from colonialism, has the capacity, the internal legitimacy, and the will to manage all resources falling within its territorial boundaries. The implica-tion is that the nation-state should be able to control the behavior of all users of all resources located within the state's (self-) declared jurisdiction, whatever the origin of the state's claim, whatever the nature of competition for those resources, and whatever the nature or origins of resistance to the state's resource control.[1]

These strategies have elicited the formal commitment of many Third World of-ficials and policymakers who, not surprisingly, stand to benefit from their in-volvement in such initiatives. Some states or state interests, however, appropriate the conservation concerns of international environmental groups as a means of eliciting support for their own control over productive natural resources. Indeed, some tropical developing states use conservation ideology to justify coercion in the name of conservation, often by using violence. The state's mandate to defend threatened resources and its monopolization of legitimate violence combine to facilitate state apparatus-building and social control. "Legitimate" violence in the name of resource control also helps states control people, especially recalcitrant regional groups, marginal groups, or minority groups who challenge the state's authority.

Excerpted from "Coercing Conservation: The Politics of State Resource Control," in *The State and Social Power in Global Environmental Politics*, eds. Ronnie D. Lipschutz and Ken Conca (New York: Co-lumbia University Press, 1993). © 1993 Columbia University Press. Reprinted with permission of the publisher.

The environmental community, perhaps inadvertently, justifies coercive-protective actions on the basis of moral high grounds which are difficult to dispute, such as the preservation of the world's biological heritage or our common security. Indeed, the recognition of the "urgent need" to defend at any cost endangered species, endangered habitats, or whole ecosystems, is becoming a more frequent part of the discourse of conservation.[2] Those who abhor state violence against its people are in some cases willing to turn a blind eye to the practice of violence or the threat of violence when conservation for (global) common security is being protected.[3] . . . Nevertheless, when a state must resort to violent means of protecting its own or the global community's claims to natural resources, it is an indicator of a failed, incomplete, or nonexistent legitimacy to govern society. Moreover, the states in question may (and often do) apply the tools and equipment they use to establish their resource sovereignty beyond the conservation endpoints envisioned by international facilitators of conservation, and appropriate the moral ideology of global conservation to justify state systems of resource extraction and production. . . .

Clashes Between Central States and Local Resource Users

It is in developing countries, many of which are still struggling to redress the legacies of colonialism and the difficulties of maintaining multiethnic nation-states, that the most difficult circumstances for conservation are found. The origins of their territorial integration lie in colonialism, and were enforced by colonial armies and arms. Though international colonial pressures may have largely died down in the wake of worldwide independence movements, world market linkages continue to influence the decisions of former colonies by increasing the returns of market activities to the national elites who control the trading links.[11] Despite their contempt for the colonial regimes that preceded them, many contemporary developing states have adopted colonial policies for land and resource control, sometimes making them even more coercive.[12] Moreover, to enforce control where state hegemony is tenuous—because of deep-seated rifts between social groups, regional disparities in resource distribution, or competing concepts of appropriate or rightful use of resources—in many Third World countries, state leaders are increasingly members of, controlled by, or strongly allied with the military.[13]

Power struggles between the state and society are played out constantly in the process of allocation, control, and accessing of resources. Both internal and external pressures on states cause them to manage resources using particular tactics to achieve conservation or (sustainable) production management objectives. A state or a faction of the state may coerce conservation under one or all of three circumstances: when the resources are extremely valuable, when the state's legitimate control of the resource is questioned or challenged by other resource users, and when coercion is considered either the last resort or the easiest means of establishing control over people and territory. . . .

The conservation agenda, which is generally depicted as being in the common interest of the entire global community, is seen by some as a justification for external intervention in what were previously the sole affairs of states.[14] From a local perspective, however, both states and international conservation groups may be seen as illegitimate controllers of local resources. . . .

International intervention or support does not guarantee the realization of environmental goals or state legitimacy, however. Replacing or strengthening power holders in order to control resources may encourage increasing local resistance or rebellion against state or international controls on local resources. State concerns with the economic value of resources may influence conservation groups to use economic terms to justify their protection and preservation strategies. Whether for intensive production or for preservation, valuation strategies for resource territories frequently disenfranchise local people who had long histories of local resource use and may have played significant, though unrecognized, roles in creating "wild" habitats. Not only does this often have the effect of undermining conservation; it also changes the way resources are perceived, defined, valued, allocated, and used. When these management strategies change who has access to and control over local resources, the use of violence becomes an expedient means of exerting state control, in the name of "conservation" or "legitimate domain."

In sum, externally based resource claimants (including the state itself) frequently redefine resources, the means by which they will be conserved or harvested, and the distribution of benefits from their protection. Such redefinitions often override, ignore, or collide with local or customary forms of resource management. When competition between external and local legitimation mechanisms is played out in the environmental arena, the result is social and political conflict, which causes environmental degradation and ultimately fails to achieve the goals of international conservation interests.

Nevertheless, the state may not "lose." Even if conservation goals are not achieved, the state may succeed in strengthening its capacity to govern via the use of force.[16] No one monitors this type of aggression or this outcome of international conservation strategy. The means of violence and the ideologies of state stewardship of global resources, obtained directly or indirectly from the international conservation community, may facilitate the state's imposition and enforcement of its right to govern. . . .

Kenya

The resources discussed in this section are the lands set aside for national parks and wildlife reserves and resources within those lands (wildlife, pasture, and water). The traditional users of these lands, the Maasai, Somalis, and pastoralists of other ethnic groups, have been excluded from access to these lands to various degrees over the past century. State claims to nearly two-thirds of traditional Maasai

lands were first made by the British colonial state at the turn of the twentieth century. In 1904 the Maasai, who used to occupy all the land from Mt. Kenya in the
north to the border with (and into) what is today Tanzania, were resettled in two
reserves. Several years later, those in the northern reserve were resettled again in
an extension of the southern reserve. By 1912, they were confined to an area of
approximately 38,000 km².[17] The British allocated some of the Maasai's traditional lands to European planters whose activities were believed by colonial officials to be "more productive."[18] Early on, however, the British did not subscribe to
the theory that the Maasai could not coexist with wildlife. Thus, in 1906 they created the Southern Game Reserve—a wildlife reserve *within* the Maasai reserve because the Maasai were not believed to threaten wildlife, having coexisted with the
region's wild game for thousands of years.[19]

It was not until the 1940s and 1950s that the colonial government gave in to
pressures from game hunters and some conservation groups to set aside rangeland exclusively for wild game. At that same time, the state wanted to settle the
Maasai in fixed places, which meant changing their traditional migratory cattle-
raising practices. The Amboseli Basin, occupying some 3,200 km of both the
Maasai Reserve and the Southern Game Reserve, was an important source of water during dry season for the region's wildlife as well as the Maasai and their cattle. Dams and boreholes to provide water outside the Amboseli basin were constructed to benefit the Maasai. As the number of Maasai cattle increased, as they
continued to migrate to areas where wild game also sought drinking water, and as
hunters threatened wildlife in a different manner, conservationist interests grew
more concerned that the wildlife dependent on the Basin waters were being
threatened. Along with big game hunters, they pressured the colonial government
to create reserves where human use would be more restricted. The Southern
Game Reserve was abolished in 1952 and four smaller reserves were created, including a new one outside the area of the old Southern Game Reserve, called
Maasai Mara. In the 1950s, hunting was first outlawed within these reserves, although the government issued permits for hunting outside the reserves. In the
early 1960s livestock grazing was also forbidden in an 80 km² area of the Amboseli reserve, which was a direct threat to Maasai lifestyles and livelihoods.[20]

The Maasai did not so easily give up their traditional patterns of migration to
seasonal water supplies; nor were water development efforts sufficient to permit
them to do so. When their principal means of livelihood was restricted by reserve
authorities, the Maasai responded by killing rhinoceroses and elephants. A decade
later, some allegedly began collaborating with ivory poachers. They also resisted
further appropriation of their access rights by increasing their use of the area surrounding the livestock-free zone, and later demanded tenure rights to all these
lands.[21]

Meanwhile, another development increased the state's direct interest in the
protection of wild game and the reservation of parklands: the increase in wildlife-
oriented tourism beginning in the 1960s. Some tourism revenues, including
hunting fees, were given to various Maasai district councils as an incentive to win

their acceptance of the reserves.[22] Fees and revenues grew through the 1960s and early 1970s, after Kenyan independence. Not all district councils, however, truly represented the interests of the people in the immediate vicinity of the reserves and parks. In Amboseli, for example, the Kajiado Council receiving park revenues was 150 km from the park boundaries. Thus some Maasai were benefitting from the Park's existence, but not necessarily those who had the most to lose from the Park's creation.

The value of wildlife tourism soon became clear to the central government. In 1974, the government designated 488 km[2] of the Amboseli basin as a national park, while still negotiating with the Maasai. In 1977 this area was reduced to 390 km[2], which was gazetted as a park and would remain free of livestock. A de facto buffer zone was to be established around the core area of the park, and group ranches—a brand-new form of social organization for these Maasai—were established to further the government's intentions of sedentarizing the Maasai. In addition, the Maasai were expected to allow wildlife to graze on these ranches in exchange for a "wildlife utilization fee," which was supposed to compensate them for losses of water and grazing area to their own livestock.[23]

By 1989, tourism in Kenya was contributing about 20 percent of the nation's total foreign exchange.[24] By 1991, tourists were spending some 50 million dollars a year to view elephants and other wildlife.[25] In this way, as Knowles and Collett have pointed out, the creation of national parks to protect wildlife has not only separated the Maasai from their livestock production base and created a mythical nature devoid of humans for tourist consumption but also provided the government with the financial means to "develop" and "modernize" them.[26] Moreover, "National Parks and Game Reserves are never justified solely in terms of the economics of tourism: both the conservationists and national governments support the creation and maintenance of these areas with *moral arguments* based on the need to conserve wildlife and the intangible benefits that conservation confers on humanity."[27]

The plans for development of the Maasai in Amboseli have not worked as well as they have in Mara. Some blame the failure on the basic conflict in the lifestyles of the Maasai and their unwillingness to allow outsiders to make decisions about their lives and their uses of resources. Collett, for example, claims that the main reason the provision of water supplies outside the park has not achieved the government's development goals is the preference of the Maasai for a migratory, pastoralist lifestyle.[28] However, a recent report by the World Bank indicates that there were also significant technical problems:

[The conflicts] may be attributed . . . to failure to implement the agreements, to the lack of an official written agreement outlining the management responsibilities of the different parties and policy changes. The water pumping system, financed by the New York Zoological Society and the World Bank, worked well for a few years and then began to fail due to technical and administrative problems which were not corrected by the central Government which had built it. An inadequate water supply left the

Maasai little option but to return to find water inside the Park. The problems were aggravated by a drought in 1984, in which the Maasai lost a substantial part of their livestock and received no assistance from the Park authorities. The wildlife utilization fees were paid regularly until about 1981, then the payments became sporadic without explanation to the Maasai. The agreement for group ranches to retain a portion of Park entry fees fell through, perhaps due to administrative changes. . . . Anticipated income from tourism did not increase as quickly as expected. . . . Construction of new lodges and viewpoint circuits on group ranch lands did not materialize as expected. Finally, the 1977 hunting ban eliminated anticipated income from safari hunting license fees.[29]

In the past few years, the basic conflicts over land and resource fights in Kenyan national parks and reserves have been reconstructed in terms of a government mandate to stop the poaching of wildlife, especially of elephants and rhinoceroses. Major international environmental organizations, including the Worldwide Fund for Nature, the African Wildlife Foundation, World Conservation International (WCI), the International Union for the Conservation of Nature (IUCN), Conservation International, and the National Geographic Society have publicized the poaching issue and its threat to global and African biodiversity. The efforts of these and other environmental groups led to the creation of the Convention on International Trade in Endangered Species (CITES). By 1991, 105 world nations had signed the CITES declaration to ban the raw ivory trade in their effort to protect elephants in Asia and Africa.[30]

A great deal, however, has been left out of the international discussion of the poaching issue, and neither the origins nor the implications of the proposed solutions to the poaching problem have received the critical analysis they merit. Two gaps in the conservation community's discussion are particularly glaring. The first is the lack of historical perspective on the political and ecological contexts within which parks were created to protect wildlife, and the resulting dismissal of local people in creating particular environments. The other is the failure to consider the political-economic implications of the provision of arms and other equipment intended (at least ostensibly) to protect wildlife.

In April 1989, Richard Leakey became the director of Kenya's Wildlife Service. Since then Leakey has made his mark by firing administrative and field staff believed to be involved in the illegal ivory or rhino horn trade, by giving raises to underpaid and overworked park rangers, and by arming these rangers with automatic rifles and helicopter gunships in order to wage war more effectively on the poachers invading Kenya's national parks. Wage war they have: within two years of his taking over, more than a hundred poachers had been killed, many of them with no chance for discussion or trial; the rangers are licensed, like military in a state of emergency, to shoot-to-kill.[31] The Wildlife Service has also reclaimed direct control over the Maasai Mara Reserve, where the combination of wildlife management with local participation and benefits had reportedly been more successful. The government claimed that the reserve had been inadequately maintained and was deteriorating, denying earlier reports that elephants and rhinoceros populations within this park had been increasing while antipoaching costs were virtually negligible.[32]

. . . In their campaigns to save animals, international conservation groups never specify who the poachers are, although some fingers are pointed and accusations made. A letter to members from the WWF, for example, says, "Some poachers, tribesmen displaced from traditional occupations by drought or civil war, use primitive methods to kill elephants and transport tusks. But most use high-powered weapons and even airplanes and various sorts of poisons."[34]

What tribe these "tribesmen" are from is not clarified, whether they are Maasai, or Kikuyu, or one of the smaller ethnic minorities within the country. Later in the letter, however, "Somali tribesmen" are directly implicated, as well as people from an apparently different social group, i.e., "Somali officials." In reference to ivory tusks sold or stockpiled within Somalia, the letter says, "These tusks were not legally confiscated. Instead, they probably were poached from Kenya's nearby Tsavo National Park by well-equipped Somali tribesmen, then smuggled out of Kenya with the complicity of Somali officials."[35] The Somali president himself also apparently wrote a letter guaranteeing his government's purchase of ivory tusks from neighboring countries.[36]

The WWF does not specifically accuse the Maasai of killing wildlife for ivory, but implies that their increasing populations are a major threat to the survival of the elephants and other wildlife. Nowhere in the letter to WWF members is it mentioned that the Maasai and other pastoral and hunter-gatherer groups coexisted with elephants and other savannah wildlife over thousands of years; or that people—as well as the elephants—play an important role in creating and maintaining the contemporary savannah habitat that supports them both. Rather, they imply that the presence of the Maasai is a new phenomenon to which elephants must adapt: "One broad cause of the decrease in elephant numbers is surely the advance of human populations into *their* habitat. . . . To some extent, elephants are able to adapt to the growing presence of pastoralists such as Kenya's Maasai."[37]

Chadwick, writing for *National Geographic,* reflects a more explicit "people versus wildlife" view, with only conservation researchers and supporters exempt:

Tusks became a sort of underground currency, like drugs, spreading webs of corruption from remote villages to urban centers throughout the world. . . . The seventies saw the price of ivory skyrocket. Suddenly, to a herder or subsistence farmer, this was no longer an animal, but a walking fortune, worth more than a dozen years of honest toil. . . . Ivory was running above a hundred dollars a pound, and officials from poorly paid park rangers to high ranking wildlife ministers had joined the poaching network. . . . Poaching gangs, including bush-wise bandits called *shifta* from Somalia, armed with AK-47 assault rifles, were increasingly turning their guns on tourists. This has all but shut down Meru National Park in the north.[38]

What is wrong with this description is its "snapshot" of a contemporary situation, with the camera angled in such a way as to keep the background out of focus. Everyone in the picture is considered equally guilty, regardless of the roots of their involvement, their power to prevent its happening, their public stance, or the historical basis of their claims to being where they are in relation to the wildlife and the lands. Both the average reader and the writer of the article are unfamiliar with the social history of these "wildlife habitats" and this gap in understanding is neither missed nor deemed necessary. The story, after all, is about people against nature. The people for nature, the heroes, are not the local people who lived alongside wildlife for thousands of years before their lands were appropriated by colonial and contemporary state agencies and carved into parks. The implicit heroes are Western wildlife scientists, environmental activists, and the conservation armies who rout the poachers. The indigenous people are implicated because of their proximity to the parks and the logistics of outside poachers gaining access, although it is unlikely that any "peasant farmer" sees one hundred dollars for any pound of ivory he has had a hand in obtaining. Peasants in this view are also guilty of "encroachment" on the elephants' habitat—the areas from which they were excluded not many decades ago: "Ultimately, though, people, not poachers, and growth, not guns, pose the most serious long-term threat to the elephant's survival."[39]

Ironically, Chadwick hints at another motive underlying the involvement of certain state and would-be state actors in this conservation drama: "To currency-strapped governments and revolutionaries alike [ivory poaching] was a way to pay for more firearms and supplies. In the eighties Africa had nearly ten times the weapons present a decade earlier, which encouraged more poaching than ever."[40]

Hence the "need" for increasing the power of the "good" government officials, particularly those working in the parks. As the WWF letter explained, "Antipoaching forces have been traditionally paid poorly, had insufficient training and equipment, and were understaffed. Moreover, they rarely enlisted the aid of nearby villagers by offering them economic incentives."[41]

As a result, WWF and its partners (IUCN, TRAFFIC, and WCI) began providing "emergency assistance to key African wildlife departments," improving ranger incentives and providing antipoaching equipment and training. They claim that "the only long-term security for elephants in Africa lies in strengthening national capabilities in wildlife conservation and management." Moreover, to its credit, WWF and other groups are "working to ensure that protected areas benefit from the income generated through access fees."[42] Leakey also asked the African Wildlife Federation for assistance, which AWF has provided, including airplanes and vehicles for antipoaching patrols in Tsavo National Park. Though it is a relatively small operation, AWF occasionally takes a more direct role in coercive wildlife protection by "mounting extra patrols when an emergency arises."[43]

That these aircraft, radios, vehicles, night-goggles, and other antipoaching equipment might serve another purpose besides conservation has been a secondary consideration in view of the emergency status of the quest to protect these wildlife. And yet, in an article appearing in January 1989, three months before Leakey's takeover and the subsequent high-powered, highly publicized crackdown on poaching, reports from Kenya showed how the government was already using its mandate to protect and manage resources to assert its authority where local people had resisted state controls on their activities since the colonial period.[44]

Ostensibly to settle a dispute over grazing rights between Somali and Borana groups residing in the north, the government sent in police, army helicopters, military aircraft and the paramilitary General Service Unit. Over 600 people were detained and "large numbers" were killed in the course of the current incident. The conflict is not a new one: a 1984 clash left 2,169 people dead, and in 1987 some 200–300 Home Guards, none of them Somali, were armed "to assist in policing grazing rights and local disputes."[45]

Many of these disputes date from the time that the Kora National Reserve was created, when Somali pastoralists were excluded from access to parklands for grazing. Whole communities of Somalis were resettled onto arid lands in Borana districts. In the course of their resettlement, they were deprived of pasture and water for their livestock. Seeking these resources in the vicinity of the reserve, they are harassed by the Kenyan security forces in the same manner as illegal Somalis engaged in the smuggling trade. The present government's harassment of both the settled and nomadic Somali in the region is couched in conservation rhetoric, but dates back to the region's efforts to secede from independent Kenya in 1967. The colonial government also had difficulty establishing its authority previously. In the course of the recent clash near the Kora reserve, it was reported that "under the state of emergency, security forces have powers to act without warrant and detain without specific reason . . . clean-up operations are commonplace."[46] Moreover, the officials involved in the political security operations now form an integral part of the antipoaching operations.

The political implications of this trend in conserving Kenyan wildlife are clear. Though equipment and funds may be allocated to protect nature, they can directly or indirectly be used by the state to serve its own political ends. In this way, the commitment to preservation of wildlife for tourism and research serves both the economic and political interests of the Kenyan government, while its actual effectiveness in doing so is questionable. . . .

Conclusion

The environmental community's tacit or explicit support of coercive conservation tactics has far-reaching consequences. First, local resistance to what are perceived as illegitimate state claims and controls over local resources is likely to heighten, and may lead to violent response, sabotage of resources, and degradation.[57] Second, and most important, the outside environmental community may be weakening local resource claimants who possess less firepower than the state. While some conservationists are also "arming" local nongovernment organizations with symbolic and financial support, their ultimate goal is as much or more to influence state policy as to empower local resource users. The ethics underlying the spread of Western conservation ideologies, without considering their inevitable transformation when accepted or appropriated by developing states, require close reexamination. . . .

[A] growing body of evidence show[s] that, wherever the state directly claims, controls, or manages landbased resources, state organizations and individual state actors have strong vested interests in the commercial exploitation of resources. Their control over the territories within which the resources occur, and over the people living within them, is a major aspect of their strategic territorial control. Militaries, paramilitary organizations, and state agencies often create or exacerbate resource-based conflicts by their participation in protective activities, their involvement as actors, or their coercive tactics. . . . Just as some military leaders can be co-opted to work for the sake of conservation agendas, conservation groups' resources and ideologies can be co-opted for separate military agendas. Once coercive conservation tactics are accepted, such co-optation is nearly impossible to prevent.

Failing to venture beyond the *concept* of thinking globally and acting locally, the writers of international conservation initiatives often brush aside or simply ignore the political implications of empowering states to coercively control access to natural resources. The militarization of resource control—whether for protection or production—leads to damaging relations with the environment, not benign ones. Whatever their approach on the ground, these conservation groups seek ultimately to change state policy and practice. Unfortunately, coercive conservation also strengthens or extends the state's military capacity—not only with the weapons of enforcement but also with new "moral" justifications to legitimate coercion in enforcing a narrowly defined "global community's" environmental will.

Notes

Introduction: Twenty-five Years of Global Environmental Politics

1. John Perlin, *A Forest Journey: The Role of Wood in the Development of Civilization* (Cambridge, MA: Harvard University Press, 1991), p. 46.

2. Zoo Daqing and Zhang Peiyuan, "The Huang-Huai-Hai Plain," in B. L. Turner II, William C. Clark, Robert W. Kates, John F. Richards, Jessica T. Mathews, and William B. Meyer, eds., *The Earth as Transformed by Human Action* (New York: Cambridge University Press, 1990).

3. Peter Brimblecombe, *The Big Smoke: A History of Air Pollution in London Since Medieval Times* (London: Methuen, 1987).

4. Turner et al., *The Earth as Transformed by Human Action.*

5. For a range of views on this theme see James Rosenau, *Turbulence in World Politics: A Theory of Change and Continuity* (Princeton: Princeton University Press, 1990); Robert Cox, *Production, Power and World Order* (New York: Columbia University Press, 1987); Benjamin R. Barber, "Jihad vs. McWorld," *The Atlantic Monthly*, March 1992, pp. 53–63; Arjun Appadurai, "Disjuncture and Difference in the Global Cultural Economy," in Mike Featherstone, ed., *Global Culture: Nationalism, Globalization and Modernity* (London: Sage, 1990).

6. Peter M. Haas, Marc A. Levy, and Edward A. Parson, "Appraising the Earth Summit: How Should We Judge UNCED's Success?" *Environment* 34, no. 8 (October 1992):7–11 and 26–32.

7. On the political implications of such a global network, see the contribution of Paul Wapner to this volume. See also Ronnie D. Lipschutz with Judith Mayer, *Global Civil Society & Global Environmental Governance* (Albany, NY: State University of New York [SUNY] Press, 1996); Thomas Princen and Matthias Finger, *Environmental NGOS in World Politics: Linking the Local and the Global* (New York: Routledge, 1994); Leslie Paul Thiele, "Making Democracy Safe for the World: Social Movements and Global Politics," *Alternatives* 18 (Summer 1993):273–305; Eric Laferrière, "Environmentalism and the Global Divide," *Environmental Politics* 3, no. 1 (Spring 1994):91–113.

8. For an overview of the Stockholm Conference, see Lynton Caldwell, *International Environmental Policy*, 3d ed. (Durham, NC: Duke University Press, 1996).

9. See National Academy of Sciences, *One Earth, One Future: Our Changing Global Environment* (Washington, DC: National Academy Press, 1990), especially pp. 15–19.

10. On the growth of scientific knowledge about the environment, see Mostafa K. Tolba, Osama A. El-Kholy, E. El-Hinnawi, M. W. Holdgate, D. F. McMichael, and R. E. Munn, *The*

World Environment, 1972–1992: Two Decades of Challenge (London: Chapman & Hall, 1992), chapter 20.

11. Riley E. Dunlap, George H. Gallup Jr., and Alec M. Gallup, "Of Global Concern: Results of the Health of the Planet Survey," *Environment* 35, no. 9 (November 1993):6–15 and 33–39.

12. On public opinion, perceptions, and attitudes see also Tolba et al., *The World Environment, 1972–1992*, chapter 21.

13. Haas, Levy, and Parson, "Appraising the Earth Summit."

14. One example of such a coalition in action can be seen in the campaign to change World Bank lending practices; see the essay by Bruce Rich in Part Four of this book.

15. See the contribution of Ruth Greenspan Bell in Part Three of this volume.

16. Tolba et al., *The World Environment, 1972–1992*, chapter 23. See also Helge Ole Bergesen and Georg Parmann, eds., *Green Globe Yearbook of International Co-operation on Environment and Development* (New York: Oxford University Press, 1997).

17. On the effectiveness of international environmental regimes, see Peter M. Haas, Robert O. Keohane, and Mark A. Levy, eds., *Institutions for the Earth: Sources of Effective International Environmental Protection* (Cambridge, MA: MIT Press, 1993).

18. Tolba et al., *The World Environment, 1972–1992*, p. 374.

19. Alan Durning, *How Much Is Enough? The Consumer Society and the Future of the Earth* (New York: W. W. Norton, 1992), p. 23.

20. Barry Commoner, *Making Peace with the Planet*, 5th ed. (New York: New Press, 1992), pp. 148–150.

21. Murray Bookchin, *Remaking Society: Pathways to a Green Future* (Boston: South End Press, 1990), p. 9.

22. Bookchin, *Remaking Society*, pp. 9–10.

23. This theme is central to much of the literature on ecological justice; see Part Seven of this book.

24. Vandana Shiva, "People's Ecology: The Chipko Movement," in Saul Mendlovitz and R.B.J. Walker, *Towards a Just World Peace* (London: Butterworths, 1987). See also Vandana Shiva, *Ecology and the Politics of Survival: Conflicts Over Natural Resources in India* (Newbury Park, CA: Sage, 1991); Ramachandra Guha, *The Unquiet Woods: Ecological Change and Peasant Resistance in the Himalayas* (Berkeley: University of California Press, 1989).

25. Shiva, "People's Ecology," p. 262.

26. On the concept of coevolution see Richard B. Norgaard, "Sociosystem and Ecosystem Coevolution in the Amazon," *Journal of Environmental Economics and Management* 8 (181):238–254.

Part One: The Debate at Stockholm

1. Mostafa K. Tolba, Osama A. El-Kholy, E. El-Hinnawi, M. W. Holdgate, D. F. McMichael, and R. E. Munn, *The World Environment, 1972–1992: Two Decades of Challenge* (London: Chapman & Hall, 1992), chapter 23.

2. Lynton Caldwell, *International Environmental Policy*, 3d ed. (Durham, NC: Duke University Press, 1996).

3. Several of these criticisms are summarized in W. D. Nordhaus, "World Dynamics: Measurement without Data," *Economic Journal* 83, no. 332 (December 1973):1156–1183. See also Julian Simon and Herman Kahn, *The Resourceful Earth* (Oxford: Basil Blackwell, 1984).

4. See Elinor Ostrom, *Governing the Commons: The Evolution of Institutions for Collective Action* (London: Cambridge University Press, 1990).

5. This theme is developed in Ronnie D. Lipschutz and Ken Conca, *The State and Social Power in Global Environmental Politics* (New York: Columbia University Press, 1992).

Chapter 1

53. See, for example, "Fellow Americans Keep Out!" *Forbes,* June 15, 1971, p. 22, and *The Ecologist,* January 1972.

Chapter 3

8. G. Hardin, ed., *Population, Evolution, and Birth Control* (Freeman, San Francisco, 1964), p. 56.

9. S. McVay, *Sci. Amer.* 216 (No. 8), 13 (1966).

10. J. Fletcher, *Situation Ethics* (Westminster, Philadelphia, 1966).

11. D. Lack, *The Natural Regulation of Animal Numbers* (Clarendon Press, Oxford, 1954).

12. H. Girvetz, *From Wealth to Welfare* (Stanford Univ. Press, Stanford, Calif., 1950).

13. G. Hardin, *Perspec. Biol. Med.* 6, 366 (1963).

18. P. Goodman, *New York Rev. Books* 10(8), 22 (23 May 1968).

20. C. Frankel, *The Case for Modern Man* (Harper, New York, 1955), p. 203.

21. J. D. Roslansky, *Genetics and the Future of Man* (Appleton-Century-Crofts, New York, 1966), p. 177.

Chapter 4

1. Tonypandy was a Welsh mining town where, in 1910, Winston Churchill sent unarmed London policemen to quell rioting strikers. The version popularly believed in Wales is that government troops shot Welsh miners who were striking for their workers' rights. In precise Tey-usage, *Tonypandy* exists when such a fiction is allowed to persist even by those people who know better. An example of Tonypandy in American history is the Boston Massacre. Josephine Tey, *Daughter of Time* (New York: Macmillan, 1951).

2. Garrett Hardin, "The Tragedy of the Commons," *Science* 162 (1968):1243–48.

3. Gordon Foxall, "A Note on the Management of 'Commons,'" *Journal of Agricultural Economics* 30 (1979):55.

4. For example, Garrett Hardin and John Baden, eds., *Managing the Commons* (San Francisco: Freeman, 1977).

5. Who could mistake the content—or inspiration—of articles such as "The Use of the Commons Dilemma in Examining the Allocation of Common Resources" (R. Kenneth Godwin and W. Brace Shepard, Resources for the Future Reprint 179), or "Legislating Commons: The Navajo Tribal Council and the Navajo Range" (Gary D. Libecap and Ronald N. Johnson, *Economic Inquiry* 18 [1980]:69–86), or Hardin and Baden, *Managing the Commons.* See also basic American government texts such as Robert Lineberry, *Government in America,* 2nd ed. (Boston: Little, Brown, 1983), in which he identifies the tragedy of the commons as "a parable about sheep overgrazing a common meadow" (pp. 579–80).

6. This is not to imply that the tragedy of the commons *never* occurred in those centuries; records are incomplete and to assert positively that something never occurred is to court contradiction and exposure.

10. Garrett Hardin, "Denial and Disguise," in Hardin and Baden, *Managing the Com-*

mons, pp. 45–52. Hardin acknowledges the injustice of the Enclosure Acts but applauds the increase in agricultural productivity that they entailed.

11. Beryl Crowe, "The Tragedy of the Commons Revisited," in Hardin and Baden, *Managing the Commons,* 54–55.

13. Richard A. Falk, *This Endangered Planet* (New York: Random, 1971), p. 48.

14. E. C. K. Gonner, *Common Land and Inclosure,* 2nd ed. (London: Cass, 1966). The first portion of this quote is quoted by Gonner without attribution. This is not, however, an outmoded or esoteric definition: basic American college dictionaries provide the same definition.

15. C. C. Taylor, "Archaeology and the Origins of Open-Field Agriculture," in Trevor Rowley, ed., *The Origins of Open-Field Agriculture* (London: Groom Helm, 1981), p. 21. See also Della Hooke, "Open-field Agriculture—The Evidence from the Pre-Conquest Charters of the West Midlands," ibid., p. 58: "Land held in common by a community is clearly in evidence by the tenth century."

16. W. G. Hoskins and L. Dudley Stamp, *The Common Lands of England and Wales* (London: Collins, 1965), p. 6.

17. Gonner, *Common Land,* pp. 3–4.

24. W. O. Ault, *Open-Field Farming in Medieval England* (London: Allen and Unwin, 1972), p. 17.

25. Ibid., p. 18. Ault gives 1246 as the earliest manor court rolls; the earliest manorial reeve's accounts are for 1208–9.

26. Joan Thirsk, "Field Systems of the East Midlands," in Alan R. H. Baker and Robin A. Butlin, eds., *Studies of Field Systems in the British Isles* (Cambridge, England: Cambridge University Press, 1973), p. 232.

28. B. K. Roberts, "Field Systems of the West Midlands," in Baker and Butlin, *Studies,* p. 199.

29. Thirsk, "Field Systems," p. 251.

30. Westminster Muniments, 1550; quoted in Ault, *Open-Field Farming,* p. 26.

31. G. Elliot, "Field Systems of Northwest England," in Baker and Butlin, *Studies,* p. 67. As an example, in Denwick in 1567 the stint of "each husbandland was 6 old beasts above two years old, 37 sheep above one year old besides lambs and other young cattle, four pigs above one year old, two geese and one horse or mare" (R. A. Butlin, "Field Systems of Northumberland and Durham," in Baker and Butlin, *Studies,* p. 138).

35. Elliot, "Field Systems," p. 83. The internal quote is from the Westmorland Record office, Musgrave D. P., Court Rolls 1695.

36. Edward Scrutton, *Commons and Common Fields* (1887; reprint ed., New York: Lenox Hill, 1970), p. 122.

39. Roberts, "Field Systems," p. 190.

40. A classic example of exploitation is the Statute of Merton (1236), which allowed "chief tenants to assart land for their own or their villeins' exclusive use, provided that 'sufficient' common land was left for the needs of the village community." June A. Sheppard, "Field Systems of Yorkshire," in Baker and Bullin, *Studies,* pp. 176–77.

41. Gonner, *Common Land,* p. 103.

43. Hoskins and Stamp, *Common Lands,* p. 55.

44. Ibid., p. 54.

46. Scrutton, *Commons,* pp. 120–21. For example, all the farmers might agree to let one field lie fallow against custom for two years. If, in the second year, one tenant decided to return to the customary management and to graze his cattle in the field, the rest were powerless to stop him, and of course, the result would be the use of the field by all the tenants.

47. Victor Rice, Frederick Andrews, Everett Warwick, and James Legates, *Breeding and Improvement of Farm Animals* (New York: McGraw-Hill, 1957), p. 16.

48. For example, between 1710 and 1790, the weight at Smithfield of cattle changed from 370 pounds to 800 pounds, of calves from 50 to 148, of sheep from 28 to 80, and of lambs from 18 to 50. This weight change is of course due to a multitude of causes. Scrutton, *Commons*, p. 121.

49. Gonner, *Common Land*, pp. 306–07.

50. Van Rensselaer Potter, *Science* 185 (1974):813.

51. Garrett Hardin, "Denial and Disguise," in Hardin and Baden, *Managing the Commons*, p. 47.

52. Hardin, "Tragedy of the Commons," in Hardin and Baden, *Managing the Commons*, p. 20.

Part Two: Ecology and the Structure of the International System

1. The term "structure" is used in this sense in Ken Conca, "Environmental Change and the Deep Structure of World Politics," in Ronnie D. Lipschutz and Ken Conca, *The State and Social Power in Global Environmental Politics* (New York: Columbia University Press, 1993).

2. World Commission on Environment and Development, *Our Common Future* (New York: Oxford University Press, 1987).

3. Mostafa K. Tolba, Osama A. El-Kholy, E. El-Hinnawi, M. W. Holdgate, D. F. McMichael, and R. E. Munn, *The World Environment, 1972–1992: Two Decades of Challenge* (London: Chapman & Hall, 1992), p. 808. This principle was reiterated twenty years later at the Earth Summit; see "Rio Declaration on Environment and Development," United Nations Conference on Environment and Development, U.N. Doc. A/CONF.151/5/Rev. 1(1992).

4. On debt, see for example the Latin American and Caribbean Commission on Development and Environment, *Our Own Agenda* (Washington, DC: Inter-American Development Bank and UNDP, 1991). On multinationals see David C. Korten, *When Corporations Rule the World* (West Hartford, CT: Kumarian Press, 1995); Jerry Mander and Edward Goldsmith, eds., *The Case Against the Global Economy and For a Turn to the Local* (San Francisco: Sierra Club Books, 1996).

5. On the role of colonialism in promoting the spread of European values, see Edward Said, *Culture and Imperialism* (New York: Random House, 1993).

6. This theme is developed in Conca, "Environmental Change and the Deep Structure of World Politics."

7. Judith Goldstein and Robert O. Keohane, eds., *Ideas and Foreign Policy: Beliefs, Institutions, and Political Change* (Ithaca, NY: Cornell University Press, 1993).

8. The term "antisystemic movement" is taken from G. Arrighi, T. K. Hopkins, and I. Wallerstein, *Antisystemic Movements* (London: Verso, 1989).

9. On the international pressures surrounding deforestation in the Amazon, see Susanna Hecht and Alexander Cockburn, *The Fate of the Forest: Developers, Destroyers, and Defenders of the Amazon* (New York: HarperCollins, 1990).

10. Ronnie D. Lipschutz with Judith Mayer, *Global Civil Society and Global Environmental Governance: The Politics of Nature from Place to Planet* (Albany, NY: SUNY Press, 1996), p. 2.

Chapter 7 (Conca)

1. See for example the comments of the Malaysian Prime Minister, Mahathir Mohamad, at the 1992 U.N. Conference on Environment and Development (UNCED), in *Environmental Policy and Law* 22, no. 4 (1992), p. 232, and Somaya Saad, "For Whose Benefit? Redefining Security," *Ecodecisions* (September 1991), pp. 59–60. See also the "Beijing Declaration of 41 Developing Countries," 18–19 June 1991, reprinted in *China Daily* (20 June 1991), p. 4, cited in the introduction to Andrew Hurrell and Benedict Kingsbury, eds., *The International Politics of the Environment* (Oxford, UK: Clarendon Press, 1992), p. 39, note 60.

2. On environmental conditionality, see Andrew Hurrell, "Green Conditionality," Overseas Development Council Policy Paper, March 1993 (Washington, DC: Overseas Development Council, 1993).

3. See Patricia Birnie, "International Environmental Law: Its Adequacy for Present and Future Needs," in Hurrell and Kingsbury, eds., *The International Politics of the Environment*, p. 84 (note 1). Birnie refers to what has been described as an emerging, bounded concept of "reasonable sovereignty."

4. On emergent global environmental values carried by transnational networks of activists and advocates see Margaret Keck and Kathryn Sikkink, "International Issue Networks in the Environment and Human Rights," a paper presented at the 17th Congress of the Latin American Studies Association, Los Angeles, California, 24–27 September 1992. See also Kathryn Sikkink, "Human Rights, Principled Issue-networks, and Sovereignty in Latin America," *International Organization* 47, no. 3 (Summer 1993), pp. 411–441, and Ronnie D. Lipschutz, "Reconstructing World Politics: The Emergence of Global Civil Society," *Millennium: Journal of International Studies* 21, no. 3 (Winter 1992), pp. 389–420.

5. For a discussion of this view, see Hurrell and Kingsbury, "Introduction," in Hurrell and Kingsbury, eds., *International Politics of the Environment*, pp. 6–8. The authors cite the work of Richard Falk and John Dryzek as representative examples.

6. Mark A. Levy, Robert O. Keohane, and Peter M. Haas, "Improving the Effectiveness of International Environmental Institutions," in Haas, Keohane, and Levy, eds., *Institutions for the Earth: Sources of Effective International Environmental Protection* (Cambridge, MA: MIT Press, 1993), especially pp. 415–417.

7. Ibid., p. 416.

8. See Riley E. Dunlap et al., "Of Global Concern: Results of the Health of the Planet Survey," *Environment* 35, no. 9 (November 1993), pp. 6–15 and 33–39.

9. One interesting result of the study by Dunlap and colleagues was the strikingly similar pattern of environmental concerns found in polling data across twenty-four countries of widely differing income levels (see Dunlap et al., "Of Global Concern").

10. These figures are from Peter M. Haas, Marc A. Levy, and Edward A. Parson, "Appraising the Earth Summit: How Should We Judge UNCED's Success?" *Environment* 34, no. 6 (October 1992), pp. 7–11 and 26–33.

11. This observation points to the basically functionalist logic of much of the ecology-sovereignty debate, a theme to which I return below.

12. For a discussion of the limits of functionalist theories, see Robert O. Keohane, *After Hegemony: Cooperation and Discord in the World Political Economy* (Princeton, NJ: Princeton University Press, 1984), pp. 80–83.

13. This list is from Ruth Lapidoth, "Sovereignty in Transition," *Journal of International Affairs* 45, no. 2 (Winter 1992), pp. 325–346.

14. Robert Jackson, *Quasi-States: Sovereignty, International Relations, and the Third World* (Cambridge, UK: Cambridge University Press, 1990), chapter 3.

15. Ibid., p. 327.

16. John G. Ruggie, "Continuity and Transformation in the World Polity: Toward a Neorealist Synthesis," in Robert O. Keohane, ed., *Neorealism and Its Critics* (New York: Columbia University Press, 1986), p. 143, as cited in J. Samuel Barkin and Bruce Cronin, "The State and the Nation: Changing Norms and the Rules of Sovereignty in International Relations," *International Organization* 48, no. 1 (Winter 1994), pp. 107–130.

17. See Ronnie D. Lipschutz and Judith Mayer, "Not Seeing the Forest for the Trees: Rights, Rules, and the Renegotiation of Resource Management Regimes," in Ronnie D. Lipschutz and Ken Conca, eds., *The State and Social Power in Global Environmental Politics* (New York: Columbia University Press, 1993), pp. 246–273.

18. Joel Migdal, *Strong Societies and Weak States* (Princeton, NJ: Princeton University Press, 1988).

19. For a discussion of this effect in the specific context of wildlife in Kenya and forests in Indonesia, see Nancy Peluso, "Coercing Conservation," in Lipschutz and Conca, eds., *The State and Social Power*, pp. 46–70.

20. I discuss this case in greater detail in Ken Conca, "Environmental Protection, International Norms, and National Sovereignty: The Case of the Brazilian Amazon," in Gene Lyons and Michael Mastanduno, eds., *Beyond Westphalia? National Sovereignty and International Intervention* (Baltimore, MD: Johns Hopkins University Press, 1995).

21. "Summit Documents Safeguard Brazilian Interests," *Daily Report: Latin America*, FBIS-LAT-92-114-S, June 12, 1992, p. 27 (supplement); original source *O Globo*, 11 June 1992, Rio '92 section, p. 1.

22. Principle 2: "States have, in accordance with the Charter of the United Nations and the principles of international law, the sovereign right to exploit their own resources, pursuant to their own environmental and developmental policies, and the responsibility to ensure that activities within their jurisdiction or control do not cause damage to the environment of other States or of areas beyond the limits of national jurisdiction." See "Rio Declaration on Environment and Development," United Nations Conference on Environment and Development, U.N. Document A/CONF.151/5/Rev.1 (1992).

23. David Cleary, "After the Frontier: Problems with Political Economy in the Modern Brazilian Amazon," *Journal of Latin American Studies* 25, Part 2 (May 1993), pp. 331–349.

24. These themes are discussed in detail in Conca, "Environmental Protection, International Norms, and National Sovereignty."

25. "Um Grito do Fundo da Selva," *Veja* (August 25, 1993), p. 27. The translation is mine.

Chapter 8

13. Although a measured activity (say, consumption of a hamburger) may occur in one place, its associated impact can be spread over many places: the rangeland where the beef was fed (maybe sustainable, maybe not; maybe on land deforested for grazing, maybe not), the rural landfill where the packaging waste will be discarded, the region where a dammed river provided the energy for cooking, the oil field depleted for energy and petrochemical feedstocks to make the plastics used in packaging, and worldwide damage from ozone depletion caused by the CFC blowing agent used to manufacture the packaging.

14. See "The Problem of Interregional Trade" in William E. Rees, "A Role for Environmental Assessment in Achieving Sustainable Development," *Environmental Impact Assessment Review* 8 (1988):271–72.

15. World Resources Institute, *World Resources 1988–89: An Assessment of the Resource Base That Supports the Global Economy.* New York: Basic Books, 1989.

Chapter 9

27. See Willis Harman, *An Incomplete Guide to the Future* (New York: Norton, 1979); Alvin Toffler, *The Third Wave* (New York: Morrow, 1980); Daniel Bell, *The Coming of Post-Industrial Society* (New York: Basic Books, 1973); Peter Drucker, *The Age of Discontinuity* (New York: Harper and Row, 1968).

28. The role of social surplus in growth and development is discussed in A. S. Boughey, "Environmental Crises—Past and Present," in Lester Bilsky, ed., *Historical Ecology* (Port Washington, NY: Kennikat Press, 1980).

29. Earl Cook, *Man, Energy, Society* (San Francisco: W. H. Freeman, 1976), p. 19.

30. The dominant social paradigm concept was developed by Willis Harman, op. cit., chap. 2; see also Dennis Pirages and Paul Ehrlich, *Ark II: Social Response to Environmental Imperatives* (New York: Viking, 1974), chap. 2.

35. Willis Harman, op. cit., pp. 25–28.

36. Willis Harman, "The Coming Transformation," *The Futurist* (February 1977).

41. See Alvin Toffler, op. cit.

51. Richard Mansbach and John Vasquez, *In Search of Theory: A New Paradigm for Global Politics* (New York: Columbia University Press, 1981), p. 5.

53. See ibid. [Mansbach and Vasquez], chapter 1.

Chapter 11 (Barker and Soyez)

1. J. C. Day and F. Quinn, *Water Diversion and Export: Learning from Canadian Experience*, Pub. Series, no. 36 (Waterloo, Ont.: University of Waterloo, Department of Geography, 1992).

2. C. Bryson, "Forest Industry in Alberta: An International Issue?" *Environment News* 13 (Summer 1991): 20–23. See, also, J. Goddard, *Last Stand of the Lubicon Cree* (Vancouver, B.C.: Douglas & McIntyre, 1991).

3. A number of press reports about the Greenpeace campaign appeared in late 1993. For example, the *Süddeutsche Zeitung* printed two articles on November 1993: "Protestaktion gegen Abholzung: Greenpeace Mitarbeiter in Kanada festgenommen" and "Kettensägenmassaker vor dem Burda-Verlag: Umweltschutzer protestieren gegen Papier, dessen Produktion die Natur zerstört." Canada reacted to the campaign with visits to Europe by forest industry and political representatives. For an exchange between Paul Heinbecker, Canadian ambassador to Germany, and Christoph Thies, a representative of German Greenpeace, see "Kahlschlag für den Kiosk? Der Streit Zwischen Greenpeace und Kanada über die Waldnutzung," *Der Spiegel Dokument*, no. 1 (February 1994).

4. See G. Wenzel, *Animal Rights, Human Rights: Ecology, Economy and Ideology in the Canadian Arctic* (Toronto: University of Toronto Press, 1991); and R. F. Keith and A. Saunders, eds., *A Question of Rights: Northern Wildlife Management and the Anti-Harvest Movement* (Ottawa: Canadian Arctic Resources Committee, 1989).

5. J. MacNeill, J. P. Winsemius, and T. Yakushiji, *Beyond Interdependence: The Meshing of the World's Economy and the Earth's Ecology* (New York: Oxford University Press, 1991).

6. The widespread diffusion of pollutants and the presence of contaminants in boreal, sub-Arctic, and Arctic environments are reasonably well documented. Examples range from the damage caused by acid rain to northern lakes and forests to the accumulation of pesticides, heavy metals, and PCBs in the far north. See, for example, Canada, Department of Environment, *The State of Canada's Environment* (Ottawa, 1992).

7. See, for example, R. R. White, *North, South, and the Environmental Crisis* (Toronto: University of Toronto Press, 1993).

8. For various perspectives on center-periphery relations in Canada and the historical role of northern resource developments, see L. D. McCann, ed., *Heartland and Hinterland: A Geography of Canada*, 2nd ed. (Scarborough, Ont.: Prentice-Hall Canada, 1987); L.-E. Hamelin, *La nordicité canadienne* (Ville LaSalle, Quebec: Hurtubise HMH, 1978); R. Page, *Northern Development: The Canadian Dilemma* (Toronto: McClelland and Stewart, 1986); and K. Coates and W. Morrison, *The Forgotten North: A History of Canada's Provincial Norths* (Toronto: James Lorimer, 1992).

9. J. R. Ponting, "Internationalization: Perspectives on an Emerging Direction in Aboriginal Affairs," *Canadian Ethnic Studies* 12, no. 3 (1990):85–109.

10. Other researchers refer to the same process as internationalization or globalization. See, for example, M. Featherstone, ed., *Global Culture: Nationalism, Globalization and Modernity* (London: Sage Press, 1990).

11. Aboriginal rights are a special case because, in both historical and recent treaties, they usually refer to limited property rights and to collective, not private, property. (The concept of individually owned property is foreign to aboriginal cultures in Canada.) For an introduction to this complex field, see M. Asch, *Home and Native Land: Aboriginal Rights and the Canadian Constitution* (Toronto: Methuen, 1984); B. Slattery, "Understanding Aboriginal Rights," *Canadian Bar Review* 66 (1987):727–783; "Collective Rights and Powers," *Inuit Studies* 16, no. 1-2 (1992); and S. Weaver, "A New Paradigm in Canadian Indian Policy for the 1990s," *Canadian Ethnic Studies* 12, no. 3 (1990):8–18.

12. A. Tanner, "Northern Indigenous Cultures in the Face of Development," in J. O. Saunders, ed., *The Legal Challenge of Sustainable Development* (Calgary, Alb.: Canadian Institute of Resource Law, 1990), 252–268.

13. For a discussion of sustainable resource use, see R. Chambers, *Sustainable Livelihoods: An Opportunity for the World Commission on Environment and Development* (Brighton, England: University of Sussex, Institute of Development Studies, 1986); and T. O'Riordan, "The Politics of Sustainability," in R. K. Turner, ed., *Sustainable Environmental Management: Principles and Practice* (Boulder, Colo.: Westview Press, 1988), 29–50.

14. See note 11 above; and A. Fleras and T. L. Elliott, *The Nations Within: Aboriginal-State Relations in Canada, the United States and New Zealand* (Toronto: Oxford University Press, 1992).

15. Hydro-Québec, *Document Synthèse: Proposition de Plan et développement Hydro-Québec 1990–1992 Horizon 1999* (Montreal, 1990); and Hydro-Québec, "Grand Baleine Complex," *Bulletin* 5 (Montreal, 1991).

16. F. Berkes, "The Intrinsic Difficulty of Predicting Impacts: Lessons from the James Bay Hydro Project," *Environmental Impact Assessment Review* 8, no. 1 (1988):201–220.

17. Comité de la Baie James sur le Mercure, *Rapport D'activités* (Montreal, 1991).

18. Grand Council of the Crees (of Quebec)/Cree Regional Authority, *Environmental, Economic, & Social Issues Related to the James Bay Phase II Project* (Ottawa, 1991).

19. Hydro-Québec, Communications et Relations Publiques, "Grand Baleine Complex," *Highlights*, no. 19 (1993); and Gouvernement du Québec, Secrétariat aux Affaires Autochtones, en collaboration avec les Publications du Québec, *Les Amerindians et les Inuits du Québec d'Aujourd'hui* (Quebec City, 1992).

20. T. Morantz, "Aboriginal Land Claims in Quebec," in K. Coates, ed., *Aboriginal Land Claims in Canada: A Regional Perspective* (Toronto: Copp Clark Pitman, 1992), 101–130; and H. Feit, "Negotiating Recognition of Aboriginal Right: History, Strategies, and Reactions to the James Bay and Northern Quebec Agreement," *Canadian Journal of Anthropology* 1, no. 2 (1980):159–172.

21. Canada, Department of National Defence, *Goose Bay EIS: An Environmental Impact Statement on Military Flying in Labrador and Quebec* (Ottawa, 1989), 3 volumes.

22. F. H. Harrington and A. M. Veitch, "Short-Term Impacts of Low-Level Jet Fighter Training on Caribou in Labrador," *Arctic* 44, no. 4 (1991):318–327; and Canadian Public Health Association, *CPHA Task Force on the Health Effects of Increased Flying Activity in the Labrador Area: Final Report* (Ottawa, 1987).

23. The Montagnais, Naskapi, and Irmo are, in fact, members of a single aboriginal people whose total population is approximately 10,000, living in small communities in Labrador and eastern Quebec. The names Montagnais and Naskapi were used by early European settlers to describe what were then thought to be distinct aboriginal groups.

24. P. Armitage and J. C. Kennedy, "Redbaiting and Racism on Our Frontier: Military Expansion in Labrador and Quebec," *Canadian Revue of Sociology & Anthropology* 26, no. 5 (1989):801.

25. See, for example, P. Armitage, *Homeland or Wasteland?: Contemporary Land Use and Occupancy Among the Innu of Utshimassit and Sheshatshit and the Impact of Military Expansion* (Sheshatshit, Nf.: Naskapi Montagnais Innu Association, 1989); idem, "Indigenous Homelands and the Security Requirements of Western Nation-States: Irmo Opposition to Military Flight Training in Eastern Quebec and Labrador," in A. Kirby, ed., *The Pentagon and the Cities* (London: Sage, 1992), 126–153; and M. Weiler, *Caribou Hunters vs. Fighter Jets*, Mundus Reihe Ethnologie Band 49 (Bonn: Holos, 1992).

26. For an overview, see A. Tanner and S. Henderson, "Aboriginal Land Claims in the Atlantic Provinces," in Coates, ed., *Aboriginal Land Claims in Canada*, pages 131–166; and Canada, Department of Indian and Northern Affairs, *Federal Policy for the Settlement of Native Claims* (Ottawa, 1993).

27. Attention is now being paid to significant differences between the scientific and traditional aboriginal knowledge systems and to their relevance for environmental management. See, for example, M. Freeman and L. N. Carbyn, eds., *Traditional Knowledge and Renewable Resource Management* (Edmonton, Alb.: Boreal Institute, 1988) and P. Usher, "Indigenous Management Systems and Conservation of Wildlife in the Canadian North," *Alternatives* 14, no. 1 (1987):3–9.

28. The Labrador Inuit Association (LIA) chose to cooperate with the consultants hired by the Department of National Defence to prepare an environmental impact statement. Extensive records of land use and ecological data were provided by LIA (J. Rowell, environmental advisor to the LIA, Nain, Nf., personal communication with the authors, 18 October 1992). Both the Labrador Innu and the Conseil des Atikamekw et des Montagnais withdrew from the formal federal environmental assessment process shortly after it was

initiated in 1986, citing lack of faith in the proceedings. Both groups participated indirectly by submitting substantive critiques of the environmental impact statement after its release in 1989 (see, for example, note 21 above).

29. A. Tanner, "History and Culture in the Generation of Ethnic Nationalism," in M. D. Levin, ed., *Ethnicity and Aboriginality* (Toronto: University of Toronto Press, in press).

30. N. Dyck, "Aboriginal Peoples and Nation-States: An Introduction to the Analytical Issues," in N. Dyck, ed., *Indigenous Peoples and the Nation-State: "Fourth World" Politics in Canada, Australia and Norway*, Social and Economic Papers, no. 14 (St. John's, Nf.: Memorial University of Newfoundland, Institute of Social and Economic Research, 1985), 1–26.

31. Inuit Circumpolar Conference, *Principles and Elements for a Comprehensive Policy* (Montreal: McGill University, Center for Northern Studies and Research, 1992).

32. See, for example, Comité de la Baie James sur le Mercure, note 17 above; and Armitage, note 25 above.

33. Networking among the various groups, including environmental and aboriginal nongovernmental organizations can take many pathways, including e-mail and Greenet. It is important to distinguish between networking as an ineffective game and communication strategies that do produce results. Cree contacts with environmentalists in the Northeastern United States did lead to a fundamental change in the nature of the electricity demand debate in New York and the New England states, which put pressure on Hydro-Quebec to justify its policies. Of course, there is always the risk that one partner in such an alliance will capture the agenda of the other partner, who then loses control over the situation.

Chapter 12 (Wapner)

4. On the concept of "global civil society," see Richard Falk, *Explorations at the Edge of Time* (Philadelphia: Temple University Press, 1992); and Ronnie Lipschutz, "Restructuring World Politics: The Emergence of Global Civil Society," *Millennium* 21 (Winter 1992).

5. There is no single, static definition of civil society. The term has a long and continually evolving, if not contestable, conceptual history. For an appreciation of the historical roots of the term and its usage in various contexts, see Jean Cohen and Andrew Arato, *Civil Society and Political Theory* (Cambridge: MIT Press, 1992); John Keane, 'Despotism and Democracy: The Origins and Development of the Distinction between Civil Society and the State, 1750–1850,' in Keane, ed., *Civil Society and the State: New European Perspectives* (London: Verso, 1988).

6. I follow a Hegelian understanding of civil society, which includes the economy within its domain. Later formulations, most notably those offered by Gramsci and Parsons, introduce a three-part model that differentiates civil society from both the state and the economy. See Talcott Parsons, *The System of Modern Societies* (Englewood Cliffs, NJ: Prentice-Hall, 1971); Antonio Gramsci, *Prison Notebooks* (New York: International Publishers, 1971). For an extensive argument to exclude the economy from civil society, see Cohen and Arato (fn. 5).

32. Michael Harwood, "Daredevils for the Environment," *New York Times Magazine*, October 2, 1988, p. 7. Also confirmed in private interviews at the time. See also Clive Davidson, "How Greenpeace Squeezed onto Satellite Link," *New Scientist* 135 (July 1992), 20.

33. For discussions on the media-directed dimension of ecological political action, see Rik Scarce, *Eco-Warriors: Understanding the Radical Environmental Movement* (Chicago: Noble Press, 1990); David Day, *The Environmental Wars* (New York: Ballantine Books, 1989); Robert Hunter, *Warriors of the Rainbow: A Chronicle of the Greenpeace Movement* (New York: Holt, Rinehart and Winston, 1979); Walter Truett Anderson, *Reality Isn't What It Used to Be* (San Francisco: Harper and Row, 1990), chap. 7.

34. Bearing witness is a type of political action that originated with the Quakers. It requires that one who has observed a morally objectionable act (in this case an ecologically destructive one) must either take action to prevent further injustice or stand by and attest to its occurrence; one may not turn away in ignorance. For bearing witness as used by Greenpeace, see Hunter (fn. 33); Michael Brown and John May, *The Greenpeace Story* (Ontario: Prentice-Hall Canada, 1989); Greenpeace, "Fifteen Years at the Front Lines," *Greenpeace Examiner* 11 (October–December 1986).

35. Hunter (fn. 33), 229.

36. Sociological perspectives on world politics have proliferated over the past few years. See, for example, Leslie Sklair, *Sociology of the Global System* (Baltimore: Johns Hopkins University Press, 1991); and David Jacobson, "The States System in the Age of Rights" (Ph.D. diss., Princeton University, 1991).

37. Joseph Gusfield, "Social Movements and Social Change: Perspectives on Linearity and Fluidity," in Louis Kriesberg, ed., *Research in Social Movements: Conflicts and Change* (Greenwich, Conn.: JAI Press, 1981) 4:326.

38. Paul Joseph, *Peace Politics* (Philadelphia: Temple University Press, 1993), 147–151; Johan Galtung, "The Peace Movement: An Exercise in Micro-Macro Linkages," *International Social Science Journal* 40 (August 1989), 377–382.

39. Gusfield (fn. 37), 326.

40. Blumer, "Social Movements," in Barry McLaughlin, ed., *Studies in Social Movements: A Social Psychological Perspective* (New York: Free Press, 1969).

41. Linda Starke, *Signs of Hope: Working toward Our Common Future* (New York: Oxford University Press, 1990), 2, 105.

42. Mathew Wald, "Guarding the Environment: A World of Challenges," *New York Times*, April 22, 1990, p. A1.

43. George Gallup International Institute, "The Health of the Planet Survey," quoted in "Bush Out of Step, Poll Finds," *Terra Viva: The Independent Daily of the Earth Summit* (Rio de Janeiro), June 3, 1992, p. 5. See, generally, Riley Dunlap, George Gallup, Jr., and Alec Gallup, "Of Global Concern: Results of the Health of the Planet Survey," *Environment* 53 (November 1993).

44. David Day, *The Whale War* (San Francisco: Sierra Club Books, 1987), 157. For a critical view of Operation Breakout, see Tom Rose, *Freeing the Whales: How the Media Created the World's Greatest Non-Event* (New York: Birch Lane Press, 1989).

45. See Council on Economic Priorities, *Shopping for a Better World* (New York: Council on Economic Priorities, 1988); Cynthia Pollock Shea, "Doing Well by Doing Good," *World Watch* 2 (November-December 1989). According to a 1991 Gallup poll, 28 percent of the U.S. public claimed to have "boycotted a company's products because of its record on the environment," and according to Cambridge Reports, in 1990, 50 percent of respondents said that they were "avoiding the purchase of products by a company that pollutes the environment"—an increase of 18 percent since 1987. Quoted in Riley Dunlap, "Public Opinion in the 1980s: Clear Consensus, Ambiguous Commitment," *Environment* 33 (October

1991), 36. See, more generally, Bruce Smart, *Beyond Compliance: A New Industry View of the Environment* (Washington, D.C.: World Resources Institute, 1992).

46. Jeremy Warford and Zeinab Partow, "Evolution of the World Bank's Environmental Policy," *Finance and Development*, no. 26 (December 1989).

47. U.S. Bureau of the Census, Statistical abstract of the United States, 1993 (Washington, D.C.: Bureau of the Census, 1993), 227, table 372.

48. The average price per seal pup skin dropped from $23.09 in 1979 to $10.15 in 1983. See George Wenzel, *Animal Rights, Human Rights* (Toronto: University of Toronto Press, 1991), 124, table 6.12.

49. This led to a further drop in price. By 1985 the price per skin had dropped to $6.99. See fn. 48.

50. Wenzel (fn. 48), 52–53; idem, "Baby Harp Seals Spared," *Oceans* 21 (March-April 1988); see, generally, Day (fn. 33), 60–64.

51. This example also demonstrates that environmental activists are not always accurate in assessing environmental threats and guaranteeing the ecological soundness of the sensibility they wish to impart. There is no evidence that harp seals were ever an endangered species. This is particularly troubling because the activities of Greenpeace, IFAW, and others produced severe social dislocation and hardship for communities as far away as Greenland, Iceland, and the Faroe Islands, as well as in the coastal communities of Newfoundland and Baffin Island. See Oran Young, *Arctic Politics: Conflict and Cooperation in the Circumpolar North* (Hanover, N.H.: University Press of New England, 1992), 128; J. Allen, "Anti-Sealing as an Industry," *Journal of Political Economy* 87 (April 1979); Leslie Spence et al., "The Not So Peaceful World of Greenpeace," *Forbes*, November 11, 1991; Wenzel (fn. 46).

52. On the issue of good conduct, see Gary Orren, "Beyond Self-Interest," in Robert Reich, ed., *The Power of Public Ideas* (Cambridge: Harvard University Press, 1988).

53. Bramble and Porter (fn. 2), 238; Porter and Brown (fn. 2), 61; Michael Parrish, "McDonald's to Do Away with Foam Packages," *Los Angeles Times*, November 2, 1990, p. A1.

54. "McDonalds Admits to Bowing to Ill-Informed Opinion on Polystyrene," *British Plastics and Rubber* (January 1991), 35; Phyllis Berman, "McDonald's Caves In," *Forbes*, February 4, 1991; Brian Quinton, "The Greening of McDonalds," *Restaurants and Institutions* 100 (December 1990), 28; John Holusha, "Packaging and Public Image: McDonald's Fills a Big Order," *New York Times*, November 2, 1990.

55. Natural Resources Defense Council, "Intolerable Risk: Pesticides in Our Children's Food: Summary," *A Report by the Natural Resources Defense Council* (New York, February 27, 1989).

56. Timothy Egan, "Apple Growers Bruised and Bitter after Alar Scare," *New York Times*, July 9, 1991, p. A1.

57. Michael Fumento, *Science under Siege: Balancing Technology and the Environment* (New York: William Morrow, 1993), 20.

58. "Revenge of the Apples," *Wall Street Journal*, December 17, 1990, p. A8. See generally Allan Gold, "Company Ends Use of Apple Chemical," *New York Times*, October 17, 1990; Adrian de Wind, "Alar's Gone, Little Thanks to the Government," *New York Times*, July 30, 1991; Lesli Roberts, "Alar: The Numbers Game," *Science* (March 24, 1989), 1430. For criticisms of the Alar campaign, see Fumento (fn. 57), 19–44; Bruce Ames, "Too Much Fuss about Pesticides," *Consumer's Research Magazine* (April 1990); and more generally idem, "Misconceptions about Pollution and Cancer," *National Review* 42 (December 1990).

59. Dave Phillips, "Breakthrough for Dolphins: How We Did It," *Earth Island Journal* 5 (Summer 1990); idem, "Taking Off the Gloves with Bumble Bee," *Earth Island Journal* 6 (Winter 1991); "Three Companies to Stop Selling Tuna Netted with Dolphins," *New York Times*, April 13, 1990, pp. A1, A14.

60. "Dolphin Dilemmas," *Environment* 35 (November 1993), 21.

61. "U.S. Law Bans Sale of Dolphin-Unsafe Tuna," *Earth Island Journal* 9 (Summer 1994), 7.

62. See CERES Coalition, *The 1990 Ceres Guide to the Valdez Principles* (Boston: CERES, 1990); Valerie Ann-Zondorak, "A New Face in Corporate Environmental Responsibility: The Valdez Principles," *Boston College Environmental Affairs Law Review* 18 (Spring 1991); Jack Doyle, "Valdez Principles: Corporate Code of Conduct," *Social Policy* 20 (Winter 1990); Joan Bavaria, "Dispatches from the Front Lines of Corporate Social Responsibility," *Business and Society Review*, no. 81 (Spring 1992).

63. For an extended discussion of NGO corporate politics that provides additional examples, see Starke (fn. 41), 89ff.

64. See, for example, Jack Doyle, "Hold the Applause: A Case Study of Corporate Environmentalism," *Ecologist* 22 (May-June 1992); David Beers and Catherine Capellaro, "Greenwash!" *Mother Jones* (March-April 1991). For sympathetic views, see Stephan Schmidheiny, *Changing Course: A Global Business Perspective on Development and the Environment* (Cambridge: MIT Press, 1992); Smart (fn. 45).

65. See, for example, Philip Hurst, *Rainforest Politics: Ecological Destruction in South East Asia* (Atlantic Highlands, N.J.: Zed Books, 1990); H. Jeffrey Leonard, ed., *Environment and the Poor: Development Strategies for a Common Agenda* (New Brunswick, N.J.: Transaction Books, 1989).

66. The relationship between the world's poor and environmental destruction is a complicated one. See, for example, Robin Broad, "The Poor and the Environment: Friends or Foes?" *World Development* 22 (June 1994); and Robert W. Kates and Viola Haarmann, "Where the Poor Live: Are the Assumptions Correct?" *Environment* 34 (May 1992).

67. See World Wildlife Fund, *The African Madagascar Program* (pamphlet) (April 1994); Nyamaluma Conservation Camp Lupande Development Project, *Zambian Wildlands and Human Needs Newsletter* (Mfuwe) (March 1990); Gabrielle Walters, "Zambia's Game Plan," *Topic Magazine* (U.S. Information Agency), no. 187 (1989); Roger Stone, "Zambia's Innovative Approach to Conservation," *World Wildlife Fund Letter*, no. 7 (1989); *WWF Project Folder #1652*.

68. Proceedings of the Workshop on Community Forest/Protected Area Management, Maumi Hotel, Yaounde, Cameroon, October 12–13, 1993, sponsored by the Cameroon Ministry of Environment and Forests; Roger Stone, "The View from Kilum Mountain," *World Wildlife Fund Letter*, no. 4 (1989); Michael Wright, "People-Centered Conservation: An Introduction," *Wildlands and Human Needs: A Program of World Wildlife Fund* (pamphlet) (Washington, D.C.: WWF, 1989); World Wildlife Fund, *1988–1989 Annual Report on the Matching Grant for a Program in Wildlands and Human Needs*, U.S. AID Grant #OTR-0158-A-00-8160-00 (Washington, D.C.: WWF, 1989).

69. Roger Stone, "Conservation and Development in St. Lucia," *World Wildlife Fund Letter*, no. 3 (1988).

70. See Vandana Shiva, "North-South Conflicts in Global Ecology," *Third World Network Features*, December 11, 1991; John Hough and Mingma Norbu Sherpa, "Bottom Up vs. Ba-

sic Needs: Integrating Conservation and Development in the Annapurna and Michiru Mountain Conservation Areas of Nepal and Malawi," *Ambio* 18, no. 8 (1989); Robin Broad, John Cavanaugh, and Walden Bellow, "Development: The Market Is Not Enough," *Foreign Policy*, no. 81 (Winter 1990); Hurst (fn. 65).

71. Outside contact may also splinter traditional associations, causing economic and social dislocation. See, for example, James Mittelman, *Out from Underdevelopment: Prospects for the Third World* (New York: St. Martin's Press, 1988), 43–44.

72. Bratton, "The Politics of Government-NGO Relations in Africa," *World Development* 17, no. 4 (1989), 574.

73. See "Whose Common Future," *Ecologist* (special issue) 22, no. 4 (July-August 1992); Robert McC. Adams, "Foreword: The Relativity of Time and Transformation," in B. L. Turner et al., eds., *The Earth as Transformed by Human Action* (New York: Columbia University Press with Clark University, 1990). For how these pressures work in one particular area, see Susanna Hecht and Alexander Cockburn, *The Fate of the Forest: Developers, Destroyers and Defenders of the Amazon* (New York: Harper Perennial, 1990).

74. Hilary French, "Rebuilding the World Bank," in Lester Brown et al., *State of the World, 1994* (New York: W. W. Norton, 1994), 163.

75. See Bramble and Porter (fn. 2); "Withdraw from Sardar Sarovar, Now: An Open Letter to Mr. Lewis T. Preston, President of the World Bank," *Ecologist* 22 (September-October 1992); James Rush, *The Last Tree: Reclaiming the Environment in Tropical Asia* (New York: Asia Society, distributed by Boulder, Colo: Westview Press, 1991).

76. Robert Livernash, "The Growing Influence Of NGOs in the Developing World," *Environment* 34 (June 1992), 15.

77. Such funding was evident in the preparatory meetings organized for the United Nations Conference on Environment and Development (UNCED). Organizations such as WWF spent thousands of dollars to bring Third World NGOs to Geneva, New York, and eventually to Brazil to attend the proceedings.

78. Michael Cernea, "Nongovernmental Organizations and Local Development," *Regional Development Dialogue* 10 (Summer 1989), 117. One should note that although the overall trend is to fund local NGOS, the amount of money going to local NGOs decreased in 1987. It increased the following year, however.

79. Cernea (fn. 78), 118, table 1. One should note that the reason for this shift in funding is a combination of the perceived failure of governments to promote development, the proved effectiveness of NGO responses to recent famines throughout Africa, and donor's preference for private sector development. See Anne Drabek, "Editor's Preface," *World Development* 15, supplement (Autumn 1987).

80. Organization for Economic Cooperation and Development (OECD), *Development Cooperation in the 1990s: Efforts and Policies of Members of the Development Assistance Committee* (Paris: OECD, 1989), 82.

81. See Fisher (fn. 14).

82. For a discussion of the interface at the local level, see Philip Hirsch, "The State in the Village: The Case of Ban Mai," *Ecologist* 23 (November-December 1993).

Part Three: The Prospects for International Environmental Cooperation

1. A classic work on barriers to cooperation is Mancur Olson, *The Logic of Collective Action: Public Goods and the Theory of Groups* (Cambridge: Harvard University Press, 1965). For a more optimistic perspective on similar questions, see Elinor Ostrom, *Governing the*

Commons: The Evolution of Institutions for Collective Action (London: Cambridge University Press, 1990).

2. For a summary of the objectives, scope, provisions, membership, and methods of these and other major international environmental agreements, see Helge Ole Bergesen and Georg Parmann, eds., *Green Globe Yearbook on International Co-operation for Environment and Development* (New York: Oxford University Press, 1997).

3. Benedick's essay was written before the 1990 London meeting of parties to the convention substantially strengthened the agreement reached in 1987 in Montreal.

4. The problem of estimating the costs of responding to climate change is taken up in William R. Cline, *The Economics of Global Warming* (Washington, DC: Institute for International Economics, 1992).

5. To its credit, the World Resources Institute, which published the tables attacked by Agarwal and Narain, acknowledged the different ways of measuring national responsibility in a subsequent publication on the same theme. See World Resources Institute, *World Resources 1992–93* (New York: Oxford University Press, 1992), box 13.3, p. 209.

6. Maurice F. Strong, statement at opening of U.N. Conference on Environment and Development, Rio de Janeiro, Brazil, June 3, 1992; cited in Peter M. Haas, Marc A. Levy, and Edward A. Parson, "Appraising the Earth Summit: How Should We Judge UNCED's Success?" *Environment* 34, no. 8 (October 1992).

Chapter 17 (Conca and Dabelko)

1. See Pratap Chatterjee and Matthias Finger, *The Earth Brokers: Power, Politics and World Development* (London: Routledge, 1994), pp. 39–40.

2. J. Baird Callicott and Fernando J. R. da Rocha, eds., *Earth Summit Ethics: Toward a Reconstructive Postmodern Philosophy of Environmental Education* (Albany, NY: SUNY Press, 1996), pp. 3–4.

3. Robin Broad and John Cavanagh, "Beyond the Myths of Rio: A New American Agenda for the Environment," *World Policy Journal*, vol. 10, no. 1 (Spring 1993):65–72.

4. Richard Sandbrook, "From Stockholm to Rio," in *Earth Summit '92: The United Nations Conference on Environment and Development* (London: Regency Press, 1992), p. 16.

5. Reg Green, "Priorities for the Future," *Earth Summit '92*, p. 35.

6. Lee A. Kimball, "The Institutions Debate," *Earth Summit '92*, p. 38.

7. The Ecologist, *Whose Common Future? Reclaiming the Commons* (Philadelphia: New Society Publishers, 1993), p. 2.

8. Tommy Koh, "Five after Rio and Fifteen Years after Montego Bay: Some Personal Reflections," *Environmental Policy and Law*, vol. 27, no. 4 (1997), p. 242.

9. Vandana Shiva, "The Greening of the Global Reach," in Wolfgang Sachs, ed., *Global Ecology: A New Arena of Political Conflict* (London: Zed Books, 1993), pp. 149–150 and 152.

10. Wangari Maathi, "A Growing Strength," *Earth Summit '92*, p. 37.

11. Wagaki Mwangi as quoted in Chatterjee and Finger, *The Earth Brokers*, p. 167. Original source: *Third World Resurgence*, no. 24/25, 1992, p. 27.

12. Tariq Banuri, "The Landscape of Diplomatic Conflicts," in Sachs, *Global Ecology*, p. 63.

13. Matthias Finger, "Politics of the UNCED Process," in Sachs, *Global Ecology*, p. 36.

14. Martin Khor as quoted in Chatterjee and Finger, *The Earth Brokers*, p. 99. Original source: *Third World Resurgence*, no. 24/25, 1992, p. 4.

15. Michael Grubb, Matthias Koch, Abby Munson, Francis Sullivan, and Koy Thomson, *The Earth Summit Agreements: A Guide and Assessment* (London: Earthscan Publications, 1993), p. 46.

16. Peter M. Haas, Marc A. Levy, and Edward A. Parson, "Appraising the Earth Summit: How Should We Judge UNCED's Success?" *Environment*, vol. 34, no. 8 (October 1992).

17. The Ecologist, *Whose Common Future?*, p. 1.

Part Four: Institutions as Though the Earth Mattered

1. See Oran Young, *International Cooperation: Building Regimes for Natural Resources and the Environment* (Ithaca, NY: Cornell University Press, 1989), p. 32.

2. Ibid.

3. A similar argument is presented by the former director of the U.S. Environmental Protection Agency, William K. Reilly. See Reilly, "The Green Thumb of Capitalism," *Policy Review*, Fall 1990, pp. 16–21.

4. Jagdish Bhagwati, *Protectionism* (Cambridge, MA: MIT Press, 1989).

5. The origins of the campaign to change the Bank are described in Pat Aufderheide and Bruce Rich, "Environmental Reform and the Multilateral Banks," *World Policy Journal* 5, no. 2 (Spring 1988):301–321.

6. Mohamed T. El-Ashry, "The Road from Rio: Implications of the UN Conference on Environment and Development for the World Bank," *Journal of Environment and Development* 2, no. 2 (Summer 1993), p. 69.

7. See for example the exchange between Paul Nelson and Rodger Payne in *Journal of Peace Research* 34, no. 4 (1997).

Chapter 22 (Cruz, Munasinghe, and Warford)

1. Specific policy measures include altering interest and exchange rates, reducing government budget deficits, promoting market liberalization, fostering international openness, enhancing the role of the private sector, and strengthening government and market institutions, as well as implementing pricing and other reforms in key sectors.

2. See Annex A of M. Munasinghe and W. Cruz, *Economy-wide Policies and the Environment: Lessons from Experience* (Washington, D.C.: The World Bank, 1995).The World Bank is also doing research in other environmentally related areas, including pollution management, natural resources and habitats, environmental valuation, sustainability indicators, environmental assessments, national environmental planning, social policy, and the global environment.

3. In this instance, the term "second best" refers to the fact that although some market reforms have been implemented, price distortions remain. Thus, "first best" conditions have not been achieved.

4. Partial equilibrium analysis involves only a limited number of economic factors and focuses largely on the direct effects of changes in policy or initial conditions. General equilibrium analysis, by contrast, includes a wider range of economic factors and attempts to account for indirect linkages within the economy.

5. Computable general equilibrium models are computer programs that perform general equilibrium analysis (see note 4 above) to provide estimates of both the direct and indirect effects of particular reforms or changes in initial conditions.

Part Five: The Sustainable Development Debate

1. For a view stressing the importance of paradigms in shaping global environmental futures, see Lester W. Milbrath, *Envisioning a Sustainable Society: Learning Our Way Out* (Albany, NY: SUNY Press, 1989).

2. This is the definition of sustainable development employed by Herman Daly; see Part Four.

3. World Commission on Environment and Development (WCED), *Our Common Future* (New York: Oxford University Press, 1987), p. ix.

4. WCED, *Our Common Future*, p. 43.

5. This argument is also presented in the statement of Malaysian Prime Minister Mahathir Mohamad at the 1992 Earth Summit; see Part Seven.

6. A similar criticism has been made of the "global change" discourse that became increasingly influential in environmental circles in the 1980s. See Frederick H. Buttel, Ann P. Hawkins, and Alison G. Power, "From Limits to Growth to Global Change," *Global Environmental Change* 1 (December 1990):57–66.

7. Timothy O'Riordan, "Future Directions in Environmental Policy," *Journal of Environment and Planning* 17 (1985):1431–1446.

Chapter 23

5. Based on data from World Bank, *World Development Report 1984* (New York: Oxford University Press, 1984).

7. FAO, *Fuelwood Supplies in the Developing Countries*, Forestry Paper No. 42 (Rome: 1983).

8. DIESA, *World Population Prospects*, op. cit.

9. Ibid.

11. W. Häfele and W. Sassin, "Resources and Endowments, An Outline of Future Energy Systems," in P. W. Hemily and M. N. Ozdas (eds.), *Science and Future Choice* (Oxford: Clarendon Press, 1979).

Chapter 24

1. Payer, C., 'Causes of the Debt Crisis' in B. Onimode (ed), *The IMF, the World Bank and African Debt: the Social and Political Impact,* Zed, London, 1989, pp. 7–16.

2. 'Action for Whose Common Future?' *Solidarity for Equality, Ecology and Development Newsletter* 1, 1989, Torggt. 34, N-1083 Oslo 1, Norway, pp. 6–7.

3. Wiebe, J. D., Vice-President, Globe 90, Executive Vice-President, Asia Pacific Foundation, in *Globe 90 Official Buyers' Guide and Trade Fair Directory,* p. 13.

4. Global Industrial and Social Progress Research Institute brochure, p. 3.

5. United Nations General Assembly, A/CONF 151/PC/2, 23 February 1990, p. 8.

Chapter 25

4. More precisely, there are ultimate limits to the stocks of material resources, the flows of energy resources, and (in the event of these being circumvented by a major break-

through in fission/fusion technologies) to the environment's ability to absorb waste energy and other stresses. The limits-to-growth debate, while not conclusive as to specifics, appears to have effectively shifted the burden of proof about the absence of such fundamental limits onto the diehard "technological optimists" who deny the existence of such limits.

5. Of course, "meeting the needs" is a rather ambiguous phrase that may mean anything in practice. Substituting this phrase with "optimizing economic and other societal benefits" (Goodland and Ledec, 1987) or "managing all assets, natural resources and human resources, as well as financial and physical assets for increasing long-term wealth and well-being (Repetto, 1986a, p. 15) does not define the objectives of development more precisely, although the importance attached to economic benefits or wealth is rather obvious.

6. It is tempting to conclude that this nine-point formulation of SD is identical with the concept of "ecodevelopment"—the original term coined by Maurice Strong of UNEP for environmentally sound development (see Sachs, 1977 and Riddell, 1981). Certainly the differences are less obvious than the similarities. Nevertheless, some changes are significant—such as the dropping of the emphasis on "local self-reliance" and the renewed emphasis on economic growth.

8. Economists have responded by suggesting that currently used indicators of economic growth (GNP in particular) could be modified so as to somehow "build in" this correlation (e.g., Peskin, 1981). To what extent this is possible and whether it will serve more than a marginal purpose are, however, open questions (Norgaard, 1989).

9. Three other "social" usages of sustainability need to be clarified. Sustainable economy (Daly, 1980) and sustainable society (Brown, 1981) are two of these. The focus there, however, is on the patterns and levels of resource use that might be ecologically sustainable while providing the goods and services necessary to maintain human well-being, and the social reorganization that might be required to make this possible. The third usage is Chambers' definition of "sustainable livelihoods" as "a level of wealth and of stocks and flows of food and cash which provide for physical and social well-being and security against becoming poorer" (Chambers, 1986). This can be thought of as a sophisticated version of "basic needs", in that security or risk-minimization is added to the list of needs. It is therefore relevant to any paradigm of development, rather than to SD in particular.

Chapter 26 (Nagpal)

1. The 2050 Project, organized by the World Resources Institute, the Brookings Institution, and the Santa Fe Institute, seeks to combine empirical analyses about critical resources, trends, and transformations with a survey of what people actually desire for the future. Instead of forecasting, the project has adopted a backcasting approach. See also the full report of the study, T. Nagpal and C. Foltz, eds., *Choosing Our Future: Visions of a Sustainable World* (Washington, D.C.: World Resources Institute, 1995).

2. World Commission on Environment and Development, *Our Common Future* (New York: Oxford University Press, 1987), 8.

3. See J. Blumenfeld, "Institutions—The United Nations Commission on Sustainable Development," *Environment* December 1994, 2; and J. Lash and D. Buzzelli, "Institutions—The President's Council on Sustainable Development," *Environment*, April 1995, 44.

4. See W. Harcourt, "Introduction," in W. Harcourt, ed., *Feminist Perspectives on Sustainable Development* (Atlantic Heights, N.J.: Zed Books, 1994), 1–5.

5. The ideas of contributors to the 2050 Project will be widely quoted throughout this article. Their home country will appear parenthetically.

6. J. H. Faulkner, "Capital Formation and Sustainable Development," *Business and the Contemporary World* 6, no. 2 (1994): 69. A similar position was adopted by the United Nations Commission on Sustainable Development in its 1994 session. The commission agreed that sustainable consumption and production objectives would be best met by "encouraging greater efficiency in energy and resource use: minimizing waste; moving toward environmentally sound pricing; and making environmentally sound purchasing decisions." See N. Desai, "The Commission on Sustainable Development," *Ecodecision* 15 (Winter 1995): 52.

7. Noted economist Herman Daly has made a similar case for development without growth but with population control and wealth redistribution. See H. E. Daly, *Steady-State Economics* (Washington, D.C.: Island Press, 1991).

Chapter 27 (BCSD)

7. World Commission on Environment and Development (WCED), *Our Common Future* (Oxford: Oxford University Press, 1987).

8. Ibid.

9. International Union for the Conservation of Nature and Natural Resources et al., *World Conservation Strategy* (Gland, Switzerland: 1980).

19. Donella Meadows et al., *The Limits to Growth* (New York: Universe Books, 1972).

20. Organisation for Economic Co-operation and Development, *The State of the Environment* (Paris: 1991).

Chapter 28 (Durning)

1. Sidney Quarrier, geologist, Connecticut Geological & Natural History Survey, Hartford, Conn., private communication, February 25, 1992.

2. Ibid.

3. Ibid.

4. Ibid.

5. Lebow in *Journal of Retailing*, quoted in Vance Packard, *The Waste Makers* (New York: David McKay, 1960).

6. Sepp Linhart, "From Industrial to Postindustrial Society: Changes in Japanese Leisure-Related Values and Behavior," *Journal of Japanese Studies*, Summer 1988; Richard A. Easterlin and Eileen M. Crimmins, "Recent Social Trends: Changes in Personal Aspirations of American Youth," *Sociology and Social Research*, July 1988; "Dynasty" from "Harper's Index," *Harper's*, December 1990; "Dallas" from Jerry Mander, *In the Absence of the Sacred* (San Francisco: Sierra Club Books, 1991); Taiwan from "Asian Century," *Newsweek*, February 22, 1988; Stephen Baker and S. Lynne Walker, "The American Dream Is Alive and Well—in Mexico," *Business Week*, September 30, 1991.

7. Billionaires from Jennifer Reese, "The Billionaires: More Than Ever in 1991," *Fortune*, September 9, 1991; millionaires estimated from Kevin R. Phillips, "Reagan's America: A Capital Offense," *New York Times Magazine*, June 18, 1990; homelessness from U.N. Center for Human Settlements, New York, private communication, November 1, 1989; luxury goods from "The Lapse of Luxury," *Economist*, January 5, 1991; gross national product from United Nations Development Programme, *Human Development Report 1991* (New York: Oxford Uni-

versity Press, 1991); member countries in United Nations from U.N. Information Center, Washington, D.C., private communication, January 14, 1992; world average income from 1987, in 1987 U.S. dollars adjusted for international variations in purchasing power, from Ronald V.A. Sprout and James H. Weaver, "International Distribution of Income: 1960–1987," Working Paper No. 159, Department of Economics, American University, Washington, D.C., May 1991; U.S. 1987 poverty line for an individual from U.S. Bureau of the Census, *Statistical Abstract of the United States: 1990* (Washington, D.C.: U.S. Government Printing Office, 1990).

8. Four-and-a-half times richer from Angus Maddison, *The World Economy in the 20th Century* (Paris: Organisation for Economic Co-Operation and Development, 1989).

9. Alan Durning, *Poverty and the Environment: Reversing the Downward Spiral*, Worldwatch Paper 92 (Washington, D.C.: Worldwatch Institute, November, 1989).

10. Estimated annual earnings per family member, in 1988 U.S. dollars of gross domestic product (GDP) per capita adjusted for international variations in purchasing power, and share of world income from Ronald V.A. Sprout and James H. Weaver, "1988 International Distribution of Income" (unpublished data) provided by Ronald V.A. Sprout, U.N. Economic Commission for Latin America and the Caribbean, Washington Office, Washington, D.C., private communication, January 2, 1992. Sprout and Weaver combined income distribution data and purchasing-power adjusted GDP per capita data to disaggregate 127 countries into five classes each and reaggregate these segments into five global classes; see Ronald V.A. Sprout and James H. Weaver, "International Dimensions of Income: 1960–1987," Working Paper No. 159, Department of Economics, American University, Washington, D.C., May 1991. Number in each class adjusted to mid-year 1992 population from Machiko Yanagishita, demographer, Population Reference Bureau, Washington, D.C., private communication, February 26, 1992.

11. Income range and share of world income estimated from Sprout and Weaver, "1988 International Distribution of Income"; Chinese appliances from "TV Now in 50% of Homes," *China Daily*, February 15, 1988.

12. Income range and share of world income from Sprout and Weaver, "1988 International Distribution of Income"; comparison to U.S. poverty line from U.S. Bureau of the Census, *Statistical Abstract of the United States: 1990* (Washington, D.C.: U.S. Government Printing Office, 1990). As used in this book, "consumers," "consumer class," and "global consumer society" are synonymous and refer to the richest fifth of humanity as measured by per capita income or lifestyle. The global consumer society, of course, does not share the institutions that a national society does, but it does share a way of life and many values.

13. Sprout and Weaver, "1988 International Distribution of Income." See also Nathan Keyfitz, "Consumerism and the New Poor," *Society*, January/February 1992.

14. Henry David Thoreau, *Walden* (1854; reprint, Boston: Houghton-Mifflin, 1957).

Part Six: From Ecological Conflict to Environmental Security?

1. See for example Lester Brown, "Redefining National Security," Worldwatch Paper no. 14 (Washington, DC: Worldwatch Institute, 1977); Jessica Tuchman Mathews, "Redefining Security," *Foreign Affairs* 67 (1989):162–177; Norman Myers, "Environment and Security," *Foreign Policy* 74 (Spring 1989):23–41.

3. Vice President Albert Gore discusses this theme in his book on the global environment, *Earth in the Balance: Ecology and the Human Spirit* (New York: Houghton Mifflin, 1992).

4. Kent Hughes Butts, "Why the Military Is Good for the Environment," in Jyrki Käkönen, ed., *Green Security or Militarized Environment* (Aldershot, UK: Dartmouth, 1994). For a discussion of how the U.S. government has operationalized environmental security ideas in a variety of ways, see Geoffrey D. Dabelko and P. J. Simmons, "Environment and Security: Core Ideas and U.S. Government Initiatives," *The SAIS Review* 17 (Winter-Spring 1997):127–146. See also all issues of the *Environmental Change and Security Project Report* published by the Washington-based Woodrow Wilson International Center for Scholars.

5. Early examples include Fairfield Osborn, *Our Plundered Planet* (Boston: Little, Brown, 1953) and Harrison Brown, *The Challenge of Man's Future* (New York: Viking, 1954).

6. For a similar critique regarding the role of the environment in causing conflict, see Marc A. Levy "Is the Environment a National Security Issue?," *International Security* 20, no. 2 (Fall 1995):35–62; Thomas F. Homer-Dixon and Marc A. Levy, "Correspondence: Environment and Security," *International Security* 20, no. 3 (Winter 1995-1996):189–194.

7. See for example Ken Conca, "In the Name of Sustainability: Peace Studies and Environmental Discourse," *Peace and Change* 19, no. 2 (April 1994):91–113.

8. Matthias Finger, "The Military, the Nation State and the Environment," *The Ecologist* 21, no. 5 (September-October 1991):220–225. See also Seth Shulman, *The Threat at Home: Confronting the Toxic Legacy of the U.S. Military* (Boston: Beacon Press, 1992).

Chapter 29

1. Thomas Homer-Dixon, "On the Threshold: Environmental Changes as Causes of Acute Conflict," *International Security*, Vol. 16, No. 2 (Fall 1991), pp. 76–116.

2. The three-year Project on Environmental Change and Acute Conflict brought together a team of thirty researchers from ten countries. It was sponsored by the American Academy of Arts and Sciences and the Peace and Conflict Studies Program at the University of Toronto.

4. For example, see David Wirth, "Climate Chaos," *Foreign Policy*, No. 74 (Spring 1989), pp. 3–22; and Neville Brown, "Climate, Ecology and International Security," *Survival*, Vol. 31, No. 6 (November/December 1989), pp. 519–532.

5. Diana Liverman, "The Impacts of Global Warming in Mexico: Uncertainty, Vulnerability and Response," in Jurgen Schmandt and Judith Clarkson, eds., *The Regions and Global Warming: Impacts and Response Strategies* (New York: Oxford University Press, 1992), pp. 44–68; and Diana Liverman and Karen O'Brien, "Global Warming and Climate Change in Mexico," *Global Environmental Change*, Vol. 1, No. 4 (December 1991), pp. 351–364.

6. Peter Gleick provides a potent illustration of the effect of population growth on water scarcity in Table 3 of "Water and Conflict: Fresh Water Resources and International Security," *International Security*, Vol. 18, No. 1 (Summer 1993), p. 101.

7. The second and third types of scarcity arise only with resources that can be physically controlled and possessed, like fish, fertile land, trees, and water, rather than resources like the climate or the ozone layer.

8. Since population growth is often a main cause of a decline in the quality and quantity of renewable resources, it actually has a dual impact on resource scarcity, a fact rarely noted by analysts.

9. James Boyce, "The Bomb Is a Dud," *The Progressive*, September 1990, pp. 24–25.

10. Bernard Nietschmann, "Environmental Conflicts and Indigenous Nations in Central America," paper prepared for the Project on Environmental Change and Acute Conflict (May 1991); and Sergio Diaz-Briquets, "Comments on Nietschmann's Paper," ibid.

11. Jeffrey Leonard, "Overview," *Environment and the Poor: Development Strategies for a Common Agenda* (New Brunswick, N.J.: Transaction, 1989), p. 7. For a careful analysis of the interaction of population and land distribution in El Salvador, see chap. 2 in William Durham, *Scarcity and Survival in Central America: The Ecological Origins of the Soccer War* (Stanford, Calif.: Stanford University Press, 1979), pp. 21–62.

28. Arthur Westing, "Appendix 2. Wars and Skirmishes Involving Natural Resources: A Selection from the Twentieth Century," in Arthur Westing, ed., *Global Resources and International Conflict: Environmental Factors in Strategic Policy and Action* (Oxford: New York, 1986), pp. 204–210.

29. See Durham, *Scarcity and Survival.*

30. Peter Gleick, "Water and Conflict," Occasional Paper No. 1, Project on Environmental Change and Acute Conflict (September 1992); and Gleick, "Water and Conflict: Fresh Water Resources and International Security," *International Security,* Vol. 18, No. 1 (Summer 1993), pp. 79–112.

31. In 1980, Egyptian President Anwar el-Sadat said, "If Ethiopia takes any action to block our right to the Nile waters, there will be no alternative for us but to use force"; quoted in Norman Myers, "Environment and Security," *Foreign Policy,* No. 74 (Spring 1989), p. 32. See also chap. 6, "The Nile River," in Thomas Naff and Ruth Matson, eds., *Water in the Middle East: Conflict or Cooperation?* (Boulder, Colo.: Westview, 1984), pp. 125–155.

33. See Thayer Scudder, "River Basin Projects in Africa," *Environment,* Vol. 31, No. 2 (March 1989), pp. 4–32; and Scudder, "Victims of Development Revisited: The Political Costs of River Basin Development," *Development Anthropology Network,* Vol. 8, No. 1 (Spring 1990), pp. 1–5.

34. Astri Suhrke, "Pressure Points: Environmental Degradation, Migration, and Conflict," Occasional Paper No. 3, Project on Environmental Change and Acute Conflict (March 1993).

35. Ibid.

45. Robert Repetto, "Balance-Sheet Erosion—How to Account for the Loss of Natural Resources," *International Environmental Affairs,* Vol. 1, No. 2 (Spring 1989), pp. 103–137.

46. This estimate does not include the economic costs of lost rooting depth and increased vulnerability to drought, which may be even larger. See Wilfrido Cruz, Herminia Francisco, and Zenaida Conway, "The On-Site and Downstream Costs of Soft Erosion in the Magat and Pantabangan Watersheds," *Journal of Philippine Development,* Vol. 15, No. 1 (1988), p. 88.

47. Ed Barbier, "Environmental Degradation in the Third World," in David Pearce, ed., *Blueprint 2: Greening the World Economy* (London: Earthscan, 1991), Box 6.8, p. 90.

70. Francis Wilson and Mamphela Ramphele, *Uprooting Poverty: The South African Challenge* (New York: Norton, 1989); George Quail, et al., *Report of the Ciskei Commission* (Pretoria: Conference Associates, 1980), p. 73.

71. See Mamphela Ramphele and Chris McDowell, eds., *Restoring the Land: Environment and Change in Post-Apartheid South Africa* (London: Panos, 1991); and Chris Eaton, "Rural Environmental Degradation and Urban Conflict in South Africa," Occasional Paper of the Peace and Conflict Studies Program, University of Toronto, June 1992.

72. World Resources Institute, *World Resources, 1992–93* (New York: Oxford University Press, 1992), p. 286.

73. Global Assessment of Soil Degradation, *World Map on Status of Human-Induced Soil Degradation,* Sheet 1, North and South America.

74. Thomas Weil, et al., *Haiti: A Country Study* (Washington, D.C.: Department of the Army, 1982), pp. 28–33.

75. Anthony Catanese, "Haiti's Refugees: Political, Economic, Environmental," *Field Staff Reports*, No. 17 (Sausalito, Calif.: Universities Field Staff International, Natural Heritage Institute, 1990–91), p. 5.

76. Elizabeth Abbott, "Where Waters Run Brown," *Equinox*, Vol. 10, No. 59 (September/October 1991), p. 43.

77. Marko Ehrlich, et al., *Haiti: Country Environmental Profile, A Field Study* (Washington, D.C.: U.S. Agency for International Development, 1986), pp. 89–92.

78. WRI, *World Resources, 1992–93*, p. 246.

79. Ibid., p. 272.

Chapter 31

2. Lester Brown, *Redefining National Security* (Washington, DC: Worldwatch Paper, No. 14, October 1977); Jessica Tuchman Mathews, 'Redefining Security', *Foreign Affairs* (Vol. 68, No. 2, 1989), pp. 162–77; Michael Renner, *National Security: The Economic and Environmental Dimensions* (Washington, DC: Worldwatch Paper, No. 89, May 1989); and Norman Myers, 'Environmental Security', *Foreign Policy* (No. 74, 1989), pp. 23–41.

3. Richard Ullman, 'Redefining Security', *International Security* (Vol. 8, No. 1, Summer 1983), pp. 129–53.

4. Hal Harvey, 'Natural Security', *Nuclear Times* (March/April 1988), pp. 24–26.

5. Philip Shabecoff, 'Senator Urges Military Resources to Be Turned to Environmental Battle', *The New York Times*, 29 June 1990, p. 1A.

7. Quentin Skinner, 'Language and Political Change', and James Farr, 'Understanding Political Change Conceptually', in Terence Ball et al., (eds.), *Political Innovation and Conceptual Change* (Cambridge: Cambridge University Press, 1989).

8. For a particularly lucid and well-rounded discussion of security, the state and violence, see Barry Buzan, *People, States, and Fear: The National Security Problem in International Relations* (Chapel Hill, NC: University of North Carolina Press, 1983), particularly pp. 1–93.

17. Ronnie D. Lipschutz, *When Nations Clash: Raw Materials, Ideology and Foreign Policy* (New York: Ballinger, 1989).

19. H. E. Goeller and Alvin Weinberg, 'The Age of Substitutability', *Science* (Vol. 201, 20 February 1967). For some recent evidence supporting this hypothesis, see Eric D. Larson, Marc H. Ross and Robert H. Williams, 'Beyond the Era of Materials', *Scientific American* (Vol. 254, 1986), pp. 34–41.

20. For a discussion of authoritarian and conflictual consequences of environmental constrained economies, see William Ophuls, *Ecology and the Politics of Scarcity* (San Francisco, CA: Freeman, 1976), p. 152. See also Susan M. Leeson, 'Philosophical Implications of the Ecological Crisis: The Authoritarian Challenge to Liberalism', *Polity* (Vol. 11, No. 3, Spring 1979); Ted Gurr, 'On the Political Consequences of Scarcity and Economic Decline', *International Studies Quarterly* (No. 29, 1985), pp. 51–75; and Robert Heilbroner, *An Inquiry Into the Human Prospect* (New York: W. W. Norton, 1974).

22. Bernard Brodie, 'The Impact of Technological Change on the International System', in David Sullivan and Martin Sattler (eds.), *Change and the Future of the International System* (New York: Columbia University Press, 1972), p. 14.

23. For a particularly lucid argument that the nation-state system is over-developed relative to its actual problem-solving capacities, see George Modelski, *Principles of World Politics* (New York: The Free Press, 1972).

Part Seven: Ecological Justice

1. For a discussion of some of these issues prior to Stockholm, see United Nations, *Development and Environment: Report and Working Papers of a Panel of Experts Convened by the Secretary General of the U.N. Conference on the Human Environment*, Founex, Switzerland, June 4–12, 1971.

2. For a discussion of the links between ecology and social justice see Alan S. Miller, *Gaia Connections: An Introduction to Ecology, Ecoethics, and Economics* (Savage, MD: Rowman and Littlefield, 1991).

3. Karen Warren, "The Power and the Promise of Ecological Feminism," *Environmental Ethics* 12 (Summer 1990):125–146; Wendy Harcourt, ed., *Feminist Perspectives on Sustainable Development* (London: Zed Books, 1994); Carolyn Merchant, *Ecological Revolutions: Nature, Gender and Science in New England* (Chapel Hill, NC: University of North Carolina Press, 1989); Irene Diamond and Gloria Feman Orenstein, *Reweaving the World: The Emergence of Ecofeminism* (San Francisco: Sierra Club Books, 1990). For a criticism of some variants of ecofeminism see Janet Biehl, *Rethinking Ecofeminist Politics* (Boston: South End Press, 1991).

4. Warren, "The Power and the Promise of Ecological Feminism," p. 125.

5. See Biehl, *Rethinking Ecofeminist Politics*.

6. Susanna Hecht and Alexander Cockburn, *The Fate of the Forest: Developers, Destroyers, and Defenders of the Amazon* (New York: HarperCollins, 1990).

7. On environmental racism see Robert D. Bullard, *Dumping in Dixie: Race, Class, and Environmental Quality*, 2d ed. (Boulder, CO: Westview Press, 1994); Robert D. Bullard, ed., *Unequal Protection: Environmental Justice and Communities of Color* (San Francisco: Sierra Club Books, 1994); Karl Grossman, "From Toxic Racism to Environmental Justice," *E Magazine*, May-June 1992, pp. 28–35; Elizabeth Martinez, "When People of Color Are an Endangered Species," *Z Magazine*, April 1991.

Chapter 34

1. This chapter is based on a longer article written for a collaborative project of the International Social Sciences Association, the Social Science Research Council, and Development Alternatives with Women for a New Era (DAWN) on 'Rethinking Population and the Environment'. I am grateful for comments on an earlier draft by Carmen Barroso, David Bell, Lincoln Chen, Adrienne Germain and Jael Silliman. The usual disclaimers apply.

2. The dissonance addressed in this chapter is between mainstream environmentalists from the North and women's health researchers and activists from both North and South.

3. My own position is that of someone who has come to these debates from a background of working on issues of gender and development, and this chapter will perforce tilt heavily towards spelling out the positions taken from within the women's movements. I do not claim to be able to explicate how the mainstream of the environmental movement (especially in the North) has come to the particular definitions it has of 'the population problem'.

4. A different theoretical approach that takes better account of the shifts in patterns of inter-generational transfers, and therefore of age-based hierarchies, is contained in the

work of Caldwell and Caldwell (1987).

5. Or, in the case of many parts of Europe, of population expansion through increased fertility.

6. For an influential early critique, see Mamdani (1974).

7. See Scott (n.d.) for a look at Norplant use in the contemporary United States.

8. Even rapid fertility decline may sometimes be indicative of a strategy of desperation on the part of the poor who can no longer access the complementary resources needed to put children's labour to use.

9. Examples of the former are Little (1992), Blaikie (1985); of the latter, Shaw (1989) and UN (1992). The latter argues, for example, that 'The failure to take fully into account the possible effects of other factors that might contribute to environmental degradation characterizes many analyses of population-environmental interrelationships at the national and global levels and thus limits their value in assessing the impact of demographic variables'.

10. An example is the well known Ehrlich-Holden identity, I = PAT, linking environmental impact (I) with population growth (P), growth in affluence/consumption per capita (A), and technological efficiency (T).

11. Personal discussion with V. Miller, co-founder of West Harlem Environmental Action in New York City.

Chapter 36 (Peluso)

1. Piers Blaikie, *The Political Economy of Soil Erosion in Developing Countries* (London: Longman, 1985); Nancy Lee Peluso, *Rich Forests, Poor People: Resource Control and Resistance in Java* (Berkeley, CA: University of California Press, 1992).

2. Daniel Deudney, "Case Against Linking Environmental Degradation and National Security," *Millennium: Journal of International Studies* 19, no. 3 (1990):461–476.; Jeffrey A. McNeeley, Kenton R. Miller, Walter V. Reid, Russell A. Mittermeier, and Timothy B. Wemer, *Conserving the World's Biodiversity* (Washington, DC: Worldwide Fund For Nature, 1988).

3. Deudney, "Case Against Linking."

11. Eric Wolf, *Europe and the People Without History* (Berkeley, CA: University of California Press, 1982).

12. Michael Watts, *Silent Violence: Food, Famine, and Peasantry in Northern Algeria* (Berkeley, CA: University of California Press, 1983); Ramachandra Guha, *The Unquiet Woods: Ecological History and Peasant Resistance in the Indian Himalaya* (Berkeley, CA: University of California Press, 1990); Peluso, *Rich Forests, Poor People.*

13. Charles Tilly, "War-Making and State-Making as Organized Crime," in Peter B. Evans, Dietrich Rueschemeyer, and Theda Skocpol, eds., *Bringing the State Back In* (Cambridge: Cambridge University Press, 1985).

14. World Commission on Environment and Development, *Our Common Future* (New York: Oxford University Press, 1987); Lester Brown et al., *State of the World 1990* (New York: W. W. Norton, 1990).

16. Tilly, "War-Making and State-Making"; Migdal, *Strong Societies.*

17. W. K. Lindsay, "Integrating Parks and Pastoralists: Some Lessons from Amboseli," in David Anderson and Richard Grove, eds., *Conservation in Africa: People, Policies, and Practice* (Cambridge: Cambridge University Press, 1987), pp. 152–155.

18. David Collett, "Pastoralists and Wildlife: Image and Reality in Kenya Maasailand," in Anderson and Grove, *Conservation in Africa*, p. 138.

19. Ibid.

20. Lindsay, "Integrating Parks," pp. 153–155.

21. David Western, "Amboseli National Park: Enlisting Landowners to Conserve," *Ambio* 11, no. 5:304; Lindsay, "Integrating Parks," p. 155.

22. Western, "Amboseli National Park," p. 305; Lindsay, "Integrating Parks," p. 154.

23. Lindsay, "Integrating Parks," pp. 156–157; Agnes Kiss, *Wildlife Conservation in Kenya* (Washington, DC: World Bank, 1990), p. 72.

24. Joan N. Knowles and D. P. Collett, "Nature as Myth, Symbol, and Action: Notes Towards an Historical Understanding of Development and Conservation in Kenyan Maasailand," *Africa* 59, no. 4 (1989):452.

25. Douglas H. Chadwick, "Elephants—Out of Time, Out of Space," *National Geographic* 179, no. 5 (1991):11, 17.

26. Knowles and Collett, "Nature as Myth," p. 452.

27. Collett, "Pastoralists and Wildlife," p. 129; emphasis added.

28. Ibid., p. 144.

29. Kiss, *Wildlife Conservation*, p. 72.

30. Chadwick, "Elephants," p. 14.

31. Ibid., pp. 26–31.

32. Kiss, *Wildlife Conservation*, pp. 71, 74.

34. World Wildlife Fund, "A Program to Save the African Elephant," *World Wildlife Fund Letter*, no. 2, 1989, p. 6.

35. Ibid., pp. 8–9.

36. Ibid., p. 9.

37. Ibid., pp. 4–5; emphasis added.

38. Chadwick, "Elephants," p. 24.

39. Ibid., p. 14.

40. Ibid., p. 24.

41. World Wildlife Fund, "A Program to Save the African Elephant," *World Wildlife Fund Letter*, no. 2, 1989, p. 7.

42. Ibid., p. 10.

43. African Wildlife Foundation, "1989 Was a Very Good Year: Annual Report," *Wildlife News* 25, no. 2:3–5.33.

44. "Kenya: Crackdown on Somalis," *Africa Confidential* 30, no. 1 (1989):6–7.

45. Ibid.

46. Ibid.

57. Blaikie, *The Political Economy of Soil Erosion*; Susanna Hecht and Alexander Cockburn, *The Fate of the Forest: Developers, Destroyers, and Defenders of the Rainforest* (New York: Verso, 1989); Guha, *Unquiet Woods*; Peluso, *Rich Forests, Poor People*.